DR. KAREN RALLS-MACLEOD, FSA Scot., Medieval historian and Celtic scholar, is author of *The Templars and the Grail: Knights of the Quest* (2003) and *Music and the Celtic Otherworld* (University of Edinburgh/St. Martin's Press, 2000). She was Postdoctoral Fellow at the University of Edinburgh for 5 years and is now based at Oxford. Karen lectures worldwide and is also founder of Ancient Quest (www.ancientquest.com) an historical research organisation.

IAN ROBERTSON is a local Scottish researcher with a special interest in Edinburgh and Midlothian history, folk traditions and legends. In 1988, upon becoming a Freemason, his research interests moved into the exploration of Scottish Freemasonry. A member of Masonic research groups, he has presented lectures to many Scottish Masonic lodges. Ian lives in the Edinburgh area and works as a trainer and youth worker.

'The reader who travels with Karen Ralls-MacLeod and Ian Robertson... will find a travelogue which enriches the mythologies and histories so beautifully told, with many newly wrought connections to places, buildings, stones and other remains which may still be viewed in the landscape and historic monuments of modern Scotland...'
REV. DR. MICHAEL NORTHCOTT, Faculty of Divinity, University of Edinburgh

'Karen Ralls-MacLeod is endowed with that rare jewel of academia: a sharp and inquisitive mind blessed with a refreshing openness. Her stimulating work has the gift of making the academic accessible, and brings a clear and sound basis to the experiential... from 'Idylls of the King' to 'Indiana Jones', the search for the Holy Grail will never be the same again. This is a 'must read' book for all who sense the mystery and magic of our distant past...'
ROBERT BAUVAL, bestselling author of *The Secret Chamber* and *Keeper of Genesis*

'This book takes us on a fascinating journey through the mystery and magic of Scotland's past. Along the way, the authors describe the people, places and traditions associated with Scotland's legends and history... the Declaration of Arbroath, the Stone of Destiny, the 'missing library' of Iona, Arthurian traditions, the Holy Grail, the Picts, the Druids... Celtic saints... Robert the Bruce... Rosslyn Chapel...the Knights Templar, and much more...'
WATKINS REVIEW

'... a refreshing look at Scotland's past. I find this style of history reading wonderful. From the Declaration of Arbroath to the Druids, leading on to Stone Circles, Early Celtic Saints and the culdees, we are presented with such a wealth of information without being overwhelmed. Arthur, the Holy Grail and Masonic and Guild traditions, all with such strong connections to Scotland, also find a home in this book. Well worth reading.'
DALRIADA, the journal of Celtic culture, heritage and traditions

The Quest for the Celtic Key

KAREN RALLS-MACLEOD
and
IAN ROBERTSON

Luath Press Limited

EDINBURGH

www.luath.co.uk

First Published 2002
First Paperback Edition Published 2003

The paper used in this book is recyclable. It is made from low
chlorine pulps produced in a low energy, low emission manner
from renewable forests.

Permission to use the Green Man image on the front cover has
kindly been granted by Rosslyn Chapel Trust.

Printed and bound by
Bell & Bain Ltd., Glasgow

Typeset in 10.5 point Sabon by
S. Fairgrieve, Edinburgh 0131 658 1763

Acknowledgements

We have been assisted in this effort by various individuals and organisations that we would very much like to thank for their time, knowledge, patience and encouragement: the National Library of Scotland, the City of Edinburgh Library, Edinburgh University Library, British Library, Bodleian library, Glasgow University library, Scottish Public Record Office, West Register House, Royal Society of Edinburgh, Society of Antiquaries of Scotland, Historic Scotland, Royal Celtic Society, National Archives of Scotland, National Museum of Scotland, New College Divinity library, Royal Historical Society, National Trust for Scotland, Midlothian library headquarters, Newbattle Abbey library, East Lothian library headquarters, West Lothian library headquarters, University of Aberdeen library, Dundee University library, University of Highlands & Islands, Dingwall public library, Inverness city library, Dumfries and Galloway regional library, Whithorn Museum, Stornoway Museum, Grand Lodge of Scotland library, Canonbury Masonic Research Centre (London), United Grand Lodge of England library, Warburg Institute, Smithsonian Institute, Prince Henry Sinclair Society, Niven Sinclair, Ian Sinclair, Robert Brydon FSA Scot., Lindsay Brydon, Goethe Institute, Peter and Sarah Dawkins, Francis Bacon Research Trust, Tom Leggett, Trades Maiden Hospital archive, Ian Fyfe, Theosophical Society library (London), The Theosophical Society in America, Ancient Mystical Order Rosac Crucis (AMORC) library headquarters, San Jose, CA, Judy Fisken, Stuart Beattie, Rosslyn Chapel Trust, the Friends of Rosslyn, the Earl of Rosslyn, Clan Sinclair, Clan MacLeod, Professor William Gillies, School of Scottish Studies, Dublin Institute for Advanced Studies, Bill Taylor of Ardival Harps, Barnaby Brown, Simon Chadwick, Professor Thomas Charles-Edwards, Dr Nerys Jones, Marianna Lines, Zin Craig, Pictish Arts Society, Susan Seright, Curator of the Groam House Museum (Rosemarkie), Netherbow Director Dr Donald Smith, the Church of Scotland, the Scottish Episcopal church, the Scottish Roman Catholic church, the Scottish Reformation Society, Domhnall MacCormaig, Scottish Poetry library, Saltire Society, Lesley Stuart, Greyfriars Kirk Gaelic service community, Yvonne Sinclair, John and Joy Millar, the Sauniere Society, the Most Rev Bishop Richard Holloway, John Algeo,

Alan Bain, Hamish Henderson, Margo Fish, John and Caitlin Matthews, Merlinda Arnold, Olivia Keith-Mitchell, Michael Newham, Anne-Marie Mullen, Dr Margaret Bennett, the late Anne Macaulay (Hon Fellow of Music, University of Edinburgh), Robert Holden, Rev Miranda Holden (New Seminary), Rev Avril Carson, Deirdre O'Flinn, Mark Dosier, Marigold Hutton, Jeremy Naydler, Michael and Seza Eccles, Simon le Fevre, Professor Gerard Leduc, Paul Falardeau, Eleri Golesworthy, Claudine Glot of the Centre de l'Imaginaire Arthurien, Chateau de Comper-en-Broceliande, Brittany, Professor Philippe Walter, University of Grenoble, Elizabeth Lane, the New York Open Center, Caroline McCausland, the late Alan Bruford, and the late Ian Ferguson (Edinburgh).

We would also like to make some special dedications and heartfelt thanks to those special family members, partners, and friends who helped us through the process of writing this book: From Dr Karen Ralls-MacLeod: 'To my husband Jon, whose special encouragement, patience, sense of fun and unshakable belief in this project were always truly inspirational, and to my other special friends, family and colleagues here and abroad who have been supportive throughout, many thanks. Also, a tribute to the ancient library of Alexandria, for inspiring us all.' From Ian Robertson: 'To my mother and father who gave me my curiosity and love of learning, my partner Vivienne who put up with me and encouraged me throughout the writing of this book and to Samantha, Kevin, and the rest of the family for believing in me even when I didn't myself.' We would both like to give many thanks, too, to Gavin and Audrey MacDougall of Luath Press Edinburgh.

We also thank you, our readers, as you embark on your own journey. The real Quest never ends, as all of us search for the Truth... now and in the future.

Contents

Introduction

We'll tak a cup o' kindness yet, for auld lang syne.

Robert Burns, *Auld Sang Syne* (1796)

'The past remains integral to us all, individually and collectively. We must concede the ancients their place... But their place is not simply 'back there', in a separate and foreign country; it is assimilated in ourselves, and re-surrected into an ever-changing present.'

Dr David Lowenthal, *The Past is a Foreign Country* (1985)

What is remembered, lives... History is a *living* memory of the past. It has always meant different things to different people and this seems to have been especially true of the history of Scotland. Travel to historic places has always been a powerful tradition the world over, to see and explore the ancient sites, medieval monastic remains and buildings that still survive today.

But places have their history and unique traditions, some from a long, long time ago. Many people today want to know much more about the origin-myth of the Scots, Robert the Bruce, Iona, Arthurian traditions, Rosslyn Chapel, the Culdees, the Knights Templar, Celtic saints, the Holy Grail or the Stone of Destiny, for example. So mainly due to the increasing popular demand for more detailed information and the fact that many aspects of these subjects have not been readily available in more conventional histories, we bring you this book.

In *The Quest for the Celtic Key* we share with you the results of our journey which started ten years ago. This began when Dr Karen Ralls-MacLeod, a Celtic scholar and medieval religious historian from the University of Edinburgh, was in the process of writing a Celtic history book and was invited to the home of a member of the Society of Antiquaries of Scotland. As it happened, a local Scottish Masonic researcher named Ian Robertson was also present and after further discussion and research exchanges, was subsequently asked to join this effort, especially regarding Masonic material for chapter 8. The resulting odyssey has taken us from our widely divergent fields to bring to light various facts and traditions of Scottish history.

To help meet the continuing public demand for more information, we have drawn together material from a wide variety of sources. In addition to examining the standard historical sources from academic books and journals, Historic Scotland, the National Library of Scotland, the Society of Antiquaries, the National Archives of Scotland and the Public Record Office, we have also made an effort to consult records from private archives, law tracts, church records, accounts of saints' lives, Masonic records, newspaper accounts, family histories, ballads, legendary accounts of specific places; chivalric libraries and archives, Highland storytellers, monastery receipts and business records to enrich and enlarge our analysis of history. We have also included some of the lesser-known, sidelined and previously unavailable or unacknowledged aspects of history that, for one reason or another, may not have made it into more conventional accounts to date.

This book largely covers aspects of Scottish history from very early times up until the year 1320 and the signing of the Declaration of Arbroath. Chapter 8, by necessity, deals with some elements of 18th C Scotland, but for us to largely go any further than the 14th C would be another work in itself. Specific chapters in this book address the history and issues surrounding the origin-myth of the Scots, the Declaration of Arbroath, the Picts, stone circles and megaliths, Druidic philosophy, Celtic saints, the Culdees, the Celtic church, Iona, Scottish Arthurian traditions, the Holy Grail, the Guild traditions of medieval Edinburgh, Masonic history in Scotland, Robert the Bruce, medieval chivalric Orders, Rosslyn Chapel and Prince Henry Sinclair's 14th C journey from Scotland to the New World.

Places associated with these subjects include Arbroath, Iona, Edinburgh, Melrose, Bannockburn, Temple, St Andrews, Glasgow, Whithorn, Aberdeen, Inverness, Stirling, Callanish, Rosslyn Chapel, villages and churches in the Highlands and Islands, Arthurian localities of Midlothian and the Borders, the Pictish stones of Fife and Angus and many, many more, far too numerous to mention here.

The factual history, customs, beliefs, myths and legends of a specific local or regional area are often intertwined with each other, layer upon layer, in early Scottish history. Of course simply because we, as authors, also include some references to mythic and legendary material in our discussions, does not mean that we necessarily endorse or advocate any particular viewpoint; we merely aim to include information from a wide variety of sources for the reader to make up his or her own mind. Although we do discuss the historical traditions of a number of places and localities, this book is not a travel book per se, as the focus is mainly on history and Celtic historical traditions, customs and beliefs.

New links between the history of the New World and Scotland are being discovered all the time, as with Prince Henry Sinclair's voyage to Nova Scotia in 1398. It is now acknowledged by an increasing number of experts on both sides of the Atlantic that the Scottish Declaration of Arbroath (1320) most likely had an influence on the American Declaration of Independence, a view put forth by Professor Ted Cowan of Glasgow University and others. A similar connection is presented by Scottish author Duncan Glen in his recent book *Printing Type Designs: a New History from Gutenburg to 2000* – that America's Declaration of Independence was typeset by printer John Dunlap in type that was made by an Edinburgh man named John Baine, from 'Calton'. He and his grandson went on to become the leading typefounders in America. These types were later referred to as 'Scotch' type in America. They were used on the first 'pirated' version of the *Encyclopedia Britannica* in early America, which was then the largest American printing production that had ever been undertaken. These types were the precursors of the typeface now known as 'Scotch Roman'.

So no matter where one comes from, history is a Quest of continuing, unfolding discovery. On our quest in this book we have explored a number of fresh new perspectives and fascinating glimpses into various areas of Scottish history and the places associated with it. Like putting together many pieces of a diverse puzzle, what lies before you may seem unusual at times, but will hopefully be an intriguing look at the past.

Ultimately, the quest for a 'Celtic key' leads to a more

'Universal key', a Truth that can propel us on, encouraging all of us to recall that history in its many different forms is a *living* memory. We hope that you, too, will enjoy the journey, keeping in mind the courage of the universal traveller:

> Two roads diverged in a wood, and I—-
> I took the one less travelled by,
> And that has made all the difference.

Robert Frost, *The Road Not Taken* (1916)

Dr. Karen Ralls-MacLeod
Ian Robertson
March 2002
Edinburgh

CHAPTER ONE

In the Beginning... the story of Scotland and its origins

IN THE BEGINNING... are the origin-myths, traditions and history of a people. The efforts by a people to define their history, origin and place in the grand scheme of things has been true of nearly every society on earth – many tribes and nations have tried to define themselves in relation to the larger Universe in some way.

Artefacts, written records, monastic manuscripts, trading receipts, laws, family history, religion, heroic poetry, saints' lives, tales, art and storytelling traditions all play a part in how history comes down to future generations. Of course, Scotland has been no exception to this – take, for example, the many traditions and legends about the Stone of Destiny.

Long before castles, whisky, golf or major scientific inventions, Scotland existed and had a history. But just how an 'image of Scotland' started, how it was shaped and evolved though time is fascinating enough. The 'tartan and shortbread' image is known to have largely been started by Sir Walter Scott in comparatively recent times. The 'Ossian controversy' of the 18th C is still being discussed among researchers today, whether James MacPherson's famous work *Ossian* was authentic or not. But given that it was known to be Napoleon's favourite reading at the time, and also that of many other prominent people on the Continent in the 18th C, perhaps it does not ultimately matter. It certainly put Scotland 'on the map' to the rest of the world at the time, much like the film *Braveheart* did in more recent times. Fact or fiction, the *effect* remains.

But there have actually been many other portrayals of early Scotland throughout the ages, and many of these come from a variety of sources, some of which might seem rather unusual to us today. Much of the major origin-myth of Scotland started in ancient times as part of oral tradition, and was then later further developed throughout the so-called Dark Ages, culminating in the famous Declaration of Arbroath in 1320.

Recently, the world was watching on 1 July 1999 as the new, devolved Scottish Parliament was opened in Edinburgh. This was a truly historic occasion, as the last Parliament in Scotland was in 1707, nearly three hundred years ago. In 1996, a stone (dubbed by some the 'Stone of Destiny') that Edward 1 took from Scone in 1296 was finally returned to Scotland. In April 2001, Sir Sean Connery, a living legend of our time, was presented with the William Wallace Award in Washington DC for his contribution to furthering American-Scottish relations, as part of the new USA 'Tartan Day' celebrations. It is now widely known that for a country of its relatively small size, Scotland has produced an inordinately high number of geniuses including Carnegie and Adam Smith. Scotland, it seems, has been in the news more than ever.

Other major Scottish symbols like the Stone of Destiny, tartan and the saltire, the national flag of Scotland, are also important to history and of which we will learn about later. But we will begin with the origin-myth, history and traditions about the origin of a people and their nation.

'The Scots' of history

So who were 'the Scots' of history? This is a complex question, as much of the whole process of defining the nation and its people started long, long ago. Dr William Ferguson of the University of Edinburgh points out in *The Identity of the Scottish Nation* that there formed in Dark Age Europe:

> ... compounds of tribal lore, of the fabulous histories of Greece and Rome, and above all, the new source of religious knowledge, the Holy Bible... the pagan West Saxon dynasty in England derived its descent from Woden, but by the ninth century the descent of Alfred the Great was traced back to Adam... tribes had relied on oral tradition... but after the acceptance of the Christian faith reliance came to be placed more on writings, though oral transmission would long continue Indeed, the written record and oral transmission began to interact.[1]

So the earlier stories that had been told for centuries were then later written down. This also happened in many other countries – Ireland, England, France, Greece, Israel, Spain, to name but a few. But as Ferguson and others believe, 'in few countries has this particular issue of the antiquity and virtue of the race lasted longer or caused more controversy than in Scotland.'[2]

Scotland has always had strong oral traditions and some of these were later incorporated into various origin-myths about who the Scots were and where they came from. As Dr Ferguson says,

> The reception and elaboration of the origin-myth of the Scots in early medieval Scotland is, in fact, shrouded in mystery. Was it transmitted by oral tradition alone? That might account for some of its vagaries... Or did the medieval Scots use their current oral versions to help preserve... earlier written sources? That is also a possibility... But, unfortunately, conclusive documentary proof of the exact provenance of the Scottish origin-myth that was advanced in medieval Scotland is not to be had.[3]

So, the exact source(s) for the major origin-myth of Scotland is still not known for certain today. Historians acknowledge that many early written sources in Scotland were either sacked by the Vikings, stolen, destroyed, or perhaps hidden away, leaving much less for modern researchers to work with than would normally be the case. But what is indisputable is the fact that the Scots in the 12th and 13th centuries were growing more and more concerned about their ethnic origins, their right to the land they inhabited, and were fearful of a growing threat from their powerful English neighbours. So, they did what many peoples in history have done in similar circumstances: they relied on the origins, history, oral and written traditions of the nation, to help solidify a feeling of national identity, a right to independence, ethnic origins, and so on. This resulted one of the most passionate, memorable and rhetorical documents of all time – the Declaration of Arbroath.

The Declaration of Arbroath

In the year 1320AD, a letter to the Pope was written that defined and outlined the character of a people and their nation. It was written in the aftermath of the difficult Wars of Independence against England which came to a head in 1314 with the Scottish victory at the Battle of Bannockburn. It has become synonymous with the terms freedom and civil liberty. It had quite an impact in its day, and is also believed to have had an influence on the American Declaration of Independence some 450 years later.[4]

This letter, also known as the *Letter from the Barons of Scotland to Pope John XXII*, was designed to influence the papacy in the favour of the Scottish king Robert the Bruce, who had been bravely fighting against the English king Edward 1 and his aggressive moves towards Scotland for some time. Bruce (Robert 1) had been excommunicated by the church primarily due to his having murdered a competitor in the past with some accomplices, something that is admittedly abhorrent, but actually was not as rare in medieval times as we may think today. So, understandably, the church took action against Bruce and then began harassing the powerful nationalistic bishops of Scotland:

> As a sacrilegious murderer and excommunicate he and his cause were ill-regarded in Rome, and The Letter of the Barons aimed to explain the situation in Scotland and to exculpate King Robert. The result was a truly remarkable document...[5]

The Declaration of Arbroath was summarised by one historian as 'one of the masterpieces of political rhetoric of all time'.[6] And indeed it was.

Who? And where?

For many years, the author of the Declaration has been assumed to have been Bernard de Linton, Abbot of Arbroath and Chancellor of Scotland, as he was the overall signatory who signed the document dated 6 April 1320. However, recent scholarship has contested this, as Professor Ted Cowan of Glasgow University explains:

Just who did mastermind the letter of 1320 is not known. An earlier generation was confident that it was composed by Bernard de Linton... [but] Professor Duncan has now demonstrated that Bernard de Linton and Abbot Bernard of Arbroath, the chancellor, were different people... The case against Bernard, however, is not absolutely conclusive... The candidate suggested for authorship by Professor Barrow is Mr Alexander Kinninmonth, a canon lawyer with considerable curial experience and future bishop of Aberdeen; he was one of the ambassadors who accompanied the 1320 missive to the papal court at Avignon... Authorship will probably never be conclusively proven...[7]

Cowan believes that whoever did write the Declaration very likely had access to important earlier documents, such as the Declaration of 1309, the Irish letter of 1317, the works of John of Salisbury, as well as other material in 1320. So, although actual authorship may never be known for certain, it is very likely that a specific group contributed to its overall rhetoric, metaphor and style.

Arbroath Abbey, in the northeast of Scotland, was founded by William I in 1178 and dedicated to St Thomas Becket. It has always been assumed that the 1320 Declaration was written at Arbroath, although it is now believed by experts at Historic Scotland to have been drafted at a council held at Newbattle Abbey, in Midlothian, near Edinburgh, in March of 1320.[8]

But it is now also being questioned by experts whether or not the Declaration was actually signed at Arbroath on the 6 April 1320, as has always been assumed. Today, the USA and some Canadian provinces have officially adopted the 6 April as Tartan Day, in honour of Scotland and its beliefs in freedom and resistance to tyranny, concepts which largely have come down to us from the Declaration of Arbroath. Exact date or not, the 6 April continues to remain symbolic of Scotland, freedom and the Declaration of Arbroath.

The origin-myth in the Declaration of Arbroath

So what did the Declaration of Arbroath say about who 'the Scots' were and where they came from? And why is it so important?

Clearly, this is a rhetorical document and passionate in its pleas. A brief summary might be something like this:

The Scottish nation had a very distinguished history, originating in Greater Scythia, in the vicinity of the Black Sea, from where they wandered through the Mediterranean to the Straits of Gibraltar for a lengthy sojourn in Spain. Then, 1,200 years after the Israelites crossed the Red Sea, the Scots were identified as a chosen people, and arrived in Scotland to defeat the Britons and Picts while fighting off constant attacks from the Scandinavians and the English. The Declaration then says that the Scottish nation had held its possessions 'free of all servitude ever since,' under the custodianship of 113 kings, 'the line unbroken by a single foreigner'. Even though the Scots existed 'at the uttermost ends of the earth', they were singled out among the first for salvation through the medium of St Andrew, the first-called of all the disciples.[9]

Then, the Declaration continues, saying that the Scots, a favoured people in the eyes of God, were protected by successive popes as a 'special charge' of St Andrew, and were living in freedom and peace until the English arrived in the guise of a friend, when in fact, they were an enemy. God intervened to save his people through King Robert the Bruce, who is compared to another courageous Maccabeus or a Joshua.[10]

Next – the most famous part – is about King Robert the Bruce and the role of the king in relation to his people, which deserves to be quoted in full:

> ... [our] king. We are bound to him for the maintaining of our freedom both by his rights and merits... Yet if he should give up what he has begun, seeking to make us or our kingdom subject to the king of England or the English, we would strive at once to drive him out as our enemy and a subverter of his own right and ours, and we would make some other man who was able to defend us our king. For as long as a hundred of us remain alive we will never on any conditions be subjected to the lordship of the English. For we fight not for glory nor riches nor honours, but for freedom alone, which no good man gives up except with his life.[11]

The Pope is then urged to 'admonish and exhort' the English king Edward II 'to leave in peace us Scots'... who are willing to concede whatever is necessary for peace, even offering to help the Pope fight in future Crusades, if peace be theirs. However, *if* the Pope will not credit their sincerity, future calamities will be laid at his door. They undertake to obey the Pope and they entrust their cause to God, and conclude by wishing the Pope holiness, health and long life. Dated 6 April 1320.[12]

The Community of the Realm: a new concept

This is an extraordinary claim – where the Scots say that if their king, Robert the Bruce, would not defend them for any reason, that they would replace him. This was a bold statement to make, and especially in those times, as European monarchs were generally perceived as ruling from 'the top down' and rarely with the consent of the people. However, here the Scots are declaring, to put it plainly: if King Robert (or his descendants) ever 'sells out' to the English, then he will simply be kicked off the Scottish throne and replaced.

The implication behind this is that the sovereign only remains a sovereign *by the will of the people*, and not merely by 'divine right' – a new idea at the time. Unlike the subjects of England, by inference, the Scots were saying that in Scotland, their view was that *all* of the people were equal in status to the king. The whole Scottish concept of 'the Community of the Realm' was further nurtured by this courageous document, akin to a type of Scottish constitution. Later, in the American Declaration of Independence, we also find the concept of governance by 'the consent of the governed'. In 1776, Thomas Jefferson wrote:

> ... that to secure these rights, governments are instituted among men, deriving their just powers from the consent of the governed; that whenever any form of government becomes destructive of these ends, it is the right of the people to alter or abolish it...[13]

In his 1993 book on the Declaration of Arbroath, James Adam says:

> It is a document remarkable for its sturdy independence expressed within a loyalty to the Pope. It is noteworthy also for its

Celtic attitude to the power of the Throne. Almost alone among the nations of feudal Europe where the accepted concept was that authority flowed downward from the crown, Scotland stated clearly and firmly that here the rights flow upward from the people. In the presence of the King, they made it plain that he had their support as long as he did not betray them and that, should he do so, they would choose another King. The Letter used exceptionally direct language to the Pope and did not hesitate to indicate potential areas of guilt and blame.[14]

This statement is the first recorded instance in European history of the contractual theory of monarchy, a fact that is taken for granted now but which originates from this unprecedented work. It is a document that takes a strong stand for freedom, especially from oppression and tyranny. In modern times, one can almost sense the spirit of this with the admittedly stereotyped image of Mel Gibson and his men in *Braveheart* shouting 'Freedom'!

The very idea that King Robert the Bruce might actually be deposed and another set up in his place was revolutionary in its time, a concept that scholars have tried to determine the precise source of. Many theories abound, from the powerful Celtic concepts of kingship that the Scots obviously already knew about, to the Arthurian ideal of the king that would 'rise again' and 'save his people', to biblical parallels, and so on.

Professor Ted Cowan mentions that the writings of the churchman Thomas Aquinas may even have been an inspiration to the clerics, nobles and barons who wrote the Declaration, perhaps especially the powerful bishops of the time, such as Bishop Wishart or Lamberton.[15] Aquinas is seen by many historians as an important link between classical thought and civic humanism, and was widely read at the time. He observed that 'the state is nothing but the congregation of men' and 'lesser evil follows from the corruption of a monarchy than from the corruption of an aristocracy'.[16] Aquinas addressed the problem of tyranny, and in some of his writings, implied that tyrants may be removed by public authority and that the king's power must be limited – points that are also evident in the Declaration of Arbroath.

The Scottish Wars of Independence

The Declaration was obviously written in reaction to what had been happening in the period leading up to 1320, which had been a most difficult and challenging time for the Scots. In spite of the Scots' stunning victory over the English at Bannockburn in 1314, Edward II carried on the hostilities that his father Edward I had started in 1296 in his attempts to conquer Scotland. In 1296, Edward I attempted to show the Scots that they had become annexed to England – as had already happened to the Welsh.

The annexation of Wales resulted from the Statute of Wales in 1284; in 1301 it was finalised by the creation of the title of 'the Prince of Wales', which is still in use today by the heir to the throne. Ceremoniously, Edward also carried the most powerful talismanic symbols held by the Welsh on his Scottish campaign in 1296, including the important relic of a piece of the True Cross and the legendary Crown of King Arthur. These were then later taken to Westminster to humiliate the Welsh even further.

Edward I was astute in that he clearly saw the value of such symbols to a nation's pride and identity. After subduing the Welsh, he then tried to break the will of the Scots, by having the national seal broken and carrying off special symbols of power – the Scottish Coronation Stone of Scone, the Holy Rood of St Margaret, other precious relics, and national records. Understandably, the Scots angrily retaliated with an aggressive series of battles to save their independence. These would last for some time.

The 1320 Declaration by the Scots was an appeal to the Pope against continued aggression from the English. The problem was that the Pope acknowledged the sovereignty of Edward I, but not that of Robert the Bruce, as he had murdered his opponent to the Scottish throne, John 'the red' Comyn, in the Greyfriars Kirk of Dumfries on 11 February 1306.

As a result of this, Robert became king. However, as this act had also defiled the church as a sanctuary, he was understandably excommunicated by the Pope. But by doing so, Bruce was obviously aware that this would have probably been a likely result, as historians now note. It is also interesting that the powerful nationalistic bishops, especially Wishart and Lamberton, had what we might call today a rather 'muted response' to this. Bruce was clearly acting in deliberate defiance of the papacy in a number of ways early on.

Robert the Bruce as 'a Maccabean hero'

Robert the Bruce was certainly a courageous leader and in the Declaration of Arbroath, the Scots compare him to the great hero of the Maccabees of Israel. From a rare 1850 book by William Livingston entitled *Vindication of the Celtic Character*, we read that:

> ... our Prince and King, Robert, who, in delivering his people out of the hands of their enemies, as another Maccabee or Joshua... whom also, by Divine Providence, and the right of succession, according to our laws and customs, which we will maintain to the utmost, and with the due consent of all of us, have we made him our Prince and King...[17]

Here the Scottish king, Robert I, is compared to the great hero of the Apocryphal first book of Maccabees, Judas Maccabeus. The confident tone of the words that follow are perhaps not too unlike the message of the Declaration of Arbroath. The account is from 1 Maccabees 3: 2-6:

> He had the support of all his brothers and his father's followers, and they carried on Israel's campaign with zest. He enhanced his people's glory. Like a giant he put on his breastplate and girt himself with weapons of war. He waged many a campaign from a camp well guarded with the sword. He was like a lion in his exploits... while the cause of freedom prospered in his hands.

Slightly further on in 1 Maccabees 3: 19-22, it says:

> Victory does not depend on numbers; strength is from Heaven alone. Our enemies, inflated with insolence and lawlessness, are coming against us; they mean to kill us... But we are fighting for our lives and for our laws and customs, and Heaven will crush them before our eyes; you have no need to be afraid of them.

The spirit of the wording in these biblical passages does seem to parallel certain sentiments of the Declaration, especially regarding King Robert the Bruce as a leader of an oppressed people, blessed by God, to fight for their freedom no matter what the cost.

Who were the Maccabees?

But who, then, were the Maccabees? The books of the Maccabees were known to many throughout Europe at the time the Declaration was written, with the Jewish martyrs already having an established cult. The *Oxford Dictionary of Saints* tells us a bit more about the Maccabees, who fought and died rather than compromise their beliefs:

> The cult of these Old Testament martyrs in the Christian Church is both ancient and widespread... They are believed to typify the Christian martyrs who found themselves in similar circumstances and the cult may be held to reveal the close connection between Jewry and early Christianity and to show Christian sympathies for the sufferings of Jewish martyrs in the Roman Empire.[18]

Interestingly, earlier, in 1301, *Edward I himself was compared to the tyrant Antiochus, the infamous defiler of the Temple of Jerusalem,* by Scottish envoys at the papal court. This notorious action of Antiochus is widely believed to have been the primary cause of the whole Maccabean revolt. The envoys alleged that like the biblical tyrant Antiochus, Edward I afflicted Scotland with many atrocities, and, 'like Antiochus he defiled despotically with sacrilegious recklessness [its] church abominations of numerous kinds'.[19]

Robert the Bruce, knighthood and chivalric values

The chivalric ideal of the Crusading knight, brave, loyal and courageous, has also influenced Scotland's values. For example, when historian Walter Bower repeated the charges against the English king, 'he explicitly evoked the chivalric ethic, claiming that Edward began to stir up strife 'as soon as he became a knight'...'[20] Robert the Bruce, after Bannockburn, was known by the epithet 'First Knight of Christiandom'.

Regarding the Declaration of Arbroath, 'the widespread admiration in which Joshua and Judas Maccabeus were held in the Middle Ages was a notable aspect of the cult of chivalry and, from an early stage, chivalric writers had ranked these two – and the latter in particular – foremost amongst the heroes of Christian chivalry'.[21] Indeed, in the tradition of the devout French Knight Templar Geoffrey de Charney, Judas Maccabeus represented the pinnacle of courage and knightly achievement and was seen as representative of the highest honours of chivalry.[22]

As King of Scotland, Robert the Bruce also destroyed the previous alliance that he had enjoyed with Edward I in earlier times, and so naturally Edward then became a formidable enemy. The decisive victory over the English army in 1314 at Bannockburn finally assured his reign and brought together the Scottish people as a confident force, and a stronger feeling of nationhood emerged.

The 'right to anointment'

However, years were to pass before England, or the papacy, actually accepted that outcome. A truce wasn't established until 1323, nine years later. In 1328, when Robert the Bruce was finally recognised as the king of an independent realm by the Treaty of Northampton, he asked the Pope to grant him and his successors the 'right to anointment', i.e. the right to anoint successive kings of Scots. Although Robert was recognised as king of Scotland, he didn't yet have the right to anoint a successor, which needed to come from the Pope. But the Scots still had to wait quite some time before this was done; finally, Pope John XXII issued his bull of 13 June 1329 which authorised the anointing of the kings of Scots. This was the same year that Robert the Bruce was gravely ill and finally died.

Strangely enough, this bull never mentions anything about Scotland still being a 'papal fief', as that previously oft-repeated claim seems to have rather suddenly lapsed. Unfortunately Robert the Bruce died before the actual anointing ceremony could take place. But it was the Declaration of Arbroath in 1320 that eventually achieved, among other things, the full recognition of the Scottish king and his right to anoint successive kings of Scots

As Dr William Ferguson puts it (emphasis ours): 'The origin-myth was *the linchpin that held the Scottish case together*, and it figured prominently in the long disputes from 1290 to 1329.'[23] Truly, the power of assorted historical myths and legends to literally 'make history' is evident in this case.

Early Scottish origin legends

Of course, received wisdom says of the Declaration of Arbroath that most of it was merely very clever rhetoric, an assortment of various myths and legends. Certainly this would appear to be the case. But upon learning that we were working on this book, and of hearing about the origin-myth in the Declaration of Arbroath, a friend of one of the authors, a trial attorney, asked: But perhaps there might have been 'a kernel of truth' in their case somewhere? After all, it doesn't seem that the Scots would have had any motive to simply lie outright to the papacy – especially when trying to make a good impression and seeking the Pope's help on behalf of their excommunicate king. They would have wanted to put their 'best case forward'. So, did the Pope ever actually dispute their claims? If he felt they were lying, he would certainly have every reason to be angry and tell them so, and even take action. The English would certainly have exploited that, too. So, what did he say in response?

Ironically, we had to admit that we didn't know, but acknowledged that these were interesting, provocative points, perhaps typical coming from a trial lawyer who loves to argue!

But we also had to admit that we had rarely seen this particular issue addressed directly in the established histories, as complicated issues like this are often dealt with as footnotes in fine print, or sidelined in relation to other larger issues. We did acknowledge, however, that it is widely known that the Declaration was deliberately constructed by those in favour of Bruce, so, in a sense, it was, at the very least, a brilliant 'medieval spin doctor' document, in modern-day parlance.

We also knew that the Pope did not deny the important connection of the Scots to St Andrew, for example. This was only one point about one of the claims by the Scots in the Declaration. St Andrew was said by the Church to have gone to Asia Minor and also to parts of the Scythian area to spread the gospel – precisely where the Scots claimed they came from. Clearly, much more research needs to be done regarding the specific arguments used in both directions about these claims, for clarification.

Admittedly, in our modern times, it does seem quite unusual – or even outright bizarre – for the Scots to have stated that they originally came from Greater Scythia by the Black Sea, and that they had travelled a very great distance for centuries, finally arriving in what is now Scotland. A strange tale indeed. But, to be fair, every nation has its myths. The Americans have the cherished legend of George Washington and the cherry tree, for instance, and so the Scots have stories of their Scythian origins, the Stone of Destiny, and so on.

However, whilst 'myth-bashing' has been common in modern times, much of this type of material has not been studied in any great detail at all. However, an increasing number of serious scholars are now acknowledging that *the belief systems of a people* – which, like it or not, do include their historical tales, legends and myths – have been found to have influenced the core political, economic and legal aspects and values of society in a much larger way than has been previously believed. They are worthy of serious study in their own right, as history has shown that their effect has been great and enduring. After all, Heinrich Schliemann *did* shock the world when he actually found the ancient city of Troy, based on clues in Homer's *Iliad*, years ago.

Historical facts and legends are often so intertwined in early history that it is often difficult to distinguish between the two. But does this then mean that *all* myths and legends are automatically false, or that all history is true? No, it does not, as it all depends on who wrote it, and what their viewpoints and intentions were. Usually, as we know today, the victor ends up writing the history. So, their worldview and values predominate, whether accurate or not.

The important thing here is to try to get into the mind of the medieval Scots in order to really understand where *they* were coming from. In medieval times, people believed differently than we do now, and we must remember this, difficult as it may seem to us today.

'Greater Scythian' origins

As historians have noted, in telling the Pope in the Declaration of their conversion by St Andrew, and of their arrival in Scotland 1,200 years or so after 'the outpouring of the peoples of Israel', the Scots – incredibly – seem to be implying to him that they were actually connected to Israel in some way. This legendary origin-myth of a 'chosen people by God' is one that other peoples in history have also claimed, for various reasons. Of course, this is a seemingly fanciful area to explore, but it cannot be denied that the many existing legends about, for example, the Stone of Destiny, Scottish kingship, and for some reason *seem to relate to biblical or Old Testament themes and legends*. The question is: why? And why is this emphasis so persistent?

The 9th C Welsh writer Nennius mentions early migrations to the north, where the Scots come from Egypt via Spain before landing in Ireland:

> According to the most learned among the Scots... Ireland was a desert and uninhabited when the children of Israel crossed the Red Sea, in which ... the Egyptians who followed them were drowned. At that period, there lived among this people, with a numerous family, a Scythian of noble birth who had been banished from his country, and did not go to pursue the people of God. The Egyptians who were left, seeing the destruction of the great men of their nation, and fearing lest he should possess himself of their territory, took counsel together and expelled him.[24]

The expulsion of this Scythian noble man and his family, who is later said to have led his descendants into Spain, and then further north to become the Scots, is the crux of the matter here. However, the overall idea of the Scots being 'a wandering people' or nation remains consistent. That certain tribes of Israel constitute this 'wandering nation' are also part and parcel of other traditions:

> These Jews were, in fact, not the people that Moses led out of Egypt but the remnant of Judah taken to Egypt by Jeremiah, following the fall of Jerusalem in 586BC.[25]

So why is 'Scythia' mentioned so often?

Again and again we seem to be faced with the term 'Scythia' and reference to the 'Greater Scythia' area. These terms have been much debated through the years. The term Scythian has been linked with more than one early people from the British Isles in their early histories. The Scots, Picts, Irish, Britons and Anglo-Saxons all have ancient accounts of ancestors supposedly coming from Scythia, near the Black Sea, and also from an area called 'Greater Scythia', as stated in the Declaration of Arbroath, which incorporates a larger area in the same vicinity.

The Welsh, who rightly identify themselves with the ancient P-Celtic speaking Britons, still refer to themselves as the Cymry. The term Cymry equates with the Cimmerians in early accounts, who are related to the Welsh and the lowland Scots, and they, too, have claimed descent at various times from the Scythian area:

> Homer tells: 'And it (Ulysses' ship) reached the extreme boundaries of the deep-flowing ocean; where are the people and city of the Cimmerians covered with shadow and vapour, nor does the shining sun behold them with his beams, neither when he goes towards the starry heaven, nor when he turns back again from heaven to earth; but pernicious night is spread over the hapless mortals.' Historically the Cimmerii lived to the east of the Black Sea, in what was called Sarmatia... according to Herodotus, the Sarmatians themselves were a horse-riding people descendants of the Amazons by Scythian fathers... the (Scythian) men failed to learn the language of the women and the women learned that of the men imperfectly, and thus 'Sarmatian' was a corrupt Scythian.[26]

Interestingly, as we will see in chapter 6, one of the more controversial academic theories currently being debated is about the possible origins of many of the Arthurian themes supposedly coming from a Scythian tribe called the Sarmatians, near the Black Sea.

Many writers have concluded that rather than just being simply a reference to ethnic origins, 'Scythian' is also a term that has been used to designate a migratory or a wandering people in general. Sandford, Lancaster Herald of Arms in the time of James II, states that when Edward I brought the coronation stone from Scotland, there was a piece of wood attached to it, on which were cut in Latin the following lines:

Ni fallst fatum Scoti hune quocunque locatum, Inyeniunt lapidem regnare tenentur ibidem.

If fates go right, where'er this stone is found, The Scots shall monarchs of that realm be found.

Sir Walter Scott, in a translation of Irish lines into English regarding the same stone, writes:

Unless the fates be faithless grown, or prophet's voice be vain, Where'er is found this sacred stone, the wanderers race shall reign.[27]

Here Scott is referring to a *'wanderers race'*. The following translation, made by the Scottish historian Hector Boece in 1537, is interesting in that Boece gives a translation of the Gaelic original which we are told read:

If the prophecy is not false, Wherever the hoary pillow is found, By right out of the free nation of Scots Kings will be taken.[28]

Boece here refers to the stone as *'the hoary pillow'*, thought by many to be a reference to Jacob's Pillow and the implications that has regarding the Stone of Destiny.

The Picts were, according to some accounts, 'descended from a colony of 'Scythian' or 'Thracian' seafarers who took wives from among the Irish before settling in the Orkney Islands and northern Scotland'.[29] Early writers like Herodotus, Bede and Nennius all mention this. We will learn more about the enigmatic Picts in chapter 3.

The term 'Scot' can mean many different things to many different people, an issue which we will explore at various points throughout this book. In ancient times, northern Britain was also called 'Alba', a named still referred to by some as Scotland today.[30]

Dr Vittorio Bertoldi, a highly regarded language scholar, has shown that the prefix 'alb' is actually *pre*-Indo-European, and that it is found in the largest concentrations around the Caucasian mountains near the Black Sea area. He believes that the prefix 'alb' probably entered Latin as a loan word with a connotation of 'white', acquired by an association with snow-capped mountains in the area. So, consider the theory of some: Did these very early pre-Indo-European 'wanderers' somehow end up in early Scotland?[31]

Ancient human habitation in the Black Sea area

Ironically, in September 2000 a highly unusual discovery was made by professional archaeologists twelve miles off the coast of Sinop, Turkey, in the Black Sea, which could possibly significantly change history regarding early migrations into Europe.

Dr Robert Ballard, Director of the Institute for Exploration and the expert marine geologist who discovered the wreck of the Titanic, has now discovered signs of ancient human habitation 300 feet *below* the current surface of the Black Sea. Emmy-award winning science and medical journalist Linda Moulton Howe explains:

> Never before in world archaeology has any human habitation been found so deep under water. He has been using submersion vessels to look for old river beds beneath the Black Sea where people might have lived before a great flood inundated the region about 7,000 years ago... using that river bed strategy, he found the remains of a stone house with fireplace and grooved wooden beams...[32]

Many cultures have stories and legends about a great flood, and of course, the Black Sea is no exception. Dr Ballard himself states 'What you have in the Black Sea flood, is a permanent flood that would have driven people away forever who would have to have settled a new land...'[33] Dr Ballard and his colleagues believe that these people had no choice but to flee, and that they possibly went into Mesopotamia, as well as further west and north. This Black Sea flood was 7,000 years ago, having occurred in about 5000BC.

But, of course, we are not implying that this necessarily means anything in relation to the ancient Scots, or Celts, per se, but, nonetheless, it would seem that this new discovery cannot be totally discounted either. The important issue here is that the very idea of early peoples migrating into Europe, saying that they had been a 'travelling people' from very far away, seems to have been a rather common phenomenon in early times, and may have been for very good reasons. Even now, there are many refugees in Europe who come from many faraway locales, sometimes due to a natural disaster, for example.

Many ancient peoples in their traditions and legends say they migrated from somewhere far away, and it appears that the early 'Scots' – or, more accurately, those who were *called* 'the Scots' – seem to be no exception to this. But it seems rather ironic that a leading international archaeological expert is now saying that certain early peoples were obviously forced to flee from the Black Sea area, i.e. Greater Scythia, by a great flood that is known by scientists today to have occurred around 5000BC.

Linguistic and genetic research: 'Greater Scythia'

Linguists – and now geneticists – have known for some time that the Indo-Europeans, of whom the Celts are a part, are thought to have originated in Turkey, then migrated from the Caucasian mountains area near the Black Sea in the southern steppes of Russia, into Europe. This theory has been put forth by Dr Colin Renfrew of Cambridge University and others. The early Kurgan culture is known to have been located in the southern Russian steppes, and to have been a major area from which Indo-European languages spread, as argued by archaeologist Dr Marjia Gimbutas and shown by modern-day genetic research. New excavations have shown that horses and war chariots were a key part of this culture, and, of course, we know that they are frequently mentioned in many early Celtic tales and legends.

One prominent geneticist and cultural historian, Professor Luigi Luca Cavalli-Sforza, states that:

...it may be useful to refer to the original Indo-European spoken in Turkey 10,000 years ago as the primary Indo-European, pre-proto-Indo-European, and to that spoken 4,000 or 5,000 years later in the Kurgan region as secondary or proto-Indo-European. It is clear that, genetically speaking, peoples of the Kurgan steppe... immigrated there from Turkey. To arrive north of the Black Sea, farmers from Turkey may have expanded west of the Black Sea, through Romania, and/or along the eastern coast of the Black Sea... Shortly after their arrival, these Neolithic farmers domesticated the horse... [later]... with the first development of bronze (around 5,000 years ago) they were on the brink of an expansion... there were many expansions, both eastward to Central Asia and westward toward Europe...[34]

The Celts came from the western part of the Kurgan area, originally from Turkey, very early on, he and other experts now believe. The Celtic languages are part of one of the major Indo-European branches of languages, along with Balto-Slavic, Italic, and Germanic subfamilies, as linguists and geneticists acknowledge. But, of course, there were also indigenous peoples present in Europe already, before these 'waves' of conquering Indo-Europeans arrived, of which little is known about today.

The strange case of the 'Tartan Mummies' of Takla Makan

If the Black Sea archaeological discovery mentioned earlier doesn't seem surprising enough, consider this: another archaeological discovery was finally made public in the 1990s, involving the almost perfectly preserved 3,500 year-old mummies of an unknown, extinct people in China's Takla Makan desert. This desert lies along the ancient 'Great Silk Road' between Kazakhstan, Kyrgyzstan and Tibet. It is still one of the driest places on earth, so these mummies and their graves were incredibly well preserved for scientists to study.

This extraordinary discovery was featured in Britain on the BBC and in a Channel 4 documentary two years ago. With their reddish-blond hair, pale skin, long noses, round eyes and finely woven tartan clothing, these extraordinary mummies were *scientifically proven to have had undeniably European roots*. They are believed to be those of an early Indo-European people called the Tocharians, who migrated east from the southern steppes of Russia in earlier times.

But, understandably, this discovery has also caused a major political storm in China, as the mummies are clearly not of Chinese origin as they obviously have Caucasian features. The government there has called a halt to all excavation in the area. However, a team of western archaeologists did study them throughout the 1970s and 1980s, the results of which have more recently been made public.

But it is the *tartan* (or twill) woven clothing that was found on the mummies that is of special interest here. Specialist textile experts were also among the archaeological teams that were allowed to examine and test the mummies. In *The Tarim Mummies*, Archaeologists Dr J P Mallory and Dr Victor H Mair state:

> ...the earliest twills known derive from the region between Turkey and the Caucasus where they are dated to the late 4th and 3rd millennium BC, and they are found in abundance from the late 2nd millennium BC in Europe... true twills are unknown in China until well into the 1st millennium BC. The Qizilchoqa twill is virtually identical to the textile fragments recovered from Hallstatt... the earliest Indo-Europeans would have known plaid twill and carried it west into central and western Europe, where it would later emerge among the Celts of the Hallstatt culture... [35]

Highly regarded ancient – textile expert Dr Elizabeth W Barber commented on the great similarity to Scottish tartan, saying:

> Not only does this woollen plaid twill look like Scottish tartans, but it also has the same weight, feel and initial thickness as kilt cloth, and as the Hallstatt materials... If the Bronze and Iron Age ancestors of the historic Celts wove woollen plaid twills so similar to modern ones, clearly the prenationalist Scots in the intervening centuries wove this sort of thing too... [36]

Perhaps the references to the early Scythians, the Black Sea area, and so on, may now be better clarified in light of these recent scientific discoveries. The word 'tartan' itself derives from the French *tiretaine*, a cloth that was half wool and half linen. The oldest tartan in Scotland dates from about 325AD, the early part of the 4th C. It was found near Falkirk and is now housed in the National Museum of Scotland.[37] Not many tartans have survived in Scotland, mainly because cloth on the whole doesn't preserve too well in its climate and soil conditions.

But as the Takla Makan desert is still one of the driest places on earth, tartan cloth from much earlier times has survived there that is very similar, if not nearly identical, to the Scottish type of tartan, which has greatly intrigued archaeologists and other scientific experts today.

Princess Scota, Tamar Tephi and the Stone of Destiny

In addition to references to 'Greater Scythia' and the Black Sea area in these early origin legends, we also find that the Prophet Jeremiah and the Scots are linked by another powerful tradition – the legend of the *Lia-Fail*, also known as 'the Stone of Destiny'. This stone, said to be the Coronation Stone of the early Irish and Scottish kings, is also called Jacob's Pillow, or Pillar. Scottish tradition says it originally came from Israel with 'a wandering people', eventually reaching Ireland and then Scotland. In old accounts of this legend, the prophet Jeremiah brings this most holy relic of the people of Israel, Jacob's Pillow, to Ireland.

Jacob's Pillow, also called the Stone of Scone and the Coronation Stone by some, has a very special place in British history. It is internationally famous 'as the sacred stone on which successive English, and after the union of the English and Scottish crowns in 1603, British monarchs have been crowned. This symbolic role stretches across the centuries from the coronation of Edward II in 1308 until, most recently, the coronation of Elizabeth II in 1953.'[38] The stone is very ancient and arguably the most powerful symbol of Scottish nationhood today.

The story of this stone, so famous in Scottish legend and history, begins in the Old Testament, when the patriarch Jacob rests his head on a stone on his way to Harran. The account is in Genesis 28, 10-22:

> Jacob set out from Beersheba and went on his way towards Harran. He came to a certain place and stopped there for the night, because the sun had set; and taking one of the stones there, he made a pillow for his head and lay down to sleep. He dreamt that he saw a ladder, which rested on the ground with its top

reaching to heaven, and angels of God were going up and down upon it...

This may sound rather familiar, perhaps from Sunday school, for example, the well-known story of 'Jacob's ladder'. Next, the Lord speaks to Jacob:

> The Lord was standing beside him and said, 'I am the Lord, the God of your father Abraham and the God of Isaac. This land on which you are lying I will give to you and your descendants. They shall be countless as the dust upon the earth, and you shall spread far and wide, to north and south, to east and west. All the families of the earth shall pray to be blessed as you and your descendants are blessed... Jacob rose early in the morning, took the stone on which he had laid his head, set it up as a sacred pillar and poured oil on the top of it. He named the place Beth-El...

In other words, after such an extraordinary dream about the blessings of the Lord upon his people, he understandably felt that the stone – 'Jacob's Pillow' – was also very special; so he then anointed it with oil. The Bible tells us next:

> Thereupon Jacob made his vow: 'If God will be with me, if he will protect me on my journey and give me food to eat and clothes to wear, and I come back safely to my father's house, then the Lord shall be my God, and this stone which I have set up as a sacred pillar shall be a house of God...

This symbol of a 'Chosen People', a special stone of some type, forms much of the basis of the Irish and Scottish origin and kingship legends, and it is also present in the legends and history of other peoples. The early kings of Israel were said to be in close contact with the pillar stone, 'Jacob's Pillow':

> ...a tradition was being kept that the kings of Israel received their crowns in the Temple and in close contact with the Pillar Stone set there by their forefather.[39]

Scottish coronation ceremony

This same practice was continued by the kings of Scotland during their Coronation ceremony, making the stone central to the inauguration of a Scottish king. Dr Louise Yeoman, of the National Library of Scotland, in *Reportage Scotland*, includes a description of the formal inauguration of Alexander III in 1249. Written by the Canon of Inchcolm, Walter Bower, writing about 200 years later, it includes a description of the main aspects of the Scottish coronation ceremony:

> With due reverence they installed him there on the royal seat which had been bedecked with silk cloths embroidered with gold... the king was solemnly seated on this royal seat of stone, with his crown on his head and his sceptre in his hand, and clothed in royal purple, and at his feet the earls and other nobles were setting down their stools to listen to a sermon...[40]

The stone – here described as a 'royal seat of stone' – was obviously a key focus of the entire coronation ritual.

Some chronicles say that many years after the destruction of Solomon's Temple, Gaythelus, a Scythian prince living in Egypt together with his Egyptian Princess Scota, travelled further north with the stone. Certain versions say that it journeyed via Spain and Ireland while others recount that it was brought to Scone directly from Egypt.

The mention of a 'Princess Scota' is interesting, as two of them are mentioned in early Irish and Scottish annals, and they have a connection with Scythia. Her name Scota, and that of Scythia, were probably both pronounced with a hard 'C', sounding like a 'K' to our ears now. The earliest Scota was said to have been the daughter of an Egyptian pharaoh named Cinciris,

> Originally, she was Akenkheres' daughter Merytaten, who had married Prince Niul of Greater Scythia. Hence, she became Princess of Scythia (pronounced 'Scota')...[41]

We then learn more about the second Princess Scota mentioned in early legends, the one who is said to have ended up in Ireland:

> ... a descendant Prince of Scythia married the sister of Pharaoh Psamic II (595-89BC) who sent a fleet of Phoenician ships to circumnavigate the African continent. This sister duly became Princess of Scythia (Princess Scota). Her husband was Prince Galamh (known also as Milidh), and their son was Djer Amon

(Beloved of Amon), cited in the Irish annals as Eirhe Ahmon. It was Eirhe Ahmon's son Eochaid, High King of Ireland, who married Tamar Tephi, the daughter of King Zedekiah of Judah, in about 586BC. With her father a captive in Babylon, and her brothers murdered by Nebuchadnezzar, Tamar had escaped to Ireland with the prophet Jeremiah, and with them came the Stone of Destiny...[42]

We then find out that this escape to Ireland 'coincided with the Jerusalem Temple Guard's instruction to remove sacred treasures from the grasp of the invading King of Babylon...'[43]

So the implication is: where did these sacred treasures end up?

What this legend is essentially saying is that at the time of Zedekiah, King of Judah, the prophet Jeremiah is said to have brought the stone to Tara in Ireland along with his scribe and a princess of the royal bloodline descended from the house of King David and King Solomon. This Princess, we are told, was called Tea or Tamar Tephi and tradition also says that she established the holy bloodline of the kings of Scotland. We learn in Jeremiah 1.1 that Jeremiah was the son of Hilkiah, the High Priest who found the Mosaic *Book of the Law* hidden within the temple (2 Kings 22.8).[44]

To put these legends into context, it is worth taking a brief look at biblical history leading up to the fall of Judah:

- Abraham became the father of the chosen people by a promise to him from God;
- Abraham's grandson Jacob has a dream while resting on the stone, in which God repeats the promise that his heirs will be the chosen of God;
- Jacob changes his name to Israel and twelve of his sons set up families that become known as the twelve tribes of Israel;
- One of the sons was not given any land in Palestine but instead became the head of the priestly family of Levi;
- The tribe of Judah became the ruling tribe of Israel and on their banner their symbol appeared as a lion;
- David brings the Ark of the Covenant to Jerusalem but leaves the building of the great Temple to his wise son King Solomon;
- Solomon builds the first Temple at Jerusalem and is known throughout history as the 'wisest of all' the kings of Israel;

- After the death of King Solomon, his kingdom was split in two with Israel in the north and Judah in the south;
- In 722BC the Assyrians scattered all of the tribes of Israel, except for Judah and Benjamin, and the so-called 'lost tribes' then disappear from biblical history;
- In 586BC, Zedekiah, the last King of Judah was overthrown by Nebuchadnezzar king of Babylon;
- The fall of Judah is said to have been a punishment by God for the disobedience of the people in not keeping his laws;
- The prophet Jeremiah and his scribe Baruch warned the king about the exile of the people, challenged the false prophets and spoke of the promise of the restoration;
- Zedekiah did not heed the words of the prophet Jeremiah and was overthrown;
- Nebuchadnezzar killed all of Zedekiah's sons, leaving no male heirs of the royal line;
- Jerusalem and its Temple were destroyed by Nebuchadnezzar, and he carried off the holy treasures along with captives into Babylon;
- The captives included Jeremiah, his scribe Baruch, and according to Scottish and Irish legends, also Zedekiah's daughter, who was Princess Tea or Tamar Tephi.

Legends of Jeremiah and 'Jacob's Pillow'

Returning to the various Irish and Scottish myths and legends about the Stone of Destiny, an interesting question is raised:

Nebuchadnezzar freed Jeremiah, who promptly rescued several items from the Temple – the Tabernacle and the Altar of Incense are mentioned – and hid them in a cave near Pisgah. He also rescued Zedekiah's daughters, one of whom was the Princess Tea, and with them fled to Egypt. The law of inheritance in Israel, since the time of Moses, had included the right of women to succeed to the throne. Princess Tea was of David's line, and of the blood royal. Having taken such care, would he have left the central item around which the Temple and his people's culture had been built – the Stone Pillar of Jacob?[45]

Well, probably not, it is implied... This legend later states that Nebuchadnezzar then planned to enter Egypt. On hearing of this threatening news, the party understandably fled and took to sea. The tribe of Dan, often called 'Phoenicians' by the Greeks, are said to have been the seafarers responsible for bringing Tea, Jeremiah, and his scribe Baruch (also called Simon Brec in old chronicles) to Ireland.

Jeremiah then completely disappears from Biblical history with no mention at all of where he went after being in Egypt. In the Irish tales, an illustrious man called Ollam Fola shows up, and he is said to be identified as the prophet Jeremiah in some traditions. The word *ollamh* in Old Irish means a professor, a most learned one, or a master of something that requires a great deal of knowledge and skill.

After arriving in Ireland, Princess Tea or Tamar Tephi marries the sovereign, a man named Heremon (other accounts say Eochaid) at the royal centre of Tara. Tradition states that Irish kings were crowned at Tara on the Lia Fail (Jacob's Pillow) for the next 1,000 years, until its departure to Scotland with King Fergus. This great dynasty was said to have been descended from Israel in these early accounts.

The Stone of Destiny

The Stone of Destiny has been shrouded in many myths and legends. It is mainly thought to be the coronation stone of the ancient kings of Israel, and later, of the Irish and the Scottish kings, having been 'Jacob's Pillow'. The stone that was returned to Scotland in 1996 from Westminster is a large piece of very old red sandstone, more than 400 million years old, and it is known to be similar to other rocks that have been found in the Scone area. It is now housed in Edinburgh Castle, along with the Scottish crown and regalia. The stone is roughly rectangular in shape, and has iron rings at each end, as if it were once carried. It is obvious that a start was made to cutting a rectangle on the top surface at some point, and it is also known that two crosses were once etched on the stone. Frankly, as many have admitted, it is rather lacking in aesthetic appeal.

The most unusual aspect of this stone, experts admit, is the obvious smoothness of its upper surface. Stone conservator Peter Hill has stated that this may be because people had once walked or kneeled on it, implying that it may have been an object of veneration by pilgrims for centuries, which is clearly a possibility. There is no question that this stone is an ancient one, and may, as some believe, be the Stone of Destiny itself. Indeed, this is the official position of Historic Scotland and other authorities.

But others aren't so sure. Some controversy still exists in Scotland as to whether this is – or was – *the* authentic Stone of Destiny or not, and critics have claimed that Edward I was actually given a 'fake' stone in 1296, and that the authentic one still remains hidden today, supposedly only to be revealed when Scotland is independent again.

Others counter with the argument that as two of Edward's senior officials were present at the inauguration of John Balliol, the 'King John' of Scotland, in 1292, they would have seen the stone he was crowned on, and would have known if it was a fake. They also point out that as this stone has a rather rough-hewn, complex form, it would actually be quite hard to fake in reality. Others believe that this stone was more likely to have been an ashlar, a large, square-cut block of masonry that may have been intended for a church. The idea of a 'foundation stone' is very important in Old Testament and Masonic traditions, which will be discussed later in chapter 8. 'Unused masonry carries a powerful Christian symbolism; Jesus is 'the stone rejected by the builders that became the keystone' (Mark 12.10; Acts 4.11-12).[46]

A chair, or royal seat

However, in many of the medieval and later chronicles, the stone is specifically described as a chair, i.e. *not merely a stone, but a chair or royal seat* of some kind. For example, on several of the seals of Robert the Bruce, one of which is appended to the Melrose Charter dated 1317, the King is clearly portrayed as sitting on a chair or seat of some kind. The stone described in early writings and shown on old seals often seems to be considerably larger than the one at Edinburgh Castle, critics point out. There are also a number of references to it being made of dark or black marble, having certain hieroglyphics or carvings on it, and that it stood on legs, making some question the authenticity of the stone that was in Westminster, as it does not appear to have any of these characteristics.

Most experts believe that the stone now in Edinburgh Castle is indeed the genuine article. In recent years the stone was debated in the British Houses of Parliament at which time it was decided to send it back to Scotland. Representing HRH Queen Elizabeth II, Prince Andrew returned the stone 'on loan' to the Scottish people on St Andrew's Day, 30 November 1996. This event was reported around the world by national and international news groups.

From its arrival in Scotland from Ireland, said to be around the year 500AD in some legendary accounts, the stone has since been regarded as a most holy and mystical relic. All the kings of Scotland from King Fergus until its removal to England in 1296 were crowned upon it. When Edward I removed it, it was then later placed under the Coronation chair in Westminster Abbey. Ever since, all the subsequent Kings and Queens of England, and Great Britain, have been crowned on it.

Stone stolen from Westminster in 1950

Barrister, advocate and writer Ian Hamilton is most famously known as the Scottish student who broke into Westminster Abbey with three others on Christmas Day 1950. Their mission, which they accomplished, was to return the stone to Scotland, as Edward I had taken it by force from Scone Abbey long ago.

A national police search understandably followed as a result of the act which lasted for several months. In April 1951 the police eventually retrieved it from Arbroath Abbey, where Hamilton and his accomplices had significantly placed it to remind the public of the importance of this national symbol and also of the Declaration of Arbroath of 1320 with its message of nationhood.

This statement from Hamilton himself sums up his sentiments for wanting to return the Stone to Scotland.

Every nation needs its symbols as well as its songs... you will seldom see an English Church which does not fly the St George's Cross flag from its tower on St George's Day. For Scotland our most potent symbol is the Stone of Destiny. I care not a fig for the argument that it is not the real one that Edward I, who tortured our greatest hero Wallace to a terrible death, was palmed off with a false one. I pay even less heed to people who say that I myself was party to returning a false one to Arbroath Abbey. You do not counterfeit the very emblem of your own nationality. The stone takes us back to Scone and the Celtic kings of Iona and to the first of our forefathers who landed on Ard Gael, now called Argyll, and to the very roots of our race itself. It may be nonsense. It may be as legendary as the story of King Arthur, the Briton who, if he ever lived, fell fighting not for the English but against them. What matters is what people believe, and we Scots believe in the Stone.[48]

Indeed, the power of legends are often greater than we realise.

Even today, there are rumoured to be more than one Stone of Destiny in existence, but obviously only one of these is the ancient coronation stone that tradition states is Jacob's Pillow. But there are different ancient descriptions of stones that may have become associated with the Jacob legend over the centuries. A key one is described as dark marble and throne – like, with inscriptions on it, which does not fit the one that was in Westminster, critics allege.

One of the most fervent arguments is presented by Archie McKerracher:

It is obvious Edward I realised he had been tricked, for on returning to London he had ordered Master Adam the Goldsmith to encase the Stone in a bronze chair. The work was only half complete when he had work stopped, and in August 1298, sent a raiding party of knights back to Scone where they tore the abbey apart in a desperate search for something. They returned empty handed and a furious Edward ordered Walter the Painter to make the present wooden chair at a cost of 100 shillings. He declared this was no longer for the monarch's use, but only for the priest celebrant, although it has been used as the Coronation Chair ever since. There is further evidence in the preliminary negotiation for the Treaty of Northampton in 1328, which finally sealed Scotland's independence. The English offered to return the Stone, but, strangely, the Scots did not insist this clause be included in the final document. The stone was offered again in 1329 and 1363 but again the Scots did not bother to reply. So the sandstone block in London remained where it was, and the real Stone remained hidden in Scotland...[49]

Many, of course, scoff at this and state that the stone returned from Westminster was the real one. Other rather persistent legends say that there are actually four different 'Stones of Destiny', and that one of them is known to be in the possession of a modern order of the Scottish Knights Templar. But whether the particular stone now housed in Edinburgh Castle is the 'real one' or not, is certainly not for us to say.

However, to be sure, the stone that sits beside the Scottish regalia today is a most powerful symbol, an important emblem of Scottish nationhood and history. It is what it ultimately *symbolizes* that is really important, and the sheer number of traditions, myths and legends about this stone also says something in and of itself. But, as some allege, you never know when the real Stone of Destiny will come out of hiding... so this powerful legend still lives on today, apparently waiting to reveal itself. Again it is not so much what is literally true, but what people *believe* to be true.

St Andrew and the Saltire

St Andrew is the patron saint of Scotland. The Catholic Church states that St Andrew spread the word of the gospel to Scythia and Asia minor after the Crucifixion. An ancient claim is that the relics of the Saint were brought to 'Pictland', also known as 'Caledonia', and later, 'Alba', before being named 'Scotland' in the days of the early church in the 9th C.

Accounts state that the relics were brought to the Picts in the 4th C by a man called Regulus or Rule. Regulus, the keeper of the Saint's relics, lived at Patras in Greece, the town where St Andrew was martyred. At the time of Regulus, the Roman Emperor Constantine, the first to embrace Christianity as the principal faith of Rome, ordered that the relics to be brought to his new centre for the Eastern Orthodox church, which he named Constantinople after himself. This legends states:

Regulus had a strange dream in which he was visited by an angel. The angel told him that the bones of Saint Andrew should be taken, not to Constantinople, but to a faraway country at the edge of the world. Regulus should take them there and build a church. Regulus obeyed the angel rather than the Emperor. He travelled across Europe, with the remains of Saint Andrew kept in a chest. It was a long difficult journey. At last he came to the east coast of Caledonia.

This 'faraway country at the edge of the world' is Scotland, according to this legend, and the specific location where the bones of St Andrew were taken is now modern-day St Andrews.

Next, it says:

There, at a place called Muckros, he and his companions landed and set up a church. Beneath the altar, it is said, he buried the chest containing the bones of the Apostle. As the years went by, the name of the place was changed. Regulus himself became a saint, and Muckros became known as Kilrymount – the hill of the church of Regulus. Later still, the fame of the greater saint over took that of Regulus, and the place became known as Saint Andrews.[50]

More will be said about St Andrew himself in chapter 5, so we will now take a look at St Andrew in relation to the national flag of Scotland – the saltire.

The Saltire, the Flag of St Andrew, is a silvery white X cross on a blue background. It is the oldest flag in the British Commonwealth and dates back to a battle fought in the year 756AD. It is interesting, though, that contrary to popular belief:

Andrew was not nailed to a Saltire but crucified by being tied to a Y-shaped olive tree... The Saltire has its origins in the Chi Rho, a cross resembling the first two Greek letters of Christ's name. It appeared as a vision to the Roman Emperor Constantine before his victory in battle and helped in his conversion to Christianity.[51]

As is well-known today, Constantine was said to have seen 'a cross in the sky', interpreted as a miracle, before winning his most famous battle. This legend also has many parallels in Scottish lore.

The village of Athelstaneford in East Lothian is the setting for one of these, which tells of a battle against the Angles that became a defining moment in Scottish history, a tale of miraculous divine intervention that is said to have given the Scottish nation its saltire. It is also the first report of the saltire appearing in the sky over Scotland at significant times. From a leaflet found in the church at Athelstaneford:

> A reporter in one of our leading newspapers has written that the day in the year 756, when the Scots and Picts defeated the Angles in battle, was the day in which Scotland was born, and that the turning point in the history of Scotland was not Bannockburn, nor Flodden, or Culloden, but that great and glorious day over twelve hundred years ago, when the brave and valiant Scots routed their enemies.[52]

Bold words, and yet a viewpoint which Sir Thomas Innes of Learney, although writing much later in the 18th C, strongly supported, as he declares: 'Probably the history of Scotland may truly derive from the victory gained in East Lothian in the late Autumn of 756.'[52] Again, the tradition lives on about the appearance of the saltire in the sky to motivate the Scots in battle.

In this particular battle of 756AD, the Picts, who occupied the land beyond the rivers Forth and Clyde, joined forces with the Scots, who then occupied Dal Riata on the west coast (now modern day Argyll) in an attempt to prevent the Angles from inhabiting the area south of the River Forth. The king of the Picts at the time was named Oengus or Angus. The tale associated with this king prior to the battle is very similar to that of the story about the Emperor Constantine:

> Before the battle, St Andrew spoke to him in a vision, and when the Chi Rho appeared in the sky with the morning sun, Oengus's army attacked and was victorious. A grateful Oengus set up a shrine at what is now St Andrews in Fife. There the saint's relics, more likely to have come to Scotland via Constantinople, Rome, Hexham in Northumberland, were given a new home.[53]

It is curious to note that it was the Picts and not the Scots after this battle who appear to have adopted St Andrew as their patron and to have dedicated a shrine to him. This tale surrounding the victory at Athelstaneford and the miraculous divine intervention of St Andrew is repeated down through Scottish history, but most notably during the Wars of Independence.

At the battle of Roslin in 1302/3, we are told that Abernethy, the Prior of Carlops, reported seeing a fiery cross appear above the Pentland Hills, a clear omen that was believed to guarantee the Scots army of only 8,000 men victory over the larger English force of 30,000 men. Looking to the top of the Pentland Hills, the Scots army allegedly called out 'a miracle, a miracle, the cross, the cross of heaven is on the hill, to arms, to arms!' on seeing it glittering in the sun.[54] Local Midlothian tradition asserts that the 'fiery cross' was a saltire and to this day, there is a place near the village of Roslin still referred to as Monks Marle, or 'Monks Miracle', said to be the place where the miraculous saltire vision in the sky was seen.

William Wallace and his vision of Scotia

The bard known as Blind Harry, writing in about 1478, refers to a tale about the Scottish hero William Wallace and his vision of Scotia, the 'mother of Scotland':

...he suddenly fell into a deep sleep... Wallace had a dream in which an old man came up to him and grasped his hand, saying he had a message for him. He gave Wallace a sword of burnished steel and told him to make good use of it. He then took Wallace up a high mountain... He could see Scotland... the whole realm was in a state of war and turmoil... As he brooded on the sight, he saw a great luminous ball coming down from the sky towards him, coming nearer and nearer till it filled the whole of his vision and landed right beside him. Then he saw the light was in fact a lady, dazzlingly bright. She handed him a wand of red and green, and taking a sapphire of dazzling blue she made the sign of the saltire cross upon his face. 'My love, she said, I have chosen you to be my champion, and God will grant you the power... Then she gave him a book and was gone in a ball of light up into the sky again. Wallace opened the book and noticed that it was written in three parts. The first part was in big brass letters, the second was in gold, and the third in shining silver. In his eagerness to read the writing, Wallace came out of his trance. Seeing the priest nearby, he told him of his vision and asked what it might mean. 'My son', said the priest, 'who am I to unravel such mysteries of God... Yet I would risk saying that it seems to me that the old man who gave you the sword was St Andrew, patron saint of Scotland, and he means you to fight for your country's cause. I am uncertain who the lady is. She might be Fortune – she might even be Our Lady Mary, mother of Our Lord. That seems likeliest, though she might be Scotia, the mother of our people...[55]

Other traditions and legendary accounts also state that the word 'Scotland' comes from Scotia, the mother and guiding light of Scotland.

Bannockburn, St Andrew and the relics of Saints Fillan and Columba

At Bannockburn, prior to the battle, divine support was sought again by the Scots from St Andrew and other saints. It is known that the Abbot of Arbroath solemnly carried the relics of St Columba and St Fillan with him into the battlefield. Specific prayers were dedicated to St John the Baptist, on whose feast day (24 June) the battle was fought, along with St Thomas Beckett and St Andrew, to assist the Scots in their cause. The Saltire flag and the Lion Rampant Standards were on display at the battlefield. The day of the battle, 24 June, is St John the Baptist's Day. It was also known to be an important date to the medieval Knights Templar, leading to further speculation and various legendary accounts about a possible surviving Templar remnant at Bannockburn to assist Robert the Bruce, who is said to have been sympathetic to the plight of the Templars, discussed further in chapter 8.

It is interesting to note that St Andrew was originally a disciple of John the Baptist before he met Jesus, according to the Bible in John 1.40. Tradition says that as the Scottish army was kneeling in prayer at Bannockburn, King Edward II supposedly mistook their devotions for surrender – something that he was later to learn was not the case, as history has shown.

The relics of St Andrew

During the Reformation in 1559, a Protestant mob attacked St Andrews Cathedral and the saint's relics were lost. In 1879, however, another of the St Andrew relics was brought to St Mary's

Roman Catholic Cathedral in Edinburgh from Amalfi in Italy. Again, in 1951, yet another of his relics was brought from Amalfi, this time to the ancient burgh of St Andrews and placed in the church of St James. More recently, in 1969, Pope Paul VI visited Scotland and gifted a new relic of St Andrew to Scotland at St Mary's Cathedral in Edinburgh. The gift was brought from St Peter's in Rome by Cardinal Gordon Gray, with the Pope's message, which said: 'Peter greets his brother Andrew'. In 1982, the current Pope, John Paul II, put Scotland on the world stage by praying before the relics of St Andrew at St Mary's Cathedral in Edinburgh during his visit to Scotland.

Ancient traditions, whether based on fact or not, clearly still have their influence on modern events. Today, the Scottish saltire, with its blue and white colours, is still to be seen in Scotland, along with the Lion Rampant and the Union Jack. In 1999, at the opening of the first Scottish Parliament in 300 years, jet planes crossed the sky over Scotland to produce the ancient emblem of the saltire, clearly an important symbolic gesture. Once more in the blue skies above Scotland, the Scottish people were invited to contemplate the saltire, by now a well-entrenched symbol in the Scottish psyche.

Clearly, to simply sideline or discount the wealth of traditions that surround many significant people, places and dates in history is to ignore an important part of the cultural identity of a people.

In this chapter, we have learned not only about known, verifiable historical facts, but also about many of the traditional customs and beliefs that surround Scottish historical issues. We have seen how symbols such as the saltire and the Stone of Destiny have been around for a very long time and are still important in Scotland today.

We will now take a look at the Druids and Druidism in early Celtic history, and about the legacy they have left us centuries later.

Notes

1   Ferguson, W, *The Identity of the Scottish Nation*, Edinburgh University Press, Edinburgh, 1998, 3.
2   Ibid.
3   Ibid, 16.
4   Murphy, AC Rev, *The Declaration of Arbroath* – 1320, (booklet), Midlothian privately printed, 1999, 4.
5   Ferguson, op cit, 41.
6   Her Majesty's Stationery Office, HMSO, *The Declaration of Arbroath* – 1320, 1980.
7   Cowan, EJ, 'Identity, Freedom, and the Declaration of Arbroath' in *Image and Identity: The Making and Re-making of Scotland through the Ages*, [Ed.] by Broun, D, Finlay, RJ, & Lynch, M, John Donald, Edinburgh, 1998, 51.
8   *Scotsman* newspaper, Edinburgh, 10 July 2000, 1.
9   Cowan, op cit, 40.
10   Ibid, 40.
11   Ibid, 41.
12   Ibid.
13   Jefferson, Thomas, *Declaration of Independence* (as orig. written by Thomas Jefferson), USA, 1776, ME 1.29, Papers 1.315.
14   Adam, J, [Ed.], *The Declaration of Arbroath*, Herald Press, Arbroath, 1993, 8
15   Barrow, GWS, 'The Clergy in the War of Independence', *The Kingdom of the Scots: Gov't., Church, and Society from the 11th to the 14th century*, London, 1973, 248-254.
16   Cowan, op cit, 57.
17   Livingston, William, *Vindication of the Celtic Character*, Greenock, 1850.
18   Farmer, DH, *The Oxford Dictionary of Saints*, Second Edition, Oxford University Press, Oxford, 1987, 273.
19   Bower, W, *Scotichronicon*, Watt, 6, 135.
20   Edington, C, 'Paragons and Patriots: National Identity and the Chivalric Ideal in Late-Medieval Scotland', in *Image and Identity*, [Ed.] by Broun, D, Finlay, R.J., & Lynch, M., John Donald, Edinburgh, 1998, 73.
21   Ibid.
22   'Le Livre de Chevalerie par Geoffroi de Charny', in *Oeuvres de Froissant*, [Ed.] le Baron Kervyn de Lettenhove, 26 vols, Brussels, 1867-77, I: part 2, 463-533; also 508-10.
23   Ferguson, op cit, 41.
24   Filmer, WE, *Who were the Scots?*, Kent, not dated, 2.
25   Ibid, 2.

[26] MacLagan, RC, *Our Ancestors, Scots, Picts, and Cymry*, Foulis, Edinburgh, 1913, 115.

[27] Gawler, JC, *Our Scythian Ancestors*, Commonwealth Publishing, Utah, 1994 reprint of 1875 orig., 9.

[28] Livingston, op cit, 17.

[29] Dunbavin, P, *Picts and Ancient Britons*, Third Millennium Publishing, Nottingham, 1998, 93.

[30] Mowat, F, *The Alban Quest*, Weidenfeld & Nicolson, London, 1999, 46.

[31] Bertoldi, V, 'Problems of Etymology', *Zeitscrift fur Romanische Philologie*, vol. 56, London, 1936, 179.

[32] Howe, Linda M, 'Evidence of 7,000-year-old Flood and Human Habitation Discovered Beneath the Black Sea', Earthfiles.com, 2 Nov 2000, 1.

[33] Ballard, R, 'Interview with Dr Robert Ballard', by Linda Moulton Howe, Earthfiles.com, Science, 2 Nov 2000.

[34] Cavalli-Sforza, LL, *Genes, People, and Languages*, Penguin, Harmondsworth, 2000, 161.

[35] Mallory, JP, and Mair, V, *The Tarim Mummies*, Thames & Hudson, London, 2000, 218.

[36] Barber, E, *The Mummies of Urumchi*, Macmillan, London, 1999, 138.

[37] Bruce-Gardyne, T, 'Tartan Truths', *Caledonia*, Edinburgh, April 2000, 34.

[38] Aitchison, N, *Scotland's Stone of Destiny*, Tempus, Stroud, 2000, 8.

[39] Gerber, P, *Stone of Destiny*, Canongate, Edinburgh, 1997, 45.

[40] Yeoman, L, *Reportage Scotland*, Luath Press, Edinburgh, 2000, 21.

[41] Stewart, HRH.M.J., *The Forgotten Monarchy of Scotland*, Element, Shaftesbury, 1998, 69.

[42] Ibid.

[43] Ibid, 70.

[44] Ibid.

[45] Gerber, op cit, 28.

[46] Aitchison, op cit, 52.

[47] Gerber, op cit, 22.

[48] 'The Story of Scotland', *Daily Record*, Glasgow, 1986, 86.

[49] McKerracher, A, *Perthshire in History and Legend*, John Donald, Edinburgh, 1988, rev ed. 2000, 216.

[50] Turnbull, A, *St. Andrew: Scotland's Myth and Identity*, St. Andrew Press, Edinburgh, 1997, 9.

[51] Ibid, 9.

[52] Athelstaneford Church and Parish, church leaflet, privately printed, no date.

[53] Turnbull, op cit, 9.
[54] Jackson, J, *Tales of Roslin Castle*, Edinburgh, 1836, 152.
[55] Scott, T, *Tales of Sir William Wallace*: Guardian of Scotland, Gordon Wright Publishing, Edinburgh, 1981, 63. [Adapted from *The Wallas of Blin Hary*].

CHAPTER TWO

The Druids: Their History and Legacy

THE DRUIDS AND THEIR history have fascinated many for centuries. Even today, at the summer solstice on the 21 June, media coverage portrays white-robed, modern-day Druids conducting Midsummer rituals at Stonehenge. But who exactly were the Druids in earlier times? What did they believe? And, for our purposes here, what are the *Scottish* aspects to this complex subject?

Druidism in Scotland has often been neglected or reduced to footnotes in the major works that have been written on the subject, which have usually tended to focus on Gaul, England, Ireland, and Wales. But much of the reason for this is understandable, as not much material has survived about the early Celts or the Druids on the whole. However, some writers in the past did make an effort to examine the subject of the Druids and Druidism in Scotland, and we will take a look at them shortly. But first, let us see what is known about the Druids in general.

The word 'Druid'

The word 'Druid' has been debated by scholars concerning exactly where the word itself came from. In Old Irish the word is *Drui* and the plural form is *Druid*.[1] The celebrated language scholar Rudolf Thurneysen derived the word 'Druid' from the Old Irish *dru* prefix, meaning 'thorough', and *vid*, meaning 'know', so that a Druid was seen to be a person of great knowledge and wisdom. Early classical writers such as Pliny believed it was related to the Greek word for oak, *drus*.

So the word Druid has generally come to mean a 'wise man or a priest of the oak'. The female equivalent is 'Druidess'. The ancient Irish writers generally wrote of their Druids in the same way as they referred to those on the Continent, using the word *Drui* for both. Latin writers usually translated the word 'Druid' as 'magus', and this term 'magus' would be translated by the Irish as *'Drui'*. A 'magus', as we know, is a wise man akin to one of the famous 'magi' of the Bible, a gifted seer or prophet.

The Druids, although they did not directly put their secret teachings into writing, did use Greek letters for more mundane types of communication, as we learn from Caesar. So, clearly they were not 'illiterate savages', as has often been the stereotype. The famous Old Irish tale of Etain and Midir tells of a Druid who could read ogham characters, and the medieval manuscript, the Yellow Book of Lecan, describes how St Patrick at one time burned 180 books of the Druids.

Druidism was monotheistic in nature and their philosophy was sophisticated and greatly respected in ancient times. The Druidic order was tripartite in nature and the number three, that of a trinity, was very important to them. Respected Celtic scholar Dr Anne Ross explains:

> The words used for this tripartite order, which is found in Europe and in the British Isles, are Gaulish as recorded by the classics: Druides ('priest-philosophers'), Vates or Manteis ('diviners and prophets'), and the Bardi ('panegyric poets')... [This] was clearly common to the entire Celtic world and these were the most powerful elements and the most influential in the whole of Celtic society. Indeed, the power of the Druids was so great that the Romans, who spent much time in trying to deprive the Celts of their political and military powers and make them subordinate to the will of Rome, issued an edict the intention of which was greatly to weaken the political influence of the highest order of this trilogy of learned men.[2]

This power rested with the Druids and the Romans understood this and took action accordingly.

Druidic teaching and education

Celtic society was tribally organised and depended on this threefold group of learned men (and women) in many ways. Ross continues, telling us about their long and difficult training process:

...scholars who had spent, in the case of a Druid – Irish *Drui*,

Welsh *Derwydd, Dryw* (the latter also means 'wren', a sacred Druidic bird) – some *twenty years* mastering his subject, and thus qualifying to teach his acolytes orally – for the Druids did not use the written word for educational purposes, believing that it weakened the memory... It took some twelve years to become a Vatis (Irish *Faith*, Welsh *Gweledydd*). Poetry was sacred to the Celts and the three degrees of learned men must master the highly complex poetic metres... It took seven years of practice in composition to become a Bard (Irish *Bard*, Welsh *Bardd*) who was accredited with great powers of praise and of satire and was thus feared... Women, too, could be trained in all three orders, and like the men, were taught the highly secret language known in Irish as *berla na bfiled*...[3]

However, most Druidic teachings were done by oral transmission in schools or colleges, as we learn from the esteemed French historian Jean Markale:

Again the supporting text comes from Caesar: 'Many come, in their own right, to entrust their education in their [the druids] hands, but many are sent by their parents and relatives; it is said that they learn a very great number of verses there by heart; thus some remain in school for as long as twenty years' (Caesar, VI, 14) Another confirming text comes from Pomponius Mela (first century AD)... 'They have... masters of wisdom that they call druids... They teach many things to the nobility of Gaul in secret, for twenty years...'[4]

Even the Rig-Vedas, the ancient religious books of India that were written in about 1500BC, are known to have made several references to what is believed to be the British Isles, as a great renowned centre of religious learning in ancient times. The name Druid can also be traced to the Vedic *Dru-vid*, meaning 'knower of the wood'.[5] Druidic teaching schools, often taught in groves or caves, were said to have been quite numerous in Britain and Gaul before the Romans came, with the medieval historian Gildas claiming that at that time, there were known to be at least sixty large 'colleges' and over sixty thousand students.[6]

Classical sources

The entire process of examining the available sources and what they have to say about the Druids can be a challenging one as, unfortunately, almost everything that has survived has been the writings of the enemies of the Druids – hardly objective sources. The classical writers, such as Caesar (*Gallic Wars*) Strabo (*Geography*) and Pliny (*Natural History*) provide us with information about some of the beliefs and customs of the Druids and it is known that much of their material was taken from a lost shared source by Posidonius. These classical writers wrote about the Celts during the 1st C BC and the first few centuries AD, when the Romans were trying to defeat the Druids.

Caesar was appointed by the Roman Senate as governor of southern Gaul (modern-day France) in 59BC and immediately started a series of military campaigns to conquer the Gallic heartlands. He finally completed his task in 50BC, after much bloodshed. His own account of the Druids from Book VI of his *Gallic Wars* is the most descriptive that we have, even though it is a view from the eyes of the enemy:

> Throughout Gaul there are two classes of men of some dignity and importance. One of the two classes is that of the Druids... The Druids are concerned with the worship of the gods, look after public and private sacrifice, and expound religious matters. A large number of young men flock to them for training and hold them in high honour. For they have the right to decide nearly all public and private disputes and they also pass judgment and decide rewards and penalties in criminal and murder cases and in disputes concerning legacies and boundaries... It is thought that this [Druidic] system of training was invented in Britain and taken over from there to Gaul, and at the present time diligent students of the matter mostly travel there to study it.

Caesar then continues:

> The Druids are wont to be absent from war, nor do they pay taxes like the others... It is said that they commit to memory immense amounts of poetry. And so some of them continue their studies for twenty years. They consider it improper to entrust their studies to writing... I think they established this practice for

two reasons, because they were unwilling, first, that their system of training should be bruited abroad among the common people, and second, the student should rely on the written word and neglect the exercise of memory... They are chiefly anxious to have men believe the following: that souls do not suffer death, but after death pass from one body to another; and they regard this as the strongest incentive to valour, since the fear of death is disregarded They have also much knowledge of the stars and their motion, of the size of the world and of the earth, of natural philosophy, and of the powers and spheres of action of the immortal gods, which they discuss and hand down to their young students...[7]

Caesar and his contemporaries clearly show the Druids as having high status in society, of a rank similar to knights, who were the highest nobility below the tribal chief magistrate or king. The position of the Druids was high because in the Celtic world the priesthood was a separate, highly respected and important grade of society. Professor Stuart Piggott acknowledges that 'their position was seen as comparable with the priesthoods of other foreign peoples. Dio Chrystostom in the 1st C AD equated Druids with Persian magi, Egyptian priests, and Indian brahmins.'[8] He further says that they were viewed by the Romans as representatives of seers, prophets, healers, magicians, and diviners of the ancient world. Strabo says that in former times Druids could intervene and stop contending armies from fighting, which also shows an important peace-keeping function to the Druids.

Celtic archaeologist and scholar Dr Miranda Green notes that:

What is very striking is the difference between the comments made by writers of the first century BC and those of the first century AD. Caesar, Strabo, and Diodorus project a positive, active image of the Druids engaged in official capacities as judges, teachers and presiders over ritual matters, including sacrifice. But if we examine the testimony of Tacitus, Lucan, Pliny, and Pomponius Mela, all of whom wrote in the first century AD, we find new notes creeping in: the association of Druids with secret, hidden places such as forests, and more pejorative, emotive descriptions of savage rites. Pliny presents the Druids as magicians; Mela speaks of Druids teaching in remote and secret places, such as caves and groves. So we may be faced with the frustrating situation that almost as soon as observers from the Classical world began commenting on the Druids, the role and status of the learned class began to change and diminish. Thus, we may have no witnesses to the Druids in action at the height of their powers, influence and prestige.[9]

What is without dispute is that the Druids were especially gifted at rhetoric, poetry and all verbal skills. They were also known to be excellent teachers and it is known that thousands of students from elite families in Gaul would come to Britain for their education. The classical writers largely agreed that the Celtic elite was divided into *Bards* (lyric poets, musicians), the *Druids* (priests, philosophers, theologians) and the *Vates* (diviners and seers), the last two being religious officials.

The arrival of the Romans

As there do not seem to be any eyewitness sources on the Druids when they were actually at the heights of their powers, we need to ask: what happened to the Druids after the arrival of the Romans?

We learn from the texts of Suetonius, Tacitus and Pliny that the early Roman emperors of the 1st C AD clearly saw the very powerful Druidic priesthood as a threat and tried to suppress it. But even before the conquest, the Romans also acknowledged the power the Druids had in other areas of expertise, such as trade and commerce, and debated among themselves how to go about conquering these people in terms of a military strategy. Strabo pointed out that because Britain was a leading commercial centre outside the Roman empire, that the sensible strategy would be to trade with them on equal terms to produce more revenue for Rome, rather than have Britain be a Roman province, where Rome would have to pay for a standing army and a civil service.[10] Later, Augustus banned Roman citizens from joining the Druids; his successor, Tiberius, had an even harsher policy and issued an edict to eliminate 'the Druids and that class of seers and doctors' altogether, no matter how long it took.

Experts are divided as to the exact reasons why Druidism

declined, with most saying that the coming of Christianity itself ultimately may have had little to do with it. In a sense, by that time, the real damage had already been done. Many factors contributed to their ultimate demise. For example, the Roman University at Augustodunum (Autun) was opened in 12BC, after which, some believe, the final death-knell may have begun for the oral Druidical colleges, where the children of the elite in society at the time had gone for their training. Many scholars say that the Romans obviously perceived the Druidic priesthood with its power and many important connections to be politically subversive and therefore felt it must be eliminated.

Under the emperor Claudius the Druids did not fare well at all. Suetonius claimed that Claudius completely abolished Druidism. Pliny informs us that also during this time a Gaulish chieftain was executed for wearing a Druidic 'serpent's egg' talisman while on legal business. Again, an overview of the situation:

> ...we can infer from Tacitus that the Druids continued to have an active role as agitators in Britain during the time of the Boudican rebellion of AD60/61, in Nero's reign, when the Roman governor Paulinus attacked the Druids' holy stronghold on Anglesey... In the 'Year of the Four Emperors', AD69, when Rome itself was experiencing enormous upheavals in the imperial succession after the death of Nero, the Druids were – opportunely – engaged in inciting the Gaulish tribes to a mass uprising. Evidence for the persecution of the Druids is clear up to and including the reign of Nero. But comments about them dry up before the end of the first century AD, only to reappear in the third century, and there exists no testimony to their systematic annihilation.[11]

Oxford Professor Barry Cunliffe points out that although it seems that the power of Druidism had decreased in Gaul by the time of Caesar, it may have remained somewhat stronger in Britain. Roman legions were told to stamp out Druidism wherever possible in Britain, a process that took some time. The final, bloody 'showdown' with the Romans occurred in 59AD on the island of Anglesey, north Wales, which was a major centre of Druidism in Britain, as was nearby Bangor.[12]

Candidates 'went north' for initiations – Scotland?

Irish tradition has the Druidic religion having a focus in 'the isles of the north of the world', – to the north of Ireland, with Scotland a strong candidate. It also shows future Druids and young people going north for their initiations.[13] Some local historical accounts maintain that Iona may have been a Druidic centre of learning in very early times, but we cannot say for certain due to lack of concrete evidence as very little has survived. But in all fairness, Iona certainly has been viewed as a sacred, holy island for many centuries and has always been viewed as a place of great knowledge and wisdom. To begin with, the name of the island of Iona itself was called *Inis Druineach* or *Nan Druihean*, meaning Druid's Isle, on old maps. Even the ancient Irish hero Cuchulainn was believed to have learned the arts of war from Skatha on the isle of Skye.

But like any defeated people, small remnants of Druids survived here and there, of course, but after the Roman conquest, for them to have worshipped openly would have been highly dangerous if not deadly. Logically, some probably assimilated into certain Christian communities, but again, we cannot say for certain, but this undoubtedly did occur in some instances. It is known that there were Druidic survivors in Gaul, parts of Britain, and Ireland.

But the importance of the oak grove cannot be underestimated, however, as the main political meeting place of the Celts in Asia Minor is also known to have been a sacred oak grove. In the time of Caesar, the main centre of Druidism in Gaul was 'in the area of Carnutes, after whom Chartres is named. There, Druids met annually at a shrine believed to be on the site of Chartres Cathedral. This was the omphalos of Gaul, the sacred centre...'[14] Scholar Eleanor Hull tells us that:

> ... in ancient Irish law seven 'noble' or distinguished trees were noted, among them the oak, which was said to belong to 'the high sacred grove', and severe penalties followed upon its destruction. Even St Columba besought the Almighty to spare the sacred oak-grove at Derry, and declared afterward that much as he feared death and hell, he dreaded still more the sound of an axe in the grove of Derry...[15]

Of course in more modern times, even the comic series *Asterix* emphasizes the importance of the oak grove to the Druids – a popular view!

Celtic beliefs and the Vedas

Interestingly, a number of early Celtic beliefs seem to have similarities with early Indian Vedic culture and beliefs. This is most likely because of a possible common Indo-European heritage, as academics like Dumezil have shown regarding languages. Celtic deities included gods who often had multiple functions, who actualised nature forces like fire or thunder, promulgated ethics, justice, knowledge, arts, crafts, medicine, speech, battled forces of darkness, and there are goddesses of land, rivers and springs. The early Vedic pantheon included deities of fire, solar, and nature forces, speech, crafts, arts, medicine, ethical order, and battlers of malevolent beings. There are also goddesses of land and rivers. Like the Celtic deities, the gods are often shown as having overlapping functions. In Irish mythology, the number 17 comes up in many contexts – 17 days, 17 years, etc. Why, in an early Irish tale, does the Druid advise Maelduin to take only 17 men with him on his famous voyage? In the early *Book of Invasions*, Mil arrived in Ireland in the 'seventeenth of the moon'; the age of consent in early Ireland was generally 17, when boys became men. But why 17? The Vedas say that the heavens were divided into 17 regions, 'Prajapati is the year, so Prajapati is seventeen'. Of course 17 as an allegory or metaphor may also have other cosmological or astronomical meanings relating to the cycle(s) of time.

It appears that both the early Irish Celts and the Vedic peoples believed that the gods are particularly fond of music; both cultures highly valued music, chanting, poetry and sound, as did the Druids, with their long oral training and emphasis on the art of memory. Musicologists have examined some of these issues and suggest close correspondences between these particular cultures. The Irish music critic, Fanny Feehan, in a paper entitled *Suggested Links Between Eastern and Celtic Music* (1981) says:

In the area of vocal ornamentation East and West come close. I once played a Claddagh recording of Maire Aine (Ni Dhonnacha) singing 'Barr an tSleibhe' for an Indian Professor of Music who refused to believe, until I showed her the sleeve of the record, that it was an Irish song. She claimed, and demonstrated by singing to me, that the song bore a strange resemblence to an Indian (North) raga about a young girl being lured toward a mountain. The Professor was interested in the mode, the pitching of the voice, and certain notes which were characteristic of both the raga and 'Barr na tSleibhe'...[16]

One of the most ancient forms of Celtic music which still survives in a few areas in western Ireland is the *marbhnai*, or 'death song', part of a process called keening (caoine). These songs are sung by women and have been compared to the raga style of India, which is similarly improvised around three or four notes.

Historian Bryan McMahon plays an interesting game with every Indian guest who visits a certain hotel in County Kerry. He hums a certain Irish melody and then asks them to complete it however they like. He says that, almost every time, they will sing it like they already know the song. McMahon believes that, for him, it is an indication that Indians and Irishmen must have a common past of some kind. While one certainly cannot generalise, what can be still said for sure is that both cultures greatly value music and sound on many different levels. But the Celts and the early Indian cultures also shared a broader belief in a *special magico-religious power of music* and an awareness of the breath and of poetic verse. The Druids, with their great emphasis on sound, poetic memory and bardic techniques, very likely also believed in such unique qualities of music and sound.

Yet today we still tend to look for only written documents or hand-held artefacts to get more information about the history or culture of a people. Perhaps neglected areas like certain musical traditions, pilgrimage routes, church liturgies, and the like can also offer additional valid perspectives. We, in our modern, high-tech age, may find it rather hard to understand the importance of such notions today, yet the power of sound, music, and vibration is now documentable, as scientific research has now affirmed.

But the Druids, as their decline began in earnest, were also facing a world that had been getting much further away from the older oral traditions, the art of memory, poetic verse, and so on, something that is easy for us to forget in modern times. So it wasn't just the Roman legions, shifting economics, or the Christians, that led to the downfall of the Druids. It was also the cultural phenomenon of a great devaluing of oral traditions and therefore, of the oral methods of teaching like those used by the Druids. The great loss to western civilization of this type of sophisticated ancient knowledge based on memory and sound was acknowledged by major thinkers of the Renaissance, who attempted to try and bring back the ancient Greek 'art of memory' to European civilisation. In chapter 8, the memory of 'the lost Word' will be further explored.

The decline of Druidism

But obviously, the power of Druidism as an institution was lost compared to its former glory in earlier times. The documents known as the *Augustan Histories* describe Druid prophetesses who acted as fortune-tellers for Roman emperors such as Severus Alexander and Diocletian in the 3rd C AD, long after the final defeat of the Druids as an institution. The Druids were highly regarded in ancient times for being very good seers and magicians, especially some of the women, and a good number of early writings from the ancient world describe the Druids as the *magi* of the Celts. This must have still been true to an extent in the 3rd C as the emperors were continuing to consult the seers of a people they had defeated.

Celtic scholar Anne Ross also believes that various pockets of Druids did survive, even during or after the 3rd C, having not been altogether destroyed. They most likely practiced their religion in caves and remote places. She says that 'their survival, at this point and beyond, continued, but they seemingly ceased to have the influence which their former teaching of the offspring of the nobility had given them. Nevertheless, they were still of use to the upper classes, could help stir up revolts and impress by their powers of prophecy and spells...'[17]

So were there women Druids? Yes, scholars believe that there were female Druidesses and from various classical sources we note specific references to certain islands off the shores of Gaul (especially Brittany) and Britain that were known to be inhabited only by 'holy women'. The Druidic schools largely consisted of men but there were some women, it would appear. The 'nine maidens' folklore tradition in Scotland may be a possible remnant of these earlier times. This has been examined in greater detail by Scottish researcher Stuart McHardy. Much of this lore centres on the various legends of remaining stone circles having once been maidens but who were later turned to stone. There are a number of place-name references in Scotland, often near ancient megalithic sites, that are named 'Nine Maidens'. Even in Homer's *Odyssey*, certain 'isles of women' are referred to. Celtic literature also has a concept of certain isles being only the special province of women and usually it is implied that they are gifted priestesses and seeresses in some way. It is interesting to note that later Arthurian tradition has the wounded King Arthur being taken away by women to the island of Avalon, and in the Grail tradition, it is women who are the bearers of the Grail, subjects we will explore further in chapter 6.

Druidism and the Christian church

The Irish texts, written by Christian monks from the 5th C on when Ireland was largely Christianised, have many references to Druids in them. They are mainly portrayed as prophets or seers. Especially in the saints' lives of Patrick and Brigid, they are shown to be hostile to the new faith of Christianity. Cathbadh, the revered Druid attached to the household of Conchobar, King of Ulster, is sometimes portrayed as having even greater influence than the king himself. There is still scholarly debate about how, or whether, some of the remaining Druids might have been assimilated into the new Irish Christian monasteries.

But ultimately, as might be expected from devout Christian authors, the beliefs and magic of the Druids are seen to be clearly inferior to the new faith – Christianity – although ironically, the Christian saints are often portrayed as performing exactly the same kinds of miracles as the Druids! So it is ultimately all a matter of perspective and the belief system of the author.

Some of the early Church Councils in Gaul made decrees against Druidism in an effort to stamp it out completely, as some of the lingering traditions were a great irritation to the church, even as late as the 8th C. For example, in 452AD, the Council of Arles decreed that 'if, in any diocese, any infidel lighted torches or worshipped trees, fountains or stones, he should be guilty of sacrilege.' Clearly the people still continued on with many of their earlier traditions and customs, Druidic and otherwise.

Needless to say, many of the Christian bishops decided to adopt a strategy of not actually destroying the temples of the Druids, but to replace the old gods with their own instead. Particularly revealing is an excerpt from a letter written in 601AD from Pope Gregory to Abbot Mellitus, who was preparing a visit to England. Here, Pope Gregory gives him some advice about his upcoming meeting with Augustine in England:

> When (by God's help) you come to our most reverend brother, Bishop Augustine, I want you to tell him how earnestly I have been pondering over the affairs of the English: I have come to the conclusion that the temples of the idols in England should not on any account be destroyed. Augustine must smash the idols, but the temples themselves should be sprinkled with holy water and altars set up in them in which relics are to be enclosed. For we ought to take advantage of well-built temples by purifying them from devil-worship and dedicating them to the service of the true God. In this way I hope the people (seeing their temples are not destroyed) will leave their idolatry and yet continue to frequent the places, as formerly, so coming to know and revere the true God.[18]

So the Christian strategy was to make the traditional sacred sites their own, as well as to Christianise the ancient gods and goddesses. A clever strategy, we might say today with historical hindsight. But this was also a policy that was used by the Romans and others in early times, so it was not particularly new. For example, Bride became St Brigid, Santan, (the holy fire) became St Anne, and Sinclair (the holy light) became St Clare.[19] Many Christian feasts and festivals were put on the same day as pagan ones and new churches were built on earlier pagan sites. Not in all cases, of course, but this did happen in many of them.

It is known that 25 December was said to be the birth date of not only Jesus Christ but also that of Mithras, the founder of a cult that was a powerful rival to Christianity in earlier times. St Columba of Iona died in 597AD, and within a matter of only a few months, also in 597AD, Augustine shows up in England to begin his conquest of the pagans and also of the Celtic church, which was still quite strong at that time.

In 658AD in Gaul, the Council of Nantes ordered the destruction of all remaining Druidical monuments. So clearly there were some Druidical survivors and the church felt it must take appropriate action, even up into the 7th and 8th centuries. This may seem surprising to us today, given that Christianity was the dominant religion. But by-and-large Druidism was officially defeated by that time and any survivors were likely to have gone underground in secrecy for fear of their lives.

Druidism and Scotland

In Scotland there are certain places believed to have possible Druidic associations, either through their place-names, local history or connections with certain stone circles and other megalithic sites. But due to the woeful lack of written historical records from early Celtic times, we will of course never know exactly what the situation was. However, we can at least try to sift through what is available, keeping in mind that some authors have their own particular axes to grind about the Druids, depending on their beliefs.

But having said that, it is interesting to examine what has been written, debated and thought about Druidism and what are described as possible remnants of Druidic customs and beliefs in Scotland. One must also remember that the Romans never really conquered Scotland north of the Antonine Wall, as the Pictish tribes were viewed as especially effective warriors by the Romans who eventually retreated from their territory.

One area of likely remnants of Druidic customs and beliefs in Scotland are traditions surrounding certain *wells and springs*. Water has long been held as sacred by many early peoples and the Celts are no exception. Rivers, lochs and especially wells and springs were highly revered by the Celts. Many wells were considered to be special holy wells and even today in parts of Wales, Ireland, Brittany, Cornwall and Scotland, certain wells are 'dressed' and revered at special times of the year. In 1861 one antiquarian writer observed that

...the well of Strathfillan in Scotland is also resorted to at certain periods of the year. The water of the well of Trinity Gask in Perthshire is supposed to cure anyone seized with the plague... Not only a reverence, but actual sacrifices are offered to some of these wells and to the saints which preside over them, or to the spirits which are supposed to inhabit them.[20]

Further,

...that the Highlanders still believe in spirits which inhabit their lakes is easily proved. In Strathspey there is a lake called Loch nan Spiordan, the Lake of Spirits. When its waters are agitated by the wind and its spray mounts whirling in the air, they believe that it is the anger of this spirit whom they name Martach Shine, or the Rider of the Storm.[21]

One famous well from the early past in Scotland is that of Innis Maree, in Loch Maree, Ross-shire. It is dedicated to St Maelrubha who founded a church at Applecross, after whom both the loch and the island are named. The island of Innis Maree, or Mourie, has an enclosure, a stone dyke, in which there are the remains of a chapel. Thomas Pennant, who visited Innis Maree in 1772, describes the appearance of this well:

The shores are neat and gravelly; the whole surface covered thickly with a beautiful grove of oak, ash, willow, wicken, birch, fir, hazel, and enormous hollies. In the midst is a circular dyke of stones, with a regular narrow entrance, the inner part has been used for ages as a burial place, and is still in use. I suspect the dyke to have been originally Druidical, and that the ancient superstition of paganism had been taken up by the saint, as the readiest method of making a conquest over the minds of the inhabitants. A stump of a tree is shown as an altar, probably the memorial of one of stone; but the curiosity of the place is the well of the saint; of power unspeakable in cases of lunacy.[22]

Whatever Pennant may have meant by 'Druidical', he obviously felt that the site was a scene of pre-Christian, pagan worship and that it still had a powerful hold on the residents of the area. He says that St Mourie, or Maree, was in his day the patron of the district and that 'the oath of the country is by his name'.[23] Sir Arthur Mitchell in the fourth volume of the *Proceedings of the Antiquaries of Scotland* says that it was customary in the parish to sacrifice a bull to St Mourie. This was done on the saint's day, 25 August, a practice that was still in existence in the late 17th C and which was denounced as idolatrous by the kirk, the presbyterian Church of Scotland.

Church action against remaining Druidic customs

The church was understandably not happy with such strong survivals in certain areas of earlier pre-Christian customs and beliefs in Scotland. In 1656 the Church Presbytery of Applecross took action against certain persons for sacrificing bulls on 25 August 'which day is dedicate, as they conceive, to St Mourie, as they call him.'[24] In 1678 the Presbytery of Dingwall took similar disciplinary action against four men for sacrificing a bull in an island in Loch Maree. Near the island stood an oak tree, into whose trunk nails and coins were left as offerings, which were, of course, viewed by the church as idolatrous customs. The ruins of the chapel were said to be circled by the devotees in dance; the custom of circle-dancing was also seen as a remnant of earlier times and as idolatrous by the church. Dancing was viewed suspiciously or even outright banned at various places and times by the church.

Martin Martin, in his *A Description of the Western Isles*, tells us about the ancient Highland seership rite of *taghairm*:

> ...a seer was wrapped in the hide of a newly-slain bull and stretched himself beside a waterfall or at the foot of some wild precipice believed to be haunted by spirits, who communicated to him what he desired to know regarding the future. The rite persisted until the middle of the 18th century and is in consonance with what we know concerning descriptions of Druidic augury in Ireland, and in the Welsh Mabinogion, there is a reference to a similar belief in the tale 'The Vision of Rhonabwy', in which a warrior of that name had a vision while sleeping on the skin of a yellow heifer.[25]

In early Ireland, a similar custom was also related to auguries and dreams relating to kingship. In the Scottish Highlands, the unique phenomenon of 'Second Sight' is acknowledged to be still occurring with some people today but this is not the same as Druidism. In 1628 the Church of Scotland Assembly prohibited visits to Christ's well at Falkirk on May mornings and passed a law sentencing offenders to a fine of 'twenty pounds Scot' and the humiliation of being 'exhibited in sackcloth for three Sundays' in church. A similar act put the offenders in prison for a week on bread and water. Clearly, the kirk had a difficult time with surviving Beltane May rituals and customs in certain areas and felt that more punitive action was necessary to stop them.[26]

Place-names with Druidic associations

Some Scottish place-names are believed to have Druidical associations, however legendary. For example, certain small stone huts on the isle of Skye, which can hold only one person, like a hermit's cell, have long been referred to by the natives as *Teg-nin-druinich*[27] or 'Druid's House', as we are informed by Martin Martin.[28] Many of the Highlanders in earlier times called Iona *Inis Druineach*, or, *Nan Druihean*, 'Druid's Isle' and the Irish called it *Eilean Drunish*. But not everyone agrees, however, judging from the irritation of the Rev Dr William Reeves with the 'silly tales of the Druids vended in Iona' in his *Vita Columbae*. Obviously, as a Christian minister, he found them offensive. As many of these Druidic associations in Scotland occurred long before the theories of the 18th and 19th centuries 'Druidic enthusiasts' of the Celtic revival, one cannot automatically blame their influence for these early Highland Druidic associations, as has been attempted before.

Such tales and beliefs were in existence for centuries long *before* their theories came to light, as noted by Lewis Spence and others.[29] Even to this day, the debate continues as to whether and to what extent certain sites and historical place-names should ever be called 'Druidic' or not. The question is, exactly what does one mean by 'Druidic'? Or, for that matter, 'Celtic', 'Scottish' or 'Pictish'? Experts are still debating these issues today.

What should not be overlooked, however, is another major

point – an apparently rather strong desire by modern-day people in the 21st C to maintain a connection with the ancient Druidic and Celtic past, with a cultural and ancestral lineage. This increasing trend, in spite of the many efforts to stamp it out through the centuries, seems to show no sign of abating in a larger proportion of the public than has been previously acknowledged. It used to be that a good number of people were happy to discuss such matters privately, but never publicly. However, this seems to be changing in more recent years.

But perhaps the important question we should really be asking ourselves, especially with declining traditional church attendance numbers, is *why*? That in and of itself is worth looking at as a serious study, to examine why the 'pull' of the ancient past still so strong, even in our modern scientific, rationalistic, high-tech age. What does the romanticisation of the Druids or the Celts in modern times really signify? What are people really seeking or feel they are missing? Such issues are being discussed by many today.

Stone circles, megalithic sites, and Druidism

Unfortunately, some early antiquarian writers often interchanged the word 'Druid' for 'Pict'. So one cannot assume in some instances exactly who is being referred to, as those being described as 'Druidic' in some instances may in fact have been 'Pictish' and vice versa. For our purposes here, we are simply discussing some of the sites, place-names and customs in Scotland that are known to have had early origins, *possibly* going back to Druidic times. But one is basically left to decide for oneself when reading this material. Sadly there is not much written material that has survived about the Picts and their culture either, but we do have their enigmatic carvings left on standing stones, which are still being analysed today by experts, as we will see in chapter 3.

Throughout the centuries, many people have persistently believed that stone circles have a Druidic origin or association. Many of the antiquarian writers claimed that the Druids themselves actually built Stonehenge, which archaeologists now know not to have been the case. But in spite of this, the association still seems to linger on between the Druids, stone circles and megaliths.

In Scotland there are many stone circles, the most famous of which is Callanish on the isle of Lewis. Long viewed as an early ceremonial centre and lunar observatory, it has been called 'the Stonehenge of the North'. It contains a huge setting of upright stones from the late Neolithic era and at the centre of this landscape is a ring of stones which surround a massive monolith and a tiny chambered burial cairn. Callanish is aligned north-south, which means that whoever built it at that time had no North Pole Star in the position it is in now to assist them in orientating the stones. The Rev Dr Gordon Strachan says of this unique north-south orientation of Callanish, 'in pointing north, they point toward the pole of the heavens. It was part of the mythology of all holy mountains that their summit touched or led to the celestial North Pole around which the stars rotated.'[30] Indeed it is obvious that the builders of this magnificent complex and others like it were certainly not 'mere savages', judging from the mathematical and geometrical complexity that some believe must have been involved in building such a site. We will learn more about Callanish and other megalithic sites in the next chapter.

Druidic philosophy and theology

So what did the Druids believe? What was their overall cosmology? A number of classical writers comment on their role as wise philosophers, priests, judges, healers, astronomers and theologians. Pomponius Mela said the Druids were *magistri sapientiae,* 'Masters of Wisdom'. Ammianius, quoting the first century BC Timagenes, says that the Druids investigated 'problems of things secret and sublime'. Diodorus Siculus, writing in his *Library of History Vol 31:1*, said that they were 'philosophers, as we may call them, and men learned in religious affairs... are called by them Druids.' The Alexandrian writers commented on the brilliance of the Druidic system; for example, Dio Chrystostom compared the Druidic philosophy with that of the great civilizations of Egypt, Persia and India.

Dr Miranda Green comments on their impressive knowledge of astronomy and natural science:

Clement of Alexandria went so far as to consider that the study of philosophy had its genesis among the Celts. The Alexandrians admired what they perceived as the native wisdom of the 'Noble Savage'... Ammianus speaks of euhages (seers) who 'strive to explain the high mysteries of nature'. Cicero commented that the Druid Divitiacus had knowledge of natural phenomena. Mela said that the Druids considered themselves knowledgeable about the size and shape of the earth, the Universe and the motion of the stars. Lucan mentions the Druids' claim to understand astrology, as well as the secrets of divinity... The astronomical observations of the Druids had one very practical purpose – that of mathematical calendrical calculation. Caesar and Pliny both speak of the Druidic reckoning of time by the moon. The Christian author Hippolytus says that the Druids were capable of foretelling certain events by means of Pythagorean reckoning and calculation...[31]

Also, it was known in the ancient world that the Druids definitely believed in the immortality of the soul. St Augustine declared that their philosophy almost exactly approached that of Christian monotheism, as the Druids believed in one divine spirit. Caesar says that the Druids attached great importance to the belief that after death the soul passed from one body to another. He goes on to comment that this taught young men not to be afraid of death in battle as they believed they would definitely live again.

Diodorus comments that they had heard that at funerals the Druids would throw letters on the pyre written to the dead by their family, as they believed that the dead would be able to read the letters when they were alive again. As Dr Green comments, 'in view of the apparent virtual illiteracy of the pre-Roman Celts, this is a curious remark'.[32] It was also known that the Druids were so certain about the immortality of the soul that if one loaned money to another, it was understood that the debt could be repaid in the next world.

The Druids held a particular reverence for the number three, believing it to be magical and sacred, and they also taught some of their philosophy in triadic form. Some of the important early Irish and Welsh poetry is in a three-fold form, for example, the Triads. The Druidic symbol of the Awen is threefold, as is the Christian trinity. It is also rather intriguing to note that some of the sculptures of Europe called the 'three nails of Christ' are nearly identical to the Druidic Awen symbol. Geo Cameron, an Edinburgh-based shaman-priest, leads interesting workshops on Celtic shamanism, the Awen, and old Gaelic chants. She carries a family Celtic shamanic tradition as focussed on dàn, the process by which we can co-create our lives with the sacred.

The Druids were known to be very effective doctors and healers and they had special veneration for the mistletoe and the oak tree. There has been much speculation about the secret wisdom that the Druids possessed, but their policy was never to write any of it down, preferring instead to emphasize the art of memory and oral teachings to specially prepared candidates. Sun worship also likely played an important part in Druidic philosophy. We know from the classical writers that the Druidic mysteries were taught in three divisions (Vate, Bard, and Druid) and that they were monotheists, believing in one divine spirit, while deeply venerating the sun, moon, stars and nature spirits.

Archaeological sites and the Druids

Recently, in the 1990s, archaeologists discovered a 4,700-year-old temple in mid-Wales that is the largest Stone Age structure ever found in Western Europe. This is being supervised by the Clwyd-Powys Archaeological Trust. More than a half a mile across and covering 85 acres, the site is thirty times the size of Stonehenge.

A six-year research programme has revealed that the huge, egg-shaped complex consisted of 1,400 obelisks, each up to 23 feet high, that were made of oak – the tree of the Druids, as some observers have noted. The site has baffled archaeologists in that it appears to have been kept extraordinarily clean, as the area inside the complex was kept completely clear for over 3,000 years, indicating an especially sacred area. The site remained untouched by normal secular human activity from its construction in 2700BC through the late Neolithic, the entire Bronze Age and the Iron Age, which ended after the Roman invasion of 43AD.

The absence of debris from any human activity from the earlier parts of the Neolithic era suggest the area may have been taboo for even longer. Ordinary people were almost certainly barred from the site, and archaeologists believe that the temple was almost certainly kept exclusively for the use of the priesthood. But was it necessarily a *Druidic* temple? We cannot assume anything, of course, but it is interesting that when the Roman invaders arrived, its very sanctity seems to have made it a definite target as the site appears to have been deliberately violated. The Romans seem to have chosen to insult the local populace by building a marching camp on one part of the sacred site and a permanent fort on the other.

This site at Hindwell is now being seen as one of the most important early sites in all of Europe, certainly on a par with Stonehenge and Callanish. Such sites often have an astronomical alignment to the sun or moon, making some people think they were actually constructed by the Druids. But, in fact, *this is very doubtful*, as it looks like the Druids 'adopted' these already existing ancient megalithic sites for their own rituals and ceremonies as they recognised their value and sanctity.

The recent discovery of 'Seahenge' off the Norwich coast in England is currently being examined in great detail and may also shed more light on the early past. In Scotland, another large circle that originally had timber obelisks has recently been found in the Dumfries and Galloway area and much archaeological information has yet to be learned about this site. Many of these sites and the areas around them have traditions and folklore attached to them, some of which have been labelled 'Druidic', whether accurate or not.

A good number of the lingering Scottish customs that have been called 'Druidic' may not actually have come from the Druids at all, but the beliefs may have seemed quite similar. So in time, people probably just assumed that they were Druidic in origin. We also know precious little about the Picts and their beliefs, but hopefully, future excavations may shed some more light on their culture. But with Druidism, we cannot say for sure, as very little extant writings about Druidism in Scotland exist and we still have much to learn from the archaeological record about the early peoples of Scotland. So, in popular jargon, 'the jury is still out'.

Druidism, the Old Testament and Freemasonry: the 'Celtic Revival'

Enthusiasm for the Druids and a romanticism of the past had led many antiquarian writers in recent centuries to formulate various theories about their beliefs and rituals. Much of this material was written in the 17th, 18th, and 19th centuries by authors such as William Stukely, John Aubrey, Rev Henry Rowlands, Godfrey Higgins, John Toland, Rev R.W. Morgan and William Blake. Just as the classical writers were divided into 'pro' and 'anti' Druid camps, so were the antiquarians. Some were quite obsessed with the Druids and bordered on the fanatical, others have been largely discredited by scholars for various reasons, and some continue to be valued today for some of their early insights and research at sites like Stonehenge and Avebury. Although their ideas may seem quite unusual to us today, their writings have had quite an effect, for better or worse.

John Aubrey was probably the most influential of the 17th C antiquaries; he made a systematic, detailed archaeological survey of both Stonehenge and Avebury, making him the first writer to link the Druids with Stonehenge. But Aubrey himself did acknowledge that his work was speculative and stated that he had 'gone further in this Essay than anyone' to date. More writers would later go much further than him, however! Although archaeologists now know that the Druids did not build Stonehenge, this impression still persists with much of the public.

One especially popular theory at the time of Aubrey was that the Druids were 'of Abraham's religion' and so associated with both the Old Testament and with Christianity. These antiquarians were building on some of the earlier commentaries that the Roman and Alexandrian writers had made about the Druids and attempted to take these ideas even further. They also wanted to defend ancient British history and Druidism, believing it to be as good or as respectable as the Judeo-Christian, Greek, Indian or Persian traditions of 'wise men'. One of the major proponents of this theory was William Stukely, a Lincolnshire doctor who was born in 1687, and took holy Orders and became Vicar of

Stamford in 1729. He was influenced by Aubrey's work and became more and more convinced of the connection between the Old Testament, the Druids and Christianity:

> In attempting to reconcile Christianity with the existence of the Druids, Stukeley constructed an elaborate pedigree for both Druids and Christians. According to him, the Druids first arrived in Britain with the Phoenicians, shortly after the Flood. He described the Druids as being 'of Abraham's religion', and thus considered them to be associated with both the Old Testament and the Christian Faith. The origins of such a notion were not peculiar to Stukeley but echoed 18th century perceptions in which Christianity went back to the time of the Creation, and the 'Natural Religion', as practised by the Druids, was akin to Christianity. By 1726, Stukeley was coming to the view that the beliefs of the Druids were 'near to the Christian doctrine'... For Stukeley, the Druids were 'Noble Savages', thinking profound thoughts and practising Natural Religion in their sacred groves. Their closeness to Christianity was proved, he said, by their consciousness of the sanctity of the number 3 and thus their recognition of the Trinity: 'As once of old in groves, so here in their representative fabrics, we adore the three sacred persons of the Trinity'.[33]

Other writers took the whole idea of Druidism being connected to the Old Testament Patriarchs even further, with special attention being given to Noah. In an effort to glorify the early Celts and put early Britain and Druidic philosophy on a par with other famous ancient civilizations, these writers pieced together bits of fact, local traditions, folklore, archaeological information, biblical comparisons, mythology and even Masonic lore to make their points.

Yes, some of these ideas may certainly seem bizarre, or even preposterous to us today, but *at the time*, these were the preoccupations of the learned in society and were taken very seriously, largely as part of an effort to show that ancient Britain was just as great as Greece, Rome, Egypt or Babylon, for instance, a seemingly noble enough idea. But we have to at least attempt to try and understand historical material *from the viewpoint of the era in which it was written*. Bearing this in mind, we will now take a look at some of these antiquarian writings, bizarre or outrageous as some of them may seem.

Helio-Arkite theory

We begin with the Rev G.S. Faber, who wrote *Dissertation on the Mysteries of the Cabiri* (1803). His work emphasizes that many of the gods of ancient Greece and Rome could ultimately be identified with Noah. It was his thesis that when the veneration of the Patriarchs (Abraham, Shem, Noah, etc.) was combined with sun-worship, this produced what he called his helio-arkite theory.[34] This theory, in turn, influenced others writers of the time. Probably the two most enthusiastic supporters of this concept of the Druids were Rev R.W. Morgan, an Anglican clergyman with strong Celtic sympathies, whose *St Paul in Britain* was published in 1922, and antiquarian Dudley Wright, who wrote *Druidism: the Ancient Faith of Britain* in 1924.

R.W. Morgan's controversial theory regarding the Druids lays heavy emphasis on the helio-arkite theory, the biblical Patriarchs, the Flood, and Noah. Regarding what he felt to be the origin of Druidism, he said:

> Druidism was founded by Gwyddon Ganhebon, supposed to be the Seth of Mosaic theology, in Asia... from Asia, Druidism was brought into Britain by Hu Gadarn, or the Mighty, its first colonizer, a contemporary of the Patriarch Abraham...[35]

He goes on to say, regarding the Druidic trinity:

> This was the Druidic trinity, the three aspects of which were known as Beli, Taran, Esu or Yesu. When Christianity preached Jesus as God, it preached the most familiar name of its own deity to Druidism; and in the ancient British tongue 'Jesus' has never assumed its Greek, Latin, or Hebrew form, but remains the pure Druidic 'Yesu'. It is singular thus that the ancient Briton has never changed the name of the God he and his forefathers worshipped, nor has ever worshipped but one God.[36]

Noah, Druidism and Freemasonry

Antiquarian Dudley Wright, whose *Druidism: The Ancient Faith of Britain* (1924) made comparisons of the ceremony of initiation of the Druids with certain Masonic symbolism, a path that other writers had previously attempted to explore. They believed that Freemasonry may have derived from the ancient British system of Druidic beliefs. Wright states:

> The ceremony of initiation, as far as can be gathered from the sources, was solemn and arduous. The candidate first took an oath not to reveal the mysteries into which he was about to be initiated. He was then divested of his ordinary clothing, crowned with ivy, and vested with a tri-coloured robe of white, blue and green – colours emblematical of light, truth, and hope. Over this was placed a white tunic... The tonsure was one of the ceremonies connected with initiation... All the hair in front of a line drawn over the crown from ear to ear was shaved or clipped... The initiation took place in a cave because of the legend which existed that Enoch had deposited certain invaluable secrets in a consecrated cavern deep within the earth... After taking the oath the candidate had to pass through the Dolmen, or perforated stone, an act held to be the means of purging from sin and conveying purity... The candidate was next placed in a chest or coffin in which he remained enclosed – apertures being made for the circulation of air – for three days, to represent death. From this chest he was liberated on the third day to symbolise his restoration to life... When the aspirant emerged from the tomb... he was pronounced regenerated, or born again...[37]

The purpose of this, Wright tells us, was that the candidate was to be subject to a solitary confinement for a prescribed period of time. He was to reflect seriously in seclusion and darkness on what he was about to undertake and be reduced to the proper state of mind for the reception of great and important truths by a course of fasting. This was a symbolic death, and after this experience, the candidate was ready to go to the sanctuary for further ceremonies. Wright continues:

> The sanctuary was then prepared for the further ceremonies... the candidate, blindfolded, was introduced to the assembled company during the chanting of a hymn to the sun and placed in the charge of a professed Druid, and another Druid, at the same time, kindling the sacred fire... Still blindfolded, the candidate was taken on a circumambulation nine times round the sanctuary in circles from East to West, starting at the South. The procession was made to the accompaniment of a tumultous clanging of musical instruments and of shouting... and was followed by

the administration of a second oath, the violation of which rendered the individual liable to the penalty of death.[38]

Then, the Noah theme comes in next:

Then followed a number of ceremonies which typified the confinement of Noah in the Ark and the death of that patriarch, the candidate passing eventually through a narrow avenue, which was guarded by angry beasts, after which he was seized and borne to the waters, symbolical of the waters on which the Ark of Noah floated. He was completely immersed in this water, and, on emerging from the water… he found himself in a blaze of light. The most dismal howlings, shrieks, and lamentations are said to have been heard during the progress of this ceremony… The candidate, on arriving at the opposite bank, was presented to the Arch Druid, who, seated on his throne or official chair, explained to the initiate the symbolical meaning of the various ceremonies in which he had just taken an active part.[39]

Wright believed that this initiation ceremony was similar to that of the Egyptian rites of Osiris – a descent into hell, a passage through the infernal lake, followed by a landing on the Egyptian Isle of the Blessed. By this means men were believed to become more holy and just. The cave in which the candidate was placed for the purpose of meditation before he was permitted to take part in the sacred mysteries was guarded by a frightening divinity figure who was armed with a sword to keep away all possible intruders. After the initiation the novice returned to the forest where the period of his novitiate was spent.

Importance of symbolism, the cube, and the sun god 'Hu'

Wright further says that the Druids were known to have a veneration for the cube, which they regarded as a symbol of truth, because it presented the same appearance whichever way it turned.[40] This was considered to be one of the symbols of Mercury. Manly P. Hall, a respected Masonic researcher of the early 20th C, wrote that US Masonic writer Albert Pike said that the Lost Word of Masonry is concealed in the name of the Druid god Hu. He further goes on to say that:

...the meager information extant concerning the secret initiations of the Druids indicates a decided similarity between their Mystery school and the school of Greece and Egypt. Hu, the Sun God, was murdered, and after a number of strange ordeals and mystic rituals, was restored to life. There were three degrees of the Druidic mysteries, but few successfully passed them all.[41]

These three degrees were Ovate, Bard and Druid. He also says that it was known that the cross, the serpent and the egg were sacred symbols to the Druids and that they held the sun in special reverence. The 'Serpent's Egg' was also known to be highly revered by the Pythagoreans. Strangely enough, as is known today, the sound 'Hu' is still highly revered by certain Sufi orders in modern times.

Thomas Paine, Druidism and Freemasonry

Thomas Paine, best known for his 18th C works *The Rights of Man* and *Age of Reason*, may have also believed that there were philosophical similarities between Freemasonry and the Druidic philosophy of the ancient British Isles. A little-known essay entitled *The Origin of Freemasonry* bearing Paine's name as the author appeared in New York in 1818. In it Paine claims that Masonry and Christianity have a similar common origin, in that

...both are derived from the worship of the sun... In Masonry many of the ceremonies of the Druids are preserved in their original state, at least without parody. With them the Sun is still the Sun, and his image, in the form of the sun is the great emblematical ornament of Masonic Lodges and Masonic dress. It is the central figure on their aprons, and they wear it also [as a] pendant on the breast in their lodge, and in their processions. It has the figure of a man, as at the head of the sun, as Christ is always represented... As the study and contemplation of the Creator is in the works of the creation, the Sun, as the great visible agent of that being, was the visible object of the adoration of the Druids; all their religious rites and ceremonies had reference to the apparent progress of the Sun through the twelve signs of the zodiac, and his influence upon the earth. The Masons adopt the same practices. The roof of their Temples or Lodges is ornamented with a Sun...[42]

He goes on to emphasize that the reason the Masons have a policy of secrecy is that this understandably originated from a fear of persecution, as those of a new religion tend to become the persecutors of the old. He gives several examples of this, saying that

...when the Christian religion overran the Jewish religion, the Jews were the continual subject of persecution in all Christian countries. When the Protestant religion in England overran the Roman Catholic religion, it was made death for a Catholic priest to be found in England... [so that when]... the Christian religion overran the religion of the Druids... the Druids became the subject of persecution. This would naturally and necessarily oblige such of them as remained attached to their original religion to meet in secret, and under the strongest injunctions of secrecy. Their safety depended upon it. A false brother might expose the lives of many of them to destruction, and from the remains of the religion of the Druids, thus preserved, arose the institution which, to avoid the name of Druid, took that of Mason, and practiced under this new name the rites and ceremonies of Druids.[43]

Paine, well-known for his views on liberty and concerns with the brotherhood of man, probably did have some interest in Freemasonry as a philosophy, although it is known that he himself was not a Freemason. However, given the prominence of Freemasons in both the French and American revolutions, it is known that many of his contemporaries were Freemasons and he undoubtedly knew this. Paine's intimacy in Paris with Nicolas de Bonneville and Charles Frangois Dupuis, whose writings are replete with Masonic speculations, may sufficiently explain his interest in the subject. After Paine died, the executrix of his will was Madame de Bonneville, and she published the first version of this essay in New York, which was entitled *The Origin of Freemasonry*.

Some doubt that Paine himself wrote this work, implying that either de Bonneville, or someone in that circle, did. That, of course, is possible. The point is that the pamphlet illustrates the nature of the philosophical issues thinking men like himself were grappling with at the time. Although this admittedly is a rather controversial work, it is interesting to read *regarding the ideas and concepts popular at the time*, and can be useful as a case study in *the evolution and use of belief systems*, especially in the 18th C. Put another way, as the old maxim states: it doesn't always matter what is ultimately true, it is what people believe to be true that matters. On the other hand, perhaps he did write it. But although the authorship may never be known for certain, the effect this pamphlet had, for better or worse, is evident.

It is widely known that Masonic lodges and other 'gentlemen's clubs' and societies had a great influence on well-known people, especially in the 18th C, which has been dubbed 'The Age of Freemasonry' by some respected historians. This is due to the large numbers of prominent men in society who are known to have been members of Masonic lodges and other similar clubs at the time. These issues will further examined in chapter 8.

William Blake: Albion, Druidism, Noah

The famous visionary and painter William Blake and his wife moved to Poland Street in London some time after his father died in 1784, and remained there until 1790. It is known that in 1781, Henry Hurle created a new association called The Ancient Order of Druids and that they met at the Kings Arms Tavern on Poland Street, a few houses away from where the Blakes resided. This neo-Druidic group came to enjoy considerable prestige, an illustrious membership, and great expansion throughout the world at the time because philosophically 'it established itself in the Judeo-Christian sphere by placing the Bible upon the altar of its closed temples... [they were] creating a whole social system of mutual insurance, far ahead in time of the National Health Service. This social system was committed to visiting sick people at home or in hospital, widows and orphans...'[44] Many of our modern-day building societies, insurance companies, friendly societies and banks have their origins in much earlier times.

The Kings Arms Tavern on Poland Street was a place of lively philosophical discussions, and possibly, according to Blake biographer Peter Ackroyd, where Blake may have acquired 'a new antiquarianism' which was both popular and scholarly at the time and 'which was rewriting British history.'[45] Ackroyd believes that Blake's sense of what he meant by Empire, whose ruler he named

Albion, came from this 'new antiquarianism' of the time. Blake believed that the ancient Druid past of England was established by Adam, Noah and Abraham, all similar ideas to other writers and philosophers of the time.

Philip Carr-Gomm, psychologist, writer, and Chief of the modern Order of Bards, Ovates and Druids in England today, has written about the history of the modern-day Druid resurgence in his latest book, an edited anthology. In it Dr Michel Raoult comments that:

> ...the first known writer of the Renaissance to have written about Druids is Annius di Vitero, in 1498. His work was popularised in 1510 by John White of Basingstoke, who also used the writings of Geoffrey of Monmouth. From that time, there has been an almost uninterrupted stream of authors who invariably publish their own opinions on Druids, rather than the real content of the tradition.[46]

The Druidic resurgence of 1717

It has also been noted by some that the major Druidic resurgence of 1717, which began in September 1716 with the famous 'Call to the Druids' by antiquarian John Toland on Primrose Hill in London, seems to generally coincide with the creation of the Grand Lodge of England (24 June 1717), in that all of this happened in the same year. This Lodge merged together four existing speculative Masonic lodges of London, and it is said that one of them used to hold its meetings at the Apple Tree Tavern, Charles Street, Covent Garden, London – the very same venue of Toland's Druidic group. But English Masonic scholars today say that as many early lodge records are not extant, such claims are difficult to prove. But clearly, 1717 was an active year for many such organisations and fraternities, as was much of the 18th C and undoubtedly some members of each of these groups may have known each other. Such clubs, fraternities and associations are known to have had a definite effect on many of the Enlightenment thinkers of the day. As safe havens, they provided a place for freedom of expression and lively discussion.

Modern-day Druidic revival

But even today, interest in the Druids has not waned; if anything, it has increased. We live in complex times, with religious topics sometimes featuring as newspaper headlines. Issues such as whether or not the modern-day Order of Bards, Ovates and Druids should have the right of access to Stonehenge on the summer solstice (21 June) for their ceremonies are featured in the media, and their popularity in books and films continues. Christian parents worry about their children getting involved in pagan groups, and pagan parents claim that Christians are trying to convert their children, so it seems to be all a matter of perspective.

But media coverage certainly does not mean that the portrayals of Druids are necessarily accurate ones. Nor for that matter is what has been written by the antiquarians of the past, which many consider to have been propaganda, or, at worst, even deliberately inaccurate. Those who attempt to rewrite history clearly have their own agendas and some of the antiquarians were no exception to this, perhaps similar to modern-day media spin doctors. But ironically, this also does not mean that *everything* that they wrote or thought was wrong either. Obviously, one must be very careful about sources and their contents.

John Matthews, a popular modern author on subjects relating to the Celts and Druids, is also a member of the Order of Bards, Ovates and Druids. He states in the introduction to his anthology *The Druid Source Book* his honest views about some of the rather outlandish claims some of the antiquarian writers made about the Druids and their history:

> ...I hold no particular brief for or against much of the material presented here. As a Druid myself, I acknowledge the contribution of writers such as Godfrey Higgins, John Toland and Edward Davies to contemporary practice, while as a writer and researcher into the ancient mysteries of this land, I may have reservations about both their scholarship and the conclusions they draw... Modern-day Druids are not gullible, uncritical beings who will accept any written wisdom as fact...[47]

Any writer is faced with the difficult task of having to separate out 'the wheat from the chaff' as to the reliability of sources. Of course, that is what good research is about. But generally what has happened is that some scholars have declared *all* of the writings of the antiquarians to be unreliable. While this may be admittedly true in some cases, basically, the 'baby has been thrown out with the bathwater', so to speak, which has left other scholars reticent to pursue such matters further for fear of their credibility being endangered. This has been certainly understandable given the circumstances.

However, the public continues to want more information and because these subjects in the past have not been dealt with by the experts of the day, many popular, but not necessarily accurate, books have come in to fill in the gap. Now, it seems, more academics and scientists are willing to address some of these issues, partly due to increasing public demand for more information and the impact of some of the more accurate popular books in the field.

Sir Isaac Newton and Sir Winston Churchill

But this situation isn't unique regarding Druidism. Take Sir Isaac Newton for example. We hear a lot about his job at the Royal Mint and his brilliant scientific inventions, but never about his serious interest in alchemy, at which he also spent a large amount of his time and left many papers to posterity which have been proven to be genuine. One has to ask: why?

Another example is Sir Winston Churchill, who clearly achieved many great things. Although it has been known that he was a Freemason for quite some time now, it has recently also come to light that he was also a member of a Druidic order and took it seriously. Surprised? We were, too, as this wasn't widely known until more recently. But history is full of such examples of selective information, where the reader only gets part of the picture for a number of reasons. But it is important to realise that some of this may not even be deliberately done; in certain instances, it can be just as much a case of simple neglect or oversight. The problem, though, is that the effect is the same – the reader only gets part of the story and history remains incomplete.

As modern professional historians are finding, the 'image' previously believed about someone famous may not in fact be an accurate portrayal of them. The real issue is 'who decides' what information is put forth and what is withheld. But is it necessarily right that just because something doesn't happen to fit one's worldview, for whatever reason, that it is simply tossed aside and left out altogether? This is hardly representative of 'scientific' research methods.

Antiquarian sources a challenge

The thorny issue of the reliability of the antiquarian writers of the Celtic revival has clearly posed a difficult dilemma for many researchers. Much of what the antiquarians wrote was simply a product of certain belief systems of their time, and they should be analysed as such. And yes, a lot of it is admittedly quite bizarre. But in many cases, all of their writings have simply been automatically disparaged, often by those who haven't even taken the time to read them, akin to the so-called expert 'film critic' who rubbishes a film in a review without actually ever having seen it himself.

The Rev Dr Gordon Strachan comments on the typical pillaging of the antiquarian Celtic revival writings by such renowned scholars as Professor Stuart Piggott (emphasis provided):

Piggott follows T.D. Kendrick in *The Druids* of 1927, who appears to be just as damning of the helio-arkite tradition as Piggott. Nevertheless, he in fact does leave the door open to the possibility of there having been a genuine continuity between the ancient Druids, the medieval Welsh bards and the Celtic revivalists saying 'this is not by any means an extravagant or ridiculous belief.' Piggott accepts this, admitting that the medieval Welsh and Irish bards had 'genuine roots in the ancient past of the Celts and Druids'. He also admits that 'the links of this tradition in the 18th century with that of the Middle Ages were genuine enough.' Now, if this is indeed the case, that there were genuine links among the Celticists of the 18th century, the bardic tradition of the Middle Ages and the ancient bards and Druids, why don't we hear more about them?... Surely, if there was any trace of truth in the assertion that there was a genuine element of continuity, then that should be presented to us as an option. But it is not. All we get is an endless catalogue of criticism which implies... that there were no reliable scholars in this field at any period...[48]

So although Piggott is right in that much of the information used by the antiquarians was for their own agendas and is therefore not reliable, he still acknowledges that there likely were genuine links. Yet he says that this can never be definitively proven, due to no reliable scholars, a rather vicious circle. But the romanticised, stereotyped image of the 'Noble Savage' and the 'Primitive' has remained with the public about the Druids, whether deliberately intended or not, into quite recent times. However, this view has become much more outdated in recent times.

The classical writers and early Church Fathers who believed that the vast philosophical knowledge the Druids possessed was as great as that of ancient Persia, India, Egypt or Babylon would probably be astounded to see to what extent they were later belittled, reduced by some to 'mere illiterate savages'. On the other hand, they would also probably be equally surprised to see to what outrageous lengths some of the antiquarian writers went in making their points.

Great interest in the 'archaic past' today

The challenge to make one's way through this minefield of various sources is obvious enough. But one thing seems certain: interest in the Druids and Druidism seems even more popular than ever in modern times. As to why, we can only conjecture; the allure of the Druids from the archaic past remains with us today, whether our modern-day perceptions of the Druids and Druidism are necessarily accurate ones or not. Perhaps this all really says more about our culture than that of the Druids.

This is a 'myth in the making' and perhaps, in some ways, it always has been since time immemorial.

We will now further explore the stone circles, megaliths and the sacred sites of Scotland, whose legacy is also still with us today.

Notes

[1] Thurneysen, R, *A Grammar of Old Irish*, Dublin Institute of Advanced Studies, (D.I.A.S.) Dublin, 1980, 124.

[2] Ross, A, *The Druids*, Tempus, Stroud, 1999, 16.

[3] Ibid, 17.

[4] Markale, Prof J, *The Druids*, Inner Traditions, VT, 1999 English transl. of 1985 French orig. [*Le Druidisme, Traditions et dieux des Celtes*], 32.

[5] Gildas, *Cottonian MS*, British Library.

[6] Frawley, D, *Gods, Sages, and Kings*, Passage Press, UT, 1991, 223

[7] Caesar, J, *Gallic War* VI, 13-14.

[8] Piggott, S, *The Druids*, Thames & Hudson, London, 1968, 102.

[9] Green, M, *The World of the Druids*, Thames & Hudson, London, 1997, 14.

[10] Ellis, P.B, *The Druids*, Constable, London, 1994, 68.

[11] Ibid, 15.

[12] Cunliffe, B, *The Ancient Celts*, Oxford University Press, Oxford, 1997, 191.

[13] Markale, J, op cit, 20.

[14] Jones, P, & Pennick, N, *A History of Pagan Europe*, Routledge, London, 1995, 85.

[15] Hull, E, *Folklore of the British Isles*, London, 125-7.

[16] Feehan, F, 'Suggested Links Between Eastern and Celtic Music', *The Celtic Consciousness*, [Ed. R. O'Driscoll], Celtic Arts Board of Canada, George Braziller Inc, New York, 1981, 334.

[17] Ross, A, op cit, 43.

[18] Rigby, G, *On Earth as it is in Heaven*, Rhaedus, Guernsey, 1996, 119.

[19] Ibid.

[20] Reade, W. Winwood, *The Veil of Isis or the Mysteries of the Druids*, C.J. Skeet, London, 1861, 208.

[21] Ibid, 209.

[22] MacKinley, J.M, *Folklore of Scottish Lochs and Springs*, Wm. Hodge & Co, Glasgow, 1893, 29.

[23] Pennant, T, *A Tour in Scotland & Voyage to the Hebrides*, Vol. 2, Chester, 1774, 330.

[24] Spence, L, *The History & Origins of Druidism*, Rider & Co, London, 1947, 37.

[25] Martin, M, *A Description of the Western Isles of Scotland circa 1690*, Edinburgh, 1716 & 1934, 110-12.

[26] Spence, op cit, 38.

[27] Bonwick, J, *Irish Druids & Old Irish Religions*, London, 1894, 240.

[28] Martin, M, op cit, 166.

[29] Spence, op cit, 38.

30 Strachan, G, *Jesus the Mystery Builder: Druid Mysteries and the Dawn of Christianity*, Floris Books, Edinburgh, 1998, 258.
31 Green, M, op cit, 50.
32 Green, op cit, 51.
33 Green, op cit, 143.
34 Owen, A L, *The Famous Druids: A Survey of three centuries of English literature on the Druids*, Oxford University Press, Oxford, 1962, 211.
35 Morgan, R.W, *St. Paul in Britain*, Marshall Bros, London, 1922, 54.
36 Ibid, 55.
37 Wright, D, *Druidism: The Ancient Faith of Britain*, J. Burrow & Co, London, 1924, 63.
38 Ibid, 64.
39 Ibid, 65.
40 Ibid, 34.
41 Hall, M. P, *The Secret Teachings of All Ages*, Philosophical Research Society, Los Angeles, 1977 ed. (of 1928 orig.), 23.
42 Paine, T, 'Origins of Freemasonry', New York, 1818, 3.
43 Ibid.
44 Raoult, M, 'The Druid Revival in Brittany, France and Europe', in *The Druid Renaissance*, (Ed.) P. Carr-Gomm, Thorsons, London, 1996, 108.
45 Ackroyd, P, *Blake*, Random House, London, 1996, 302
46 Raoult, op cit, 105.
47 Matthews, J, (Ed.), *The Druid Source Book*, Blandford, London, 1996, 9.
48 Strachan, G, op cit, 58.

CHAPTER THREE

Stone Circles, Megaliths and Early Sacred Sites

NEARLY FOUR CENTURIES AGO the Scottish historian George Buchanan said that the purpose of history was 'to restore us to our ancestors and our ancestors to us.'[1] There have been various traditions about the Stone of Destiny, for example, that have helped shape the history of a nation. Here we will also take a look at the very early history of Scotland, of the geology, stone circles and early sites, as they, too, form a fascinating history.

Stones have always been thought to have special qualities in many early cultures and Scotland is no exception. It is easy for us in modern times to forget to what extent early peoples made great efforts to build early stone monuments, often bringing huge monoliths many, many miles at tremendous effort, as with Stonehenge for example.

Early geological history of Scotland

Scotland is famous for its stunning scenery, beautiful landscape and unusual rocks. Many tourists have come to visit the Highlands and hillwalkers have climbed Ben Nevis or the Cairngorms, probably not realising that these mountains, made largely of granite, were created millions and millions of years ago. The red sandstones of Orkney and Caithness were formed in a huge freshwater lake as many layers of sand, mud and pebbles were gradually deposited. Arthur's Seat, which today still dominates the skyline of Edinburgh, was formed sometime between 360-290 million years ago and it was once an active volcano. Other very early active volcanos in Scotland were on the islands of Arran, Skye, Mull, Rum and St Kilda. So many of Scotland's most famous tourist attractions are actually among the earliest rocks on the planet today.

For its size the land of Scotland itself has the most varied geology and natural landscape of any country on earth, a result of all of the cataclysmic earth activity through the centuries. Geologists worldwide come to study Scotland's rocks; especially, for example, the ancient gneiss formations on the isle of Lewis, located on the outer Hebrides, which were created around three billion years ago in the Precambrian period. It is not widely known that up until around 410 million years ago, as Scotland's rocks were still being formed, it was still connected to North America by a continent called Laurentia.[2] By 2.4 million BC, Scotland had gradually drifted away from North America. An Ice Age with its glaciers followed and this period did not really end until about 9500BC. The advance and retreat of these ice sheets affected the land and resulted in the raised beaches on the islands of Jura and Islay and the world-famous links golf courses on the east coast of Scotland.

James Hutton, the father of geology, was born in Edinburgh in 1726 and studied chemistry and medicine at the University of Edinburgh. He laid the basis of the science of geology as we know it today. He wrote his famous *Theory of the Earth* in 1788. Hutton's theory, unusual in its time, was of a cycle in which weathering destroyed old rocks while new ones formed from their sediment. Certains places where Hutton studied are still visited by geologists from around the world today, such as Siccar Point on the Berwickshire coast and Salisbury Crags, part of Arthur's Seat in Edinburgh. As is often the case, his findings were not universally accepted until after his death in 1797.[3]

So perhaps it is not surprising that the idea of a 'Stone of Destiny' would come to be especially associated with Scotland, as it seems that stones, rocks and their perceived power throughout the course of time are well established in its history.

As we can see from the early geological history of Scotland's ancient land mass, it may come as no surprise that anthropologists believe that many early peoples often thought of the earth as constantly changing through the cycles of time, as having a life of its own, and of rocks and stones as being somehow 'alive'. The concept of a living earth, and of stones in particular as being a special marker or acknowledgement of the cycles of life, was present in many early societies. Some stones were believed to have special magical and protective properties. The dead were commemorated with cairns made of stones, for example. Even today, most graves are still marked with a stone, as it lasts for a long time and is symbolic of remembering a person or event. Church foundations, too, were often started with the laying of the foundation stone – an old tradition that goes back to ancient times, through to the building of the Temple of Solomon and Chartres Cathedral, etc. This same idea also appears in certain church, Masonic and Templar writings, which will be discussed later in chapter 8. The high crosses of Ireland, Scotland and Wales, with their ornate Celtic designs, were also made of stone, as are many commemorative markers today.

Callanish: the isle of Lewis

Early sites like Callanish (Gaelic: Calanais) on the isle of Lewis, the Ring of Brodgar in Orkney, or Cairnpapple Hill in West Lothian are all examples of the Scottish equivalents of sites like Stonehenge or Avebury in southern England.[4] Archaeological excavations in Scotland have revealed field systems and other structures beneath the peat near the famous stone circle of Callanish. According to Historic Scotland archaeologist Ian Armit, the major stone circle at Callanish is one of the finest examples of the 'old order' of the Neolithic period in Scotland and can be dated to around 3000BC, which would have been about 5,000 years ago. He adds that

> Around 3000BC it seems that the ridge was given over to arable ground, although there are tantalising hints of earlier, dismantled structures on the site. Between 2900 and 2600BC, however, the stones were dragged into place and set up to form the main elements of the monument as we see it today. This dating places Calanais only slightly later than the Stones of Stenness, and rather earlier than the great stone circle at Stonehenge. The builders used Grooved Ware pottery, closely similar to the types found at these other centres.[5]

Shortly after this, a small chambered tomb was erected in the centre of the main circle and was apparently in use for several centuries later. Pottery remains have been found there, but unfortunately, archaeological excavations have shown that the chamber was ransacked and ruined around 2000-1750BC. The main stone circle at Callanish consists of 13 monoliths. It is approached from the north by a double avenue of stones and has shorter single lines leading off to the east, west and south, making the whole main circle complex in the shape of a huge cross, as seen from the air.

But there are also a number of other important 'minor' stone circle sites around the main circle at Callanish. Nineteen other sites have been located near the main site. Ian Armit comments that there are at least three other stone circles, various lesser alignments and single stones, which are all worth a visit in their own right. Researchers Ron and Margaret Curtis, who live in the village of Callanish, claim to have shown by their research that the builders of the Callanish sites were especially interested in the movements of the moon. They point out that at such a northernly latitude (58 degrees north), a rather rare lunar event known as the 'southern extreme of the major standstill' is known to have occurred at Callanish for thousands of years. The moon skims low across the southern sky, with only a few hours passing between moonrise and moonset. At the June full moon, the effects are most pronounced, as it shines at a very specific point between the stones. It is a rare astronomical event that occurs once a month over a period of several months, but then it is not repeated again until 18.6 years later.[6] This process is still going on today.

A number of archaeologists say that it is likely that the builders of such sites as Callanish did have a clear awareness of celestial events and the movements of the stars, sun and moon, that is that they weren't simply 'mere savages' who were only concerned with so-called 'barbaric rites and superstitions', a rather outdated view as more evidence comes in.

Callanish a 'lunar observatory' to the ancients?

Others, though, go even further. The leading proponent of the 'astro-archaeology' school of thought was retired Oxford Professor of Engineering, Professor Alexander Thom, who rocked the archaeological establishment in 1967 with his *Megalithic Sites in Britain*. It was published by Oxford University Press, and caused quite a stir with its premise that the megalithic builders were expert astronomers and intelligent surveyors with a unified code of science based on number and geometry. Thom analysed many stone circles and found a common unit of measure, a 'megalithic yard' of approximately 2.72 feet, derived from his own surveys of many British stone circles. The megalithic yard theory is dependent on precise geometric patterns fitted within the stone circles. Some researchers believe that they are based on Pythagorean geometry. Since Thom's death, leading researchers such as the late Anne Macaulay, Honorary Fellow, University of Edinburgh, Keith Crichlow and John Michell, for example, have done further research along these lines. The pioneering research of the late Anne Macaulay (d.1998) will be edited by experts and issued as a series.

But critics of Thom state that such alignments in these monuments generally occur by chance alone and that erosion and displacement of the stones makes any attempt to evaluate these sites by detailed measurements very difficult, especially after thousands of years. One critic even went so far as to say that 'the megalithic yard is a figment'.[7] Obviously, supporters of the theory strongly disagree, so the debate continues today.

It seems that a good number of professional archaeologists are somewhere in between. They believe that observation of the heavens was undoubtedly an important part of activities at sites like Callanish and that these early builders probably were a lot more sophisticated than we have previously given them credit for. However, they add that this doesn't necessarily mean that they consciously knew about mathematics and geometry and built the sites around it; they believe that as more research is being done all the time, one cannot say for certain about the role of astronomical alignments at megalithic sites like Callanish, Stonehenge, or Newgrange, for instance. But they also do not deny the obvious celestial alignments at some of these sites. This means that while not everyone agrees that it can be proven, it can no longer be completely disproved either, meaning that 'the jury is still out', so to speak. However, as many who visit these sites will attest, one seems to get the clear impression that the early builders did have a definite awareness of the sun, moon and stars, and especially at the solstices and equinoxes.

Similar connections between ancient monuments and sun, moon and star cycles have also been discovered in a number of other countries where more research is still being done. This has as its focus the effects of the light of the sun and moon at the solstices and equinoxes. Dr Anna Ritchie, a leading Scottish archaeologist, states in her book *Scotland BC*, that although it is difficult to prove that the early megalithic builders of sites like Callanish knew about geometry, astronomy or more sophisticated mathematics,

> This does not lessen the impact of sites where a deliberate alignment on sun or moon is obvious. The design of the recumbent stone circles of north-east Scotland shows a consistent interest in the rising or setting of the moon in the southern sky: they are built in places where there is an open view to the south, and the recumbent slab with its flanking pillar-stones is arranged so as to frame the moon when viewed from inside the circle.[8]

Callanish is certainly an old site and some researchers believe that it may have been referred to by the classical writer Diodorus Siculus when he wrote in 55BC about the legend of the Hyperboreans, those who were said to live on an island 'beyond the north wind'. In a famous passage that has perplexed many experts about exactly who he meant by the mysterious Hyperboreans, Diodorus states that:

> Of those who have written about the ancient myths, Hecateus and certain others say that in the regions beyond the land of the Celts (i.e. Gaul, modern-day France) there lies in the ocean an island no smaller than Sicily. This island... is situated in the north and is inhabited by the Hyperboreans, who are called by that name because their home is beyond the point whence the north wind (Boreas) blows...[9]

He continues:

> There is also on the island... a notable temple which is... spherical in shape... The moon, as viewed from this island, appears to be but a little distance from the earth... The god (i.e. light) enters the earth every nineteen years...[10]

The 18.6-year cycle and the importance of '19'

It is now known scientifically that every 18.6 years the unique astronomical lunar phenomenon called the 'southern extreme of the major standstill' occurs, only in the very northern latitudes. When this happens, the moon seems to be very large and bright and especially close to the horizon. At Callanish, some researchers believe, this event is marked by the alignment of the stones. One is tempted to ask whether the ancient world, through shipping and maritime travel, was well aware of northern Britain, an island 'beyond the north wind'? For example, we know that the Phoenicians were great navigators and that they knew about the British Isles early on. This idea has been postulated by a number of authors, both professional and amateur, in recent years. We also know that the ancients certainly were aware of the Druids and their powerful priesthood, from the writings of the Romans and others from the classical period. Perhaps they heard of this special place with its spherical temple from early travellers or had visited it themselves.

Diodorus also mentions that every 19 years when this 'god' visits the island of Hyperborea, he plays the cithara (similar to an ancient lyre) and dances continuously all through the night, from the vernal equinox to the rising of the Pleiades. This 'god' may also have a Scottish component, judging from folklore collected in the Hebrides, which includes the island of Lewis where Callanish is located. On Midsummer Day (21 June) it was believed that 'the Shining One' walked down the northern avenue at Callanish. Some researchers believe that this may be a reference to Lugh, the bright, shining, Celtic sun-god, while others believe that it refers to a personification of fertility, from a long lost ritual or folk memory from very early times. Later Christian legends say it is St Michael.

With many older customs and beliefs, we often see several layers of various traditions superimposed one upon the other. Nonetheless, it may seem rather striking to us today how some of these old Scottish beliefs seem to sound quite similar to what Diodorus seems to be referring to. Again, we obviously can't prove that Diodorus was referring to Callanish specifically, of course, but we cannot discount it entirely, either, as we do not have any written documents or people from that ancient time to interview one way or the other! Archaeologists now believe that some of these early stone circles are also connected to distant, prominent hills and that these early sites must be viewed within the context of the entire landscape itself, in addition to any sun, moon and star connections. So whether or not Diodorus was specifically referring to Callanish per se, must remain as interesting speculation only, although it seems that there is some circumstantial evidence for it being a good candidate. There are also 19 smaller sites around the central main stone circle at Callanish.

A 19 year cycle as a way of marking time was also known in other places in ancient times and in the early church regarding the dating of the Easter cycle. Eusebius (Hist Ecc.7.20) studied the matter and mentions the Cycle of Dionysius of Alexandria, which was produced in 268AD which was an 8 year cycle. But he also mentions Anatolius, an Alexandrian Christian mathematician, who:

> ...about the year c.280, introduced, or rather reintroduced, an old (originally Attic) cycle of nineteen years. It was called a Metonic Cycle, for it had originally been drawn up in Athens (for purposes other than deciding the Passover, of course) when Meton was Archon...[11]

Throughout the early centuries of the western Christian church, some calendars were merged and various modifications were made in an effort to accurately calculate the dating of the Easter cycle. Finally, in 525AD, the Table of Dionysius Exigus, which was based on a return to the old, Alexandrian, 19 year Metonic Cycle, was written in Rome. Now, for the first time, Rome and Alexandria (which had followed this Cycle ever since about the year 300) were agreed upon their Paschal Table for the dating of the Easter cycle. It was not officially adopted, however, due to the death of Pope John I. And as is known today, the issue of the dating of Easter is believed to have been a rather contentious one between Rome and the Celtic church in 644 at the Synod of Whitby, discussed in chapter 5.

But for our purposes here it seems that the basic idea of a 19 year cycle of marking time was a very old one and perhaps especially in Scotland, where it was related to the lunar cycle. But the case for the lunar observatory theories about megalithic sites must still be regarded as 'not proven'. However, it is clear that sites were likely to have been set up for a variety of purposes – alignments with lunar events would not preclude the marking of solar or planetary events, even with the same stone circles.

Placing his research emphasis on the experiences of the builders of megalithic sites, archaeologist David Trevarthen has been looking at the interactions between the original unweathered colours of the stones, the surrounding landscape and seasonal movements of the sun. The resulting interplay of light, shadow and colour built into the monuments produces some carefully designed and visually stunning effects. As part of his experiential method, Trevarthen visits sites for extended periods to witness these effects for himself in their natural setting. A detailed description of one of these studies has been published in the *Cambridge Archaeological Journal*.[12]

Traditions about Scottish stone circles and megaliths

Various legends about Callanish from the past remain. One of them says that the stones are giants that refused to allow St Kieran to baptise them, so they were turned into stone as punishment. Another says that a great priest-king arrived in Lewis long, long ago and that he and his fellow priests wore robes made of bright, colourful feathers and the skins of birds. The chief's robe was white with feathers on it, and he was said to have always been accompanied by a wren, a bird that had great importance to the Druids. His assistants wore multi-coloured robes. Ironically, this type of dress sounds similar to that of certain shamans of northern Siberia, Lapland, and Asia. In early Irish literature, there are also descriptions of the highest poets, the *fili*, wearing bird feather robes to symbolise their shamanic flights to the Otherworld.

It was said that a group of black men came with the priests who wore robes with feathers on them to Callanish and that they built the stone circle and then departed with some of these priests.

The other priests were said to have remained at Callanish, teaching their religion to natives of the area. Later traditions say that Beltane rituals were also held at Callanish on May Eve.

One popular misconception about Callanish, as with Stonehenge, is that the Druids built it. This is not true. This idea was largely popularized in the 18th C, when new antiquarian theories were all the vogue. But of course the Druids, as well as the early Celts, undoubtedly knew of these powerful ancient places that they encountered from earlier times. They very likely worshipped there and had communal rituals at these sites, as many archaeologists now believe. But they did not build them – as the time frame doesn't fit, as these sites were built even earlier during the time of the megalithic peoples, of whom experts are still learning more about today. We do know that the megalithic peoples during Neolithic times were generally much more communal than those in the later Bronze Age, when a more hierarchal social structure began to predominate, with chieftains' and kings' graves being singled out, thus putting more emphasis on the individual than the group.

Another common misconception is that all early megalithic circles were built of stone, i.e. 'stone circles'. Not true. Actually, the earliest circles in Scotland were made of stone, but some were built only of timber. Others had both, with parts of these megalithic stone constructions also being made of timber. For example, a timber circle of 63 posts enclosing a U-shaped setting of huge timbers was built at Machrie Moor on the isle of Arran around 3000BC, in the middle of what was clearly a well-populated landscape at the time. Nearby are two tall stone circles, leading many archaeologists to conclude that the timber circles may have been built for the living and the stone circles to commemorate the dead.[13] The Twelve Stones of Stenness on Orkney were also built around 3000BC, about the same time.

A new site has been recently discovered in southwest Scotland, dubbed 'Scotland's Stonehenge', at Dunragit, near Stranraer. The indentations of hundreds of wooden totem poles which formed three concentric circles have been left across fields, revealing the largest ceremonial settlement of its kind ever found. Archaeologists in Scotland are currently excavating the site and believe that it could be as important as Stonehenge, especially in terms of analysing the Neolithic period in Britain. The Dunragit site was built around 2500BC, and may also have astronomical alignments associated with it. The Neolithic timber enclosure is formed by three concentric rings, one inside the other, which were entered through a wide avenue pointing to a hill in the distance. It will be interesting to see what emerges from this excavation in the future.

Skara Brae

But the stone village of Skara Brae, on Orkney's western mainland, is even older, having been built about 3100BC – nearly half a millennium before work started on the Great Pyramid of Cheops in Egypt. Skara Brae is the finest and best-preserved Neolithic village in northern Europe, with high-quality, dry-stone houses made of local flagstone. It was uncovered by a storm in 1850. The village was inhabited by a farming community for 600 years or so, from 3100BC until about 2450BC. Ten houses are visible today, although it is likely that many more lie buried underneath the main complex.[14]

Two of the houses are particularily interesting, as stated by Ian Armit, Historic Scotland archaeologist. One of them stands a bit away from the main group and lacks beds and a dresser. Armit surmises it might have been a workshop, a communal meeting area or something similar. Carved balls were found there. The other may have been some kind of a religious or special ritual area, as although it was part of the main group of houses, it was accessed only by a winding side passage that was bolted shut from the outside, rather than the inside. This house yielded more and stranger material than the others. A bull's skull lay on one bed, while dishes of red pigment, beads, pendants and other debris lay strewn around, and the bodies of two women were buried beneath the floor. Armit rightfully wonders whether this house may have possibly been 'a house for the ill or dying, for childbirth, for widows, or for worship, confinement or meditation?'[15] He then adds that only in these two houses were carved stones found, again suggesting that there must have been some special function to these two houses. No doubt certain shamanic rituals were probably performed there.

Mysterious stone balls with geometric patterns

Probably one of the greatest enigmas of early Scotland are the mysterious stone balls dated to at least 5,000 years ago that are found mostly in Aberdeenshire, in northeastern Scotland. These stone balls are in the Museum of Scotland today. Most are about the size of a tennis ball and have unusual geometric patterns on them which have confounded experts. Some researchers believe they are designs based on Pythagorean geometry, while others believe they were probably some kind of a weapon. But in any case, the exact use of these balls is unknown. They are carved from a variety of rocks and are decorated with raised knobs on them; some have 3, 5 or 7 raised knobs on them, and some even have over 100 on them. No one really knows what they were used for and why they are only found in this area of the world, in northeast Scotland.

But they do appear to have definite, mathematically accurate geometric and numerical designs on them, making it hard to see how such objects could be made by 'mere primitive savages', as was believed in earlier times. As it would have taken considerable skill and time to carve them, no doubt they would have been prestigious to own. One was even found in a Viking grave in Norway – akin to a 4,000 year-old souvenir, perhaps? Hopefully in the future, someone will be able to 'crack the code' of these mysterious objects that have baffled experts and tourists alike for centuries.

Maes Howe

An elaborate chambered tomb nearby in Orkney, Maes Howe, has a passage pointing approximately towards midwinter sunset and was built on a clay platform. Maes Howe, which lies in the rural community of Stenness, is thought by archaeologists to be a key example of the Neolithic cairn-building tradition and is believed to date from about 2800BC. It has a 24 foot high domed mound 115 feet in diameter, and has a standard of design and quality of workmanship not seen north or west of the Mediterranean. It seems that sunlight at dawn and dusk during the midwinter months played an important part of the beliefs of those who built Maes Howe, judging from the orientation of the passage of the site. The Stones of Stenness, however, according to archaeologists, do not seem to show quite the same type of significant astronomical alignment as Maes Howe or Callanish, for example.

At Balnuaran of Clava, near Inverness, a tall stone circle surrounds two chambered burial cairns and a ring cairn that date between 2000BC and 1700BC. In the square kilometre around the monuments at the Clava stones, there are at least six other similar sites and many more are scattered around the Moray Firth. The passage of the northerly chambered cairn at Clava is orientated towards the midwinter sun.

In recent years a tourist 'took' one of the stones from the Clava cairns, an ancient burial site, and upon bringing it home, a series of unexplained accidents and disasters began to occur in his life and those around him. He then actually sent the stone back to the tourist office in Inverness with an explanation of what had happened to him. This is reminiscent of some of the famous stories of 'mummies curses' on certain Egyptian tombs. Perhaps surprisingly, some highly-regarded archaeologists even today will privately state that they are firmly convinced some of these are real. So, one is obviously advised not to take anything from ancient sites and to try not to damage the area.

Acoustic effects: ancient Scottish megalithic chambers

These are only a few major examples of early megalithic sites in Scotland. There are many more. But probably some of the most unusual results ever to emerge are those from a recent professional study of these sites by archaeologist Aaron Watson, University of Reading, and sound expert David Keating. They tested the acoustic properties of ancient Scottish megalithic chambers and the results were startling. Using a combination of electronic measuring and experiments on volunteers, Watson found that specific pitches of chanting or drumming inside the cairns produced eerie effects. From a research paper published in the respected journal *Scientific American*, Watson said

> I found that many of the Neolithic monuments possess unusual acoustic properties that give sounds strange, otherworldly aspects... These monuments from the distant past were not the remote and silent places we visit today; they may be best understood as gateways through which people of the Neolithic period passed to gain access to dimensions far beyond the reality of their everyday lives... Many surviving sites yield evidence of rituals. These were probably highly theatrical events, perhaps involving singing or chanting and primitive musical instruments. The larger the chamber, the lower the pitch needed to create the resonance effect.[16]

Tests have shown that the chambered cairns were built to create sonic effects which include what we call today the Helmholtz Resonance – the sound created when one blows across the top of a glass bottle – and also sub-sonic vibrations, which may have altered the mental states of worshippers. Today, for instance, it is well-known that scientists have proven in the laboratory that ELF (extra-low frequency) sounds certainly do alter people's behaviour and moods.

Overall, in the experiments conducted by Watson and his team, certain pitches of chanting and drumming were used inside the cairns. The volunteers experienced a range of unusual sensations and effects, such as 'sensations of ascent', occasional dizziness, a disquieting feeling that some sounds were actually coming from inside their head and body, changing pulse rates, vibrations, balance disturbance and even altered states of consciousness in some. Watson argued in his research article that the nature of the sound waves created shows that the chambered cairns were probably built as awe-inspiring cathedrals of stone where ancient man could feel touched by the gods.

The detailed studies initially involved two of the early megalithic sites in Scotland, Maes Howe in Orkney and Camster Round Cairn in Caithness. At Maes Howe, discussed above, the researchers used a drum and found that the correct pitch was of 'infrasonic frequency', notes so low that they cannot be heard by the human ear. However, they can be 'felt' by humans as a physical or psychological sensation, suggesting that they could have a profound effect on anyone exposed to them for a prolonged period. Certain frequencies do affect humans, even though we cannot actually hear them, as scientists now know.

Camster Round Cairn is one of a group of three stone cairns, dating from the third or fourth millennium BC, in moorland near the village of Lybster. It is a nearly-intact round structure of loose stones, 55 feet in diameter and 12 feet high. Both Maes Howe and Camster Round Cairn have long narrow passages leading into the inner burial chambers where the experiments were done.[17]

Scottish traditional literature also has a lot of material referring to unusual, otherworldly music and sounds, some of which are described as occurring near stones circles. In *Music and the Celtic Otherworld*, one of the key Scottish tales about otherworldly music is presented, that of Thomas the Rhymer. In one Scottish Borders version of this famous story, Thomas the Rhymer of Ercildoune is a talented lute player who is 'abducted' by the Elf Queen and taken away to her otherworldly realm:

> [He] plucked idly at his lute strings, and heard above his own music a distant sound like the trickle of a hill-side stream. Then he started to his feet in amazement; for down one of those green pathways rode the fairest lady in the world... 'Play your lute to me, Thomas,' she said; 'fair music and green shade go together.' So Thomas took up his instrument again, and it seemed as though he had never before been able to play such lilting tunes...[18]

He is then taken by the Elf Queen to her Otherworld home, but under the condition that he not speak one word while there for a period of seven years, a taboo. He manages to not speak a word and returns rewarded with not only great musical skills, but the gift of prophecy as well. He then became famous as a seer who always told the truth, 'True Thomas'. This tale, like others of its kind, illustrates the awareness of the early Celts of a special connection between the Otherworld and the effects of music and sound. Judging from the scientific experiments of archaeologist Aaron Watson and his team, it seems highly likely that the ancient megalithic peoples of Scotland also believed in such a connection, something similar to what these old folklore accounts seem to indicate. Even into more modern times, some composers, like Mozart for instance, claimed at times to have 'heard' beautiful music and then said they 'merely wrote it down', implying special inspiration from elsewhere.

The connection between otherworldly music and stone circles is also present in world folklore, as shown by an example from Brittany. Breton folktales describe the *corrigans*, little dwarfish-like beings akin to some of the fairies or *sidhe* beings described in Celtic folklore. The corrigans were believed to live under the dolmens, menhirs, and tumuli of megalithic sites, especially at Carnac. They are portrayed as singing and circle-dancing by moonlight and to be especially effective at enticing unsuspecting mortals to join them.[19] Once they disappear and the mortal is left alone after what seems like only an hour or two, he soon discovers that many years have passed and that all of his friends and family have died. This motif is found in folklore accounts (Rip van Winkle, for example) the world over.

Scottish customs and beliefs involving stone circles

Areas around certain megalithic monuments seem to have been viewed by the ancients as places where special events or gatherings could occur. Although it may surprise us today, stone circles were places where *legal* courts were once held in Scotland. This old custom is mentioned by Homer and apparently survived in Scotland into historic times:

> In 1349, the Bishop of Aberdeen held a court at the Ring of Fiddes, where William de Saint Michael was called upon to explain the seizure of certain Church property; in 1380, the Wolf of Badenoch, a natural son of Robert II, held a court at a circle to which the Bishop of Moray was summoned in connection with his claim to certain lands in Badenoch; in the fourteenth century, the king's steward held a court at Strathearn in Perthshire, and similar courts [at stone circles] are recorded at Crieff, Perthshire, and at Huntly, in Aberdeenshire.[20]

Evidently, certain stone circles were also viewed as important places well into medieval times, echoing earlier beliefs about them as sacred places. Dancing, music and May weddings are also known to have taken place at many of the early monuments, according to early customs and beliefs. One antiquarian, commenting on the Stanton Drew henge in Somerset, said 'I have observed that Weddings, Brides, and the like, is not peculiar to this place, but applied to many others of these Celtic monuments about the land'.[21] In Scotland, too, Beltane rituals at or near stone circles have continued on, even into the present day.

One rather unusual account in more modern times is about a complex of submerged megalithic standing stones that was said to have been discovered by marine archaeologists and located underwater at lochend, the tip of Loch Ness. This submerged underwater megalithic site is believed by some to have been located on a major 'ley line' that runs right through the centre of Loch Ness. It is also believed to have been a possible reason why the eccentric black magician Aleister Crowley, who called himself 'The Beast', bought Boleskine House on the shores of Loch Ness. As there has been no official publicity about this find, and mainly vague village rumours, it is impossible to know whether or not it is true or merely hearsay. But who knows? Perhaps there are various submerged stone circles at certain places worldwide that are now underwater, probably due to large earthquakes in the distant past or some other natural catastrophe, for example. But regarding such matters in Scotland, we cannot say for sure until more research is done by professionals.

Perhaps even more enigmatic are the Newton Stone inscriptions, which no one seems to really understand or agree on as to their proper origin or interpretation. Located on private land in the Grampian area in the northeast of Scotland, this tall standing stone was believed by one prominent professor and antiquarian in 1925 to be evidence of what he called 'an Aryan Phoenician language of the early Briton or Gothic type'. On the same stone are ogham inscriptions which basically say pretty much the same translation, causing some early antiquarians to conjecture that this stone may be akin to a Scottish Rosetta Stone, a bi-lingual version of the same historical record. If so, then it would be of great historic importance. The script was written left to right, not right to left, like many Semitic languages, and it does not have pictorial or geometric designs on it. It is also not believed to be Pictish. Some experts in the past have thought that this stone means that Scotland may have had early foreign visitors who knew their own language and also that of ogham and traded with the native peoples here.

The Newton Stone was dated earlier this century to roughly 400BC by Professor Waddell, a Fellow of the Royal Anthropological Institute in London. The main surprise for everyone at the time was what he claimed the inscription said:

> This Sun-Cross was raised to Bil (or Bel, the God of Sun-Fire) by the Kassi... of Kast of the Siluyr (sub-clan) of the Kilani (Hittite-palace dwellers), the Phoenician (named) Ikar of Cilicia, the Prwt. ('Brit'-on)...[22]

Preposterous, one may be tempted to think today. Yet, strangely enough, Bel is acknowledged by scholars to have been one of the earliest, most prominent Celtic deities, with evidence of worship of him all over Europe, especially Gaul. Also called Belenus, the term was an epithet or descriptive surname given to the Celtic sun-god in parts of Gaul, northern Italy, and parts of Britain. The word 'Belenus' is believed to mean 'bright' or 'brilliant' by scholars, many of whom have also pointed out that the word 'Beltane' means 'bright fire' or 'goodly fire', and has the same prefix. So the question of a stone with a possible dedication to Bel, the god of sun-fire, seems interesting and perhaps may not be all that surprising. Providing Waddell's translation is accurate, some may ask: Could it be that the Phoenicians, who are known to have been great mariners, or some other sea-faring people from far away, left inscriptions here in the past, for example?

But if so, the question is – were they also familiar with ogham script? Or were they travelling with Celts, or frequently trading with them? Or, perhaps the inscription is by a largely unknown people? Obviously one cannot say for sure. Yet it seems that very little has been researched, or said, about this stone since 1925, and most archaeologists, we have found, usually say that they themselves know little about it, which is often true, and imply that someone else does. But so far, unfortunately, we have found nothing else about this stone from more recent times, and this strange inscription remains an enigma today.

Professor Stuart Piggott in *Scotland Before History* comments about the early megalithic sites and their people, saying that we do not know, nor can archaeology tell us for sure, the beliefs and rituals that actually happened there. So ultimately, one can only speculate.[23] After all, who are we, in modern times, to 'automatically assume' what early peoples thought? This is especially true for the very early sites. It is only in more modern times that any records have survived at all about what possibly went on at these sites in later times. Early church records sometimes describe remnants of pagan rituals and customs, but of course this is from the viewpoint of those who wanted to stamp them out, hardly objective sources! Some of these involve stones and the beliefs about them, such as certain stone charms are 'evil'. We must keep an open mind as to what the early stone circles may have meant to those who built them. We also cannot automatically assume that our modern view of things is necessarily 'superior' to those of the ancient world, including the megalithic builders.

Pictish stones and crosses

Undoubtedly some of the most beautiful and elaborately carved stones in Scotland are the Pictish stones and crosses. The legacy of the Picts and these stones have fascinated many for centuries. The Picts (unlike the Gaels, Angles, Vikings or Britons, who are shared with other nations) belong to Scotland alone. Yet little is known for sure about them, except that they defied the might of the Roman Empire – no small feat indeed!

When the Romans first came in 84AD, the Picts were not mentioned in any of their reports as they did not distinguish between the tribes of the south and those of the north. But by 297AD, there is mention of the 'Picti', the Latin word for Painted Ones, as these northern warriors still painted their bodies blue with woad, a custom which had died out earlier in the south. Elaborate tattooes are also described by the Romans. So what essentially happened was that a cultural difference emerged between those tribes of the south who became more 'Romanised' and those who lived further to the north who didn't.

The Picts were known to be very resilient warriors, the last of the free peoples of the island of Britain. They did a good job of keeping the Roman legions at bay, partly, it seems, by a policy of 'united we stand, divided we fall'. As the Roman conquest continued, though, we see a gradual coalescence of all of the tribes beyond the empire, yet the Picts are still mentioned at the time of the withdrawal of the Romans. Dr David Breeze, Chief Inspector of Ancient Monuments, Historic Scotland, describes this situation in *Roman Scotland*:

> The native States alone were no match for Rome and from the earliest days combined to oppose this new force in the north. Tacitus described this process at the battle of Mons Graupius. It is... significant that, as the years progress, we see a gradual coalescence of of the tribes beyond the empire. Twelve were listed by Ptolemy in the second century, though presumably representing the situation at the time of Agricola. At the end of the second century only the Caledonians and Maeatae are mentioned, and Dio states that 'the names of the others have been included in these'. A century later, in 297, we first hear of the Picts... the Emperor Constantine... refers to 'the Caledonians and other Picts', demonstrating their ancestry... The Verona List of 314 mentions the Scoti, Picti, and Caledonii...[24]

A series of Roman emperors were involved in the conquest of Britain. Reports of persistent trouble along the northern frontier – Hadrian's Wall – by the Caledonians, Picts, and other tribes, caused what we might call today 'a real nightmare' for the Roman officers and generals, many of whom were probably hoping to finish this conquest quickly and move on elsewhere. Breeze continues:

> Dio stated that they stood their ground with great determination and Herodian that they were fearsome and dangerous fighters... It took Agricola two years to bring the Caledonians to defeat at Mons Graupius and at first they had the better of the war, surprising the Roman army by attacking one of its forts and then nearly destroying the ninth legion in a night attack on its camp... Severus at the end of his first campaign thought that he had conquered the Caledonians, only to have them rise against him. During both wars, the Caledonians appear to have adopted guerilla tactics, their most sensible approach to the discipline of the Roman army.[25]

Of course, it was no doubt in the Romans' interest to exaggerate the fighting qualities of their opponents, but clearly, they ran into far more than they expected north of Hadrian's Wall. As we have seen, they directly commented on the fearsome qualities of the Picts and Caledonians. Accounts of some of the famous northern warriors like Calgacus ('The Swordsman') and Argentocoxos ('Silver-Leg') prevented the Romans from getting a permanent hold on the lands north of the Firth of Forth.

Many of the Pictish attacks were carried out by ship, leading Gildas, a historian of the early Britons, to refer to them as 'transmarini', people from overseas. This, according to the now established view, caused later chroniclers to mistakenly believe that the Picts had come from abroad, like the Saxons or the Irish Gaels.

However, it seems that no one is absolutely certain exactly where the enigmatic Picts did come from. It is now thought by Historic Scotland archaeologist Sally Foster that they were actually native tribes that were already here, that they didn't come from abroad, and also that they probably did speak some form of an Indo-European language, contrary to what was thought before:

> Myths and legends which have clouded modern perceptions of the Picts have been reassessed and current learned opinion largely favours the view that they were 'a typical northwest European barbarian society with wide connections and parallels' (Alcock 1987, 90); at least they were accepted by their neighbours on this basis... we are now fully confident that the Picts were simply the descendents of the Iron Age tribes of Scotland... The considerable achievements of the Picts are recognised as having laid the foundations for the 'birth' of this new nation. Rather than being a 'lost people', it is argued that aspects of Pictish society continued, including the kingship... The ill-founded notion that the Picts, unlike their neighbours, spoke a non-Indo-European language is a present-day myth firmly dispelled by modern research...[26]

The concept that an early brilliant or especially talented people need not necessarily be automatically assumed to have come 'from somewhere else', that the native tribes may have been just as capable of brilliance themselves, is a noble enough idea. However, if the Picts were simply descendents of 'typical Iron Age peoples' who had already been here, then why is their art and its symbols still such an enigma? Why is nothing similar found in other nearby cultures? Why is their language still not well-known or understood?

Other researchers believe that there is still much more work to be done overall before anything definitive can be concluded. Some authors maintain that the Picts were not Celts, as many past scholars automatically tended to assume, but Scythians, and that at least one of their dominant tribes were actually Finno-Ugrian immigrants from the Baltic.[27] The ecclesiastical historian Bede, who wrote in the 8th C, and Nennius, in his *Historia Brittonum*, says that the Picts originated from Scythia, near the Black Sea, and that they obtained wives from among the Irish. Nennius also said that the Picts settled first in the Orkneys, from where they then occupied the northern half of Britain.

Later historical accounts usually quote from these two earlier sources, giving rise to various myths and legends about the Picts. We also must remember that when chroniclers like Bede or Nennius used the word 'Scythian', it was in the broadest possible sense, so this could conceivably include a whole possible range of peoples said to have originated from the greater Black Sea area, such as the Germans, Balts, Slavs and others. Also, as some chroniclers used the terms 'Scot' or 'Pict' interchangeably, this can make it very difficult to figure out exactly which tribe(s) they are referring to. However, this is not to say that they are necessarily wrong, it is simply that one must be very careful when looking at this material. Other scholars also now say that the Celts may have originally come from the Scythian area before eventually moving into central and northern Europe, but others disagree. So the debates about these matters will no doubt continue for some time.

Still other researchers believe that both the Celts and the Picts, as separate peoples, may have originated from the same general Greater Scythian area long ago, before moving into Europe in *separate waves* at different times. The tartan cloth found with the nearly perfectly preserved, 4,000 year-old mummies in China, who have reddish-blond hair and were found to be Caucasian, is apparently of a nearly identical weave to tartan found in Scotland. As we saw in chapter 1, these mummies have bone structure similar to the ancient Celts and Saxons, and the Chinese authorities have now stopped western archaeologists from conducting further research on this find. This discovery certainly raises some intriguing questions about early peoples and their migrations and clearly more research is needed.

We also saw how the Scottish origin-myth, the Declaration of Arbroath and its reference to the 'Scots' having come from 'Greater Scythia' have resulted in a rather contentious debate in some quarters today. The 'Greater Scythian origins' theory of the Picts seems to continue to persist today, in spite of the more established view that they were merely descendents of the indigenous Iron Age tribes that were already here. More research is being done and so this debate continues today.

Other myths abound about the Picts, too, which unfortunately have resulted in various ridiculous stereotypes about them through the centuries. Scottish archaeologist Anna Ritchie tells us that an anonymous Norwegian historian wrote in the 12th C, saying that:

> The Picts were little more than pygmies in stature. They worked marvels in the morning and evening building towns, but at midday they entirely lost their strength and lurked through fear in little underground houses. This vision of tiny Picts living underground persisted into this century, colouring both Robert Louis Stevenson's ballad 'Heather Ale', and John Buchan's story 'No-Man's Land'. Folklore insists that the first Vikings who came to Rousay in Orkney dared not land because of beings like elves or trolls bearing shining spears, and even Sir Walter Scott believed that the galleries in the walls of the brochs were low and narrow because of the size of the Picts (in common with his generation, Sir Walter mistakenly believed these prehistoric stone towers to be Pictish).[28]

Mere 'pygmies'? Who were also able to keep back the Roman legions? We think not! Obviously many legendary accounts about the Picts exist and some have even lasted down to the present day, in spite of evidence to the contrary.

What about Pictish documents?

But one thing does seem certain, however, and that is the extraordinary stone carvings with their enigmatic designs that the

Picts have left us as their legacy. They were known to be a literate people, but strangely enough, every single one of their documents has disappeared, except for a Pictish kings list, the 10th C one preserved in the National Library of France. The Picts were known to have eventually accepted Christianity and built monasteries. It is also known that St Columba needed an interpreter when conducting missionary work in Pictland in the late 6th C.

One major question remains, and that is why *no documents at all exist from Pictland*, even though it is known that Pictish monasteries, also like the Gaelic ones, were also scriptoriums and produced written documents. Dr Sally Foster, an archaeologist with Historic Scotland, in *Picts, Gaels and Scots*, mentions that 'the rare survival of a carved Latin text from Tarbat [a Pictish monastery] implies that this monastery had the capacity to produce books in an accomplished Insular script'.[29] Obviously, then, the Picts were a literate people. Dr Anna Ritchie continues:

> We can only speculate about other manuscripts of Pictland, although a strong case has been made for allowing the possibility that the illustrated gospels known as the *Book of Kells* was created in a monastery somewhere in eastern Pictland. The stylistic links between the *Book of Kells* and Pictish stone carvings are certainly very impressive. If such documents were being produced in Pictland, what happened to them?[30]

A very good question indeed. It is possible that a good number of records may have been destroyed after the Dalriadic Scots took over, as any Pictish annals might have been suppressed then for political reasons, as Anna Ritchie and other experts acknowledge. The rest probably fell foul of the zeal of the Vikings, or of the reformers in the 16th C when many documents and artefacts were destroyed, but the fact remains that no one really knows what happened to many of the early records of Scotland. Because of this woeful lack of early extant written records, it is understandably difficult for experts today to properly reconstruct what early Scotland was really like for certain. But it is believed that the Picts used an alphabet similar to ours for writing and a few inscriptions, mainly ogham ones, have also survived, but none of the manuscripts remain.

What happened to the ninth legion?

Speaking of disappearances, Scottish tradition has it that 'no one really knows what happened' to the ninth Roman legion in northern Scotland, with one writer commenting that 'None of the men, or their equipment, were seen again.'[31] It is now known that the decimation of the ninth Roman legion, as we saw earlier, was due to a surprise attack by the Picts. This incident is also featured in popular historical novels such as those by Rosemary Sutcliffe and the late Nigel Tranter. That a tribe of so-called 'barbarians' could attack and destroy an entire Roman legion may seem surprising to many today, but it is basically true, in that the unsuspected night attack caught the Roman legions off guard. Some scholars now believe that Agricola may have been tipped off and sent his fastest cavalry to the rescue, therefore preventing the complete demise of the ninth legion. But no one disputes that in any case, it was very nearly completely destroyed and memory of this incident has remained in Scottish tradition to this day.

Eventually the Romans finally decided to leave Britain for a variety of reasons, beginning a gradual process of withdrawal starting in about 350AD. They are believed to have left Britain for good by 410AD. This very likely had as much to do with problems within the Roman Empire itself as it did with difficulties they experienced in the north.

Pictish symbols

But in spite of no written Pictish manuscripts having survived, the heritage they left in stone remains. Frankly, if it wasn't for these elaborately carved sculptured stones, we might know precious little at all about their culture today. The earliest Pictish carved stones date to about the 6th C. The mysterious designs on them continue to baffle many experts today – the double-disc, the crescent-and-V rod, the notched rectangle, and the Z-rod, for instance – while others represent more concrete things in their environment, such as the horse, boar, wolf, eagle, stag, snake, salmon, mirrors and combs. One unusual portrayal of an unknown water creature, a so-called 'swimming elephant', is shown consistently throughout the Pictish carvings. Obviously there is nothing Christian about these particular designs and no one really can say for sure what they mean, but they do seem to be a specialised writing system that used symbols of some kind. Some archaeologists think they might represent personal names, but again, no one can say for certain.

The stones that they used were rough, upright boulders set up in certain places in the landscape. Pictish symbols have also been found on objects of metal and bone and on the walls of caves, but

> they principally occur carved on stones which have been grouped into two classes. Class I, natural slabs or pillars with incised symbols, and Class II, shaped slabs which are carved in relief with a cross and sometimes other sculpture in addition to the symbols... The ornamentation of some symbols has led some scholars to date Class I from c650 to c850AD and Class II from c800 to c1000, but both are earlier. Some Class I stones may have been carved before the Picts accepted Christianity, and the Class II slabs are unlikely to have continued in use very long after the Picts lost their identity as a separate nation. Class I may be fifth or sixth-century to the eighth and Class II mid or late seventh to the ninth.[32]

So, it is likely that the transition from the earlier Class I stones to Class II stones began not very long after the introduction of Christianity to Pictland.

The St Andrews Sarcophagus

Probably one of the most elaborately carved examples of all Pictish art and one of the best examples of early medieval sculptures in Europe, is the magnificent St Andrews Sarcophagus. It was discovered in the 19th C in the graveyard of St Andrews Cathedral. This Pictish royal shrine is one of the major artistic achievements of the early medieval period and gives us some more insight into the cultural sophistication of Pictish culture, especially during the 7th and 9th centuries AD. The sarcophagus is dated to the late 8th C and may have housed the bones of the great Pictish king, Unust, who died in 761, but experts do not yet know for certain.

Pictish kings looked to the model of King David; he is shown in exquisite carvings on the sarcophagus killing a lion and is also depicted on the Dupplin Cross. Many biblical motifs are shown on the sarcophagus and on other Pictish stone carvings; they tend to feature Old Testament scenes such as the story of Jonah and the whale, Daniel in the Lions' den, or specific scenes of Hell.

It is clear that the Picts were not an unsophisticated, isolated people living in a northern backwater, but well connected, as attested by expert archaeologist Isobel Henderson, who says that there is:

> ...irrefutable evidence that Pictish society was not an inward-looking, self obsessed 'lingering Iron Age survival'... but one aware of, and fired by, all the cultural stimuli that came with their membership of European Christiandom. If one accepts that the natural force of the Picts (not to mention the political acumen necessary for a people who shared frontiers with three different races) led to travel and contacts, the diplomatic exchange of gifts, and the desire to emulate, then the availability at Pictish centres of exotic models, whether classical or oriental is neither wishful thinking nor a mystery... the nature of the art of the Sarcophagus suggests that these exotic influences were not received by the Picts only at second-hand from the south or west... but were physically present to be copied from, the consequence of 'princely gifts' to a religious foundation or its elite patron... It should also be said that acquisition on the continent by Picts for Picts need not necessarily be ruled out.[33]

Also in the late 8th C we see other insular regions like Northumbria, Mercia and Ireland also responding to exotic influences from many other places and incorporating these into their artwork, a prime example being the ornate *Book of Kells*, which is believed to have been created at Iona. Some of the blue pigment for the *Book of Kells* is now known through scientific research to have come only from Afghanistan, indicating that a great deal of travel and cultural interchange was obviously going on in early times. The St Andrews Sarcophagus is a fine example of this principle at work in Scotland in early medieval times.

The Picts were united with the Scots in 843AD when Kenneth mac Alpin of the Dalriadic Gaels, who were from Ireland, came to power. This resulted in the powerful new Scottish kingdom of

Alba or Scotia. However, recent scholarship is challenging the conventional view that this was a 'union' between Pict and Scot in which it was implied, if not always stated, that the Picts were the senior partners. This is a view that came to prominence in the 18th C by historian Thomas Innes. It probably had everything to do with the politics of the Union of Parliaments in 1707, as some scholars now believe, saying there are:

> ...a number of historians who, within the last decade or so, have been moving away, in other words, from the notion of a Scoto-Pictish kingdom, towards a consensus which sees Alba as a military creation of the Scots supported by the Columban church but at the expense of the Picts.[34]

But although nearly everything about Pictish culture was destroyed, their stones still stand today, a fascinating glimpse at what remains of early medieval Scottish sculpture. They, too, like the stones of Callanish, Maes Howe or Skara Brae, are a living testimony of the power of the past.

In the next chapter we will explore what is known about the Celtic saints of Scotland, who had a great influence on early Christianity in the British Isles.

Notes

[1] Cowan, Prof E J, *Scotland's Story*, Vol. 1, First Press Publishing, Glasgow, 1999, 3.

[2] Ibid, 7.

[3] Ibid, 6.

[4] Armit, I, *Celtic Scotland*, B.T. Batsford/Historic Scotland, London, 1997, 19.

[5] Armit, I, *Scotland's Hidden History*, Tempus, Stroud, 1998, 61.

[6] Ponting, G & M, *The Stones Around Callanish*, self-published, Callanish, 1984 (rev. in 1993), 9.

[7] Pitts, M, *Hengeworld*, Century, London, 2000, 228.

[8] Ritchie, A, *Scotland BC*, Historic Buildings and Monuments, HMSO, Edinburgh, 1988, 54.

[9] Curtis, R & M, *Callanish: Stones, Moon and Sacred Landscape*, self-published, Callanish, 1994, 30.

[10] Ibid.

[11] Hanson, R P C, *Saint Patrick: His origins and Career*, Oxford University Press, Oxford, 1968, 67.

[12] Trevarthen, D, 'Illuminating the Monuments: Observation and Speculation on the Structure and Function of the Cairns at Balnuaran

of Clava', *Cambridge Archaeological Journal*, Vol 10, No 2, October 2000, 295-315.

13 'Stones that Stand the Test of Time', no author listed, *Scotland's Story*, Vol. 1, First Press Publishing, Glasgow, 1999, 23.

14 Armit, I, *Hidden History*, op.cit, 32.

15 Ibid.

16 Mowat, B, 'Ancient Stone Burial Chambers', *Scotland on Sunday*, 5 March 2000, Edinburgh, 5.

17 Ibid.

18 Ralls-MacLeod, K, *Music and the Celtic Otherworld*, Edinburgh University Press, Edinburgh, 2000, 41.

19 Ibid, 128.

20 MacNeill, F.M, *The Silver Bough: Scottish Folklore and Folk Belief*, Vol. I, Wm. MacLellan, Glasgow, 1957, 86.

21 Dames, M, *The Avebury Cycle*, Thames & Hudson, London, 1977, 154.

22 Waddell, Prof L, *The Phoenician Origin of Britons, Scots and Anglo-Saxons*, Williams and Norgate, Ltd, London, 1925, 32.

23 Piggott, S, *Scotland Before History*, Polygon, Edinburgh, 1982, 37.

24 Breeze, D, *Roman Scotland: Frontier Country*, Historic Scotland, B.T. Batsford, London, 1996, 115-6.

25 Ibid, 97.

26 Foster, S, 'The Picts: Quite the Darkest of Peoples in Dark Age Britain', *The Worm, The Germ, and The Thorn*, Ed. By David Henry, Pinkfoot Press, Balgavies, Angus, 1997, 6-7.

27 Dunbavin, P, *Picts and Ancient Britons: An Exploration of Pictish Origins*, Third Millennium Publishing, Nottingham, 1998,

28 Ritchie, A, *Picts*, HMSO, Edinburgh, 1989, 5.

29 Foster, S, *Picts, Gaels, and Scots*, Historic Scotland, B.T. Batsford, London, 1996, 96.

30 Ritchie, A, op.cit, 7.

31 *The Roman Empire*, website article, www.lighteningfoundry.com/scotland/history.

32 Mack, A, *Field Guide to the Pictish Symbol Stones*, Pinkfoot Press, Balgavies, Angus, 1997, x.

33 Henderson, I, 'Primus Inter Pares', in *The St. Andrews Sarcophagus*, Ed. By Sally Foster, Four Courts Press, Dublin, 1998, 98.

34 Bannerman, J, 'The Scottish takeover of Pictland and the relics of Columba', *Spec Scotorum: Hope of Scots*, Ed. By D. Broun & T. Clancy, T & T Clark, Edinburgh, 1999, 71-2.

CHAPTER FOUR

The Early Celtic Saints of Scotland

LIKE THE STONE CIRCLES and megaliths of the ancient past, memory of the saints of Scotland lives on today. Kentigern, Ninian, Columba of Iona, Brigit... these are but a few of the names of the early Scottish saints. Today we usually tend to think of them as being dedicated missionaries, devoted hermit monks or nuns and lovers of God's creation in nature. Sometimes they are portrayed as devoted ascetics, as lovers of religious poetry and music, or perhaps even as special shining examples of a 'lost Golden Age' of Christianity. Accurate or not, the saints and the powerful legacy they have left us remains, with places like Iona or Lindisfarne still being popular places of pilgrimmage and the beautifully illuminated pages of the *Book of Kells* and the *Lindisfarne Gospels* continuing to inspire many today.

But who, exactly, were these early saints of Scotland? In this chapter, the saints will be presented by geographic region, so that some of the local place-names and regional traditions about them can be included. We will learn more about the saints of the Scots of Dalriada, the early British kingdoms (Galloway, Strathclyde, Northumbria), and the northwestern and southeastern areas of Scotland. Many of the early saints in Scotland, such as St Ninian, for example, often travelled and did their missionary work in both Pictish and non-Pictish areas, but have often been placed in either one category or the other. So there is often a considerable overlap between the two. The early Celtic saints were widely known for their extraordinary missionary work to far-flung corners of the globe and were famous in medieval times for their dedication to pilgrimage.

The terms 'Celtic saint' and 'Celtic church'

The term 'Celtic saint' is often used in a very general way, usually referring to the Welsh, Gaelic, Irish, Cornish, Breton and/or

Pictish saints. But actually, all this term really means is that the saints lived or worked in a 'Celtic area'. Today the debate continues as to what exactly is meant by the term 'Celtic', as it really refers to many different diverse people, communities and tribes. In later sources the term 'Culdee' is also used in this same general way, something that we will further explore in the next chapter.

The popular idea of a single, unified, organised 'Celtic Church' is actually quite misleading, as it implies that there was a rather neat uniformity throughout all of the Celtic parts of Europe, which wasn't the case. Also, it doesn't properly acknowledge the very real organisational differences between the early 'Celtic churches' and their often quite diverse communities. To simply lump them all together and imply a unity is to do a disservice to the great complexity of this topic. The term 'Celtic church' has also been used in reference to its having been different in traditions or customs from another church. Some of these early, diverse Christian communities were clearly thought to have been somehow different in certain aspects from those of the Roman church in particular.

We should acknowledge the many real differences that these various early Celtic religious communities had. Dr Ian Bradley in *Celtic Christianity* describes them as 'the early indigeneous Christian communities of the British Isles', which is much more accurate than merely saying 'Celtic Christian' communities.'

An unfortunate tendency has developed in recent years towards viewing the Celtic saints as highly romanticised personality cults, like those of Columba and Patrick, for example, which really doesn't do justice to the hard work of the other now largely forgotten saints who also did major missionary work in Scotland. Although part of this reason may be due to promotion by the tourist industry, we have to remember that there are many unacknowledged saints in this story too, the 'unsung heroes and heroines' of medieval times.

It is also for this reason that the saints are presented by geographical region, so as to also include some of the lesser-known, yet important, saints. We will not only look at the facts that are known about the early saints of Scotland, but also some of the local traditions and legends, many of which have had an important bearing on how certain saints have been remembered through the centuries. As history has shown, legends and traditions have had a tremendous power that for better or worse has often far exceeded the mere facts themselves. Many of these are highly localised stories about a particular saint and are often preserved in the place-lore, for example. Sometimes it is very difficult to sort out fact from legend.

Legendary accounts of saints

Although it is true that the hagiographers, those who wrote the Saints' Lives, sometimes deliberately embellished or made up a tale about a saint for their own reasons (i.e. to glorify a certain monastery and its founding saint), this doesn't necessarily mean that all legends and place lore tales are false or that the study of such traditions has no value for our lives today. In this sense, the medieval hagiographers may be no more guilty of embellishing facts than some of our modern-day media 'spin-doctors'.

The modern tendency to blatantly disregard all legendary accounts and local traditions as essentially unimportant or untrue is to ignore the fact that often it is *the legends themselves* that have best preserved the memory of a particular saint. Sometimes, iron-ically, 'mere legends' have even been proven to be true in the end – such as the famous case of archaeologist Heinrich Schliemann's discovery of the ancient city of Troy from his analysis of reading the works of Homer. Even if we find out that they aren't true in the end, it is still worth examining why they have held such power for so long.

This book, while presenting the known facts, will also acknowledge the major legendary accounts about certain saints – not by ignoring them or attempting to disprove them – but by honouring their rightful place in the history of a particular saint. However this is not to overromanticise them; it is simply to include these legends and not try to censor them, unusual as some of them may seem to us today. In so doing, we are also giving power to the many often overlooked local traditions about certain saints and about some of the lesser-known local place-names or artefacts that may have a particular saint's legends affiliated with them.

Like the legends of the Stone of Destiny, many of these saints' legends also simply 'refuse to die', often lingering on for centuries. Many of these were an important part of oral tradition in Scotland. Keeping all of this in mind, we will now take a look at the saints of the Scots of Dalriada.

St Columba of Iona: his early life

There are a number of saints who lived and worked in the kingdom of Dalriada, beginning with probably the best known, St Columba (Columcille) of Iona (b.521 – d.597AD). As there are many well-researched books already available about St Columba, his missionary work and community, we hope to present here some additional aspects about him and his life.

The Dal Riata were a Gaelic tribe from the coastal districts of what is now County Antrim in Northern Ireland who played a key role in the early history of Iona. Most of the information we have about Columba's life comes from Adomnan's *Life of Columba*. Adomnan was the Abbot of Iona and it is believed he wrote this work about 690AD, nearly a century after Columba's death.

The other major source of information about Columba comes from Bede, who wrote about forty years after Adomnan. Oral tradition among the monks of Iona was also a source of information and it is also believed that Adomnan had access to an earlier *Life of Columba* written by his predecessor Abbot Cummene (657-669).

Born in Ireland about 521AD, St Columba's father was Fedlimid, son of Fergus, an aristocrat of the family called the Cenel Conaill which ruled over much of county Donegal. When he was young Columba was fostered to a priest and learned from some of the greatest teachers in Ireland at the time, including St Finnian. Little is known for sure about Columba's life in Ireland prior to coming to Iona, where he built his famous community. Columba was an extraordinary missionary and was greatly respected in his time.

The exile of St Columba and his arrival at Iona

Even less is known about two rather mysterious events in his life in Ireland. The first is the battle of Cul Drebene, which was 'fought and won in 561AD by Columba's kin and their allies against the ruling southern Ui Neill... Much has been made of his connection with the battle by both medieval and modern commentators, especially in the light of his departure for Britain two years later. Was Columba involved in some inappropriate way in the battle?'[3] No one seems to know for sure. Dr Thomas Clancy and Rev Gilbert Markus in *Iona* describe the second event surrounding Columba:

> Adding to the mystery is Adomnan's story of Columba being excommunicated by a synod at Tailtiu (Telltown, in the Boyne Valley) 'on a charge of offences that were trivial and very pardonable... improperly as afterwards became known.' What these offences were we do not know. Is it an accident that the synod was held in the territory of the same Southern Ui Neill who had been defeated in the battle? The persistent feeling one gets from these two events is that Columba was somehow caught up in accusations of collusion of violence, and partisanship – a suspicion that is not allayed by the partisanship he shows in Adomnan's *Life*.[4]

In 563AD, two years later, Columba came to Iona accompanied by twelve monks and was given the island by Conall son of Comgall, the king of the Scottish Dal Riata. There were other foundations that were part of Columba's missionary activity besides Iona. These were the mysterious island of Hinba, the exact location of which still hasn't been identified for certain, and Mag Luinge, on the island of Tiree, where it is known that Columba sent penitents who came to him. There are also churches referred to on an unidentified island of Elen and on the mainland at a place called Cella Diuni.[5] Clancy and Markus further comment on what is known about Columba's life from then on:

> Columba returned to Ireland on a number of occasions, on one of which he founded a monastery at Durrow, in the territory of the southern Ui Neill. He visited other prominent churchmen in Ireland, and such people are in turn frequently found visiting the saint on Iona or elsewhere... it is probably true that Columba

was sought out by leading churchmen, such as Comgall of Bangor and Colman mac Beognae... Columba's involvement in politics did not end when he left Ireland. He appears to have had an important role in a 'conference of kings' in 575, with Aed mac Ainmirech, king of Cenel Conaill and later of Tara, and Aedan mac Gabrain, king of Dal Riata.[6]

Columba went to Iona in 563AD and the way of life that he developed for the monastery on Iona became a model for other Celtic monasteries. According to Bede, the Iona community was characterised by their purity of life, love of God and loyalty to the monastic rule. Little is left today of the original monastery and as early as the 8th C, imported stone was used for the manufacture of the large, free-standing Celtic crosses, which are so famous today.

The current Iona Abbey was restored in more recent times from the early 13th C Benedictine Abbey. The wood and stone buildings of the original monastery were replaced. The Augustinian Nunnery on Iona, like the Benedictine Abbey, appears to have been founded about 1200AD by Reginald, son of Somerled, ruler of the Isles, and the dedication was to St Mary the Virgin. The mother-house of this nunnery is unknown.

The chapel and burial ground on Iona take their dedication from St Oran (Odhran), a cousin of St Columba, who died in 617 AD. This little chapel is the earliest surviving building on Iona, and its burial ground dates from the early Christian period. It is said that many kings and other prominent individuals, from Scotland and elsewhere, were buried there in earlier times. Today, Iona is still one of the major visitor attractions in the Highlands and Islands, as it has been for centuries.

The death of St Columba

It is also known that Columba, the 'Dove of the Church', died on 9 June 597, age 75, on Iona, after many years of dedicated service to God. We know this from St Adomnan's testimony in his *Life of Columba*. One of the most enduring anecdotes about the life of St Columba is the account of his last days and hours, as described by Dr Alan Macquarrie in *The Saints of Scotland*:

Adomnan describes how, in the month of May... Columba was

taken in a cart to visit the monks who were at work in the western parts of the island. He told them that his end was drawing near, and blessed them... on the Saturday after that, he and his personal attendant Diarmait went out for a short walk, but Columba's age (he was in fact 75) prevented him going further than the nearest farm-buildings. These he blessed, while he told the sorrowing Diarmait that he expected to die that same night. On the way back to the monastery he sat down... While he sat resting, he was approached by one of the monastery's horses, 'an obedient servant who was accustomed to carry the milk-vessels between the cow pasture and the monastery'. The horse placed its head in the saint's bosom and seemed to weep, as if it knew that its master would soon be taken from it. Diarmait wanted to drive the beast away, but Columba would not allow this; rather he allowed it to nuzzle against him, before 'he blessed his servant the horse, as it turned sadly away from him.'[7]

Here Columba is portrayed as having special sensitivity to animals, an image that has remained with the public about the Celtic saints today, similar to St Francis. Scottish painter John Duncan featured this episode in the life of St Columba in his now famous painting of Columba with this white horse shortly before his death. It is known that in earlier times on the Hebridean islands of Benbecula, South Uist and Barra, at Beltane (May eve) the people dedicated their hymns to not only the holy Trinity, but also to St Columba, as guardian of their cattle.

St Columba and music

In addition to being very devout and inspirational leader of his community, St Columba was also believed to have been a good poet, musician and singer. In *Betha Coluimb Cille* (*The Life of St Columcille*), a 16th C manuscript, the boy Columba's singing is portrayed as having very unusual, far-reaching effects. The young Columba was with his tutor alongside a road, who fell asleep, so Columba began to chant his lesson:

And so diligent was the memorising and so loud the voice that a convent of nuns who were a mile and a half away from him heard the sound of his voice; for it was usual to hear him so far, as the poet said: 'the sound of his voice, Columcille's, much its melody beyond every choir. For twelve hundred paces, mighty the courses, was the distance it was audible...[8]

In the *Amra of Columcille* it says that Columba had a voice that could be heard up to 1,500 paces and that it was like a melodious lion. John Purser in *Scotland's Music* speaks of this and comments, 'Mere fancy, one might say. And Adomnan admits Columba rarely did this, and only when he was inspired. But it is quite possible that Columba had mastered some esoteric vocal techniques such as emphasising the harmonics that exist in everyone's voice.'[9] Today, such special vocal techniques might be similar to something like Tibetan harmonic overtone singing. Perhaps a similar technique was known to the early Celts. Indeed, in earlier times, certain of their chants were known to be unique and it is quite possible that they knew of special techniques that emphasized harmonic overtones, which are known to project the voice much further than would normally be the case.

Musicological analysis has shown that some of the early Celtic chants, especially the Gaelic ones, are known to be similar in style to certain Ethiopian and Coptic chants. Adomnan also wrote that when St Columba and his brethren were trying to convert the Pictish King Brude, they were approached by what are referred to as 'hostile Druids'. Upon seeing them, Columba began to sing the 44th psalm, and his voice was said to be so unusually loud, like pealing thunder, that the king and people alike were struck with terror and amazement. Again, he seems to be portraying Columba's musical abilities and perhaps may be implying his great skill at overtoning, which to those unfamiliar with it, would certainly sound quite loud and frightening.

The death of Columba is also described with a musical analogy in the *Amra of Columcille*, a late 11th C manuscript. Here, we have a description of the departing soul of St Columba being summoned to Heaven, accompanied by music, as his community mourns his loss:

The whole world, it was his:
It is a harp without a key,
It is a church without an abbot...
he reached the plain where they know the custom of music,
where sages do not die...
He went with two songs to Heaven after his cross.[10]

Columba was also known to have gone to Ireland to defend the rights of the bards at the Convention of Drum Ceat in 575AD.

St Columba the scribe

There are many other references to events in the life of St Columba. One of the more well-known concerns a strange accusation of plagiarism, where supposedly Columba was said to have made 'a secret copy' of a psalter belonging to another cleric without getting the owner's permission – evoking images of scenes from Umberto Eco's *The Name of the Rose*! This was obviously considered to be a serious infraction, and it is said that at a special ecclesiastical court he was found guilty and was ordered to hand over the copy he had made to the owner of the original. Some believe that this incident may have been one of the reasons Columba eventually left Ireland for Iona, but of course no one can say for sure. On the other hand, it could be simply an exaggeration by his competitors of a minor incident of some type.

But even so, the accusation itself seems rather unusual, as some believe that the precious psalter that Columba supposedly copied from was alleged to have been done in a Coptic style – something that would have been considered to be quite special or different at the time. (The Coptic church was based in Egypt, and had a strong desert father tradition). Perhaps Columba knew it had an unusual style, valued it, and wanted to preserve it but 'got caught in the act', so to speak. He was a very learned man, so he understandably would have wanted to make sure that something that unique would be preserved and probably would have wanted to have a copy for himself. But, again, scholars cannot say for sure exactly what occurred here as there isn't enough concrete evidence. But St Columba is distinguished from other saints in that he is often portrayed as *a scribe himself*, the implication being that writing was an especially holy task and he apparently did a lot of it. Other accounts of the learned Columba say that many of his books, although immersed in water, would remain dry and intact due to the intervention of God.

The Cathach of St Columba is part of a psalter dated about the late 6th C and is among the oldest examples of Irish Latin script in existence. It is of a unique style in that the initial letters are sometimes surrounded by little red dots, something that was also found in Coptic manuscripts in earlier times, as well as in other traditions. The Coptic church was Egyptian, naturally leading one to wonder about various 'desert father' connections with the early Celtic monasteries in Ireland, an issue which serious scholars have addressed in the past. Some say that this Egyptian connection may have been due to the influence of the Coptic church and of Alexandria. Others believe that the early Syrian monastic communities, which were known to have a strong emphasis on the Anchorite 'desert fathers' hermit tradition (such as that of St Anthony) may have been one of the major monastic ideals for the early Celtic saints. The place name of Dysart in Fife, for example, is believed to be named after this concept of the desert fathers and their monastic ideal. Other similar place-names in Ireland also refer to the desert fathers.

The black coronation stone of Iona and St Aidan

The many legends around possible 'Celtic-Egyptian' and/or 'Celtic-Judaic' connections are varied and apocryphal in nature, but are nonetheless fairly numerous. We learned of some of these in the first chapter. Recall, as an example, the one apocryphal legend relating to the Stone of Destiny, which says that Eochaid, high King of Ireland, married Tamar Tephi, the daughter of King Zedekiah of Judah, in about 586BC.

> With her father a captive in Babylon, and her brothers murdered by Nebuchadnezzar, Tamar had escaped to Ireland with the great prophet Jeremiah, and with them came the Stone of Destiny... This event coincided with the Jerusalem Temple Guard's instruction to remove the sacred treasures from the grasp of the invading king of Babylon, and it is therefore apparent that Jeremiah is more than just a prophet...[11]

Earlier we learned about the legend of Scotia and possible Egyptian connections to early Ireland. Again, these legends seem to simply 'refuse to die', remaining embedded in local traditions.

One of the key events in St Columba's life as chief ecclesiastical leader was the bestowing of formal benediction and inauguration on Aidan in 574AD. Aidan was seated on a black coronation stone that was said to be at the entrance to the church of Iona. Columba anointed his head with oil and proclaimed him the successor to Conall as king of Argyll. Some say that this black stone may explain some of the medieval references to a 'black coronation stone' regarding the Stone of Destiny, but again, no one can say for sure. St Aidan went on to do much missionary work in Northumbria and is still honoured today on Holy Island and by the Lindisfarne community.

There are also many accounts of Columba having various magical contests with Druids. No doubt such hostile encounters took place, especially when the Christians tried to convert pagan areas. Other early legends say that there was a Druidical college on Iona in earlier times which later came under the protection of St Moluag. There exists a tale about this legendary rivalry between Columba and Moluag, as to who would dominate the island of Lismore, which is described in full in the next chapter on the Culdees.

Customs and beliefs about St Columba

St Columba's Day (9 June) was on Maundy Thursday in earlier times in the Highlands. It was celebrated in a number of different ways. It was looked upon as a lucky day for all activities, including setting out on a journey. Celtic scholar Anne Ross states:

> On the eve of St Columba's Day, the woman of the house used to make a bannock of oats or rye and she would place a small silver coin in this. The cake was then toasted in front of a fire which had been kindled from one of their sacred woods – oak, yew, or rowan. On Maundy Thursday the head of the house would take the cake and cut it into as many pieces as there were children in the family, all of the same size. These were placed in a basket and each child helped himself to a piece; the child who got the coin was given the crop of lambs for the year, or at least part of them.[12]

The Mull of Kintyre is also an important area of St Columba, as it is said that his first footprints and landfall was at Keil Point, where a later church and St Columba's Well can still be seen. The large rock footprints, only one of which is genuinely old, have a ritual significance that is believed to have been connected to king-ship. Caves to the west mark an early settlement. Dr Donald Smith also points out that 'before its absorption into the empire of Clan Campbell, the main town of Kintyre was Kinlochkerran – the head of the loch of St Ciaran, an early missionary from Ireland. On one of his journeys Columba encountered a trading ship here from Gaul – modern-day France.'[13]

Clearly early Scotland was not a marginal place on the edge of the known world. Christianity also brought a sense of interna-tionalism and of being connected to other countries, regardless of national boundaries, and even before Christianity, there was much important trade going on with other areas of the world.

The monastery and scriptorium of Iona

Iona became a great centre of scholarship and learning in medieval times and was especially renowned for its scriptorium. At a time that has been labelled the so-called 'Dark Ages', one of the greatest libraries in all of Europe (and some of its finest art) was based on Iona. The famous library of Iona contained the Vulgate Latin Bible, many Christian classics, Jerome's commen-taries on biblical books, works by Pope Gregory I, Augustine, Athanasius, and many Lives of the saints and writings of the early church fathers, among others. The learned monks there were clearly well connected with the mainstream of European Christian theology. It is also now believed by a increasing number of schol-ars that the beautifully ornate *Book of Kells* was created on Iona by monks and then taken to Ireland around 800AD to protect this precious illuminated book from the Vikings, who badly devastated Iona in 795AD

But it does not seem to be widely realised that the *Book of Kells*, so famous today, was actually never completed! It is a very complex manuscript with many fine details that took a long time to create with great effort and skill. Minerals were brought from enormous distances to provide colours for the manuscript, such as the blue pigment that is known to have come from the lapis lazuli from Afghanistan. The *Book of Kells* is now displayed in Trinity College Dublin where its pages are turned at the rate of one a day.

A facsimile is housed in the National Library of Scotland in Edinburgh.

Iona was also associated with St Oran. St Oran's Chapel and its burial ground is believed by some to be an even earlier foundation than that of the church of St Columba. It is known that Columba's original monastery was to the north of the present restored Abbey. Iona was called by some of the Highlanders, even into this century, as *Inis Druin-each*, or 'Druid's Isle'; the Irish called it *Eilean Drunish*. Many of the early kings of Scotland were buried at Iona.

As part of practical daily living, monasteries were often fairly self-sufficient communities, with the monks working hard and tilling the land. It is known from the 7th C *Life of Columba* that the monks of his community built many stone enclosures. This was because in quite windy places like the western plain of Iona, which was probably the harvest field for the Iona monastic community, the corn needed protection. Some aerial photographs show small fields surrounding the early monastery at Iona and also at other Celtic Christian sites.[14]

The 'missing library of Iona'

Iona, later famous for its scriptorium, as we've already seen, has a curious legend associated with it about a very early collection of precious books there – *before* the arrival of St Columba. Subsequent accounts have arisen around this story about the 'missing library of Iona':

> In Iona, in very ancient times, a great collection of books was made, and it is an interesting fact of history that Fergus II of Scotland, who in his youth assisted Alaric the Goth at the sack of Rome, 410AD, brought away, as part of the plunder, some valuable 'geir', and a chest of books which he afterwards presented to the monastery of Iona, then known as Inis-nan-Druidneach (Isle of Druids). This presentation was made 164 years before St Columba's date... [furthermore]... Eneas Silvius, afterwards Pope Pius II, sent a legate to Scotland to ascertain if the lost book of Titus Livy should be found among them. At a later date (1525) Master John Campbell, Treasurer to the King, found five old books which then consisted of nothing but broken leaves and very difficult to read. Boece says that 'the reading

sounded more like the eloquence of Salustius than of Livy'.[15]
Fergus II is not to be confused with Fergus mac Earc, 6th C., who
with his followers from Ireland settled in Scotland. Fergus II
(grandson of Ethodius, who was banished from Scotland and
received by the King of Denmark) succeeded in recovering his
birthright possessions and the crown of Scotland.[16]

This does make one wonder what books from ancient times
may have actually been housed at Iona. Because it was so far
away, on 'the edge' of the known world, it may have also been
viewed as a safe haven for certain very valuable books. Dr William
Ferguson, Honorary Fellow of Scottish History at the University
of Edinburgh, studied this matter in detail. In his insightful work,
The Identity of the Scottish Nation, he states:

> Still, the stories about the wondrous books at Iona circulated;
> and finally, through the promptings of Bishop Elphinstone of
> Aberdeen, who was agog to see them, and the help of John
> Campbell, who was treasurer to James V, the mysterious books
> were carried from Iona to Boece at Aberdeen in 1525. Some were
> found to be too perished to be decipherable, but disappointment
> was tempered by the discovery of unexpected treasure. Boece
> claims that the same messenger from Iona brought with him the
> 'History of Veremundus', who was allegedly archdeacon of St
> Andrews in the late eleventh century. Veremund, a Spaniard,
> had, it was said, compiled a chronicle that covered the history of
> the Scots from earliest times until the reign of Malcolm III or
> Canmore, 1058-93. Or so, at least, Hector [Boece] claimed.[17]

The problem, though, was that Veremund's history was never
found, as its existence is only known about from Boece's alleged
use of it. Ferguson goes on to say that the 19th C Scottish historian
W.F. Skene believed that the existence of Veremund's *Historia* was
not simply a mere figment of Boece's imagination, as he believed
that such a history of the Scots from earliest times until the reign
of Malcolm Canmore had indeed existed and that it was probably
written sometime in the late 13th C. Skene based this on the fact
that certain St Andrews charters granted at Falkland in 1267 were
witnessed by one 'Ricardus Veyrement or Veriment'. Yet many
scholars today have still not found the proof they are seeking to
clear Boece of charges of a questionable version of Scottish history,
in spite of many tantalising clues.

Ferguson tells us that 'Professor Barrow has identified a Richard Weyremont or Vairement who was a Culdee of St Andrews about that time, but finds no evidence to link him with Skene's supposed historian.'[18] Some believe that this may indicate that this so-called *Veremund's History* of Boece came from a Culdee-orientated source, and that this has been ridiculed by those with other vested interests past. Still, nothing can be said for sure about this matter. Ferguson concludes:

> All the same, the possibility cannot be avoided that something known as *Veremund's History* does seem to have existed, if only fleetingly, and of what exact nature is not known. Boece says he had use of it, but what use he might have made of it is also unknown. Not being a critical or scientific historian any more than his great mentor Livy was, Hector Boece would gratefully make use of whatever was available, glossing and embellishing to suit himself. That was the method of his day, and while it would be pleasant to think that such crude practices are now unknown, no working historian today would be likely to regard that as certain.[19]

So, as it is commonly acknowledged that most history ends up being 'written by the victors', so to speak, this point is worth contemplating. Perhaps Boece is no more guilty of this kind of thing than some modern day media 'spin doctors'. We must remember than all history is written by someone, at some time, with certain interests in mind, and that often what remains centuries later is a genuine mish-mash of facts and legends. Then, if a country or place is conquered, it is well known that the history of that place is often rewritten to suit the vested interests of the 'victors', whoever they may be.

With the above example of the 'missing library of Iona', there seem to be few scholars who actually doubt the existence of old, precious books on Iona; most of the criticism is directed at Boece's alleged source not actually being found. No doubt there were many old and valuable books there, but we cannot say for sure what they were or where they went. But many believe that after the death of Columba, certain books may have been taken back to Ireland. Nonetheless, the connection between books, learning and Iona, persistently comes up in many accounts of early Scottish history. Even English poet William Wordsworth visited Iona in 1835 and commemorated his visit with four poems.

But important as it was, Iona was also part of a much larger network of early Christian settlements. Travel had a particular significance to the early saints, and the Celtic saints in particular were well-known for literally attempting to take the Gospel to 'the ends of the earth'. They were great missionaries, both at home and abroad. A highly recommended booklet, by Dr Donald Smith, entitled *Celtic Travellers*, was produced in 1997 by HMSO in Edinburgh to mark the 1,600th anniversary of the first mission to Whithorn and the 1,400th anniversary of Iona. It is an excellent guide for those visiting Scotland and tells more about the travel of the Celtic saints, and has interesting details of place-names.

Much of the following material is a summary of the various places that have been associated with the Celtic saints. (For a general map, please consult the Appendix or, for specific details, see *Celtic Travellers* which is listed in the Bibliography.) Specific saints' names are listed, with the associated places and local traditions listed that apply to them in that area.

The Hebridean islands and the Argyll area

Saints Baithene and Cainnech

The monastery at Kildalton was dedicated to St Baithene 'the fosterling' who is believed to have been Columba's foster son, St Baithene. Other scholars believe he was actually Columba's cousin as the Columban church was very much a 'family affair'. It is said that Columba's final words as he died transcribing the 34th psalm were 'let Baithene finish it'.

Between Kildalton and Port Ellen is the little island of Texa which was an early monastic site and visited by St Cainnech (Kenneth). Dunadd, nearby, was the main fortress of the Kingdom of Dalriada. A local legend says that Columba may have installed Aidan as King on the rock where a large carved footprint is located, which probably already had some ritual significance anyway. Also at Dunadd there are other carvings associated with inauguration, like a boar, a rock-cut stone basin possibly for libations, an inscription in Ogham, and possibly a rock-cut throne. To the east of Dunadd is the church of Kilmichael Glassary, where in 1814 workmen discovered a bronze bell shrine containing a 7th C Celtic handbell, which is now housed in the National Museum in Edinburgh. It may be the bell of St Moluag of Lismore. Kilmartin Church has an important collection of early carved stones, and Kilmartin House is an attractive visitor centre with an interesting display on Celtic sea travel.[20]

St Brendan

The now-uninhabited islands of Garvellach and Scarba were once places of penance and spiritual contemplation for the early saints. At one time they were certainly as spiritually important as Iona. The Garvellachs in particular have a connection with St Brendan, the famous voyager saint of Ireland. Before Columba, it is believed that St Bernard of Clonfert established the monastery of Ailech on Eilean An Naoimhe ('the Saint's Isle') in the 6th C. Others believe that St Brendan founded this monastery himself. This site has beehive cells, a chapel and an underground store; a nearby island is called Cuil Breanainn ('Brendan's Retreat'). The larger island, whose main hill is called Dun Breannain ('the hill of Brendan') is also rough and rocky, surrounded by the constant sound of the sea.

Saints Moluag and Columba

Lismore, in the mouth of Loch Linnhe, was an important burial place in earlier times and was a connecting point between the Pictish territories to the north and the Kingdom of Dalriada. Lismore actually has few remains left on it today, but there is a ruined chapel associated with Columba on the southwest end of the island. Portmoluag is where Lismore's patron saint Moluag is said to have first landed and his principal monastery and burial ground were at Clachan around the surviving church. It and the visible foundations remaining around it, however, belong to the later Cathedral of the Isles which stood within the 'great enclosure' or 'lios mor' of Moluag's monastery from which the island takes its name. The surviving staff of St Moluag is kept today by its Hereditary Keeper on Lismore. The famous *Book of the Dean of Lismore* was created here in the 16th C in which St Moluag is commemorated with praise.[21]

Saints Catan of Bute, Fintan, Donnan and Beccan

Ardchattan Priory on the north shore of Loch Etive is a medieval foundation on an earlier Celtic site, dedicated to St Catan of Bute. East of Ballachulish in Loch Leven is Eilean Munde, the island of St Munnu or Fintan, a cousin of Columba who is believed to have been a leper. As we have noted, the Columban church was very much a 'family affair', with relatives of Columba having prominent positions within his community. The chapel on this island is also a burial place of the MacDonalds.

The northwestern areas were also important ones for the early Celtic missions. The isle of Eigg was the scene of the earliest recorded maryrdom of a Celtic saint, when St Donnan and his community of monks were massacred here on Easter Sunday, 16 April 618AD, it is said, by a Pictish queen who who resented their settlement there. The ruined chapel of Donnan still exists on Eigg today. St Donnan's mission was mainly to the northern Picts. Rum is associated with the hermit saint Bec (or Beccan) but there is little trace of his occupation there today. Sadly, Rum was cleared of its entire population in 1826 and only partially resettled. The island of Canna is associated with Columba and Iona; there is a ruined chapel of St Columba there, as well as an early carved cross shaft in the modern church. There is also a monastic ruin on the southern coast below Am Beannan, isolated by rocks and sea, with the name Sgor nam Ban-Naomha ('Skerry of the Holy Woman') and suggests a woman's 'dysart' or spiritual retreat. The modern-day Catholic chapel is on the tidal island of Sanday.[22]

Saints Columba, Comgan, Oran, Maelrubha, Fillan and Kentigerna

Skye is associated with several Celtic saints, beginning with St Columba, who is commemorated on a tidal island off Portree, the main town today on Skye. South of Kilmuir lies the drained Loch Chaluim Chille, or St Columba's Loch. A stony mound now marks the former island of Columba, on which can still be seen the foundations of the enclosing wall, beehive cells and two chapels. In the mouth of the river near Skebost is St Columba's Island, with the ruins of a medieval chapel. Believed to be an original Columban foundation, the island was the headquarters of the Bishopric of the Isles from 1079 to 1498, and the burial place of the Nicolsons. One of the oldest Christian settlements on Skye's northern peninsula, Vaternish, is called Annait, or 'Mother Church'. This site has not been excavated yet, and its founding saints remain unknown.

Duirinish, also on Skye's northern peninsula, is the ancestral home of the MacLeods of Skye at Dunvegan. The valley of Glendale nearby includes several crofting communities as it opens out to the sea and the outer isles. In early times, Glendale was a known to be a particularly strong centre of the Druidic religion, and remaining legends tell of how St Columba came here to establish Christianity... but not without quite a fight, it seems! An early graveyard stands at the foot of the valley and on the level ground beside the river are the displaced boundary stones of a lost monastery. The earliest known dedication at this location is to St Comgan. In the southwest of Skye, at Borline on Loch Eynort, is another important site of early Christian settlement. Kilmoruy was St Maelrubha's church, related to the famous monastery at Applecross.[23]

The isle of Ornsay, named after St Oran, is in the Sound of Sleat, on the eastern side of Skye. To the north, the isle of Raasay features St Moluag, with a ruined chapel dedicated to him there. On the shore beside the chapel is a Celtic cross carved in the rock, while beside Raasay House is a Pictish symbol stone with a Maltese cross and the vestiges of the chi-rho symbol of Christ on it.

On the mainland of Skye in the district of Lochalsh, the early church sites of Kilchoan and Kilillan are dedicated to St Comgan and St Fillan, respectively. St Comgan's sister, St Kentigerna, was an Irish princess and the mother of St Fillan, who also worked in the area as part of this remarkable family of saints that were related to the royal house of Leinster in Ireland.[24]

Fillan and Comgan were cousins. The father of St Fillan was Feredach, also of the royal house of Dalriada. St Fillan is also famed throughout parts of Perthshire, especially Strathfillan and Killin. The name Fillan means 'wolf cub' or 'little wolf'. It is said that both mother and son became missionaries, with his mother Kentigerna retiring to Inch Cailleach, meaning 'Isle of the Old Women, or Nuns' on Loch Lomond, where she died in 734AD. As the influence of the old Celtic church gradually waned and became more absorbed into the Roman, more land was removed from St Fillan's chapel to other dioceses. But an Abbot still presided over it and the custom of sanctuary being offered for hunted men was still honoured.

In 1306, fugitive King Robert the Bruce came to St Fillan's Chapel with a few of his men for sanctuary after escaping a superior force near Tyndrum shortly after his coronation. There's no doubt that he credited his deliverance to the intercession of St Fillan as he specifically requested one of his relics, the left arm bone, prior to the Battle of Bannockburn in 1314.[25] There were five Dewars, or guardians, of the relics of St Fillan, which were the pastoral staff, the bell, the arm bone, and perhaps his portable altar and his manuscript. The actual Bell of St Fillan, the Bernane, is said to be in the National Museum of Scotland today.

The monastery at Applecross

St Maelrubha's main monastery was at Applecross, which was linked with Bangor in Ireland rather than Iona in Scotland. The burial ground is all that is now visible of this once major and important non-Columban monastery. Applecross was destroyed by the Vikings within a century of St Maelrubha's death.

Unfortunately, however, this was to be the fate of many a

Celtic religious settlement. Dr. Sally Foster, an Inspector of Ancient Monuments, Historic Scotland, in *Picts, Gaels and Scots*, says that Iona was closely involved with the development of the early church in Ireland, and that Applecross also had an important role. As Iona was the major monastery in Argyll, 'much material was probably transmitted there (including the *Senchus fer nAlban*) due to links between the churches on both sides of the North Channel, particularily when Ionan monks fled to Ireland at times of political pressure and Viking threats. From about 675 to the 740s there may also have been a source at Applecross monastery.'[26]

Historian Dr Dauvit Broun comments on the very real problem of the lack of contemporary chronicles for this period in Scottish history, adding that his academic colleague 'Isabel Henderson has also made a cogent case for regarding some entries in the Annals of Ulster as derived originally from a chronicle kept at Applecross from c.675 to no later than c.750... Unfortunately, nothing at all survives from a Scottish chronicle between c.750 and c.850...'[27] This is also the era of the St Andrews Sarcophagus, an elaborate Pictish royal shrine unearthed at St Andrews in the 19th C. So, no doubt Applecross was important and more might be discovered about this in the future.

Not far from Applecross is the Isle of Maree, which lies close to the north side of Loch Maree, and has the remains of an early chapel and a well. This is said to be the burial place of St Maelrubha. This well of Innis Maree, has been famous from an unknown past and is dedicated to St Maelrubha. Thomas Pennant, in *A Tour in Scotland*, visited Innis Maree in 1772, and described its unusual appearance:

> In the midst is a circular dike of stones, with a regular narrow entrance, the inner part has been used for ages... I suspect the dike to have been originally Druidical, and that the ancient superstition of Paganism had been taken up by the saint, as the readiest method of making a conquest over the minds of the inhabitants...[28]

St Mourie

Whatever Pennant may have meant by Druidical, there is reason to believe that this place was regarded by him as a location of pre-Christian rites that lasted way into Christian times and that St Maelrubha cleverly made use of this fact. We saw more of his comments about Innis Maree in chapter 2. Early writers of the Society of Antiquaries documented that 'the people of the place speak often of the God Mourie instead of St Mourie, which may have resulted from his having supplanted the old god.'[29]

It is also known that the Loch Maree area was known for bull-sacrifices, and that even as late as the year 1656, the Church Presbytery of Applecross took action against certain people for sacrificing bulls on 25 of August, St Mourie's Day. In 1678, the Presbytery of Dingwall took similar disciplinary action against four MacKenzies for sacrificing a bull in Loch Maree, sacred to St Mourie:

> This island Innis Maree has an enclosure, or stone dyke, in which are the remains of a chapel. Near it stands an oak tree ... Mourie was the successor of a 'divine king' connected with the oak and the sacred well at Innis Maree, the god or spirit of which was incarnate in him. The sacrificed bull may have incarnated the spirit of the god...[30]

Although some material about Loch Maree was referred to in the earlier chapter on the Druids, this bit is included here to show the connections to St Mourie and the Applecross area. It is possible that such customs are reminiscent of the 'Holly King' or 'Oak King' of much earlier times. In the early Highland rite of *taghairm*, a seer was wrapped in the hide of a newly-slain bull and slept beside a waterfall or at the foot of some wild precipice, where it was believed that spirits would communicate to him and foretell the future. This rite persisted until the middle of the 18th C in certain areas, which is quite late. That it was also practised in Wales is a possibility, as in the *Mabinogion*, a tale called 'The Vision of Rhonabwy' has an episode where Rhonabwy, a warrior, had a vision while sleeping on the skin of a yellow heifer.[31]

Saints Finbarr, Bethog, Clement and Ronan

On the isle of Barra is the ancient religious centre of Kilbarr, dedicated to St Finbarr (or Barr), the patron saint of Cork, Ireland. In the words of a very old Irish poem:

> Barr, the fire of wisdom, loves
> Humility to the men of the world;
> He never saw in want
> A person that he did not assist.[32]

On the Carinish peninsula on North Uist, Trinity Church was built by St Bethog, a medieval Prioress of Iona. At Rodel in the south of Harris, St Clement's church stands today. It was built by Alexander MacLeod (d.1546) chief of the MacLeods of Harris and Dunvegan and it houses his tomb today. On the isle of Lewis, in the Uig Sands, the famous Lewis Chessmen were found in 1831 after a storm. They can now be seen in the summer months in the Museum Nan Eilean in Stornoway. The church at Eorpaidh on Lewis was dedicated in Norse times to St Olaf.[33]

But in St Moluag's time, on the isle of Lewis, there was also a strong belief in Shony, a sea god:

> Eorpaidh was the cultic centre of a sea god called Shony whose festival was observed here, centuries after the arrival of Christianity, on 1 November, when a cup of ale was symbolically cast into the water to ensure fertility. The Saint himself was believed to heal both limbs and lunatics. Little remains of another chapel at Eorpaidh, Teampull Ronain... Even at Eorpaidh, Ronan's companions were mainly the birds and the seals, but he pushed north seeking 'a desert place in the sea', and was carried to Ronan by a sea monster.[34]

Southeastern areas of Scotland

Saints Cuthbert, Abb and Aidan

The southeastern areas of Scotland, including Edinburgh and the Lothians, as well as parts of Strathclyde, form a large area that is rich in the history of the saints. Lindisfarne in Northern England was later known as Holy Island, is a tidal island north of Bamburgh, ancient capital of the Anglian kingdom of Northumbria. The first monastery on Lindisfarne was founded from Iona a the invitation of King Oswald who had spent several years there in exile... the most famous Prior of Lindisfarne was St Cuthbert, who also had a chapel on the tidal Hobthrush Rock southwest of the village. Cuthbert's body was reverenced here until the Viking onslaught forced the monks to take their saint's relics on a tortuous pilgrimage, ending up finally at Durham where Cuthbert's shrine can be visited today.[35]

St Cuthbert was born in 635AD in the region of the Lammermuir Hills in the Scottish borders, where he worked as a shepherd. One day he had a vision of angels taking a soul to Heaven. He later found out that on that very day, St Aidan, Bishop of Lindisfarne, had died. So in 651, that same year, he answered his call and entered the monastery of Old Melrose. Cuthbert later became Bishop of Lindisfarne and also preached in Galloway, with the largest county there named after him. The village of Kirkcudbright is the modern-day use of the old term of 'Kirk-Cuthbert', meaning the church of Cuthbert.

St Cuthbert was greatly honoured by the gushing forth of springs both during his lifetime and after his death. In his *History of St Cuthbert*, Archbishop Eyre remarks that there is a legendary tradition that when the bearers of St Cuthbert's body journeyed northwards from Yorkshire and came to Butterby, near Croxdale, they put down his coffin and immediately a spring burst out upon the spot. This was said to have happened several more times. Even while at Lindisfarne, it is said that when Cuthbert withdrew to Farne Island to pray, a spring gushed forth from under the floor of his cell.[36]

Lindisfarne is also famous for the *Lindisfarne Gospels*, the beautifully illuminated manuscripts that were a product of its Anglo-Saxon and Celtic culture. What doesn't seem to be widely understood today is that St Cuthbert is not really a 'Celtic saint' in the strictest sense; he is thought to be more properly a Northumbrian saint who also conducted missionary work in Celtic areas. In fact, the name 'Lothian' is only first found in contemporary use towards the end of the 11th C, which is quite late, as in earlier medieval times it wasn't originally even considered to be a part of the kingdom of Scotland![37] As far as church organisation, the Edinburgh area was originally considered to be in the northern part of the See of Northumbria.

St Abb's monastery, near Lindisfarne, was named after an Anglo-Saxon princess named Ebba, after she was shipwrecked with her two sisters. We are reminded that 'despite her Anglo-Saxon origins, Ebba's monastery was a thoroughly Celtic foundation combining men and women, which may be the reason for later criticism of her 'laxness'. Cuthbert used to stay here, slipping down to the shore to spend the night hours in penitential prayer...'[38] After the Viking onset St Abbs was destroyed, but St Margaret's son King Edgar re-established the monastery inland at Coldingham, where extensive remains of Coldingham Priory can still be seen.

Saints Serf and Kentigern

Legend has it that King Loth, of whom it is said the Lothians got their name, threw his pregnant daughter Thanew down the hill of Trapain Law in a chariot, as she had refused to marry a British prince by whom she had been mercilessly raped. But, it is said, she somehow survived this terrible ordeal, so she was then next cast off in a boat at Aberlady by her father's men. But she also survived this, it is said, having managed to sail over to the Isle of May, followed by all of Aberlady's fish, and then on to Culross, where her baby was brought up by St Serf, the mentor of St Kentigern.[39]

The Isle of May is intriguing for many reasons, one of them being the fact that a scallop shell from the great medieval pilgrimage centre of St James of Compostela, in northwestern Spain, was found in the mouth of a man buried before the high altar there. It was also known to be important to the medieval Scottish Knights Templar, who had their headquarters at Balantradoch, now the village of Temple in Midlothian, which is not all that far from the Firth of Forth.

St Serf is a rather mysterious figure, as not much is known about him; but it is thought that he was a mentor of St Kentigern. He is also associated with various miracles and legends, such as his staff turning into a blossoming apple tree after he threw it across the River Forth from his cell at Culross. He is also credited with miracles involving islands: 'Given the Celtic idea of Avalon (the Island of Apples) where Morgan took the wounded Arthur to be tended by her and her eight sisters, this idea is suggestive.'[40] As you can see, local saints are credited with any number of extraordinary feats.

Other legends about St Serf include his fame for dragon-slaying. It is said that he killed a dragon at Dunning in Strathearn and also at the Dragon's Cave on the south side of Kinnoull Hill, Perth. According to the Breviary of Aberdeen, it was at Dunnyne where he performed the miracle of slaying the ferocious dragon, armed 'only with the breastplate of faith he entered its lair and slew it by a blow of his pastoral staff.'[41]

St Serf was also associated with the Culdees, as he was given the large island in Loch Leven that still bears his name.[42] Dr Alan Macquarrie also comments about St Serf:

> A firm *terminus ante quem* for the historical St Serf is probably provided only by the Lochleven notes, which indicate that the church there was in existence by c.950. If, as appears virtually certain, the church at Culross was in existence before that at Lochleven, then St Serf must have lived and worked before the mid-tenth century. The early Christian fragments of sculpture at Culross, of ninth or tenth century date, point in the same direction. If, as appears likely, he was Pictish or (less likely) British, then he must have been ninth century or earlier... he is unknown to Bede, which may not indicate anything; but it must 'be remembered that Bede's friend Trumwin was an Anglian 'bishop of the Picts', operating from a cathedral at Abercorn, for a few years up to 685... it may not be possible to date him [i.e. Serf] more precisely than to the seventh, eighth, or ninth century; but... c.700 seems the most likely.[43]

St Kentigern is the patron saint of the church of Glasgow. Unfortunately, there aren't many existing records about him. However, it is known that he did exist. There are no surviving writings by him, or anything resembling an early Life such as Adomnan's *Life of Columba*. He is unknown, or not mentioned, by Bede. We do have a 12th C *Life of St Kentigern* by Jocelin of Furness, a highly-regarded writer in his time.

The first historical record of Kentigern is the note of his death in a Welsh chronicle, the *Annales Cambriae*, around the year 612. There is a gap of about 550 years until two 12th C lives were written, one of them Jocelin's *Life*, mentioned above.[44] No other Kentigern is known, and the older form of the name Kentigern, Conthigerni, means 'Hound-Lord'; the later Welsh Cyndeyrn being a variation of his name. His beloved name of 'Mungo', meaning 'most dear one', is similar to what an affectionate nickname would be to us today.

According to legend, St Kentigern was a 'star' pupil at the Culross monastery, often incurring the jealously of the other students of St Serf. He is described as performing many miracles. For instance, one time when it was his turn to watch the fire, he fell asleep and it went out, obviously a very serious problem for the community in midwinter. However, the young Kentigern put some frozen leaves on the hearth and kindled the fire with his own breath, thus saving the monastery of bitter cold. Kentigern was said to have major influence over animals, at one point even ploughing the fields with a wolf and a stag yoked together. It is said that Kentigern went to the area around Stirling – but legend says he got there by the miraculous parting the waters of the Forth, much like Moses! After this, he continued on, and was led by God to the Glasgow area.

It is widely believed that Kentigern founded a new church here by the Molendinar burn in Glasgu, the 'green hollow', a name which accurately describes the original setting.[45] This location was just a few kilometres away from the royal residence of the British Kings of Strathclyde at Partick. He was consecrated Bishop of Glasgow, but was exiled to Cumbria during a period of political unrest. Kentigern later returned to meet with Columba; it is said the two exchanged staffs with each other, a symbol of friendship. Kentigern is believed to have evangelised in the areas of Glasgow, Annandale, Dumfriesshire and Cumbria. He died in 612AD. He was buried in the church of his monastery in Glasgow, which became a major place of pilgrimage.

Intriguingly, as stated by archaeologist Peter Yeoman in the Historic Scotland publication *Pilgrimage in Medieval Scotland*, Edward 1 of England was the only king known to have made offerings at the shrine, and possibly because of this no Scottish royal gifts are recorded, other than the favours of David I, who presumably had acted at least partly out of devotion to Kentigern. James IV, however, did also favour the cathedral, having become a canon at an early age.[46]

Another rather unusual comment about St Kentigern and his family is from Scottish folklore researcher Stuart McHardy:

> Although we know little about Kentigern's father, his mother's family were straight out of the great Celtic hero tradition. Her mother is said to have been Anne, daughter of the great Uther Pendragon, and thus sister of King Arthur. [King] Loth himself is mentioned in all the earliest Arthurian sources and his two sons, Kentigern's uncles, were major Arthurian figures. They were Modred and Gawain...[47]

Such legendary accounts that refer to Arthurian characteristics of St Kentigern seem to 'refuse to die' even today. Although mythic in nature, such stories are quite persistent, including some local associations of St Kentigern with Merlin, to be discussed later in chapter 6.

St Kentigern and North Wales

St Kentigern was also believed to have made a sojourn to Wales, and is said to have had encounters with both St David and St Asaph. Although now believed by some scholars to be largely legendary, such tales, again, seem to 'refuse to die'. Dr Alan Macquarrie, respected historian the medieval period in Scotland, states in his informative book *The Saints of Scotland*:

> The cult of St Kentigern is found in Wales, however, and it must be asked how it got there, since in 'triadic' tradition he is placed yn y gogled , i.e. 'in the North'. There is good reason to believe that some Strathclyde aristocrats left Scotland and settled in Gwynedd, c.890, when they refused to conform with the increasing integration of Strathclyde into the kingdom of Scotia. Presumably, these aristocrats took the cult of St Kentigern with them, and subsequently, legends about Kentigern developed in Wales; these could have been written up in the early twelfth century, transferred back to Glasgow, and have found their way into

F. [an early manuscript re: Kentigern]... Their intention is to connect Kentigern with major Welsh saints, David and Alsaph, and with Gwynedd, but the relationships described are not to be taken literally.[48]

Others aren't so sure, however. There is, for example, a Masonic lodge dedicated to St Kentigern in Wales, an issue to be discussed in chapter 8. If this is all just mere legend, the story goes, then 'why bother', so to speak, with any dedications to him as far away as Wales? But, like many saints' dedications, perhaps he simply visited the area, like many saints were known to do, or just as likely, the Strathclyde aristocrats who left the area in the 9th C for north Wales were likely to have brought their tales about St Kentigern and his miracles with them. What we do know, though, is that the Strathclyde aristocrats likely felt a definite kinship with the people of north Wales – the Cymry. Given that the Strathclyde and Lothian areas in early times both spoke a Brythonic P-Celtic language similar to Old Welsh, perhaps this isn't so surprising to imagine after all.

A number of scholars now believe that Kentigern did go to Wales. Some believe he even may have been somewhat reluctant to return from his foundation at Llanelwy in North Wales, now known as St Asaph's, to Glasgow, when summoned by the Strathclyde king Rydderch Hael in 574AD. Rydderch Hael had defeated a pagan chieftain in the area, yet he was a Christian and needed help in evangelising the area again. So Kentigern did return, it is said, with a number of his followers, including St Nidan and St Finan, and they then did successful missionary work all over Scotland, including as far away as Aberdeen and the province of Mar. St Kentigern is highly regarded in Scotland and Wales today.

St Kentigern and new Trapain Law research

Ironically, new archaeological research at Trapain Law in east Lothian may actually lend some credence to the legends about Kentigern's mother being 'banished' from Trapain Law, a large fortress and hill, after discovering that she was pregnant by the angry King Loth. This is another variation of Kentigern's birth tale, but in fact scholars have never known exactly where he was born – perhaps, until now. Archaeologist Fraser Hunter, Curator of Iron Age and Roman Collections at the National Museum of Scotland, said in a recent article:

> We have found unexpected evidence for the later use of the hill, after its abandonment as a major settlement around the 5th century. A typical early Christian burial has been uncovered, providing evidence of some religious use. These findings lend some legitimacy to the myths which link the birth of St Mungo to events on Trapain... Although at this stage it can't be proven, this could be connected with a church or shrine to St Mungo.[49]

Lothian and Borders areas associated with St Kentigern

Innerleithen, a small Peebles-shire town on the Tweed in the Scottish Borders, also has an old church there dedicated according to early folklorists, to St Kentigern. The town received from Malcolm II (1003-1033) the right of sanctuary because the body of the king's son, drowned in the Tweed, had lain there for a night before burial. Innerleithen also has St Ronan's Well, and the unusual, beautifully carved Anglian cross shaft is called by some the Innerleithen stone.

Another town associated with St Kentigern is Lanark, which received her charter in 1140AD. Around 564AD or so, it is thought that St Kentigern built a church here, and in 978AD, Kenneth III held an assembly for dispensing justice. Later, Lanark would take her place with Edinburgh, Stirling and Linlithgow as one of the Four Royal Burghs. Various privileges were conferred on her by visiting sovereigns. A more grisly memory in Lanark's past is that of the murder of the beloved wife of William Wallace, Marion Bradefute, by English troops. On that night the streets were filled with tumult and slaughter.[50]

Saints Kentigern/Mungo, Bega, Llolan, Ronan and Baldred

At Penicuik, the early church and a well are dedicated to St Kentigern. This whole area is associated with four important early missionaries: Kentigern/Mungo, Bega, Llolan and Ronan. St Llolan's bell and staff were once kept by the Earls of Perth. Into this century, local villages often have celebrations relating to early saints, for example, the Procession of the Boy Monks in honour of St Ronan, held at Innerleithen. Even Sir Walter Scott celebrated St Ronan in his novel called *St Ronan's Well*. These are but a few examples of how local folklore often involves a saint from much earlier times, with some villages still celebrating their memory in different ways even today.

In the east Lothian area, there are dedications to St Baldred. He is said to have been a prior or a monk at Lindisfarne who was sent to minister to the people of east Lothian in the 8th C. He is believed to have had a monastery at Tyninghame; the most famous place of retreat associated with him is the Bass Rock, which is now a major visitor attraction and bird sanctuary. A cave is dedicated to him at Seacliff Beach. Local legend has it that St Baldred's Cradle, a rock off the coast at Tyninghame, was once located between the Bass Rock and the shore, but that in response to St Baldred's prayers, God moved it to the south!

Whitekirk: an important place of pilgrimage

In later medieval times, 'Baldred's cult was overshadowed by the magnification of another of his churches as a major pilgrimage resort, at Whitekirk, only 1.5 km (1 mile) northwest of his monastery at Tyninghame.'[51] The great healing powers of the well dedicated to Our Lady there brought great fame to Whitekirk during the 13th C. But probably the most famous Whitekirk pilgrim was an Italian diplomat named Piccolomini, later to become Pope Pius II, who was shipwrecked near Dunbar while on a mission to Scotland in December 1435.

About this same time, James I is known to have had a number

of guest houses built for the increasing number of pilgrims to Whitekirk. An exciting archaeological discovery was recently made of the barn on the site, according to Dr Peter Yeoman of Historic Scotland:

> ...when fragments of a shrine or altar, decorated with the Cistercian rose motif and an encircled cross, were found. It is even possible that this was part of the shrine dedicated in 1309, and broken up as a building stone at the Reformation. Further archaeological work has confirmed that the no longer visible site of the well is as marked on Ordnance Survey maps. It is not known whether a separate chapel stood here, although this is quite possible. Healing rituals would have taken place at the well, and pilgrims would have been given the holy water to take away in return for their offerings.[52]

Whitekirk was close to Edinburgh; it is known that James IV was a regular visitor, sometimes taking lodgings in the guest houses, and, it is said, 'partaking of cards and other entertainments during his short stay.'[53] No pilgrim's badge or token has ever been identified directly with this site, although Dr Peter Yeoman says regarding Whitekirk that 'it is possible that a 15th C badge depicting the Assumption of the Virgin Mary, found at East Castle on the Berwickshire coast east of Whitekirk, may have originated from the East Lothian shrine.'[54] This badge is made of tin alloy. The sacred well is now blocked up, and today, a yearly modern-day pilgrimage tradition continues, beginning at Whitekirk and ending at St Mary's Church, Haddington, reminiscent of earlier times.[55]

Whitekirk means 'white church' and has associations with the 'White Monks', the Cistercians. The Cistercians, of whom the founder of the medieval Knights Templar, St Bernard of Clairvaux, was a member, built important monasteries in Britain, including the famous Scottish ones of Melrose (1136) and Newbattle (1140). The headquarters of the medieval Knights Templar in Scotland was nearby at Balantradoch, now called the village of Temple, close to where early saints such as Cuthbert and Kentigern did their missionary work.

St Baldred of Tyninghame is stated in the *Historia Dunelmensis Ecclesiae* by Symeon of Durham to have died in 756

AD. It was said that Baldred was St Kentigern's disciple, and that he had committed to memory the facts of the life of St Kentigern. Scholars know that there was a lost *Life of Kentigern* in regular use at Glasgow Cathedral which may have incorporated material attributed to Baldred.[56] These issues are still being researched, but scholars now believe that it is possible that St Baldred was a likely source for some of the information about St Kentigern that made its way into later works.

St Triduana's Well

St Triduana's Well, also called St Modwenna, is located at Restalrig in Edinburgh, and is one of the earliest religious sites there. A church has existed at Restalrig from the 12th C, but it was likely a place of pilgrimage and worship long before then. Legend has it that the beautiful young lady, Triduana, grew tired of the unwanted attentions of a Pictish prince. Marianna Lines, in *Sacred Stones, Sacred Places*, elaborates:

> ...the King sent some messengers to ask for her hand in marriage, whereupon Triduana asked what it was that the prince so admired. The answer was 'the transcendent beauty of your eyes.' Her reply was a macabre refusal, as she plucked out her eyes and put them on a thorn stick with the words, 'Accept what your prince desires.' Triduana subsequently wandered south, ending up in Restalrig, Lestalryk as it was known, in Lothian, the kingdom of Loth. Having secured her chastity in a rather extreme manner, she devoted the rest of her life to fasting, prayer and caring for a holy well... The name Triduana is holy, meaning 'lady of the three days' fast – it is derived from triduanum ieiunnium, a three days' fast, a well known institution in the Celtic church.[57]

So, a cult of the virgin saint grew around the site of this sacred spring at Restalrig and St Triduana's Well became a popular place of pilgrimage for healing any eye diseases in medieval times.

In 1477, King James III began the transformation of the church known as the Shrine of St Triduana into one of the Collegiate Churches of the time. A hexagonal building next to the rebuilt parish kirk houses this holy well today; the spring under the floor is now operated by a pump, where the water flows through Edinburgh and out of the well head at St Margaret's Well in the Queen's Park in Holyrood, near the Palace, and Arthur's Seat.[58]

Melrose Abbey: Saints Waltheof, Cuthbert and Aidan, and the heart of Robert the Bruce

The earliest monastery of Mailros, or Melrose, was founded at Old Melrose in the mid-7th C. It is thought that Old Melrose was founded by St Aidan and his monks of Iona, when they colonised the site from Lindisfarne. Cuthbert was the son of a local Anglian farmer, and as we saw before, he entered Old Melrose monastery in 651AD, after having a vision of St Aidan. Old Melrose was later destroyed by the Scots in 839AD.

It is known that another monastery was built here again by the 12th C. 'David I invited the Cistercians of Rievaulx to build their monastery here at the place sanctified by St Cuthbert, but they preferred the site 4 km (2.5 miles) to the west, taking the place-name with them. A chapel at Old Melrose continued to function as a place of pilgrimage.' [59] Waltheof was the stepson of David 1 and became a monk; in 1148, he became the second Abbot of the Cistercian monastery at Melrose. The *Melrose Chronicle* was written in medieval times and tells of cures affected by placing the afflicted part of the body next to the same part of the sculpted effigy of the saint. When Jocelin became Bishop of Glasgow (1174-99), head of the diocese which included Melrose, he carried on the campaign to have Waltheof canonized.

Archaeologist Dr Peter Yeoman, in his Historic Scotland book *Medieval Pilgrimage in Scotland*, describes the excavation work that has been done at the site of Melrose Abbey:

> It is difficult to know how significant this cult was, and to what extent Melrose Abbey was a place of pilgrimage. An exciting clue, however, was discovered during the clearing of debris from the site in the 1920's, when fragments of a tomb-shrine were uncovered... These pieces, along with the possible fragments found at Glasgow Cathedral, represent the only surviving tomb-shrines of later medieval saints to survive the Reformation. The Melrose fragments have been reconstructed to form one end of a

tomb chest of local stone... The chapter house at Melrose is also reputed to have been a royal shrine, housing the heart of King Robert I... What may well be a Melrose pilgrims' badge can be found in the collections of the National Museum of Scotland...[60]

The issue of the death of King Robert I (Robert the Bruce) and the story about his heart being brought back to Scotland by Sir James Douglas, we have the following:

> In 1329, Bruce died, to be succeeded, as he had arranged, by his grandson Robert II, the first of the Stuart dynasty. Before his death, he had expressed the wish that his heart be removed, placed in a casket, taken to Jerusalem and buried in the Church of the Holy Sepulchre. In 1330, therefore, Sir James Douglas, Sir William Sinclair, Sir William Keith and at least two other knights embarked for the Holy Land, Douglas carrying Bruce's heart in a silver casket hung around his neck. Their itinerary took them through Spain, where they made the acquaintance of King Alfonso XI of Castile and Leon, and accompanied him on his campaign against the Moors of Granada. On 25 March 1330, at the Battle of Tebas de Ardales, the Scots, riding in the vanguard, were surrounded. According to 14th century chronicles, Douglas removed from his neck the casket containing Bruce's heart and hurled it into the attacking host... Having hurled Bruce's heart at the foe, however, he and his fellow Scots did proceed to follow it, charging headlong into their adversaries. All of them died, with the exception of Sir William Keith... [who] is said to have retrieved the heart from the field, miraculously intact in its casket, and to have brought it back with him to Scotland. It was buried in Melrose Abbey...[61]

However, historian Dr Alan Macquarrie believes that 'it was not a reckless suicide charge which cost Douglas his life (the story of throwing the king's heart into the midst of his foes is a later invention – Barbour states that the casket containing the heart was found beside Douglas's body); it was a simple tactical error which cost him dearly. He and his men advanced too far from the rest of the attackers and were isolated and easily cut down...'[62] Again, we cannot say for sure today exactly how this whole drama unfolded, but the legend of the heart of the Bruce resting at Melrose lives on.

The incredible dedication and valour of Douglas and his men was extraordinary indeed. The medieval custom of a separate burial of the heart from the body was not only confined to this case, as it was also a custom among other European royalty at the time. Bruce's heart was said to have been buried at Melrose, while his body was buried at Dumfermline Abbey.

Melrose was also part of a larger group of Cistercian monasteries in Scotland, including Dundrennan (Dumfries and Galloway), Newbattle Abbey (Midlothian), Kinloss (Moray), Coupar Angus (Perth and Kinross), Balmerino (Fife), Culross (Fife), Deer (Aberdeenshire), Glenluce and Sweetheart (Dumfries and Galloway), among others.[63]

St Ninian of Whithorn

Another well-known Scottish saint is St Ninian of Whithorn, in Galloway. Ninian was a British bishop who lived sometime in the late 5th – early 6th C. Ninian is largely credited with evangelizing the southern Picts. Whithorn has been called the earliest cradle of Scottish Christianity by some. It is also known that there were already Christians to the north of Hadrian's Wall, judging from the writings of Tertullian and others, and this area may have included Galloway.[64]

The name Whithorn (Hwit Aerne) also known as Candida Casa, means 'shining white house'. It is likely that Ninian built his famous church in the very late 5th C and that his reputation as a great saint made Whithorn a major pilgrimage centre for centuries, right up to the time of the Reformation.

Archaeologists, in conjunction with the Whithorn Trust, have recently done excavation work at Whithorn which has virtually changed previous ideas about St Ninian. For example, it is now doubted that he actually ever went to Rome. This traditional legend of Ninian was based mainly on the works of Bede, who described how Ninian was taught at Rome, and then spent time under the famous Martin of Tours who died in 397AD. After this Ninian is supposed to have returned to Scotland to found his monastery and church. Bede also says that Ninian converted the southern Picts to Christianity and that his death and burial were within his church at Whithorn in 431AD.

But Dr Peter Yeoman, archaeologist, tells how these earlier legends of Ninian are now being questioned:

Almost all of this has been called into doubt in recent research, and it is certainly the case that Bede's sources were imprecise, and that he had something to gain by talking up the cult and the place to help his friend, Pecthelm, who had just been appointed as first Northumbrian Bishop of Whithorn. The alternative version suggests a pre-Christian origin for the Candida Casa placename, and that Whithorn was already established as a centre of trade and power for the local British population, within the sphere of Roman Carlisle. This version discounts Ninian's travels to Rome and Tours, and any missionary work outwith the southwest; a church, yes, but nothing we would recognise as a monastery. What remains constant is that Ninian was a local sub-Roman Briton, who became the first Bishop... [he was] reverenced by the Christian population, whose burial-place did become a focus for pilgrimage soon after his death, in the fifth or early sixth century. What was thought to be a fragment of Ninian's church is now believed to date from the eighth century.[65]

So was Bede a particularily effective medieval 'spin doctor' with good intentions, helping out his friend? Or did he really go to Rome? We may never know for sure; but the fact remains that much of what was assumed about Ninian for certain has now been challenged by new archaeological evidence, something that is difficult to ignore. However, nothing absolutely definitive can be said yet. The cult of St Ninian was a quite a phenomenon in medieval times and it really put Whithorn 'on the map' for pilgrims from far away places.

Whithorn was unique, as from the time of the earliest records on, it was associated with healing by direct contact with the relics of St Ninian and was reputed to be one of the best places for the healing of leprosy, paralysis and blindness. Amazing stories of miraculous cures of leprosy even drew the attention of King Robert the Bruce, who endured a long and painful journey to Whithorn in 1329 three months prior to his death.[66] By the time the *Aberdeen Breviary* was printed in 1510, Ninian 'was at the height of his popularity, and the subject of national devotion to rival that of St Andrew.'[67] No small feat indeed. Whithorn also has a museum which houses an important collection of early carved stones. Nearby is Ninian's Cave, where many of the carved cross slabs were found.

Saints Medana and Patrick

Near Whithorn on the Rhinns of Galloway is Kirkmaiden, the Chapel of Medana. Again we have a story very similar to that of St Triduana, where the young maiden plucked out her eyes rather than go with an Irish prince who was entranced with her beauty. It is said that her eyes were thrown out to sea, where they became the Scares rocks halfway across to Whithorn.[67] The southwest of Scotland is full of many dedications to St Patrick, and it is clear that there was much communication between Ireland and Galloway. But it is not widely realised that St Patrick wasn't really an 'Irish saint', as is commonly thought, as he was actually of Romano-British stock.

Kilwinning and St Wynnin/Winnin

At Kilwinning is the church of Wynnin, or Winnin, the British form of Finan, its Irish form. The abbey at Kilwinning, like Kilbirnie Old Kirk, is a later building on or near the original foundation.[68] The primary source of information about St Winnin is in the *Aberdeen Breviary* (1510) which was written by William Elphinstone, Bishop of Aberdeen, possibly at the prompting of James IV. It is believed that St Winnin died on 21 January 715AD, and 21 January is his feast day. Kilwinning is also famous as the location of one of the very earliest Masonic lodges in Scotland called 'Mother Kilwinning', to be discussed in chapter 8.

There remains a piece of a Celtic cross said to have been erected by St Winnin in honour of St Brigit outside of the church which he is said to have built on the present site of Kilwinning Abbey. The fragment of the cross is preserved in the North Ayrshire Museum, Saltcoats, but unfortunately no trace of the original church or settlement survives. Here we see an implied connection between St Winnin and St Brigit.

St Brigit

St Brigit in Scotland is mostly associated with the Hebridean islands, but she is also known from very early times in Ireland. The *Annals of Ulster* give the year of her birth as 452AD and report her death at the age of 70. She is thought to have founded a major church at Kildare in about 500AD, and there is evidence of popular devotion to her into the late 6th C. But there isn't any actual evidence of a Christian historical abbess named St Brigit; the earliest references to a Brigit are to a goddess. Two Lives of St Brigit, one by Cogitosus and the other called the *Vita Prima*, are dated to about 680AD and are the earliest known Lives of an Irish saint in existence. 'The *Vita Prima* closely identifies Brigit with the cause of the kings of Leinster, the province in which Kildare was situated... *Cogitosus' Vita Brigiti*... is rather a string of miracle stories intended to illustrate her sanctity, her great faith...'[69]

One of the main focuses of her posthumous miracles was 'a huge millstone, which she had, after death, helped the prior of Kildare to find, and which was later placed near the gate of the monastery where, we are told, 'it cures diseases of the faithful who touch it.'[70] Another miracle-legend uses fire imagery. Here, St Brigit was caught in a sudden rainstorm while tending sheep, took off her soaking wet cloak and hung it 'on a sunbeam' to dry. St Brigit was also famous for giving away many of her father's prized possessions to the poor, much to his chagrin. Later, she joined a religious community, answering God's call.

Kildare was renowned in early Ireland for having a fire that never went out, tended by the faithful nuns and holy women of St Brigit. This idea of a perpetual fire, or flame, is very central in accounts of St Brigit, as is the concept of many miracles of food and drink, a Celtic 'cauldron of plenty' theme. Brigit was patroness of fire, smith-work, poetry, leechcraft (healing) and the arts.

It is obvious that a number of the stories about St Brigit seem to incorporate a great deal of material from earlier accounts of the goddess Brigit, as many scholars now note. It is likely that the holy women of Kildare may have been the Christian inheritors of a college of women who were once attendants at the shrine of Brigit the goddess in earlier times. Even in ancient Rome, the vestal virgins, who kept the perpetual flame burning in their special shrine, were a popular devotional cult. 'Brigit the goddess is not a single figure, however. There seem to have been several different Brigits, many of whom have an association with fire. Three Brigits, daughters of the Dagda, are described in Cormac's Glossary as the goddesses of poetry, leechcraft, and smithcraft.'[71]

The number 19

An intriguing, yet highly speculative, correlation may exist with the number 19 and some earlier goddess and lunar-orientated societies. For example, Callanish, if you think of it as an ancient lunar observatory or temple, also has a possible connection with the number 19 in terms of a cycle of years. As we saw in chapter 3, at Callanish every 18.61 years a rather rare astronomical phenomenon called 'the southern extreme of the major standstill' occurs. The Greeks said the sun god of the north, 'whom they called the Hyperborean Apollo, visited the northern temple of the moon goddess once every 19 years, a mythic expression of the coincidence of solar and lunar calendars.'[72] Callanish, some archaeologists now believe, must be viewed in its entirety, and the landscape around it should be considered as part of the site as well. It is possible that the ancients who built it may have perceived the landscape itself as being female. As the number of Brigit's priestesses at Kildare was said to be 19 in some accounts, is this perhaps a remnant of some kind of early lunar or goddess tradition(s) somehow involving the number 19? Of course, this cannot be confirmed or denied for sure, but in other folklore traditions around the world, there also exist connections between the number 19 and various goddess or and lunar themes.

The number nine also comes into play, with other accounts saying that the number of attendants at Brigit's fire at Kildare was nine, a number known to have been connected with the triple goddess and the famous 'ninth wave' of illumination in early Celtic sources.

Bride and St Brigit in the Hebrides

St Brigit is connected with the early Celtic festival of Imbolc, the eve of the first of February. She is also mentioned in early Welsh accounts, associated mainly with healing and certain sacred wells.[73] Brigit was a major Celtic goddess with shrines dedicated to her having been found all over mainland Europe in addition to Scotland, Wales, England and Ireland.

In Scotland, especially the Hebrides, there has always been a strong tradition of Bride in earlier times. Bride was the goddess of Summer, the opposite of the old winter hag, the Cailleach. In the east of Scotland, the Cailleach was called the Carlin. In earlier Scottish tradition, the connection between these two goddess figures is evident. The Cailleach herself said to have created the Hebrides; the very name 'Hebrides' is thought to have come from I-Bride, the islands of Bride. As Stuart McHardy notes, there are also references to Bride in other parts of Scotland:

> There are in Angus alone several Bride-names that are not associated with Christian sites which is what we would expect if the idea of St Bridget came in with Gaelic-speaking priests... Chadwick is said to have believed that Bride originated in Scotland... and Small... mentions that Bride originated in Glen Esk in Angus... [His] statement about Glen Esk is corroborated by a place-name, Bride's Bed, attached to a strange circular excavation at the foot of Craig Maskeldie at the head of Glenesk, and the neighbouring glen, Glen Clova, too, has an interesting Bride place-name, Bride's Coggie...[74]

He continues with more information about the Nine Maidens tradition:

> St Bridget is associated with a particularly Pictish group at Abernethy. These are the Nine Maidens who are variously said to have come to Abernethy from Glen Ogilvy, a few miles north of Dundee... and to have arrived with St Bridget from Ireland. These Nine Maidens, unusually, crop up as a group of Pictish saints in *Forbes' Breviary*, but I have found no reference to them as such in Irish sources... the cult of the Nine Maidens with its associated wells lasted until a century ago when the farmer at Pittempton, just outside Dundee, covered up the Nine Maidens Wells in the late 1870s because too many people were visiting it...[75]

The great importance of oral tradition in early Celtic society, including Scotland, can yield some interesting information about subjects like this. The place-name of Bride's Bed mentioned above is also interesting in light of certain Hebridean customs that survived even into the late 18th C, where on 1 February it was usual to

> make a bed with corn and hay, over which some blankets are laid in a part of the house near the door. When it is ready, a person goes out and repeats three times *'a Bhrid, a Bhrid, thig an nall's dean do leabaidh'* (Bride, Bride, come in; thy bed is ready.) One or more candles are left burning near it all night.[76]

So St Brigit in her many manifestations is one of the more interesting Celtic saints regarding how the old and new traditions were often merged together. By incorporating, rather than ignoring, some of these earlier traditions, it seems that the church enabled communities to accept Christianity with more ease that would have otherwise been the case. But overall, St Brigit remains a genuine enigma even today.

Saints Beya, Michul of Bute, Kessog, Catan, Marnoc, Mirren and Convall

Other Scottish saints that we also don't know a lot about, but know existed, include Beya, Michul of the isle of Bute, Kessog of the Loch Lomond area, Catan, Marnoc, Mirren of Paisley and Convall of Renfrew. Commenting on the unfortunate lack of records about many of Scotland's early saints, Dr Alan Macquarrie says 'there can be no doubt that, whether as a result of neglect or systematic destruction, the vast bulk of Scotland's liturgical and hagiographic writings have been lost. What survives, mainly the 12th C vitae and the *Aberdeen Breviary*, provides a tantalizing glimpse of what must once have existed in a nation proud of its saintly traditions.'[77]

Glasgow's Govan Old Parish Church

In Glasgow's Govan Old Parish Church, an ornately carved stone sarcophagus may have formed part of St Constantine's shrine, as the church is dedicated to St Constantine. However, there has been much speculation among scholars as to exactly which Constantine this refers to. Dr Alan Macquarrie argues that the founder of Govan was either the Scottish king Constantine, son of Kenneth, who reigned from 862-878AD, or, his son Donald, who reigned from 889-900.

Archaeologist Anna Ritchie, in *Govan and its Carved Stones*, believes that the sarcophagus can be dated to the latter half of the 9th C, saying 'this is the only sarcophagus carved from solid stone known from pre-Norman northern Britain, and there are few parallels even from southern Britain.'[78] In addition to the sarcophagus, there are two magnificently carved crosses and two cross slabs at Govan, and a very unique group of 'hogback' carved stones. A 'hogback' is a personal memorial designed to lie along the grave at ground level consisting of a solid block of stone carved into a long hump-backed shape.

Govan has a remarkable heritage of early Christian carved stones, generally dating from between the 9th and 11th centuries. The existing church was built in the late 19th C; the original Old Govan Parish Church was probably built in the late 9th C. Two skeletons excavated at Govan Old Parish Church have recently been carbon-dated to some time between 434 and 601AD. This discovery makes them among the *earliest known Christian remains that have been found in Scotland*, possibly seriously challenging Whithorn. More research needs to be done.

Recently, however, a much more controversial theory about exactly who might have been buried in the stone sarcophagus at Old Govan Parish Church has come to light. Local researcher Hugh McArthur of Glasgow claims that it is not St Constantine who was buried there at all, but King Arthur! He bases this claim on several things: that it is a Dark Age sarcophagus, that there isn't a single Christian symbol on it and that there is a Celtic warrior carving on the side engraved with a letter 'A' on it. Experts can't say for sure who was buried in it, though, as the lid and skeletal remains associated with the sarcophagus disappeared long ago. Scholars understandably scoff at such suggestions, saying that there is no way anyone can prove anything about the historical King Arthur from such meagre evidence. But this example shows again how the power of tradition and legend in relation to early Scottish sites is still with us today, factual or not. Like the various stories of the Celtic saints, Arthurian legends have also always been popular in Scotland, something to be be further discussed in chapter 6.

But now we will take a closer look at those Scottish saints who evangelised the areas called the southern and northern kingdoms of the Picts. Much of this is a story that has been largely untold or misunderstood – that of the Culdees, or Celi De. Let us begin our journey.

Notes

[1]   Bradley, I, *Celtic Christianity*, Edinburgh University Press, Edinburgh, 1999, ix.

[2]   Macquarrie, A, *The Saints of Scotland*, John Donald, Edinburgh, 1997, 75.

[3]   Clancy, T, and Markus, G., *Iona: The Earliest Poetry of a Celtic Monastery*, Edinburgh University Press, Edinburgh, 1995, 10.

[4]   Ibid.

[5]   Ibid.

[6]   Ibid, 11.

[7]   Macquarrie, op cit, 84.

[8]   Henebry, R., 'The Life of Columbcille', ZCP III, London, 1901, 566-7.

[9]   Purser, J., *Scotland's Music*, Mainstream, Edinburgh, 1992, 33.

[10] Ralls-MacLeod, K., *Music and the Celtic Otherworld*, Edinburgh University Press, Edinburgh, 2000, 101.

[11] Stewart, M, *The Forgotten Monarchy of Scotland*, Element, Shaftesbury, 1998, 69-70.

[12] Ross, A, *The Folklore of the Scottish Highlands*, Batsford, London, 1976, 132.

[13] Smith, D, *Celtic Travellers: Scotland in the Age of Saints*, HMSO, Edinburgh, 1997, 13.

[14] Hughes, K, and Hamlin, A., *Celtic Monasticism*, Seabury Press, New York, 1981, 41.

[15] Boece, H, *Scotorum Historiae*, ed. By J. Bellenden, 1531, 252.

[16] Elder, I. H, *Celt, Druid, and Culdee*, London, 1947, 110-1.

[17] Ferguson, F, *The Identity of the Scottish Nation*, Edinburgh Univ. Press, Edinburgh, 1998, 64-5.

18   Ibid, 66.
19   Ibid.
20   Smith, op cit , 15.
21   Ibid.
22   Ibid, 44.
23   Ibid, 45.
24   Ibid.
25   McKerracher, A, *Perthshire in History and Legend*, John Donald, Edinburgh, 1988, 4.
26   Foster, S, *Picts, Gaels, and Scots*, Historic Scotland/B.T. Batsford Ltd, London, 1996, 20.
27   Broun, D, 'Pictish Kings 761-839: Integration with Dal Riata or Separate Development?', in *The St. Andrews Sarcophagus*, ed. By S. Foster, Four Courts Press, Dublin, 1998, 72.
28   Pennant, T, *A Tour in Scotland, Vol. II*, Chester, 1774, 330.
29   Macinlay, J, *Folklore of Scottish Lochs and Springs*, Wm. Hodge & Co., Glasgow, 1893, 30.
30   Spence, L, *The History and Origins of Druidism*, Rider, London, 1947, 37.
31   Ibid.
32   Smith, op cit, 46.
33   Smith, op cit, 48.
34   Ibid.
35   Smith, op cit, 18.
36   Macinlay, op cit, 130.
37   Anderson, M O, '*Lothian and the Early Scottish Kings*', *The Scottish Historical Review*, Vol. xxxix, Thomas Nelson & Sons, Edinburgh, 1960, 98.
38   Smith, op cit, 20.
39   Smith, op cit, 21.
40   McHardy, S, *Scotland: Myth, Legend and Folklore*, Luath Press Edinburgh, 1999, 50.
41   *Historic Dunning: A Brief History of an Old Perthshire Village*, Dunning Community Council, Dunning, 2.
42   McHardy, op cit, 50.
43   Macquarrie, op cit, 156-7.
44   Yeoman, P, *Pilgrimage in Medieval Scotland*, Historic Scotland/B.T. Batsford, London, 1999, 16.
45   Ibid.
46   Ibid, 28.
47   McHardy, S, *Strange Secrets of Ancient Scotland*, Lang Syne, Glasgow, 1989, 30.
48   Macquarrie, op cit, 133.
49   'Was Glasgow's St. Mungo really a Lothian Boy?', *Edinburgh Evening News*, Monday 2 September 2000, 4.

50 MacNeill, F M, *The Silver Bough*, '*The Local Festivals of Scotland*', Volume 4, Stuart Titles Ltd, Glasgow, 1968, 108.
51 Smith, op cit, 21.
52 Yeoman, op cit, 50-1.
53 Ibid.
54 Ibid.
55 Smith, op cit, 21.
56 Macquarrie, op cit, 121.
57 Lines, M., *Sacred Stones, Sacred Places*, St. Andrew Press, Edinburgh, 1992, 72-3.
58 Ibid.
59 Yeoman, op cit, 45.
60 Ibid.
61 Baigent, M & Leigh, R, *The Temple and the Lodge*, Little, Brown & Co, New York, 1989, 39.
62 Macquarrie, A, *Scotland and the Crusades*, John Donald, Edinburgh, 1997, 74-5.
63 Fawcett, R, *Scottish Abbeys and Priories*, Historic Scotland, B.T. Batsford, London, 1994, 127.
64 Brooke, D, *Wild Men and Holy Places: St. Ninian, Whithorn, and the Medieval Realm of Galloway*, Canongate, Edinburgh, 1994, 10.
65 Yeoman, op cit, 33.
66 Ibid.
67 Smith, op cit, 10.
68 Ibid.
69 Bradley, I, op cit, 10.
70 Clancy, T O, 'Columba, Adomnan, and the cult of Saints in Scotland', *Spec Scotorum: Hope of the Scots*, [Ed. By D. Broun and T. O. Clancy], T&T Clark, Edinburgh, 1999, 6.
71 Low, M, *Celtic Christianity and Nature*, Edinburgh University Press, Edinburgh, 1996, 158.
72 Walker, B, *The Women's Encyclopedia of Myths and Secrets*, Harper & Row, San Francisco, 1983, 117.
73 Green, M, *Celtic Goddesses*, British Museum Press, London, 1995, 202.
74 McHardy, S, 'The Wee Dark Fowk o' Scotland, The role of oral transmission in Pictish studies', *The Worm, the Germ, and the Thorn*, [Ed. By D. Henry], Pinkfoot Press, Balgavie, 1997, 110.
75 Ibid.
76 Hutton, R, *The Stations of the Sun*, Oxford University Press, Oxford, 1996, 137.
77 Macquarrie, Saints, 10.
78 Ritchie, A, *Govan and its Carved Stones*, Pinkfoot Press, Balgavie, 1999, 16.

CHAPTER FIVE

The Culdees: Servants and Companions of God

MANY OF THE EARLY SAINTS in Scotland flourished between the foundation of Whithorn around 400 AD and the sack of Iona by the Norse Vikings around 800 AD. The period from the 5th to the 8th centuries has often been thought of as a 'Golden Age' of Celtic Christianity, when much of Europe was still in the so-called 'Dark Ages'.

We are told more about this by Professor Michael Lynch in *Scotland, A New History*:

> The search for Scotland's history is almost indistinguishable from the quest for Scotland's faith... The revival in the Irish church in the 8th century of the cult of asceticism, a return to the purity of the Columban-type pilgrim, was also felt in Pictland. In the next two centuries, new communities of Celi De (servants of God) were established, but they were no longer confined to minor centres such as Loch Leven; they were now also attached to major royal and religious centres such as Kilrimont and Dunkeld. The Culdees, as they are usually called, are the symbol of a Celtic revival in a post-Columban church...[1]

What we now call 'Scotland' did not actually officially emerge until the 9th C. It is known that before then there were four main racial and cultural groupings, each of which maintained their independence: the British of Strathclyde and Galloway, the Picts, who occupied the largest part of Scotland, the Scots of Dalriada who raided and then settled in Argyll from Ireland, and the Anglo-Saxons of Northumbria who pushed into southern Scotland. 'From about 800AD, a fifth group, the Norse of Norway and Denmark, harried and then colonised large areas of northern Scotland and the Western Isles.'[2]

So given this situation, putting together the story of the early church in Britain, let alone those who are later called 'Culdees', is understandably a challenging one. Ian Armit of Historic Scotland comments that the early kingdoms of 'Strathclyde and Rheged, under the influence of Rome, seem to have adopted Christianity even before St Ninian's arrival at Whithorn, around 400AD...'[3] Other scholars have agreed with this viewpoint. But this leaves us with the tantalising question: But where exactly, then, *did* they get Christianity from? Again, scholars are still divided about this issue, too.

He further comments that although the Romans were in parts of lowland Scotland, 'their empire appears to have contributed little to the social institutions, settlement forms or material culture of the Picts.'[4] For example, it is also known that later on in the 6th C, St Columba needed an interpreter when he visited Pictish areas, as they still spoke their distinctive language.

The Culdees, or Celi De, are generally thought of as 'servants of God', as devout religious men and women, or, even as the last, romanticised 'holdouts' against an encroaching Roman church. However, the term 'Celi De' in the manuscripts can often mean a great variety of things: an acetic monk or nun, a reference to religious celibates in general, an indication of married men who adopted a religious life, or a reference to someone who is bound by obligations of poverty or self-denial.

In short, although the term is generally understood to mean a devout servant of God, the question, with historical hindsight, is exactly *what type* of servant of God were they referring to? Pictish? Gaelic? Northumbrian? The answer seems to be that it depends on the writer of the manuscript, and also the region or area that they're talking about. Frankly, it ends up leaving us with more questions than it answers, as the history of early Scotland is complex. So it isn't really possible to exactly define the term 'Culdee' uniformly, as we shall soon see.

The term 'Culdee'

The word 'Culdee' is found in manuscript references to holy men and women in Ireland, Scotland, Wales and England. In each area, the term was used according to the prevailing beliefs and customs of that time. But *it is not found outside of the British Isles*, which is interesting to note. The widespread erroneous assumption in the past has been that the term 'Culdee' meant those churches or monasteries that were founded or started in honour of St Columba of Iona, but that doesn't appear to actually have been the case at all, as the term had much wider connotations than only the Columban church. One often sees terms like 'early British church', 'Culdees', and 'Celtic communities', all of which have often been presumed to mean the same thing. Those called 'Culdees' were also found in Anglo-Saxon and Northumbrian areas as much as they were in 'Celtic' areas, according to medieval sources.

In fact, Culdees are recorded in church documents 'as officiating at St Peter's, York, until 936AD. And... the Canons of York were called Culdees as late as the reign of Henry II. In Ireland, a whole county was named Culdee, declared with emphasis when reference was heard at a court hearing in the 17th century.'[5] There are references to Culdees in Scotland up until around the time of David I in the late 11th C, often spelled as 'Keledei' in manuscripts.

Jocelin's *Life of St Kentigern* is the earliest Scottish record of the name of Celi De.[6] Although Jocelin's history of Kentigern was written in the late 12th C, it was compiled from much earlier sources. In it, the term Celi De is Latinised as Calledei, and we learn that

> ...they were understood by the Scotch, in the 12thC, to have been a religious order of clerks who lived in societies, under a superior, within a common enclosure, but in detached cells, associated in a sort of collegiate rather than coenobitical brotherhood – solitaries in their domestic habits, though united in common observance, both religious and secular, of a strict nature.[7]

Before the 12th C the whole Celtic ecclesiastical way of life was monastic in nature, with the office of the abbot exalted above the episcopate. The diocese form of church government was *not* the early form of the structure of the Celtic church. Many of the old religious communities were referred to as Keledei, or Celi De, and are generally understood to have been those communities that still kept to the older ways.

The Celtic tonsure and the dating of Easter

The Keledei were known to be distinctive about two major issues, among others, that were later discussed at the famous Synod of Whitby in 664AD. The first was their tonsure, which means the specific manner in which they wore their hair upon being initiated into holy orders. 'The Celtic tonsure, that of St John, was adopted among the Greeks, Britons and Irish, while the shaven crown, that of St Peter, an emblem of the crown of thorns, was the form agreed to by the Council of Toledo in 633AD, and was... common to the clergy and monks of western Europe... [However] Columba used white garments and the Celtic tonsure.'[8] Clearly, there are two different types of tonsure being referred to here, and the reference to St John may be particularly important, as we will later explore in chapter 8. Quite recently, in 1972, Pope Paul VI eliminated tonsure altogether so it is no longer generally practised in the Roman Catholic communities.

The other issue was the dating of Easter, which was different in the Roman and the Celtic churches, as each used a different calendar. Another clear difference was that unlike in the Roman church, some of the Celtic clergy were also allowed to be married, while others remained celibate.

The early church in Britain: Joseph of Arimathea

Some of the early Church Fathers wrote of a Christianity existing in Britain before the arrival of either St Palladius in 431AD, or St Augustine, in 597AD, two of the earliest missionaries that came to Britain.

Tertullian, the son of a Roman centurion, was born in Carthage. He became a Christian while a young man and his writings consist mainly of Christian apologetics and various homilies. He mentions in his *Adversus Judaeos*, written in about 200AD, that the extremities of Spain, various parts of Gaul, and 'the regions in Britain, which, though inaccessible to the Romans, have yielded to Christ.'[9] Origen was born in Alexandria, and was a renowned early Church Father in both Theology and the classics. He also refers to Britain in his work entitled *Against Celsus* in which he discusses how widespread the influence of the doctrine of Christianity was at the time. Writing in about 245AD, in the mid-3rd C, he said 'The land of Britain has received the religion of Christ'.[10] This means that they both thought, or had heard, that parts of Britain had already received Christianity.

In 304AD, according to the Venerable Bede, was the martyrdom of St Alban, said to have been the first Christian in Britain.[11] The modern-day English city of St Albans is named in his memory. This, then, would have been in the early 4th C.

In 313AD, the now-famous 'Edict of Milan' was issued by Constantine, after his vision of a cross at the Battle of Milvian Bridge. This Edict granted toleration to all religions in the Roman Empire, including Christianity, and was a real breakthrough for the early church in terms of stopping persecutions of Christians. The Christian Church was from that point on recognized as a legal entity and granted positive privileges. Obviously, as Constantine was not baptised a Christian until he was on his deathbed and was a previous worshipper of the sun god Apollo, there is the issue of not only matters of faith but also the fact that he surmised that Christianity could help him unify his empire further in political terms. As history has shown, he was right. Two years earlier, in 311AD, Constantine had hailed the sun, 'portraying the deity on his coins as his unconquerable ally, *Sol Invictus*. This cosmic arrangement between Emperor and solar god survived on Constantine's coinage long after the Battle of Milvian Bridge... it is certainly true that Jesus was often called *Sol Justitiae* or depicted in statuary in a form closely resembling the god Sol.'[12]

Eusebius, Bishop of Caesarea, had survived the infamous Diocletian persecution of Christians, to serve Constantine the Great. He wrote many learned works, and has preserved for us the text of a letter sent by the Emperor Constantine 'summoning the bishops of western Europe to a conference at Arles in 314AD. The names are recorded of three British bishops who were present at the Council, from York, London, and perhaps Lincoln, but more probably Colchester.'[13] This would have also been in the *early part of the 4th century*. Arles was in Gaul, which is part of modern-day, south central France.

Eusebius also attended the famous First Council of Nicaea, in

325AD, where the Nicene Creed that is still in use in many churches today was originally drawn up. This council defined orthodox trinitarian belief and also decided against the practice of celebrating Easter on the date of the Jewish Passover, as was the custom of certain eastern churches at the time.

At this Council, it is said the British bishops, in their absence, were given precedence as representing the church said to be founded by Joseph of Arimathea, causing a degree of jealousy among other churchmen, especially those from Gaul. Not surprisingly, some scholars have disputed this, leaving us no clearer about this issue today. Eusebius probably knew something of early British history from Constantine the Great, who historians know was proclaimed Emperor at York, England, by the troops on 25 July in 306 AD. As is now widely known, many legends continue to persist into modern times about Joseph of Arimathea and others coming to Britain in the first century. Many of these have Glastonbury as their focus.

Highly regarded Cambridge Celtic scholar Nora Chadwick tells us that

> ...we again find three British bishops, probably from the same sees, taking a prominent place in the Synod of Rimini summoned by Constantine in 359AD, in his efforts to formulate a unity of belief acceptable to the whole Church. Moreover, the part taken by the British bishops in continental councils is something more than a mere show of hands. The writings of both Hilary of Poitiers and St Athanasius, Patriarch of Alexandria, state repeatedly that they count the Britons among their supporters in combating Arianism.[14]

Arianism was considered a very troublesome heresy, especially in the 4th C, and it was officially declared heretical at the abovementioned Council of Nicaea. Arius, an Alexandrian priest, did not believe that God could essentially be 'three in One', a Trinity, as he believed that at some point, the Son had to have been created by the Father, implying that there was a time before that when the Son didn't exist. In doing so, he denied the true divinity of Christ in the eyes of the church, although he felt he was upholding true monotheism. This particular heresy survived down into more modern times, for example, with well-known men like Sir Isaac Newton ascribing to this belief system.

Such heresies were understandably a real thorn in the side of the early church, which was trying to find greater unity amidst its tremendously diverse communities. But we do have here what appears to be testimony from some of the early Church Fathers that there were definitely Christian communities in the British Isles in very early times. Some scholars have said that they couldn't have possibly meant any of this literally, while others insist that the idea of an early apostolic mission cannot be ruled out either. So, the whole issue is still somewhat controversial, but with academic opinion leaning more now in favour of the definitive early existence of early Christian communities in the British Isles.

It is also strongly believed that after 177AD, when intensive persecution of Christians began in Gaul, some Christians would have obviously tried to flee northwards, reaching Britain. There have also been a number of early Christian archaeological finds in Britain, from finding the Chi-Rho cross in Roman mosaic pavements, to the mural paintings in a little Christian chapel at Lullingstone, Kent, dated to about 360AD, which confirms the presence of Christians in Britain *well before* 597AD.[15] We also know that St Ninian was probably at Whithorn as early, or even earlier, than 397AD, for example.

Yet, in spite of all of this, many school textbooks, Protestant, Catholic, or otherwise, still insist that the introduction of Christianity in Britain began with the arrival of Augustine in 597 AD! Obviously, one has to wonder why.

But surprisingly perhaps, the Vatican has actually been more emphatic in correcting this erroneous assumption than many may realise. Caesar Baronius (1538-1607) was a Cardinal from a noble family who also earned a doctorate in law at Rome in 1561. He was appointed Librarian of the Vatican in 1596 and wrote his influential 12-volume historical work entitled *Annales Ecclesiastici*.[16] In it he tells of how he found in the Vatican Library an ancient manuscript in which was described the voyage of a company of our Lord's friends, travelling in an old abandoned boat that was without oars or sails, who landed at Marseilles, where they spread out over southern France and were credited with the founding of many churches. Among this company was Joseph of Arimathea, who is thought to have gone further north into Britain from Gaul, as he clearly would have had to flee after being targeted by the Sanhedrin after the Crucifixion of Christ.

The early British historian Gildas said that Joseph of Arimathea introduced Christianity into Britain in the last year of the reign of Tiberius, which would be about 37AD. Baronius dates this arrival in Marseilles as occurring in 35AD, which would make it possible for Joseph to have been in Britain when Gildas said he was. Some French church records also confirm what Baronius said. Both Baronius and another respected Vatican librarian, Alford, refer to ancient documents in the Vatican library that basically say that St Joseph was the 'Apostle of Britain'.

Early legendary accounts in Britain: Mary

The 4th C *Vindicta Salvatoris* and *Evangelium Nicodemi,* which are in the Vatican library today, both record that Joseph fled Palestine and settled outside of the Roman empire, somewhere in the far north. In 597AD St Augustine of Canterbury came to Britain at the request of Pope Gregory, and after travelling widely, wrote to the Pope telling him that on an island in the west of the country there was a church where some of Jesus' original disciples had worshipped and where it was said that Christ had built a church. It was, he said, 'sacred to Mary, the Mother of God.' Incredibly, this letter went on to imply that Augustine believed that he had actually found the church that Christ built.[17] Before the 8th C churches were usually dedicated to a saint whose bones were actually buried there, so in this case it would have been Mary, strange as this may sound to us today. Some researchers believe this church was at what is now the village of Llanerchymedd, in the centre of the island of Anglesey.

At this location there was a holy well that from very early times is known to have had great significance. We know this because the two most important Christian leaders of Anglesey just prior to Augustine's visit there, abbots Seiriol and Cybi, are said to have made a daily pilgrimage to a holy well at the centre of the island. A question, some ask, is: did Augustine discover something there relating to Mary or the early disciples, that Pope Gregory, an early advocate of the Assumption theory of Mary, decided was best to keep under wraps?

If Mary was 'taken up body and soul into Heaven', as is the essence of the Assumption dogma, then her bones cannot be found anywhere here on earth. Intriguingly, belief in the Assumption of Mary first appeared in church writings in the 6th C – at the same time that Augustine and Pope Gregory lived, although the Assumption was not officially declared until 1950 by Pope Pius XII.

After World War II, Father Giovanni Benedetti, an archaeologist attached to the Vatican Museum, researched and concluded, like most historians, that there was no evidence that the tomb in the Valley of Jehosophat, to the east of Jerusalem, was really Mary's tomb, as many then believed.

But he did, however, say that he had uncovered persuasive evidence for her tomb elsewhere – *possibly in Britain*, which had long since been forgotten. When he reported back his findings to the Vatican,

> ...he was summoned to appear before... the Holy Inquisition... On pain of excommunication, Benedetti was instructed to discontinue his work and was forbidden to publish or speak publicly about his research. A good Catholic and an employee of the Vatican, he complied... The Holy Office position... was evidently that... the second tomb was simply a Dark Age legend; they considered that any further investigations into the subject by a Vatican official would appear divisive.[18]

Benedetti also believed that Mary, the Holy Mother, was the Holy Grail. Obviously, there had been many legends around and the church was apparently only trying to sort out fact from fiction. But if there was a persistent 'Dark Age legend' about a so-called tomb of Mary being in Britain, and there was nothing at all to it – this being only a harmless tale, so to speak – then why go to all of the trouble of silencing Fr. Benedetti? One can only wonder.

After this, he remained completely silent about his research for the rest of his life. In 1950, when Benedetti was just about to publish his findings, Pope Pius XII declared the Assumption dogma, which meant that there was no tomb of Mary to be found anywhere on earth, as she was said to be taken up body and soul to Heaven. Obviously, there have been many legends throughout the centuries about a possible early arrival of certain of the disciples of Jesus to Britain and/or Gaul. Perhaps understandably, the Vatican only wanted to research the matter further, to stop false rumours from proliferating any further, a noble enough aim.

But for there to be total silence about the issue altogether is unusual, especially considering the fact that according to the respected 12th C historian William of Malmesbury, Augustine left his assistant Paulinus behind at the church on Anglesey to help with its repair. There is also a marker stone on Anglesey about four kilometres from Llanerchymedd, near Tre-Ysgawen House, which dates from the period of Augustine's visit in the late 6th C. This stone has on it a contemporary inscription which confirms Paulinus' presence in the area.[19]

Today, it would appear, no one seems to know for sure what to think about this controversial issue, but once again, we have yet another legend about early Christian arrivals in Britain. It is also hard to believe that Augustine and Paulinus, being educated, devout churchmen of their time, would 'waste their time' on something that had absolutely no consequence or import.

In fact, it is likely that they were trying to carefully investigate everything in order to get to the bottom of the situation in Britain and would therefore have had no reason to lie or exaggerate their claims, especially to their superiors in the Vatican including the Pope. And Fr Benedetti would obviously have had no reason to lie either. So we are left to wonder about this strange incident, or, as some believe, a possible cover-up. No one can say for sure; the Vatican says that as the Assumption dogma has already been officially declared, there is obviously no reason to inquire any further as to a possible tomb of Mary. So, the legend remains.

Again, at the very least, what this all seems to illustrate is the acknowledged power of certain legendary accounts to stay quite consistent over the centuries. Also, as St Augustine's claims in his letter to Pope Gregory *have never been officially denied or disproved*, we are left with no definitive information about this situation, only speculation.

But if the early church in Britain *did* have some claim to an early apostolic mission of some type, then this clearly wouldn't have been in the best interests of Rome, for a number of reasons.

Some maintain that all of these legends are just that – mere legends. Others retort with the fact that there seem to be quite a few of them from a number of different places that have brought up issues that have still not been adequately explained. So, 'the jury is still out', it would seem.

Early British legends about St Paul

Another persistent legend through the centuries is that it was St Paul who may have first introduced Christianity to Britain. For example, St Paul's Cathedral in London is named after him. As is also widely known, St Paul's mission was to preach to the Gentiles and to go to the 'ends of the earth' to do so. Back then, Britain was considered to be literally near the ends of the known world. The following account illustrates the continuing tradition about the importance of St Paul in early British church history into the 20th C:

> In 1931, Pope Pius XI received at the Vatican the visiting English Roman Catholic Mayors of Bath, Colchester and Dorchester, along with a hundred and fifty members of the Friends of Italy Society. In his address to them, the Pope said that St Paul, not Pope Gregory, first introduced Christianity into Britain.[20]

Pope Gregory, as we know, sent St Augustine to Britain to preach the gospel in 597AD, the late 6th C. St Paul, then, if he did so, obviously would have travelled to Britain much earlier than that. Britain was also said to have been proclaimed Christian by King Lucius, at the National Council of Winchester in 156AD. Winchester was a known early Druidic centre of Britain which was said to have had its own Druidic college. It is said that Lucius declared at this council that Christianity was the 'natural successor' to Druidism.[21] This would have been in the mid-2nd C, quite early on, if it occurred as stated in this legendary account.

'British church' and 'Celtic church'

But the issue of what appear to be very early Christian communities in Britain brings up another key question: but were they necessarily *Celtic Christian* communities? The term early 'British church' is a very broad one, and the term 'Celtic Christian' can mean many different things. In certain writings, authors like to automatically link them together, which is not accurate. After all, the term 'Culdee' itself isn't found until the 8th C in Scotland. So, as one can see, the situation about the early church in the British Isles is quite complex.

It is also believed by some scholars that other Christian communities from elsewhere sought refuge in the British Isles, especially Ireland. Professor Adam Loughridge writes in the *New International Dictionary of the Christian Church* that the 8th C Irish author of the *Didache Litany* in Ireland, whose name was Oengus the Culdee, commemorates the fact that large numbers of scholars from the Middle East sought refuge in Ireland in the 8th and 9th centuries. Oengus provides lists of Bishops and Pilgrims who are said to have lived in groups of seven.[22] He says that the influence of the East Syrian Church, the Nestorians, on the monastic life of the Celtic church is quite evident.

It is also interesting to note that the *Didache Litany* and the *East Syrian Liturgy* of Mari and Addai follow the same form as the *Stowe Missal, and this contrasts with all other forms of the Eucharistic Liturgies that developed separately in the west.* Differing from the rest of the western church, Celtic Christian communities in certain places are likely to have embraced a theology, some say Johannine, that was probably taught to them by their Coptic and Syrian teachers. The Johannine tradition had as its focus the writings of St John.[23] Others disagree with this, but it is clear that not all so-called 'Celtic Christian' communities were alike, which is important to note in and of itself.

It also appears that in the early Irish Celtic church at least, there was what you might call a 'tribe of the church' with differing orders, grades, and functions, and this seems to have been consciously modelled on the Tribe of Levi, many of whose institutions it made its own. Some of the early Irish Celtic hermit monks were even called 'Judaic refugees' by some, as they still used the old calendar. The Irish church was highly respected in all of western Europe and beyond.

Also, the earliest music believed to have been sung by the Celtic Christians dates from the 3rd C. It appears that the isolated Ethiopian Church retained the most ancient of Christian music, possibly from original Palestinian or Temple sources, some scholars believe. Additional recent evidence of a fusion of a certain Celtic-Hebraic chant form is the result of the systematic deciphering by Haik Vantoura of the notation existing in the ancient Masoretic Hebrew *Old Testament* of the 9th C. The Masoretic author, Moses Ben Asher, noted in the text that the notation was 'delivered to him as passed down from the prophets of old'. Analysis by Vantoura reveals that there are many similarities in the embellishments, modes and melodies of the early Irish Psalmody and the Hebrew Temple chant of the *Book of Psalms*.[24]

So as one can see, the overall situation regarding the early church in the British Isles is quite complex, providing a necessary background before we look at the Culdees in Scotland. As we have seen, there have been many legendary accounts describing early Christian communities, as well as definitive factual ones. However, it does seem clear from these early references that an early Christian church of some type, with diverse communities, certainly did exist in the British Isles before 597AD. It also seems clear that they were viewed as being somehow 'different' from those of Rome, issues that were discussed at the Synod of Whitby in 664AD.

The Culdees in Scotland

Rev William Reeves, in his exhaustive 1864 work entitled *The Culdees of the British Isles* states that 'among the Cotton manuscripts in the British Museum is preserved a catalogue of the religious houses of England and Wales, at the end of which is a list of the Scotch sees... It is annexed to Henry of Silgrave's *Chronicle*, and as that compilation comes down from the year 1272...'[25] It lists the specific instances where the term 'Keldei' or 'Keledei' occurs in the record as pertains to Scotland. They are:

St Andrews	Episcopatus S. Andree	Canonici nigri	Keldei
Dunkeld	Episcopatus Dunkeldre	Canonici nigri	Keldei
Brechin	Episcopatus de Brechin		Keledei
Rosemarkie	Episcopatus de Ros		Keledei
Dunblane	Episcopatus de Dublin		Keledei
Dornach	Episcopatus de Katenesio		Keledei
Lismore	Episcopatus de Arguil		Keledei
Iona	Episcopatus in Insula		Keledei

In modern-day terms, the Scottish locations associated with what were major Culdee centres in earlier times are St Andrews, Dunkeld, Brechin, Rosemarkie, Dunblane, Dornach, Lismore and Iona.

These are the only cases where the specific terms 'Kelei' or 'Keledei' are used. The term 'Canonici nigri' refers to the regular canons of St Augustine, and are shown as existing at St Andrews and Dunkeld, and as *co-existing with* the 'Keldei', the Celtic clergy. In the other instances one can see that the term 'Canonici nigri' is not listed, meaning that at that particular location, the Keledei clergy predominated.

As Dr Ian Bradley points out in *Celtic Christianity*: 'relations between the Celi De and members of the new monastic orders seem to have been uneasy at St Andrews and Loch Leven and there was particular tension at Dunkeld where Cormac, bishop of the recently created diocese from 1114 to 1123, angered the existing Celi De community by his attempt to subordinate them to the newly installed Augustinian canons.'[26] Clearly, at this point, the Celtic clergy were beginning to feel that their identity was being submerged and understandably felt threatened.

Reeves goes on to say that after the major Keledei sites listed above, that there were also other important non-cathedral monasteries, who still adhered to the old ways, information that he gleaned from the charter sources. They are:

Lochleven	Kinross (esp. St Serf's island, Loch Leven)
Abernethy	Perthshire
Monymusk	Aberdeenshire
Muthill	Perthshire
Monifieth	Forfarshire

He further says that there were other churches which resembled these, like Scone, Montrose, Dull and Melrose, and that they could conceivably be added, but he says that his object is to only focus on the names of the particular churches or communities listed in the records as being specifically associated with the 'Keledei'. So, the ultimate number is probably even higher than the Reeves list. We will now take a more detailed look at each of the above places and their Celi De connections.

St Andrews

The original Celtic name of St Andrews was Cennrigmonaid (Kinrimont). Scholars now use Kilrymont, meaning 'the Head of the King's Mount'. It referred to the settlement on the promontory at the mouth of the Kinness Burn. The name Kinrymont was still in use in 747AD. The remains of 8th and 9th C religious activities have been found within the Cathedral precinct around St Rule's tower and also close to St Mary's church, Kirkhill. By 1144 Kinrymont became known as St Andrews.[27] Now known worldwide as the home of golf and site of Scotland's oldest university, St Andrews was also 'on the map' in medieval times, as it was considered the major ecclesiastical centre for much of the Middle Ages in Scotland. The cult of St Andrew was established in the 9th C, scholars believe.

The earliest bishop of St Andrews was Cellach in the 10th C. In 906AD, St Andrews became the major ecclesiastical centre of Scotland over Dunkeld. Also in 906AD, a major meeting was held at Scone on Moot Hill, called the 'hill of faith'. This was the same location where Robert the Bruce would later be crowned king of Scotland. This meeting was something akin to a 10th C church assembly. Present were King Constantine II and Cellach, the bishop of St Andrews. It was attended by both the clergy and laity, and the object of this national meeting was that 'the rights in churches and gospels should be kept in conformity with [the customs of] the Scots.'[28] This implies that they wanted to try and maintain, to some degree, what were viewed as their own native customs.

Also in the 10th C, the first version of the St Regulus Legend of St Andrews was recorded, and in 1070AD, St Rule's church was built. Even around the time of St Margaret, there were actually two churches at St Andrews – one was the Roman Church of St Andrew, which was used mainly when the king and bishop visited the city, and the other, the old foundation of St Cainnech, which was served by 13 Celi De clergy, was the more popular church at the time with the people.[29] In 1144AD the name of 'St Andrews' was in use, and by 1160AD, the building of the Cathedral was started. 1180AD also saw the earliest representation of a special cross associated with St Andrew, the Chapter seal of St Andrews. By 1318AD, the St Andrews Cathedral building was completed, four years after the Battle of Bannockburn.

Whether or not the relics of St Andrew ever were at St Andrews remains a debatable topic. Dr Sally Foster of Historic Scotland says:

> It is mere speculation that relics of St Andrew may have been at Kilrymont. Skene argues that they were brought from Hexham (also dedicated to St Andrew) in 732, when, or so he alleges, political instability in Northumbria led to Bishop Acca spending a period of exile in Pictland. Yet it is improbable that Acca had been at St Andrews... there is an absence of early dedications to St Andrew. The eastern origin of the foundation legends is certainly implausible, but throughout Europe the idea of the reborn Christian Roman Empire became popular after c.750, and this is mirrored in Pictland in the series of kings called Constantine. This might provide support for the existence of an 8th C cult of St Andrew in Scotland...[30]

Foster also says that it is unknown exactly how early the Culdee influence was felt at St Andrews, but that it was definitely known as a Culdee centre in early times. There are two major foundation legends that were written about St Andrews, dubbed by scholars as Version A and Version B.

Version A is older and is seen as the voice of the established Gaelic-speaking church raised against powerful claims from the south, especially York. Surprising as it may seem to us today, St Andrews faced a very serious challenge from York in 1072AD.

> It is clear from the earliest known papal letter sent to Scotland that the papacy regarded Scotland as within York's province... The full text of the A version of the legend sheds light on many

aspects of St Andrews... .it is the earliest piece of homogeneous prose to survive from eastern Scotland.'[31]

Not surprisingly, then, the focus of Version A is the self-confident assertion of St Andrews' archiepiscopal status.

Version B is twice as long, and is more Augustinian in focus.

The main concern of the Augustinian Account is not so much with the Episcopal status of Kilrymont, but with the status and fortunes of the Augustinian house founded by Bishop Robert in 1144. This new establishment found itself surrounded by older, more entrenched powers and interests, such as the Celi De community...[32]

But this relationship wasn't easy, as clear tensions existed. The Keledei coexisted with the Augustinians at St Andrews until William Bell was chosen bishop in 1332. After this, the Culdees were no longer allowed any power at St Andrews, as they were 'absolutely excluded from taking part in the election... neither does the name Keledei occur again in existing records...'[33] After this time the Augustinian canons were predominant at St Andrews and the Culdees were basically finished, in an official sense.

One of the most fascinating early medieval artefacts found in Scotland is the famous St Andrews sarcophagus, dated as late 8th C, as we learned in chapter 3. This sarcophagus depicts the theme of David holding open the jaws of a lion, and features motifs that resemble those found in the *Books of Kells*. Found in 1833 by workmen digging in the area of the later Cathedral at St Andrews, it seems to suggest to Professor Michael Lynch 'a church based firmly in an established royal centre rather than a missionary one. It hints at a church of kings of Picts and Scots, rather than a pan-Celtic one.'[34] Dr Sally Foster, an Historic Scotland expert on the St Andrews sarcophagus, is currently conducting further detailed research about this important archaeological find and one of Scotland's finest examples of Celtic artwork.

The early Celtic foundation at St Andrews was by St Kenneth, a friend of St Columba, and it

...marked a centre of mission to the southern Picts called Kilrymont. The cult of St Andrew was a conscious creation of the early kings of the Scots and Picts, possibly based on some holy relics brought to Scotland by St Regulus or St Rule to whom an earlier church on the Cathedral site is dedicated. Alternatively, Regulus was another Scottish holy man already associated with this site, which seems to have grown in stages from a cave by the shore (St Rule's or Lady Buchan's Cave), to a church on Kirkhill, to St Rule's Church and the Cathedral.[35]

The history of St Andrews is fascinating indeed, intertwining a heritage of the Picts, the Scots, the Culdees and the Augustinians, among others. Its royal connection remains even today, where Prince William began his university education at St Andrews University in Autumn 2001.

Dunkeld

The church of Dun-caillenn ('Fort of the Caledonians'), now called Dunkeld, was believed to have been founded about the year 820AD. The *Annals of Ulster*, 864AD, record the death of Tuathal, son of Artgus, chief-bishop of Fortrenn, and an abbot of Dun-caillenn. Dunkeld is inextricably tied up with the history of the Picts. Fortrenn was another name for Pictland and Dunkeld was an important ecclesiastical seat of Scotland. Dr Norman Davies, in his *The Isles: A History*, sums up about the early establishment of a royal centre called Fortriu or Fortrenn:

> Bede observed that in his day the northern Picts were separated from the southern Picts. The first historical king, Bridei mac Maelcon (mid-6thC), had a father with a British name and a stronghold in the Great Glen. At some point, however, a central royal establishment appeared in a region called Fortriu or Fortrenn. The royal hall at Forteviot was located on the banks of the River Earn. In the seventh century, part of southern Pictland was occupied by the Northumbrians until recovered by Brude mac Bili (r. 672-93), the victor of Nechtansmere. This may explain Bede's observation. In the eighth century, one king, Nechtan mac Derelei (r. 706-39), overran Dalriada but failed to conquer Strathclyde. Collectively, the rulers were known as the Kings of Fortrenn.[36]

The *Annals of Ulster*, record the death of Tuathal, chief-bishop of Fortrenn and abbot of Dunkeld. His successor to the abbacy of Dunkeld, however, doesn't seem to have enjoyed Episcopal orders, for his obituary in the *Annals of Ulster* states that he was 'Flaithbertach, son of Muircertach, superior (*princeps*) of Dun-caillen.'[37]

In 964AD, also according to the *Annals of Ulster*, 'Donnchadh, abbot of Dun-caillen, was slain in the battle of Moneitir', and again, in 1045AD, Cronan, abbott of Dun-caillen, is described as losing his life in a domestic encounter. This Cronan, states Reeves, was called Crinan in the *Pictish Chronicle* and was married to Bethoc, daughter of King Malcolm II and by her was father of the Duncan who was slain by MacBeth. The abbacy of Duncaillenn had now become an appendage of the Crown, for Edmund, a younger son of Malcolm III, in a grant to the Keledei of Lochlevin, is described as 'Abbott of Dunkeld, and moreover, Earl of Fife'. In Dunkeld, while the abbacy, together with its lands, descended to the Earl of Fife, the inferior ministers retained their corporate and clerical condition as the officiating ministers of the church.[38] So, clearly, Dunkeld was an important place at the time.

Dean Mylne, who was a canon of Dunkeld about 1485, has left to us in his *History of the Bishops of Dunkeld*, the following description of their ancient chapter:

> In this monastery Constantine, king of the Picts, placed religious men, commonly called Kelledei, otherwise Colidei, that is, God-worshippers, who, however, after the usage of the Eastern Church, had wives (from whom they lived apart when taking their turn in the sacred offices) as afterwards grew to be the custom in the church of the blessed Regulus, now called St Andrews... St David, the sovereign, who was the younger son of King Malcolm Canmore and the holy Queen Margaret, having changed the constitution of the monastery, erected it into a cathedral church; and, having superseded the Kelledei, created, about the year 1127, a bishop and canons, and ordained that there should in future be a secular college. The first bishop on this foundation was for a time abbot of that monastery, and subsequently a counsellor of the king.[39]

Rev Reeves comments that in his concluding passage, Mylne seems to imply that the Keledei, who occupied the monastery which was attached to the mother church, were removed from this position, and instead downgraded to a college of secular clergy, while their former place was assigned to a society of regular canons, meaning the Augustinians. With the new arrangement, the bishop was now made head of the diocese rather than the abbot, as had been the earlier Keledei custom.

In modern terms, the Keledei were effectively 'demoted'. At St Andrews and at Dunkeld, both the Augustinian canons and the Keledei coexisted for nearly two centuries. But, as Ian Bradley points out, this was obviously not without some tensions, stating that 'several later bishops of Dunkeld apparently based themselves at Inchcolm, which had an Augustinian priory but no Celi De community. Whether this move was made to avoid the hassle of Celtic obscurantism, however, must remain a matter of pure speculation'.[40]

In time some of the early abbeys and monasteries became more secularised. It was in the reign of David I (1124-1153) that the greatest change in the structure of the Scottish church took place, as with the example cited above. Instead of the abbot being the head of the monastery, this power was transferred to the bishop of the diocese. But of the 10 new territorial dioceses created to bring the Scottish church into line with continental Catholic customs, 7 were still centred on the old Celtic monastic sites: Glasgow, St Andrews, Dunkeld, Dunblane, Aberdeen, Brechin and Whithorn. David I also revered Columba, after whom he christened his first-born son.

Dunkeld was founded by missionaries from Iona and was viewed by many as an outpost of the Columban Celtic church. St Andrews was largely an outpost of the Roman church, with the Augustinians predominating there. The earlier Pictish kingdom 'came to an end in the 9th century; their distinctive culture was gradually replaced in the far north by Scandinavian ideas and elsewhere Pictland became Scotland', states Dr Anna Ritchie in *Picts*.[41]

The story of Dunkeld is also an important one in the unfolding of Pictish history. In 844AD Kenneth mac Alpin, King of Dalriada, established himself as King of the Picts and this united kingdom was called 'Alba', also called 'Scotland'. Kenneth mac Alpin selected Dunkeld as his principal church and transferred to it some of the relics of St Columba. Despite Dunkeld being chosen as a 'safer' location than Iona for the Columban church, it wasn't immune from a later devastating Viking raid in 903AD. It is intriguing to note that the Scottish army that fought off this attack had the crozier of Columba held up aloft to inspire the troops.[42]

Such was the perceived power of saints' relics in medieval times. Eventually in 849, the precious relics of St Columba were divided between Kells in Ireland and Dunkeld in Scotland, which became the administrative centre of the Scottish church. Following another attack on Dunkeld in the 850s, the centre of the Scottish church was moved again, to Kilrymont, or St Andrews.[43]

Some of the 13th C bishops of Dunkeld chose the island abbey of Inchcolm, in the Firth of Forth near Edinburgh, as their final resting place. This community of canons on Inchcolm was only established when there proved to be difficulties in ousting the existing community of Culdees at Dunkeld.[44] So, again, there were clearly tensions in the gradual process of the Culdees being incorporated into the church of Rome

We will now turn our attention to yet another important early Culdee centre, that of Brechin.

Brechin

Brechin in Forfar was one of the churches where David I revived the Episcopal office and secured its succession. Under him the bishop and Keledei had a common interest, for by a charter he granted certain rights to 'the Bishops and Keledei of Brechin'. Reeves says that this good relationship seemed to continue as various grants were made by the bishops of Brechin between 1180 and 1222 and were witnessed by various Keledei clergy. Around 1210 AD, Malebyrd, the prior, the Keledei, and other clerks of the chapter of Brechin, ratified a donation made by the bishop to St Thomas's of Arbroath.

Reeves explains that about this time, though, the beginnings of the destruction of the power of the Keledei was starting to occur:

> The prior of the Keledei, who formerly as a witness ranked next to the bishop, now gives place to the archdeacon; and a dean presently makes his appearance, to the exclusion of the prior, until, in 1248, the dean rises to capitular supremacy, the Keledei

are ignored, and the cathedral style runs 'Dean and Chapter of Brechin'. After this, the Keledei of Brechin appear no more.[45]

Brechin is also home to an unusual early round tower, which is believed to date back to the 10th C. It is similar to the early Irish ecclesiastical round towers, and is one of only three round towers located outside of Ireland; the other two being Abernethy and Peel, Isle of Man. There are over sixty in Ireland, and all of these round towers are associated with Celtic monasteries or nunneries. The tower at Brechin is 86 feet high and is crowned by an octagonal cap which raises it another 20 feet. It has seven storeys and like other towers of its type, its entrance is raised about 6 feet above ground level.[46]

It seems clear that the Brechin and Abernethy round towers were associated with the Celtic church and also with Pictish areas. During the period after 844AD, Kenneth mac Alpin united Pictland and Dalriada. The Picts had been weakened by their struggles with the Vikings and had been defeated by the Scots. Place-name evidence shows there was an expansion of Gaelic language and settlement into Pictland and Strathclyde during the 9th and 10th centuries.

Rosemarkie

The origin of the church of Rosmarkie, known as Rosmarkin, is said to be connected with St Boniface, or Curitan. Boece calls him Bonifacius Quertinus, and also associates him with St Moluag of Lismore who died in 592AD. The legend in the Breviary of Aberdeen identifies him with Boniface the 4th, who died in 615AD. Reeves discounts this, but acknowledges that from an early date, the name of St Boniface/Curitan has been associated with the church of Rosemarkie both on seals and in records.

The day of his festival, 16 March, points to Ireland rather than Italy as the place from where the founder of this church came. Reeves further states:

> we may with safety conclude either that Boniface was an assumed name, or that the memory of some later ecclesiastic who was so called has been confounded with that of the Celtic

founder. In the Irish calendars of Tamhlacht and Marian Gorman, under the above named day, the 16th of March, is found the commemoration of Curitan, bishop and abbot of Rosmic-Bairenn, who, beyond all reasonable doubt, is the Queritinus de Rosmarkyn of the Scotch.[47]

Still, though, this St Boniface/Curitan of Rosemarkie remains an enigma in many ways.

W.J. Watson in his classic work on Scottish place names says that Curitan was 'certainly connected with Ros Maircnidh, Rosmarkie, in Rosshire', and he adds that 'Maircnidh is the name of a stream in Rosmarkie, i.e. Ros Maircnidh, and it is also a tributary of Fechlin'.[48] Reeves believes that the early church of Rosemarkie, which in the course of time became the cathedral of the diocese of Ross, was an Irish foundation, but not all scholars agree on this. There are other place-names in Scotland that refer to a Curitan, such as at the church of Bona, at the lower end of Loch Ness, and at the church of Corrimony, in Glen Urquhart, there are the names Cladh Churadain and Croit Churadain.[49]

Rosemarkie is also associated with St Moluag, as after the defeat of the Dalriada in the mid-9th C, the Gaels reverently carried the relics of St Moluag from Lismore to Rosemarkie.

A fine Pictish cross-slab, the Rosemarkie Stone, was found here and can be viewed in the wonderful Groam House Museum, which houses many fine examples of Pictish crosses and artwork today. There is a tradition that St Curitan was buried at Rosemarkie.[50] According to legend, St Tredwell, a holy virgin, accompanied St Boniface on his mission to the Picts. Dedications on Papa Westray in Orkney to them both 'suggest that a Northern Isles bishopric may have been intended for here... Boniface is also credited with building a church at Rosemarkie... The large collection of carved stones from here and other sites around the Moray Firth (Shandwick, Tarbat, Hilton of Cadboll and Nigg) testifies to the presence of a vigorous and wealthy church in this area.'[51] St Curitan's Well, at Hill o' Hirdie, is a special well that is still in use, and a spring issues from a round hole. It is still dressed with rags, as are other Clootie wells in Scotland.

Dunblane

Blaan, or Blane, the founder and patron saint of Dunblane, is commemorated in the Felire of Aengus as well as in Scottish calendars, on 10 August. According to a Life of the saint, by George Neuton, archdeacon of Dunblane, Blaan was Irish and came over to Scotland with his uncle Catan. Dunblane in Scotland is said to have been his chief monastery, and Watson says that

> he is commemorated also in Kintyre (Southend), in Inveraray parish, and at Lochearnhead... There is a Kilblain near Old Meldrum, Aberdeen. Blaan's tutor was Cattan, who is said to have been his uncle and who was a contemporary of Comgall (d. 600AD)... This would make Blaan flourish about the end of the sixth century. He was doubtless an Irish-trained Briton, and his work appears to have been mainly among the Britons of Galloway and Fortriu...[52]

Reeves tells us that St Blane's church at Dunblane was probably the seat of a small monastic fraternity among whom he was abbot and bishop, but questions whether any of Blane's successors were also invested with Episcopal orders. Silgrave's catalogue, which lists Dunblane as having Keledei clergy, is one of the few specific mentions of Dunblane and the Keledei. In 1238AD, Bishop Clement is on record as having complained to Rome that nearly all of the possessions of the Dunblane church had been 'usurped by secular persons', as the church had been vacant for 100 years or so in previous times, and although several bishops had subsequently been installed there, Clement told Rome that these possessions still weren't recovered and in fact were probably destroyed.

Upon his appointment to Dunblane he found a nearly dismantled church in a pathetic state, as there was no longer any college there, only a struggling country chaplain who bravely performed divine services in the church, which was by then stripped of its roof! Clearly, the church was not in good condition by 1238AD, when Bishop Clement arrived.

Reeves says that this Bishop Clements' 'revenues were so slender and miserable, that they scarcely yielded him a suitable maintenance for one half of the year. All this looks like Culdee appropriation. Yet before 1210AD, Gilbert, Earl of Stratherne, is said to have devoted a third of his earldom to the church and bishop of Dunblane.'⁵³ The neighbouring church of Muthill seems to have grown as a result of the decline of the church of Dunblane, as its ecclesiastics then occupied the foremost position in the diocese.

St Blane was born on the island of Bute and was active in converting the Picts. In addition to the cathedral at Dunblane, he also founded a Celtic Christian community at Kingarth, on Bute. 'The site is surrounded by an enclosure wall, and there are several ruinous buildings, including 'The Cauldron', the purpose of which is unclear, although it is recorded as being used as a place of punishment...'⁵⁴ There is also a spring at this chapel at Kingarth, said to be a wishing well, and is known today as St Blane's Well.

Today, Dunblane has a wonderful visitor's centre in Cathedral Square, as well as Archbishop Leighton's Library, and the reconstructed chapel behind Scottish Churches House.

Dornoch

Dornoch is listed among other Culdee centres like St Andrews and Dunkeld. It is believed that the church at Dornoch may have been founded by St Barr in the early 7th C. St Barr is patron saint of Cork, Ireland, and of the Hebridean island of Barra, and is commemorated on 25 September. The Irish prefix '*finn*', meaning fair, is often put before his name, thus we have references to St Finbar. The local church of Dornoch is referred to in the Sutherland charters as 'St Finber of Dornoch'. The church at Dornoch is most likely that of an Irish foundation, out of which grew in the course of time, Reeves says, into:

> that peculiar development of the ministerial office called Keledean. What the ecclesiastical process was through which it passed under Norse rule we are not informed, but David 1 accepted it as the most venerable church in the earldom when he defined the diocese of Caithness and made this its cathedral centre. Andrew, bishop of Catanes, appears on record in 1146AD.⁵⁵

Silgrave's catalogue, which lists this church as 'Keledei', probably covers the time period from Andrew, bishop of Catanes, to Bishop Gilbert, who was elevated to the see in about 1222AD. He found little money there, a church in not very good condition, and a single priest officiating – a similar situation to Dunblane. So he had a new church built and established a chapter which consisted of five canons and other dignitaries. Bishop Gilbert eventually became the patron saint of the church at Dornoch and his name is also associated with 'the virtual extinction of the Keledei in this diocese', according to Reeves.[56]

Today the earlier Celtic origins of this site are overlaid by the Cathedral of Dornoch. From Dornoch 'inland routes lead up into the mountains, straths and lochs of Sutherland. At Creich on the north side of the Dornoch Firth, east of the Pictish fort at Dun Creich, the church was dedicated to St Devenick, and 'St Devenick's Cross' still stands here. On the south side of the Firth was the Celtic monastery of Fearn, but its exact site is unknown.'[57]

Dornoch is also known as the place of *the last execution of a witch in Scotland*, which occurred in 1722. In 1563, the Scottish Parliament had passed the witchcraft statue, where the biblical 'Thou shalt not suffer a witch to live' was actually part of the Common Law of Scotland. It wasn't until the dawn of the 19th C that the fear of witches and warlocks really lost its hold in certain areas of the countryside, and even Burns and Hogg wrote about popular beliefs about witchcraft still around at their time, the 18th C.[58]

Lismore

The diocese of Argyll had as its cathedral the church of St Moluag, on the island of Lismore. In the mouth of Loch Linnhe, the island of Lismore is a strategic link between Oban, Appin, Morvern, and Ardnamurchan beyond.

It was founded by St Moluag, an Irishman, who died in 592 AD. In Irish records he is listed as 'Moluoc of Lismor in Alba'. He was commemorated in both Irish and Scottish records on 25 June; in the *Breviary of Aberdeen* he is also referred to as a bishop. His bell and staff were long preserved in his church, which are some of the oldest relics of the Celtic church in Scotland that have survived. St Moluag's own staff still survives today and is kept on the island of Lismore by its Hereditary Keeper.[59]

Even back in earlier times, Lismore was a major connection

between the Kingdom of Dalriada and the Pictish territories to the north, and so it was a really important missionary location for a church. Lismore was an important burial place and has many cairns.

An intriguing and seemingly rather fierce rivalry between St Moluag and St Columba has come down to us today as a legend. Dr Donald Smith describes this famous legend about a boat race between Moluag and Columba:

> Legend has it that Columba and St Moluag raced for possession of Lismore but that Moluag cut off his little finger and threw it ahead to ensure his claim. It is interesting that Columba and Moluag both arrived shortly after the defeat of the Scots of Dalriada by Brude, the overlord of the Northern Picts. Of the two saints Moluag has the greater claim as an apostle to the Picts with early dedications reaching from Lewis in the west to Rosemarkie and Aberdeen in the east.[60]

An old Hebridean account describes this rivalry in an anecdotal way, a real 'war of words', probably a remnant of the old Celtic poetic practice of satire. When St Moluag saw that St Columba was ahead of him, racing to claim Lismore,

> ...he seized an axe, cut off his little finger, threw it on the beach some distance away, and cried out, 'My flesh and blood have first possession of the island, and I bless it in the name of the Lord.' St Columba, seeing that he was outwitted, began to invoke various curses on St Moluag's occupation: 'May you have the alder for your firewood,' wished St Columba. 'The Lord will make the alder burn pleasantly,' replied St Moluag. 'May you have jagged ridges for your pathway,' exclaimed St Columba. 'The Lord will smooth them to the feet,' answered St Moluag. Thus it was that Lismore became the centre of St Moluag's missionary work.[61]

After the defeat of the Dalriada in the mid-9th C, the relics of St Moluag were carried by the Gaels away from Lismore to Rosemarkie. On Lismore today, Portmoluag is said to be where St Moluag first landed, and around the surviving church at Clachan are where Moluag's main monastery and burial ground were. 'It, and the visible foundations around it, however, belong to the later Cathedral of the Isles which stood within the 'great enclosure' or '*lios mor*' of Moluag's monastery from which the island takes its present name.'[62]

Although listed as having Keledei clergy in earlier times, there is a charter which shows that before 1251 a dean and chapter existed, as the name of the first dean on record is Gillemoluoc, signifying a 'servant of Moluac', the founder.

In the 16th C *The Book of the Dean of Lismore*, Scotland's greatest collection of Gaelic poetry, was compiled at Lismore, which was a great centre of Gaelic culture. St Moluag was commemorated in poetry as 'Moluag the clear and brilliant, the sun of Lismore in Alba'.[63] In the whole Argyll area, many much older customs remained as part of traditions in the early Christian communities there.

For example, the chapel at Craignish was named Kilmole in early times and is believed to have a connection with water and baptism, and also with Molluch, an old deity who was said to devour children in ancient times. Researcher David Stewart-Smith says:

> The dedication to Molluch referred to the place where the inhabitants of DunVhuilig, Craignish, and Ardfern would go to baptise their babies. [This] was known as 'proving the infants', where, at six months old, the babies were thrown bodily into the sea... In later years, the chapel became an important stopping point on the Road of the Dead, the processional path through which the funeral for the kings of Dalriada passed (circa 500-800 AD). When the King's body came to Kilmole at Craignish, it was immersed in the sea as part of the funeral ritual.[64]

Many locations have often retained their much earlier place-names, mythology or legendary meanings from very ancient times. Many places often had connections with Culdee communities and traditions from other places in Scotland. A place in Fortingall, Perthshire, which is also believed to have had a Culdee community there in the past, has been linked to St Cedd, a bishop of Iona, who died in 712AD, so showing a possible link between Culdee communities of Fortingall and Iona. Sir James MacGregor in the early 16th C was both the Vicar of Fortingall *and* also the Dean of Lismore, as Scottish historian William Skene wrote in 1862.[65]

Iona

As the story of St Columba and Iona was largely told in the last chapter, here we will focus on the earlier 'Keledei' references to Iona. It is one of the eight primary early 'Keledei' churches, according to Henry of Silgrave's *Chronicle*. Iona is listed as 'Abbatia in Insula', as having an Abbot of the Keledei, or Celtic, persuasion. In contrast, St Andrews and Dunkeld also have Keledei clergy listed, but show Augustinian canons co-existing along with them, as we have seen.

It appears that Iona was perceived as 'Keledei', most likely meaning that it had an Abbot of the Columban church, who was still following the Celtic ways of St Columba, as opposed to other influences. Dr Ian Bradley in *Celtic Christianity* says that 'It is certainly the case that Celi De communities were located at several early monastic sites, notably Dunkeld, Brechin, Abernethy, Iona, Muthill and on St Serf's island in Loch Leven...'[66]

In time, however, like at other locations, the monks were gradually persuaded to accept the Roman ways. By 703AD Adamnan had persuaded many in Dalriada, Pictland and Strathclyde to change, and finally in 716AD, Abbot Dunchad and his monks at Iona complied and accepted the Roman ways. This was 52 years after the Synod of Whitby in 664AD, where the Celtic church lost to Rome on certain issues, like the dating of Easter and tonsure.

During the reign of the Pictish king Nechtan, in 717AD – one year after the monks at Iona decided to accept Roman ways – certain Celtic monks who would not conform to the Roman practices were expelled from Pictland to Dalriada. William Skene in his *Celtic Scotland* believes the monks at Abernethy were among those driven out. This expulsion from Pictland is most curious, as Iona had already been persuaded by Adamnan and Bishop Ecgbert of Northumbria to accept the changes before this date, so perhaps this banishment occurred for other reasons too, most likely political ones. Perhaps Nechtan wanted to curtail the power of the Columban church and the powerful dynastic families that were associated with it.

But – and this may be significant, especially with historical hindsight – *it was only after this expulsion of the Celtic clergy (in 717AD) that we encounter in Scotland the term 'Keledei' or*

Culdee. It seems as though the Celtic monks that were expelled were members of a reform movement seeking to return to, or keep to, the ascetic and other traditions of Columba's monastic brotherhood. Culdees are known to have existed at Brechin, Iona, Dunkeld, Dunblane, Dornoch, Loch Leven, Abernethy, St Andrews, Lismore, Monymusk, Muthill and Rosemarkie. These Keledei clergy were gradually 'demoted' to be secular canons as time went on.

St Columba made his pilgrimage from Ireland to Iona in 563AD. and was given the island site of Iona by Conall son of Comgall, the king of the Scottish Dal Riata. There were other foundations besides Iona, such as Hinba, which is still unidentified, where anchorites lived a more solitary life and 'Mag Luinge on Tiree where Columba sent people who came to him as penitents. There are also churches mentioned on an unidentified island called Elen and on the mainland at a place called Cella Diuni.'[67]

On Iona, St Oran's chapel and burial ground of the kings of Scotland may commemorate an earlier foundation than that of Columba. Columba's monastery was to the north of the present restored Benedictine Abbey, but only its cashel or enclosing wall survives:

> Tor Abb, a mound to the west of the Abbey, is believed to be the site of Columba's own cell, while the gravestone known as 'Columba's Pillow' is housed in St Columba's Shrine in the Abbey or cathedral church. The restored Abbey buildings are the base of the 20th c. Iona Community, founded by George MacLeod to take the gospel of Columba into urban Scotland. The High Crosses of St Martin and St John, though partially restored, are among Scotland's finest Celtic artworks.[68]

There is no question that today, as in times past, the island of Iona is still revered by many as a special beacon, a place of pilgrimage.

Abernethy

Abernethy was an important Pictish centre in the period of the 5th – 11th centuries. Walter Bower, a 15th C historian who wrote his *Scotochronicon* in the 1440s, was an Augustinian Abbot of

Inchcolm, an island in the Firth of Forth. He records that he had seen a chronicle in Abernethy which stated it was the main Pictish capital and an important Christian centre.

It is well-known that the Abernethy area has a large number of Pictish and early Christian stones, and many more which have not been excavated yet. The River Tay played a very important part in the early history of the church in Scotland, for it links the three most important Episcopal centres, first of Pictland and then of Scotland in the 8th to the 10th centuries: Abernethy, Dunkeld and St Andrews. Abernethy held supreme position in 8th C Pictland, relinquishing that role to Dunkeld only after the union of the Picts and Scots in the mid-9th C. By the early 10th C, though, Dunkeld was second to St Andrews.[69]

Bede in his Ecclesiastical History refers to the year 563AD and St Columba's mission. He writes '… the southern Picts, who dwell on this side of those mountains [the Grampians], had long before (i.e. before 563AD) as is reported, forsaken the errors of idolatry and embraced the truth by the preaching of Ninian, a most reverend bishop and holy man of the British nation'. It is possible that St Ninian of Whithorn himself could have founded the church at Abernethy, as he died in 452AD. The Rev D. Butler in his book *The Ancient Church and Parish of Abernethy* (1897) states that the first church there was dedicated in 460AD to St Bridget of Kildare and was endowed with its great territorial possessions by the king of the Picts. He was not saying here that it was *founded* in 460AD, but that it was *dedicated* and endowed on that date. This could mean that it was re-dedicated then, with the original consecration by Ninian. We don't really know for sure.

Another possibility is that the founding of the Abernethy church may have been dedicated by another monk from Whithorn, but not actually by Ninian himself. For example, St Serf, the mentor of St Kentigern, is associated with churches at Dunning and Culross on either side of the Ochils and perhaps also with Stirling. Another probable founding of Abernethy would have been from an Irish mission. We are told by John Fordun's *Chronicle* that in 430AD Palladius was ordained by Pope Celestinus and sent to Scotia. One of his followers, called Ternan, may have been high bishop of the Picts, and Abernethy could have been the centre of his see. Ternan is also linked with Fordun, Brechin and Banchory, as well as Abernethy. Another persistent tradition is that St Brigid herself established a monastery here before Columba's mission to Scotland.

So it is not clear exactly when, or by whom, Abernethy was founded, or precisely when southern Pictland was converted to Christianity. William Skene in his *Celtic Scotland* says that Gartnaidh, a king of the Picts, established a monastery at Abernethy where the earlier church had been, and that he re-dedicated it to St Brigid.

King Gartnaidh reigned from about 586-597AD, and St Columba died in 597AD. We know that Gartnaidh's monastic foundation at Abernethy took place 225 years and 11 months before the establishment of the church at Dunkeld by Constantine, who was Pictish king from 789-820AD. The parish church at Abernethy is called St Bride's. It looks as though King Gartnaidh re-dedicated the church to St Bride in about 586AD, and this implies that there was an original dedication before this date. Rev D Butler also tells us that Darlugdach, St Brigid's successor as the Abbess of Kildare, was present at a dedication at Abernethy to St Brigid, probably sometime after the date of the death of St Brigid which was about 525AD. The present church at Abernethy gets its name from St Brigid. So there is obviously some kind of a connection between the traditions of Bride, St Brigid, the Picts and Abernethy that is important.

It is believed that the Pictish King Gartnaidh, described as the 'high King of the Tay', supported Columba and that together they overcame the 'fierce druids', as stated in the *Amra Columcille*. On 20 May 684AD, one of the most important battles in Scottish history took place at Dunnichen, near Forfar. The Picts, under their king Bruide, defeated the Angles and killed the Northumbrian king Ecgfrith. Bede, writing in 731AD, says that from that time the hopes and strengths of the English crown began to waver, as the Picts had recovered their own lands which had been held by the English. The early church in Pictland was influenced not only by the Northumbrian expansion, but by influences from Dalriada and Strathclyde. During the reign of Pictish king Nechtan in 717AD the Celtic monks (the 'Keledei') who refused to conform to the Roman ways were expelled from Pictland to Dalriada, and the monks of Abernethy were among those expelled. So it is clear that Abernethy also had strong Pictish connections.

But it is the *round tower* for which Abernethy is also well known. This is one of the only three similar round towers that are outside of Ireland; two are located in Scotland, at Abernethy and at Brechin. The Abernethy round tower was most likely built in the 11th C. A plaque by Historic Scotland inside the door suggests this, but also says that the door frame does exhibit some characteristics of earlier architecture. These round towers are definitely associated with Celtic monasteries or nunneries. The 74-foot high round tower at Abernethy indicates the importance which the Kings of the Scots and Picts placed on Abernethy as a religious centre. It is believed that the tower was also used as a belfry.[70]

Abernethy is an ancient Pictish site and the Scottish historian Fordun says that St Brigid and her nine virgins were granted all the lands and tithes which the prior and canons enjoyed from ancient times. The connection of Abernethy with St Bride, and its corresponding folklore, is certainly interesting and needs further examination. Abernethy is also famous for its fascinating carved stones and their Pictish designs.

Although Abernethy enjoyed prominence early on with its Keledei orientation, by about the close of the 12th C it began to become secularised and one half of the tithes were bestowed on the newly founded abbey of Arbroath. In 1214, a controversy arose between the Keledei of Abernethy and the convent of Arbroath regarding certain tithes, as Reeves tells us.

> It was decided by the arbitrator, the bishop of Dunblane, against the Keledei, and so emphatically as to forbid a recurrence of the question. Before the close of the 13th century, they had entirely disappeared. The finishing blow was struck in 1272, when, as John of Fordun relates, the priory of Abernethy, which had previous consisted of Keledei, was converted into a society of canons regular.[71]

This obviously meant that the Keledei no longer had any official power, but not without a long struggle on their part to try and preserve the old Celtic ways. By the end of the 13th C, it is believed that the Celtic church was officially no more in Scotland. As is often known to happen when a people or a culture is defeated, a process of romanticisation sets in, which may not necessarily be accurate as to the truth of the hardships that these ascetic monks and nuns endured for the love of Christ. But, their memory lingers on.

Loch Leven

Loch Leven and St Serf's island are known to be one of the earliest religious foundations in Scotland. Reeves tells us that there existed an early chartulary or donation book, written in Gaelic, an abstract of which is preserved in Latin, in the register of the priory of St Andrews.

The first memorandum in the collection states that Brude, son of Dergard, the last of the Pictish kings, bestowed the island of Loch Leven on God, St Servan, and the devoted Keledean hermits dwelling there. It also says that the Keledei clergy there gave over the site of their cell(s) to the bishop of St Andrews, providing that he would supply them with food and clothing, and that Ronan, a monk and abbot, granted the place to Bishop Fothadh, who was highly regarded all over Scotland. The bishop then pronounced a blessing on all who should uphold this covenant between him and the Keledei, and a curse on all those bishops who should ever violate or retract the same. (Yes, it seems, bishops could and did curse!)

Reeves goes on about this:

> ...this is a very interesting record, not only as affording a glimpse of the Scottish church and the Celi-De in particular, at a period where history is painfully silent. Sometime between 1037 and 1054AD, a grant was made from MacBeth and his wife Gruoch to the Keledei of Loch Leven, of certain lands. Malduin, Tuathal, and Modach son of Malmichel, successive bishops of St Andrews, appear in their order as the donors of lands and privileges to the 'Keledei hermitae'.[72]

By the time of King David I, the fate of the Keledei seems to have been sealed. David I declared that he had given and granted to the canons of St Andrews the island of Loch Leven, and that the Keledei who still resided there, if they still wanted to live there, could remain there, *but only if they agreed to be subject to the*

Augustinians. If they resisted, they would be expelled. As can be imagined, the Culdees were not happy about this at all. Robert, the English Bishop of St Andrews, who dictated this stern enactment to the Culdees, was not slow to carry out its provisions. For immediately after King David I made his declaration, he placed these Keledei clergy under the regular canons of St Andrews (the Augustinian canons), and converted their old possessions into an endowment for his newly erected priory.

Sadly, it seems, Bishop Robert even transferred the ecclesiastical vestments which these Keledei possessed, and their little library, consisting mainly of patristic and ritual books, the titles of which are listed. After this point, the separate existence of one of the earliest religious houses in Scotland declined in a major way, and not without a lot of tension, it appears. It was clearly the end of an era.

Monymusk

The founder of the church of Monymusk, in Aberdeenshire, is said to have been Malcolm Canmore. About the year 1080 AD, when leaving on a military expedition, he said that if he returned safely, he would make a liberal offering 'to God and St Andrew'. The most likely probability, however, was that he was a *restorer*, not a founder, and that he revived a dormant monastery and enlarged its endowments, as with the subsequent case of Deer.

From 1080AD, Monymusk was affiliated to the church of St Andrews, and was considered to be one of the institutions of the Keledei. Later, it received further additions from the Earls of Mar, and in various charters from 1200 on, its clergy are called '*Canonici qui Keledei dicutur*', for example. This early society of Keledei at Monymusk consisted of 13 secular priests. Its early connection with St Andrews, however, reduced Monymusk to a condition of secondary importance and deprived it of a bishop all their own. We see them excluded from all parochial functions and, as regarded the rights of the parish church, put on a footing with ordinary parishioners. By 1245, they vanish from the pages of history, and Reeves tells us that 'in their stead there appears the Prior and Convent of Monymusc of the order of St Augustine.'[73]

But Monymusk's other 'claim to fame' is the Brecbennach of

St Columba, a portable shrine for his relics. It was often carried into battle and became the most visible and potent symbol of the post-Columban church:

> The Monymusk reliquary and other emblems of Columba would be carried into battle not only by kings of Dalriada but also by later kings of Scots. His crosier or bachall would accompany the armies of Constantine II which defeated Ivar II and his Vikings somewhere in Fortriu in 903AD, and Ragnall, Norse King of York, at the Tyne in 918AD. The Brecbennach would even be carried before the army of Robert the Bruce at Bannockburn in 1314AD. But in 1314, the Scots went not with one patron saint but two, for they also carried with them the banner of St Andrew.[74]

So, ironically, even though the Celtic saints today are portrayed as having a gentle, peace-loving image, in earlier times, their relics were often major 'weapons' in warfare, carried first on to the battlefield!

Muthill

Closely associated with the church of Dunblane was that of Muthill, also spelled as Muthel, which gives its name to a large parish adjoining that of Dunblane on the north. History is silent regarding its foundation and early history. It is a place also associated in early times with St Patrick's Well, and that of Struthill with its adjacent chapel.

We know that in the 12th C there existed at Muthill a society of Keledei, who held a prominent place in the diocese of Dunblane. 'Malpol, prior of Keledeorum de Mothel' and '*Sithach et Malcolm Keledei de Mothel*' are witnesses to a charter of the bishop of Dunblane about the year 1178AD. Another charter is dated 1200AD. A Malkirg, '*prior Keledeorum de Mothle*', is witness to a charter of confirmation about the year 1214AD.

These Keledei at Muthill have been generally referred to by Scottish writers as being affiliated with the Dunblane community, but they do not really appear to have had any further connection with its church other than as occupying the adjoining parish and growing in importance when the community of monks at Dunblane began to decline.[75]

Monifieth

Next to Dundee is also the parish of Monifieth, which once possessed a house of Celi De, as we learn from a charter in 1242AD. Matilda, Countess of Angus, granted to the church of Arbroath all the land on the south side of Monifodh, which the Keledei held in the time of her father. This was the last remnant of the ancient Keledei there, whose endowments were lost in part through the administration of their secular affairs, while the remainder were handed over to a neighbouring monastery whose practice was considered more orthodox and amenable to Anglo-Norman law.[76] This is yet another example of how the decline of the Keledei gradually occurred, and by the close of the 13th C, it is believed, they were officially extinct.

The official end of the Culdees: the 13th C

So the story of the Culdees is a long and varied one. They were obviously very devout monks and nuns and were good missionaries. But by the end of the 13th C in Scotland, it is clear that they were no more. However, their memory remains, and there is an increasing interest in the Culdees today, as well as Celtic Christianity in general.

In fact, as many have noted, there seems to be a real 'explosion' of interest in Celtic Christianity, and a lot of romanticisation about certain aspects of it. Many have correctly pointed out that what is now called 'Celtic Christianity' may actually have little to do with how it was actually practised in earlier times. It is often hard to sort out the myths from the facts, especially with this subject. As we have seen throughout this book, history is usually a bit of both.

But perhaps just as important is the fact that so many people today in our modern scientific, high-tech age, would even *want* to learn more about them at all. Of course, looking back at the distant past, there is inevitably going be some romanticisation, as history has shown. Dr Ian Bradley of St Andrews University says that in spite of all of this, 'I still believe that the distinctive voice of the early indigenous Christian communities of the British Isles speaks to us through all the layers of distortion...'[77] And yes, no doubt it somehow does.

As with the enigmatic Culdees and early Celtic Christianity, the myth of King Arthur still lingers on today, many centuries later, even though little is actually known about him. It is to the world of Arthur, Merlin and Guinevere that we will now turn.

Notes

[1] Lynch, Prof M, *Scotland: A New History*, Pimlico, London, 1991, 26, 38.

[2] Smith, D, *Celtic Travellers: Scotland in the Age of the Saints*, Her Majesty's Stationery Office, Edinburgh, 1997, 5.

[3] Armit, I, *Celtic Scotland*, Historic Scotland, B.T. Batsford, London, 1997, 117.

[4] Ibid.

[5] Jowett, G F, *The Drama of the Lost Disciples*, Covenant: London, 1996 ed, of 1961 orig, 40.

[6] Reeves, Wm, *The Culdees of the British Islands as they appear in History*, Royal Irish Academy, M.H. Gill, Dublin, 1864 orig, reprint 1994 by LLarnerch Publishers, Felinfach, Wales, 27.

[7] Ibid, 28.

[8] Wise, T.A, *History of Paganism in Caledonia*, London, 1884, 251.

[9] Chadwick, N, *The Age of the Saints in the Early Celtic Church*, University of Newcastle, Newcastle, 1960, 12.

[10] Ibid.

[11] Moorman, J R, *A History of the Church in England*, A & C Black, London, 1980, 4.

[12] Thiede, C P, & D'Ancona, M, *The Quest for the True Cross*, Orion Books, London, 2000, 33.

[13] Chadwick, op cit, 14.

[14] Ibid.

[15] Moorman, op cit, 5.

[16] McBrien, R P, [Gen. Ed] *The HarperCollins Encyclopedia of Catholicism*, HarperCollins, New York, 1995, 140.

[17] Phillips, G, *The Marian Conspiracy*, Sidgwick & Jackson, London, 2000, 185.

[18] Ibid, 11.

[19] Ibid, 278.

[20] Jowett, op cit, 79.

[21] Ibid.

22 Douglas, J D, *The International Dictionary of the Christian Church*, Zondervan Publishing, Grand Rapids, MI, 1978, 723.
23 Ibid.
24 Vantoura, Haik, *The Music of the Bible Revealed*, [Ed by Wheeler, J], Babel Press, San Francisco, 1991, 105-6.
25 Ibid, 32.
26 Bradley, I, *Celtic Christianity*, Edinburgh University Press, Edinburgh, 1998, 56.
27 Batchelor, R, *Origin of St. Andrews*, Shieling Publishers, St. Andrews, 1997, 30.
28 Lynch, op cit, 28.
29 Scott, A B, *The Pictish Nation*, T N Foulis, Edinburgh and London, 1918, 512.
30 Foster, S, [Ed], *The St. Andrews Sarcophagus*, Four Courts Press, Dublin, 1998, 43.
31 Broun, D, 'The church of St. Andrews and its foundation legend in the early 12th century: recovering the full text of version A of the foundation legend', *Kings, Clerics and Chronicles in Scotland*, 500-1297, [Ed.] Simon Taylor, Four Courts Press, Dublin, 2000, 114.
32 Taylor, S, 'The Coming of the Augustinians to St. Andrews and version B of the St. Andrews foundation legend', *Kings, Clerics, and Chronicles in Scotland*, 500-1297, [Ed.] Simon Taylor, Four Courts Press, Dublin, 2000, 121.
33 Reeves, op cit, 41.
34 Lynch, op cit, 37.
35 Smith, op cit, 28.
36 Davies, N, *The Isles: A History*, Macmillan, London, 1999, 189.
37 Reeves, op cit, 41.
38 Ibid, 42.
39 Ibid.
40 Bradley, op cit, 56.
41 Ritchie, A, HMSO, Edinburgh, 1989, 7.
42 Ibid.
43 Fawcett, R, *Scottish Abbeys and Priories*, Historic Scotland, B.T. Batsford, London, 1994, 16.
44 Fawcett, R, *Dunkeld Cathedral: A Short History and Guide*, The Society of Friends of Dunkeld Cathedral, with Historic Scotland, 1990, 6.

45 Reeves, op cit, 43.
46 Toulson, S, *Celtic Journeys*, Hutchinson & Co, London, 1985, 138.
47 Ibid, 45.
48 Watson, W J, *The History of the Celtic Place-Names of Scotland*, Edinburgh, 1926 orig, Birlinn ed. reprint 1993, 441.
49 Ibid, 375.
50 Smith, op cit, 39.
51 Foster, S, *Picts, Gaels, and Scots*, Historic Scotland, B.T. Batsford, London, 1996, 91.
52 Watson, op cit, 165.
53 Reeves, op cit, 47.
54 Miller, J, *Myth and Magic*, Goblinshead, Musselburgh, 2000, 87.
55 Reeves, op cit, 48.
56 Ibid.
57 Smith, op cit, 18.
58 MacNeill, F M, *The Silver Bough*, Vol. I, Scottish Folklore and Folk-Belief, Wm. MacLellan, Glasgow, 1977 ed. Of 1957 orig, 129.
59 Smith, op cit, 17.
60 Ibid.
61 Barnett, T.R, *Scottish Pilgrimage*, John Grant, Edinburgh, 1942, 196-7.
62 Ibid.
63 Ibid.
64 Stewart-Smith, D, *Life Experience Petition*, Vermont College, August 1990, 13.
65 Dunford, B, *The Holy Land of Scotland*, Brigadoon, Aberfeldy, 1996, 9.
66 Bradley, op cit, 56.
67 Clancy, T, and Markus, G, *Iona: The Earliest Poetry of a Celtic Monastery*, Edinburgh University Press, Edinburgh, 1995, 10.
68 Smith, op cit, 16.
69 Ritchie, op cit, 38.
70 Smith, op cit, 16.
71 Reeves, op cit, 54.
72 Reeves, op cit, 51.
73 Reeves, op cit, 52.
74 Lynch, op cit, 36.
75 Reeves, op cit, 57.
76 Ibid, 58.
77 Bradley, op cit, ix.

CHAPTER SIX

King Arthur, Merlin and Guinevere: Scottish Traditions

KING ARTHUR, MERLIN, GUINEVERE, the Sword in the Stone, the knights of the Round Table... the memory lives on. Most of us have heard of and celebrated the legends of King Arthur and his knights of the Round Table. Children, too, are fascinated by the 'myth that refuses to die'. These tales still have a powerful allure today, with many books, films and documentaries written about King Arthur, the 'Once and Future King'. But because of the sheer volume of material available, this chapter will be limited to Arthur, Merlin and Guinevere, and the next chapter will include the Holy Grail and the Round Table.

King Arthur

The quest for the historical Arthur has certainly been a fascinating, yet challenging, task for many through the centuries. Many have studied the Arthurian tales – historians, archaeologists, Celtic scholars, Jungian analysts, theologians and mythologists, among others. As has been said about Arthur, one of the most enduring legends of all time, 'the power, durability and adaptability of his legends suggest that 'universal truths' may be discovered by an exploration of the legends.'[1] Yes, history has often shown that enduring universal truths turn out to be found in myths, stories and legends.

Arthur is an important cultural figure in early Celtic literature and many portrayals of King Arthur exist – as leader, warrior, chieftain, hero, and champion against the invading Anglo-Saxons, to name a few. 'By the 12th C, he becomes a Pan-European figure, a dominant motif in literary and artistic culture, a focal point for the cults of chivalry and courtly love and for esoteric mysteries such as the Holy Grail'.[2] Also by the 12th C, prominent historians of the time, like William of Malmesbury, Caradoc of Llancarfon and Giraldus of Wales were trying to sort out fact from fiction. One author tells us about the power of the 'Arthurian mythos':

> The potency of the Arthurian legends may reflect the remarkable achievements of the historical King Arthur. But undoubtedly a factor in their cultural power and adaptability was that from the earliest stages the mythos of Arthur absorbed aspects of Celtic religion and deification, such as the mysterious birth, the sword in the stone, the water deities (ladies of the lake), the cauldron of immortality and the Other World, and, most importantly, an element found in many religions, the Second Coming... The Arthurian legendary material has attracted many of the great writers of European civilisation – Taliesin, Geoffrey of Monmouth, Wace, Chretien de Troyes, Gottfried von Strassburg, Wolfram von Eschenbach, Geoffrey Chaucer, Sir Thomas Malory, Edmund Spenser, Alfred Tennyson, Thomas Hardy, T.S. Eliot...[3]

British Arthurian folklore is mainly associated with the areas of lowland Scotland, Wales, Cornwall and parts of Cumbria. Arthur's entrance into English culture as a whole comes later on, especially immortalised by the works of Tennyson and Malory; in 12th and 13th century France, many of the Arthurian and Grail manuscripts were written down.

Certainly no other hero of the Dark Ages is featured so prominently in such a vast amount of literature as King Arthur. But ironically, not much of what has come down to us speaks in consistent glowing terms of Arthur, Lancelot or Guinevere, for example. Those who wrote the Arthurian literature wrote it down much later than the early medieval period, when Arthur is believed to have actually lived and died.

Many different Arthurian manuscripts were commissioned in the 12th and 13th centuries, so we have several versions of the tales. Many of these were written in Old French, Latin or Old Welsh, for example. Little was heard of Arthur after 542AD, so this time period has been assumed to be roughly about when he died. One scholar has pointed out that 'significantly, however, youths of noble and royal birth began to bear the name Arthur after the year 542.'[4] Naturally, parents would have wanted to name their children after a hero as great as Arthur.

Scholarly controversy about Arthur

Generally, King Arthur has always been thought of as a Celtic hero, as most of the earliest references to Arthur come from Celtic areas. Scholars have said that the Latin version of his name, Arturus, does not seem to have been found anywhere else. They have come to the inevitable conclusion that it must be a name that commemorates the great deeds of a lost king or chieftain of the Dark Ages, or even prehistoric Britain. Generally, this view has been the predominant one. However, recent and quite controversial scholarship has found evidence that a 2nd C Roman officer named Lucius Artorius Castus, prefect of the VI Legion Victrix:

> ...was headquarted at York. (Eboracum) and charged with the defence of northern Britain... A passage in Dio Cassius's 'Roman History', written 225 C.E, describes how, at the end of the Marcomannian War, 8,000 cataphracti from a Sarmatian tribe known as the Iazyges (or Jazyges) were impressed into the Roman legions. Of these Iazyges 5,500 men were sent to Britain... Iazygian auxiliaries were posted in groups of five hundred to the garrisons along Hadrian's Wall... Their first commander was a Roman officer named Lucius Artorius Castus...[5]

The Sarmations and Iazyges are believed to come from ancient Scythia, the area we know now as the southern Russian and Ukrainian steppes, near the Black Sea.

Naturally, this theory is quite controversial among scholars, but the evidence of the existence of the name Artorius, they say, is indisputable. Some are even claiming that this might explain why there are more references to Arthur in this part of Scotland, in addition to any existing indigenous Arthurian folklore, while others insist that there can be no way that a Celtic hero like King Arthur could ever be modelled on a Roman officer, which seems logical enough. What all of this may ultimately mean is another story, and this is where current scholarship is having a lively debate, with some scholars claiming that elements of the Arthurian mythos come from much earlier Indo-European roots in Scythia rather than from an exclusively Celtic source, which has been the predominating assumption for centuries. They base this on what they see as some rather striking parallels in the Arthurian material with the Ossetian Nart sagas of the greater Scythian area. But, as others say, the ancient Celts were believed to have migrated from that general area anyway, so in a sense, perhaps both are right in some ways.

Although the debate goes on, what most scholars *do* agree on is the phenomenon of the legend of Arthur and how it has become 'the myth that refuses to die' – which is certainly culturally important and worthy of serious study, even in our modern age. Many believe that there certainly must have been an historical Arthur to inspire such a long-lasting legacy, although we know little about him from the existing sources. And even if there wasn't an historical Arthur, it may not ultimately really matter, as the mere fact that this powerful myth has remained with us for nearly *fifteen centuries* is important in and of itself. After all, this is one of the most enduring historical themes of western civilisation, and it still shows no signs of abating.

In fact, it seems that if anything, Arthur is more popular than ever! Psychologists and other social scientists have attempted to study why this myth 'refuses to die', pointing out that the overall theme of a 'saviour' or 'redeemer' who will one day return and make things right again, be it Christ, the Messiah, the Buddhist Maitreya, and so on, is a powerful, pervasive one in many cultures. Today, many people also tend to think of science as a 'saviour' in terms of belief system, for better or for worse. So, the world still awaits...

Arthurian legends in Wales

But it is from the writings of Geoffrey of Monmouth that we first hear of King Arthur and his amazing exploits and deeds. Geoffrey, a Welshman, wrote *Historia Regum Britanniae*, in 1132. The Arthurian legend is believed by many to be rooted in Celtic tradition, but it 'only achieved its prodigious popularity when it became a dominant theme of medieval literature in Continental Europe, first and foremost in France... However, Arthur was a known figure in Welsh tradition at least as early as the 8th C. In one of the earliest references, that of Nennius in his *History of the Britons*, Arthur is a war leader who defends his country against Saxon invaders.'[6]

Early Welsh literature has references to Arthur. In the Old

Welsh poem *Preiddeu Annwfn*, The Spoils of Annwfn, Arthur visits the Otherworld to carry off a magical cauldron of the realm of the dead. Miranda Green refers to the medieval Welsh texts, like the *Y Gododdin*, that mention the name Arthur:

> ...the Gododdin, for example, describes the warrior Gwawrddur who, while heroic, 'was not Arthur'. A spate of young princelings appeared in several Welsh kingdoms in about AD600; the sudden popularity of the name for these young noblemen may point to an early warrior named Arthur,who perhaps adopted the title 'dux bellorum' when fighting against the Saxons. Many parts of Britain have laid claim to this Arthur and Wales has its stong candidates... in truth, there is no hard evidence to link Arthur with any identifiable site. It is interesting to speculate, however, that a mobile cavalry leader might be attracted to a prominent location such as the former legionary fortress as a rallying-point. It is impossible to assign Arthur to any location, but as compelling a case can be made for Caerleon as for any-where else.[7]

The Welsh tale of Culhwch is the earliest of the Arthurian tales and may be even earlier in its first compilation than the Four Branches of the *Mabinogi*, dating to around 1100AD. The Culhwch story is basically a quest tale, 'a quest within a quest'.[8]

The magical cauldron

In early Celtic mythology, pigs, and especially boars, were con-sidered to have special status regarding the Otherworld. In the fol-lowing tale, the warrior Culhwch must find a special magic boar, Twrch Trwyth, as one of the 'impossible tasks' assigned to him by the giant Ysbaddaden, the father of Olwen, whom Culhwch has been made to fall in love with by a spell by his step-mother. He wants to marry Olwen, but her father says he can't until he finds this magic boar. So, he sets off to Arthur's court to get help with these nearly impossible tasks:

> Culhwch arrives at the court of Arthur unannounced, he is denied entry by the gatekeeper, and, in his rage at this insult, the young man threatens to utter three shouts that will cause any pregnant woman in the land to abort her foetus and that will

make all other women barren. Such an episode may be a metaphoric device to signal Culhwch's god-like power to make the land infertile...[8]

This idea of a wasteland, as many will recognise, is a theme of the Grail legends, which tell of an ailing Fisher King presiding over a bleak, infertile landscape until the Grail is found. Here we have the theme of a barren wasteland in an early 12th C manuscript where Arthur is named, and as many experts acknowledge, much of this undoubtedly comes from an earlier bardic and storytelling tradition that had already existed for centuries.

Two other medieval Welsh texts that mention the magical cauldron theme are the *Book of Taliesin* and the poem called *Preiddeu Annwfn* (The Spoils of Annwfn). *Preiddeu Annwfn* tells of a disastrous raiding expedition made by Arthur to Annwfn, the Otherworld, to plunder its magical cauldron, famous for its precious jewels and for its utter refusal to boil food for a coward! This 13th C poem is preserved in the *Book of Taliesin*. Professor Green points out that this poem has an interesting connection with 'Culhwch ac Olwen', as both stories show Arthur as a 'cauldron-rustler':

> In 'Culhwch', one of the 'impossible' tasks the... hero has to perform is the obtention of the cauldron of Diwrnach... 'to boil meat for thy wedding guests' says Ysbaddaden. The vessel is brought back by Arthur, filled with the treasures of Ireland, after a successful but bitterly contested raid. The focus of 'Preiddeu Annwfn' is Arthur's plundering of the Otherworld for its valuable cauldron, a vessel studded with precious stones... and it flatly refuses to boil food for a coward. Arthur's expedition is successful but only at immense human cost; he loses nearly all his ships and forces in the raid...[9]

Arthur is referred to in many parts of Britain, but in the Welsh sources his court is said to be located in either southeast Wales or Cornwall. According to Welsh scholars Rees and Rees: 'In the work of Nennius, Arthur appears in the place-lore of the Builth district and of Ergyng (now in Hertfordshire); in the early Welsh poem *The Spoils of Annwfn*, he is associated with the lords of Dyfed, and in the story of Culhwch and Olwen his great boar-hunt ranges over South Wales.'[10] Arthur's name is also in the 10th C *Annales Cambriae* which tells of his important victory at Badon dated sometime between 490 and 518, and it records that he was killed at the Battle of Camlann in either 515 or 539AD.

Arthur 'the bear'

The Welsh epic tale of Math son of Mathonwy, as he appears in the fourth branch of the *Mabinogi*, also has much in common with the Arthurian story. French Celtic scholar Jean Markale and others have noted the important connection of the name Arthur with a bear, or the concept of a bear title as a leader, or title of, a bear clan. Markale believes that these two epics developed side by side, from the same original myth. From the legend of Math, it is clear that he is portrayed as an impotent king, like the Fisher King in the Grail sagas. The name Math is repeated in his father's name, Mathonwy, and this name is interesting in relation to the Arthurian tales in that it corresponds to the *Gaelic Mathgamnai* and scholar de Jubainville notes that in the Irish Bible the Hebrew word *dob*, which means 'bear', is expressed in Gaelic as *math-ghamhuin*, literally 'bear cub'. There was also a Gallic name Mathugenos, meaning 'son of a bear'. Markale says:

> ...in ancient Celtic there were two words meaning bear, 'matu' and 'arto'... In Welsh and modern Breton the word for bear is 'arth' and 'arz', and the famous goddess with a bear in the museum of Berne, a divinity worshipped in Gallo-Roman times, is called Artio... So Math and Arthur have something very basic in common: the name of the bear. How Arthur developed from 'arth' or 'Arto' may be more difficult to determine, but it must be more than coincidence. Many Celtic heroes have animal names... Obviously Arthur could be traced back to other equally convincing etymological sources... in view of the fact that Arcturus derives from Arctus, the name for the Great Bear and the Little Bear, this merely brings us back to Arth, the bear...[11]

Math and Arthur have other similarities, too. Both have a nephew who is heir to the throne and who abducts their women, for instance. Markale believes that Celtic heroes like Arthur who resemble the heroes of Teutonic mythology are so closely bound up with the divine that it is often impossible to tell which of them are gods made men and which are men made divine.

Like the sword Excalibur we're familiar with, in the Welsh tales, too, Arthur has a magic sword called Kaledfwlch. He also has a magic shield, Prytwen, which he can use as a boat, if needed. He defeats all his enemies and can only be overcome by treachery, like all the heroes of ancient epic. And he has a magic invisibility cloak – whoever wore it could see others without being seen himself.

Cataloguing these kinds of amazing marvels and wonders was actually already an old established activity in medieval Wales, according to Dr Brynley Roberts of the National Library of Wales. The list of miraculous deeds, or *'mirabilia'*, in the *Historia Brittonum* (dated about 830AD) has 20 of these marvels. Two of these relate to Arthur. The first, from a 9th C manuscript, relates to Cafal, Arthur's hound:

> There is another wonder in the country called Builth. There is a heap of stones there, and one of the stones placed on top of the pile has the footprint of a dog on it. When he hunted Twrch Trwyth, Cafal, the warrior Arthur's hound, impressed his footprint on the stone, and Arthur later brought together the pile of stones, under the stone in which was his dog's foot-print, and it is called Carn Cafal. Men come and take the stone in their hands for the space of a day and a night, and on the morrow it is found upon the stone pile.[12]

Carn Cafal is a grave which gives its name to what is now called Corn Gaffallt, a hill some 1,530 feet above the upper Wye in north Brecknockshire. Dr Roberts says that 'Cafal... appears as the name of Arthur's hound... as in Culhwch ac Olwen, presumably on account of its huge size, and the unmarked place-name Carn Cabal was reinterpreted as the cairn of Arthur's hound who left his imprint on the stone' during the hunting of the magical cauldron.[13] Cafal the hound appears in Culhwch ac Olwen only in the story of the boar hunt; it's also referred to in Geraint of the *Mabinogion* as Arthur's favourite dog, the only one named in the hunting of the white stag. This theme of the hunting of a white stag, with hounds present, comes up again in Celtic folklore, such as that of the Lothian and Borders area of Scotland, where it is related to the concepts of a royal hunt and kingship.

The 'unmeasurable grave'

The second old Welsh Arthurian miracle has the theme of the 'unmeasurable grave', a grave that has no limits:

> There is another wonder in the country called Ergyng. There is a tomb there by a spring, called Llygad Amr; the name of the man who is buried in the tomb was Amr. He was a son of the warrior Arthur, and he killed him there and buried him. Men come to measure the tomb, and it is sometimes six feet long, sometimes nine, sometimes twelve, sometimes fifteen. At whatever measure you measure it on one occasion, you never find it again of the same measure, and I have tried it myself.[14]

This grave is of a man who is said to have been buried there, who is believed to be Arthur's son, who was slain by his father. Amr, however, isn't known in later Arthurian legend except for a reference to Arthur's son Amhar, one of his chamberlains in *Geraint*, in the *Mabinogion*. Dr Roberts believes that these two miracles show that by the 9th C, Arthur had already become a popular hero in folklore and was a figure of sufficient fame by then to attract so many local legends...

> these 'mirabilia' are the earliest examples which can be securely dated. How far these Arthurian allusions are due to... the *Historia Brittonum* cannot be known, but the southeast Wales and Wye and Severn valleys orientation of the most fully developed items on the list probably reflects his local knowledge. On their own, the two 'mirabilia' are not evidence that a special place should be assigned to this area in a study of Arthurian legendary origins, though they may achieve greater significance when considered with other evidence.[15]

But it does seem clear, though, that the legendary theme of a 'grave that has no limits' would obviously refer to someone perceived to be greater than a mere human, as here we have a reference to someone who goes beyond normal limits, even after death.

The myth of the 'Once and Future King'

The myth of the 'Once and Future King' – the idea that Arthur is asleep in a grave or cave and will someday return to save the country in its hour of need – is also a theme that is found in traditions across the world. The question is where, exactly, did this tradition come from? Even scholars like Professor T. Gwynn Jones have concluded that there doesn't seem to be a clear bardic tradition for the idea that Arthur wasn't really dead and would one day return to save his people, which may seem surprising to us today.

Some believe that the idea of Arthur waiting in an Otherworld realm to return one day to save his people may have originated in the 12th C with the Normans. According to authors Blake and Lloyd:

> ...the Normans ...were responsible for turning Arthur into the chivalrous king we know today. The original 'once and future king' of the Welsh was Cadwaladr, the last king of the Britons, of whom Welsh poetry tells us that he would return to rescue Prydein [i.e. Britain] from its enemies. Not wanting to encourage the idea of a native Welsh king returning to drive them out of Wales, the Normans simply replaced Cadwaladr with Arthur (whom they had already made one of their own) and used the concept to further their own cause. In the 15th century, the Welsh were to turn the Norman invention of Arthur's return against its creators, using it for their own propaganda during the rise to power of Henry VII in 1485. For the first time since Cadwaladr, a descendant of the original British royal blood line was on the throne, not only of Wales but of England as well. Henry VII named his eldest son Arthur, and the country awaited the return of Arthur to the throne of Britain, but his premature death in 1502 meant that this expected return never happened.[15]

According to Blake and Lloyd, the Norman propaganda of Arthur's return was used by the Welsh Tudors to gain acceptance in England, while in Wales poetry comparing Henry with Cadwaladr was used to appeal to the Welsh. As a consequence, 'the idea of Arthur's return was not entertained widely in Wales until the late 15th C and even then it only took root slowly. The English, however, had been fed the myth from two different dynasties – the Normans and the Tudors – and therefore the legend of the 'Once and Future King' was much stronger than in Wales.'[16]

So again we witness the long-lasting power of a legend and how it might be used by various vested interests, something that historians have noted has happened rather frequently in history at certain times.

St Arthmael

But some authors go even further into controversial territory about Arthur, with Barber and Pykitt suggesting that Henry VII may have actually known what they call 'the truth' about the historical King Arthur – that he was really the historical St Arthmael, of which there is a representation in King Henry VII's chapel in Westminster Abbey.

St Arthmael is also called St Armel in some texts, as he is known to the Bretons. It is well known that Henry VII, through his Welsh grandfather, traced his descent from the ancient British kings and proudly saw himself as the successor of King Arthur. He named his son Arthur, was born in Wales and spent his early years both there and in Brittany, thus enabling him to be immersed in the history and folklore of the Celtic people. When he went to battle he marched under the standard of the Red Dragon, which he saw as the emblem of Arthur's Britain. Henry VII made the Welsh Dragon one of the supporters of the royals arms and this was upheld through the Tudor period. Later, the dragon was replaced by the unicorn of the Stuarts. These authors say that 'it is perhaps more than coincidence that Sir Thomas Malory's book *Le Morte d'Arthur* was published in the same year that Henry Tudor won the Battle of Bosworth and became Henry VII.'[17]

Their theory is that the real Arthur was in fact St Arthmael, who is mentioned in south Wales and is known to have lived in the 6th C, the time of King Arthur. St Arthmael, whose name means 'Bear Prince', also lived at the same time as Athrwys ap Meurig, who is described in the genealogy contained in the *Book of Llandaff* as the king reigning over Morgannwg and Gwent at this time.

St Arthmael is also known as the national messiah of Brittany, remembered for the part he played in liberating the Bretons from the tyranny of Marcus Conomorus, or King March, in the 6th C.

The Arthmael Stone from Ogmore Castle can now be seen in the National Museum of Wales and is dated to the 9th C.

Barber and Pykitt go on to say:

> For some time, we had suspected that Henry Tudor knew that King Arthur was synonymous with the great soldier-saint Arthmael... Arthmael was the national messiah who delivered his people from tyranny and that he is synonymous with King Arthur. Henry Tudor believed that, in freeing his country from the tyranny of Richard III, he was fulfilling the prophecy of Merlin which foretold the return of King Arthur. Our relentless search in due course revealed several examples of the veneration of St Armel in England and it would appear that the height of his popularity was during the reign of King Henry VII, for the name and pictures of St Armel [also spelled 'Arthmael'] can often be found in prayer books of this period.[18]

They go on to say that the death of Arthur (i.e. St Armel) was in 562AD at St Armel des Boschaux, where he is buried in a stone sarcophagus. He lived to be 80 years of age and the authors claim that 'the true identity of this highly-venerated soldier-saint from Glamorgan was previously unknown to the Bretons'.[19] They also claim that after his death, during the next 11 years three of King Arthur's most important contemporaries died and spent their final years in Armorica – known as Brittany to us today.

These authors stress that most people today are sadly unaware of the historical connections between Brittany and Wales, for they have been largely forgotten. Indeed, this is true. It is particularly significant that large numbers of immigrants from Gwent and Glamorgan settled in Brittany during the 5th and 6th centuries and that they named their territory Leon, after the Caerleon in Gwent which they had left behind. No doubt they also took their stories and traditions with them.

It seems apparent to them that it was from the Bretons rather than the Welsh that the Normans derived their knowledge of Arthur. But it must be remembered that these Breton traditions originally came from Wales, from settlers who brought their own history and culture, which they transplanted onto Brittany. A 'King Arthmael' is mentioned in the *Life of St Cadoc* compiled in the 11th C by Lifricus, son of Bishop Herewald, Archdeacon of

Glamorgan, where he says that 'a grant of land, now known as Cadoxton-juxta-Beath, was made to St Cadoc by a certain King Arthmael.'[20]

Also interesting is Geoffrey Ashe's suggestion in *The Discovery of King Arthur* (1980) that Geoffrey of Monmouth was really referring to the exploits of the Dark Age king Riothamus when he described how Arthur led an expedition to Gaul to fight the Romans. Ashe believes that many details make it clear that Geoffrey based his account on the activities of Riothamus in 468-469AD, when he led a British force of 12,000 men across the Channel to aid the Romans against the Visigoths invading the Loire area. But unfortunately the Romans never showed up for this battle, leaving the British forces decimated. It is said that Riothamus and the rest of his army retreated to the friendly territory of Burgundy, eventually to a town called Aballo, now known, ironically, as Avallon. The English village name of Appleton also comes from this root. Usually, the continental chroniclers about Arthur place him as contemporary with Riothamus in the 5th C.

Arthurian legends in England: Glastonbury

We will now turn to Arthur in English history, especially regarding Glastonbury. As scholars have pointed out, the Arthur in English history was largely that of Geoffrey of Monmouth, portrayed as the active heroic king:

> On the Continent, Chretien de Troyes introduced a different Arthur: the *roi faineant* hovering in the background while his knights dominate the action... In England... the version of Arthur which prevailed... was basically that of Geoffrey of Monmouth. Only at the very end of the Middle Ages did Thomas Malory supplement Geoffrey's whole account of the rise and fall of the kingdom with materials from the French romances.[21]

But the turning point in what one scholar calls 'the historicizing and anglicizing of Arthur' was the exhumation of his relics at Glastonbury Abbey in 1191:[22]

> In that year, his body and according to some accounts that of Guinevere, too, was 'discovered' in a sarcophagus buried at great

depth between two ancient pyramids in the monks' cemetary, a leaden cross revealing the identity of the remains... Why the discovery of Arthur's body took place precisely when it did appears to have been the result of several factors. The devastating fire at Glastonbury in 1184 created a financial crisis and the community would have been sympathetic to the kind of publicity Arthur's discovery would generate. According to Giraldus Cambrensis, Henry II suggested the dig and in the 1180s Henry II would have had good reason for reminding the Welsh that Arthur was dead and buried (and in English territory at that). He might also have wished, in the aftermath of the Becket fiasco, to have promoted Glastonbury as an alternative site to Canterbury for the origins of English Christianity...[23]

Originally, it was said that *three* bodies had been found, including that of Mordred, but this was later excised, as was that of Guinevere, once Richard the Lionheart became associated with this event. The inscription on the lead cross found with the bodies was said to have been, in 1193, by Giraldus: '*Hic iacet sepultus inclitus rex Arthurus cum Wenneuereia uxore sua secunda in insula Auallonia*' – 'Here lies buried the famous king Arthur with his second wife Guenevere in the Isle of Avalon'.

Ralph of Coggeshall (c.1194) read it as 'Here lies the famous king Arthur, buried in the Isle of Avalon'. Writing a half a century later, the Glastonbury chronicler Adam of Damerham said that it read, '*Hic iacet sepultus inclitus rex Arturius in insula Aualonia*'. At the time of the Dissolution of the monasteries in the 16th C, antiquarian John Leland claimed to have actually handled the lead cross itself and said that it read '*Hic iacet sepultus inclytus rex Arturius in insula avallonia*'. It is this version which is the major one known to posterity through William Camden's engraving of 1607.[24]

So where is the lead cross today? Unfortunately, it was said to have been lost in the 18th C. So, as some have asked: did the monks 'fake' this discovery to get more pilgrims after the devastating fire of 1184? Many have believed so. Yet others say no.

Geoffrey Ashe comments:

> However, the theory of a pure fake was refuted in 1963 when Ralegh Radford re-excavated the site. He proved not only that the monks had dug where they said, but that they had got down

to a stratum of very early burials. There is no longer any doubt as to the grave. The question is simply whose it was, and this turns on the lead cross. It was lost in the eighteenth century... The problem is complex and has certainly not been cleared up.[25]

But unfortunately without the lead cross there is no way to verify that it was the body of Arthur that had been exhumed. Researchers Graham Phillips and Martin Keatman comment on this:

> Today the affair of Arthur's bones is considered so suspect that few historians take it seriously. In all likelihood, the monks discovered an unmarked grave and subsequently some had the idea to claim it as Arthur's... Whatever actually occurred, we can be sure of one thing: pilgrims came flocking and the abbey was considerably enriched.[26]

From very early times Glastonbury was an important pagan sanctuary as the Tor, the hill rising above the area of the Abbey, has a system of paths or terraces which are believed to be the remnants of a prehistoric maze. The surrounding landscape forms a zodiac pattern that may date from earlier times.

Legends state that Glastonbury was the place where Joseph of Arimathea came to Britain with the young Christ to visit his Cornish tin mines, clearly also making Glastonbury an important place with early Christian affiliations.[27] As we saw in chapter 5, in 597AD St Augustine was quite surprised to find an already existing Christian church in the west of Britain where Christ and some of the apostles were said to have come after the crucifixion.

Many believe this was at Glastonbury, or possibly, on the island of Anglesey. Celtic missionaries were said to have been trained at Glastonbury, and there is also a tradition that St Patrick went there. *The Domesday Book* called Glastonbury 'The Secret of the Lord'. One has to wonder why – clearly this indicates that there was already an existing legend about this tradition in place, probably about Joseph of Arimathea. The Holy Thorn at Glastonbury, said to have been planted from the staff of Joseph of Arimathea, is a genuine Levantine thorn, *Crataegus Praecox*, and it is known to mysteriously blossom twice a year, in May and at Christmas. These are only a few of the many legends about Glastonbury relating to Christianity.

Glastonbury also has many other legends. The pagan-Christian issue is addressed in an early legend associated with the Tor and a 'showdown' between St Collen and Gwyn, the King of the Fairies, said to live under the Tor:

> ...Glastonbury Tor, in particular, came in Welsh tradition to be associated with Annwfn [i.e. the Otherworld], and Annwfn's lord, Gwyn ap Nudd, in later tradition the fairy king... And it was on the Tor that he was encountered by Collen, the sixth-century wandering saint ... Collen had come to live as a hermit on the Tor, and one day overheard two men talking of Gwyn, who had his palace there. He rebuked them for speaking of devils... they warned him that Gwyn would not overlook such an insult, and would certainly send for him. Sure enough, a few days later, a messenger came to Collen's cell to invite him to visit Gwyn. Three times the saint refused, but at last agreed to go, though taking the precaution of hiding a flask of holy water under his cloak. He entered the hill by a secret door and found himself in a wonderful palace, where Gwyn sat in a golden chair. The king offered him food, but Collen refused it, no doubt because he knew that fairy food was perilous. 'I do not eat the leaves of a tree,' he said, and after further boorish remarks, sprinkled his holy water about him. King and palace vanished forthwith, and Collen found himself... alone on the cold hillside.[28]

This tale is from a *Life of St Collen* written in the 16th C which shows Gwyn, the King of the Fairies, already living inside the fairy mound, as he is usually portrayed in 18th C Welsh tradition. But earlier, Gwyn was a god, a son of Nudd, the British god Nodens, who was honoured in a shrine at Lydney. He was also connected early on with Arthur, as in the early Welsh tale of the hunting of the great boar Twrch Trwyth.

The boar in relation to Arthur is interesting, with Geoffrey of Monmouth telling us of Merlin, who told Vortigern – the usurper of the throne – that the terrible conflict between the Britons and the Saxons would continue *until the coming of the Boar of Cornwall*. The prophecy states that the Boar would trample the Saxons and conquer France and the island of the sea, and that his end would be shrouded in mystery. The boar is the 'sovereign beast' renown for its ferocity and courage in battle and 'the Boar of Cornwall is Arthur, and the great hero is here a figure of destiny, whose coming was foretold by a prophet and whose career was planned by unseen forces, guiding events from behind the scenes.[29]

The evolution of the myth of 'Arthur as King'

King Arthur and his legendary image as a powerful, heroic king continued long past the Dark Ages. In 1277, Edward I defeated the Welsh and forced Llywelyn ap Gruffydd, prince of Wales, to submit to him. Dr James Carley says:

> To justify their domination of the Welsh, the English represented themselves as the legitimate successors of Brutus and Arthur, both of whom held sovereignty over Scotland and Wales. By the spring of 1278 Edward faced the danger of renewed Welsh opposition, rallying under the banner of the prophesied return of Arthur, the sleeping king. This, then, is the subtext of the 1278 Easter visit to Glastonbury by Edward and Eleanor, the highlight of which was Arthur's 'second' exhumation...[30]

Adam of Damerham, believed to have been an eyewitness, describes what Edward I found in the tomb and the inscription which was put on the inside by Edward and Eleanor: 'These are the bones of the most noble King Arthur which were placed here on 19 April in the year of the Lord's Incarnation 1278 by the illustrious Lord Edward, king of England...'[31]

Dr Carley goes on to say that this was part of the process of the 'Arthurization' of the reign of Edward I, noting events such as the reburial of the bones of Arthur and Guinevere at Glastonbury in 1278, the presentation of Arthur's Welsh crown at the high altar of Westminster Abbey in 1284, the Arthurian style Feast of the Swan in 1306, and so on. 'Edward himself believed that his coronation oath gave him authority over the whole imperium and that he was entitled to exercise is control in both Wales and Scotland.'[32]

Edward I also used the power of Arthur in his confrontations with Scotland, starting with the crisis of 1290 when Edward was called upon to adjudicate the Scottish succession question:

> Unsure of his own constitutional position, Edward launched a historical inquest, sending circular letters to the monasteries in 1291 and again in 1300, in which each community was instructed

to search its chronicles and archives for evidence concerning the status of the two realms. When he came to write his letter in 1301 to [Pope] Boniface VIII outlining his position on the Scottish question, Edward – presumably basing himself on the findings of certain of the returns – included Arthur as an important piece of evidence...[33]

Edward stated in this letter to the Pope, among other things, about Arthur and Scotland:

> Arthur, king of the Britons, that most famous leader, made subject to his authority rebellious Scotland, and destroyed nearly all its people and then appointed as king of Scotland one Anguselus. When later the same King Arthur had a celebrated feast at Caerleon, all the kings subject to him attended, among whom Anguselus, king of Scotland, displaying his service for the kingdom of Scotland, bore King Arthur's sword before him and subsequently all kings of Scotland have been subject to all kings of the Britons.[34]

The Scots, of course, vehemently retaliated against this and said that while Arthur may have conquered Scotland in far distant times, the fact that he died without children meant that Scotland automatically reverted back to its independent status and that this claim was therefore irrelevant.[35]

Professor Michael Lynch, University of Edinburgh, says in *Scotland: A New History*:

> A mythology of English civilisation, which would survive as a potent vehicle of policy for centuries, was first bred as part of the successive wars of conquest... In 1284 the conquest of Wales had been marked by the removal of both the legendary crown of King Arthur and the most precious relic in Wales, a fragment of the True Cross. It was no accident that Edward took these emblems of a conquered people to Scotland on his campaign on 1296... These were wars of ideology as well as conquest... The mythology of the war was as important as the course of it...[36]

But the Arthurian connections didn't end there. When Edward I lay dying, he and his advisors were very fearful of news from a Scottish informant that dealt with *the prophecy of Merlin and the Scottish King Robert the Bruce*. Lynch describes:

> The rise of Robert Bruce after 1306 seemed to bring a new threat to the conquest of Wales as well as in Scotland: panic greeted a

rumour from an informer in Scotland in 1307, as Edward I lay dying, that 'preachers' involved with the cause of Robert the Bruce had discovered another prophecy of Merlin, that 'after the death of 'le Roy Covetous' the people of Scotland and the Britons [i.e. the Welsh] shall league together'...[37]

Naturally, this is not at all what Edward and his advisors wanted to hear – the idea of a possible Celtic unity occurring between the Scots and the Welsh. Such propaganda strategies of using a powerful legend like King Arthur are certainly something that many countries and armies have tried in times of war all throughout history, the English certainly being no exception to this. Of course, one could also argue that it appears that Bruce's supportive preachers were also brilliant 'spin doctors' at the time! The belief systems of a people are clearly important and are often used or manipulated in warfare by both sides, something that is widely acknowledged by historians today.

But problems with the Scots continued after Edward I's death, in particular after Edward III's repudiation of the Treaty of Northampton in 1330, which really increased hostilities.

Dr Carley comments about Glastonbury and Scotland in his work *Arthur in English History* that not long after the Treaty of Northampton 1330 [emphasis supplied]:

> ... just before Christmas 1331, Edward III and Philippa paid a visit to Glastonbury, thus publicly reaffirming Edward's Arthurian connections in the same manner as Edward's grandfather had done in 1278. It was roughly the period of Edward's visit, too, that the prophecy of Melkin the Bard was concocted at Glastonbury. In this cryptic text the mysterious Holy Grail of Arthurian romance tradition has been transformed into a wholly respectable Holy Blood relic, historically unimpeachable, brought to England by Joseph of Arimathea. Glastonbury thus took on apostolic status... Apart from its local interest... *the affirmation of Joseph's mission to Glastonbury served Edward's needs on the Scottish front admirably. In 'Scimus, fili', Boniface VIII had cited the special relationship between the Scots and St Andrew, and the Declaration of Arbroath (1320) stated that the Scots were converted by Andrew. Joseph at Glastonbury undermined, of course, the force of the Andrew story; and the genealogical chain from Joseph to Arthur which the Glastonbury*

writers formulated added even more potency to Edward's claims as monarch and overlord.[38]

About an historical Arthur, most historians 'now agree that an Arthur-like British warlord really did exist and that Gildas's account of a famous British victory at 'Mons Badonicus' is basically trustworthy. What they can't say with any confidence is who Arthur was, where his political base was located...', according to Oxford historian Norman Davies.[39]

But, even so, it does seem indisputable that

> James VI of Scotland had great expectations through his Tudor blood, and these were realised when he succeeded Elizabeth in 1603... He was thoroughly convinced of his historic descent from Arthur... The prophecies of Merlin were bandied about to much the same effect by Archbishop Spottiswoode and others. Ben Jonson persistently flattered James... in his 'Masque of Oberon' he speaks of the throne as 'Arthur's Chair'...[40]

Arthurian legends in Scotland

Scotland has its own intriguing group of legends and folklore about Arthur, Merlin and Guinevere that are indigenous to Scottish culture, as some scholars now maintain. The Lothian and Borders area of Scotland, near Edinburgh, has a long tradition of place-names and legends relating to Arthurian subjects. These have been persistent for a very long time. One logical question would be: Why? The dominant view regarding where Arthur's political base was, and where his battles have been fought, has largely placed Arthur in England, Wales or Cornwall, the areas that most of us are familiar with from the stories.

But, strangely enough, *Arthur's battles aren't mentioned at all in the Anglo-Saxon Chronicle.* It is now believed by Arthurian scholars that at least one and probably more of Arthur's battles were likely to have been fought somewhere in the north – in the Scottish lowlands, northern England or perhaps north Wales, for example. The problem is exactly where, and experts still do not agree. But as we will see, there are several interesting theories about this.

Back in the 5th C, at the end of the Roman period and right before Arthur's time, Scotland was an area of many different linguistic and racial groupings. The main group in southern Scotland, near Edinburgh and the Borders, was British, speaking what is called a 'P-Celtic' language related to Welsh, Cornish and Breton. The Votadini (Edinburgh area), the Selgovae (Borders/Tweeddale area), the Novantae (southwestern area) and the Damnonii (in the valley of the Clyde river, and Glasgow area) were all P-speaking tribes in early times.

The other branch of the Celtic languages is called 'Q-Celtic', which was spoken as Irish, Scottish Gaelic and Manx. So the early language that was actually spoken in the Edinburgh area, for example, was similar to what we would now call Old Welsh, one of the languages the early Arthurian material was written in.

The men of the north: The Gododdin

The Welsh poem Y *Gododdin* takes its name from the Votadini (Goddodin) who lived *around the Edinburgh area*. In this poem the warrior Gwawrddur is praised as heroic, but it is stated that he 'was not Arthur'. Clearly he is being compared to what sounds like a great warrior who was named Arthur. In the late 8th and 9th centuries, it is believed by scholars that several of the P-Celtic tribes from the Scottish lowlands and Strathclyde areas migrated into north Wales, taking their memories of Arthur with them. What is left today in Scotland are various place-names and legends commemorating Arthur and his great deeds.

One of the earliest advocates of a Scottish location for Arthur was W.F. Skene, who believed that most, if not all, of Arthur's major battles were probably fought in the lowlands of Scotland. Although most scholars do not accept this theory today, preferring instead to acknowledge that *at least one or more* of the battles were likely fought in the north, they do not accept that all of them were.

To his credit Skene did at least attempt to point out some possible sources of remaining confusion, for example, the lowland Scottish tribe 'Damnonii' being nearly identical to the Cornish 'Dumnonii', implying that this was a mistake of the early manuscript translators as to where Arthur's base was.

Kentigern/Merlin window at Stobo Church

Maiden Stone, Aberdeenshire

The Eagle Stone, Strathpeffer

Aberlemno Stone, front

Aberlemno Stone, reverse

Apprentice Pillar,
Rosslyn Chapel

Glastonbury Thorn Tree

Brechin Round Tower

Fingal's Cave, Staffa

Vanora's (Guinevere) Mound, Meigle churchyard

Monument at Athelstaneford

TRADITION SAYS THAT NEAR THIS PLACE IN TIMES REMOTE PICTISH AND SCOTTISH WARRIORS ABOUT TO DEFEAT AN ARMY OF NORTHUMBRIANS, SAW AGAINST A BLUE SKY A GREAT WHITE CROSS LIKE SAINT ANDREW'S, AND IN ITS IMAGE MADE A BANNER WHICH BECAME THE FLAG OF SCOTLAND.

Ironically, Arthur was never listed as a king, as he isn't named on any of the kingship lists. Instead he is described as '*dux bellorum*', which means he was more likely a very courageous war leader or warrior chief. Yet the popular image of him as a 'king' has persisted.

The best case for a Scottish location for one of Arthur's battles is the Scottish wood called *Cat Caet Celidon*. It is listed as the 7th battle in the *Historia Brittonum* and is one of the 12 key battle sites of Arthur. This was the Caledonian forest where Merlin was said to have wandered. It is also spelled *celyddon*, and is where the modern word 'caledonian' is believed to have come from. Today most people think of Scotland when 'Caledonia' is mentioned. In earlier times, those we think of as the 'Scots' today were often called the 'Caledonians' and the term 'Scots' in medieval manuscripts generally means the Gaelic-speaking Irish immigrants, another race of people altogether. The 'Picts' were listed as separate from both of these, and didn't speak Gaelic. Today, the Welsh in Wales are related to the descendants of the early Cymry tribe, who came from the Edinburgh and Lothians area of Scotland in early times. Skene saw Arthur as re-establishing the Cymric kingdoms in the North.[41]

Arthur's Seat, a large, imposing volcanic rock that dominates the Edinburgh skyline, has some interesting traditions associated with it. In early times, all over Scotland, numbers of young girls would rise before dawn on Beltane (May Eve) and go out to meadows or hillsides to bathe their faces in the fresh dew. In Edinburgh, this tradition survived well into the 18th C on Arthur's Seat on Beltane morning.

Even long after the Reformation, the observance of May Day was never entirely abandoned, as those who were ill 'were brought to Arthur's Seat before dawn to bask in the beneficent rays of the 'new sun'.[42] The *Scotsman* newspaper reported on 2 May 1949:

> Arthur's Seat Sunrise Service – In spite of a 'Scotch Mist', about 1,000 gathered at the top of Arthur's Seat, Edinburgh, yesterday morning at sunrise (5:30 am) to take part in the usual May Day service. The average age of the early morning climbers was 17-20, but many people were well over 60. Organised by Christian Highway, the Church of Scotland organisation for young people

keen on open-air activities, the service lasted 17 minutes... It was the ninth May Day service to be held, the numbers of persons attending having risen steadily.[43]

And indeed they have, although perhaps in a different way. Today, every year Beltane eve is celebrated on top of Calton Hill in Edinburgh. It is a large evening festival, featuring drama, music, special drumming and dancing, organised by the Beltane Fire Society. In recent years up to 10,000 people have come from far and wide to Edinburgh to attend this event on Beltane eve, 30 April.

The Stirling area also has a pervasive Arthurian legend about the site of Stirling Castle. According to tradition:

> ...this was one of the historic seats of the Celtic hero Arthur, the flat table-land which lies southwest of the Castle being identified with the Round Table on which he trained his forces. The Castle was a favourite residence of Alexander I and William the Lyon, and has associations with several of the Stuart kings.[45]

A local Scottish Borders legend says that Arthur never died but still sleeps with his knights under the Eildon Hills near Melrose, until such time as he will be needed again. This is where Arthur and his sleeping knights were said to have been seen with all their horses and gear, and were very nearly awakened by a local horse-dealer who had accidentally strayed into their cavern under the Eildon Hills. But as the horse-dealer did not correctly fulfil the awakening conditions, the knights returned to sleep and remain there undisturbed yet today, it is said. Again the focus is on the Scottish borders area in this old legend.

Alastair Moffat, in his recent book *Arthur and the Lost Kingdoms* has done interesting research on local place names, traditions and customs in the Borders area. A brief summary, which does not begin to do this book justice due to the complexity of these issues, is that the real Arthur was a cavalry leader of the Votadini tribe who lived near Edinburgh, and that Arthur and his men existed almost 1,000 years *before* chainmail and long bows. This, ironically, is the major 'image' that most of us have of Arthur and his knights today! Arthur was the courageous Dark Age leader of the Votadini, who called themselves the Gododdin, and defeated the Picts to the north and the Angles to the south.

Moffat believes that Camelot is at the ancient site of Roxburgh in the Scottish borders and that this site should be further excavated – as should many others in the area – to help clarify the situation about Dark Age Scotland. He points out that a few Dark Age princelings did leave gravestones, although rather crudely carved ones. One of them in particular, now in the National Museum of Scotland in Edinburgh, is dated to the 5th C and has an inscription of 'Coninie Ertire or Artirie'. The names are Latin genitives of the first declension, he states, and that this Erthir or Arthur was buried near Peebles in the Scottish borders. Amidst his many speculations he makes a very good case for the need for further excavations and research to be done in Scotland so that more can be known for certain about Dark Age Scotland and its history.

Moffat also points out that many of the earlier P-Celtic place-names were later changed to Q-Celtic names, reflecting the influx of the Gaelic-speaking peoples centuries later. Around Stowe, in the Borders, for example, 'there are a number of P-Celtic names which have been altered to fit... the Q-Celtic speakers who settled by the Gala Water half a millennium after Arthur. 'Tref' names, meaning settlement, became 'tor' names, a Gaelic word for a hill or sometimes a rocky hill. Torsonce Hill is where the remains of the shrine to St Mary stands, hidden by trees, but in 500AD it was a 'Tref' name, perhaps meaning the 'settlement of a prince or chief'...'[45] So naturally such changes of place names may have contributed to a lot of the confusion. Indeed, this is an area that does need more research in the future to help clarify matters. Intriguingly, he points out, the Nennius papers had said that Arthur bore or wore the image of the Virgin Mary and slew great numbers.

Michael Scot: the 'Wizard of the North'

The ruins of the magnificent medieval Melrose Abbey in the Scottish Borders stood very close to the large Roman fort of Trimontium, on the Great North Road from London to York up to Stirling, in central Scotland. The fort was called Trimontium because of the triple peaks of the Eildon hills, an exceptionally dramatic panorama. Almost no traces of Trimontium, now called Newstead, exist today.[46]

Melrose Abbey has a fascinating history. It was built by the Cistercians and it is said that the heart of Robert the Bruce is buried there. Another association with Melrose, although rather unusual, relates to the mysterious Michael Scot, dubbed the 'Wizard of the North' in medieval times. Scot's grave is said to be at Melrose Abbey in the south transept chapel nearest the presbytery, and it has a cross on it, as Scot was a cleric. Born in Scotland, he was celebrated all over 12th C Europe and was later associated with the court of Emperor Frederick II of Sicily. It was acknowledged that he was a very learned man and widely read in the serious study of philosophy, mathematics, alchemy, astrology and magic, in addition to medicine, earning him the title of 'wizard' at the time. Others believe his real grave is still to be found, along with his valuable library of rare books.

The 'city of the legion' that Nennius names in relation to Arthur has been thought by some to have been Chester, an enthusiastic case made by Robert Stoker in 1965.[47] Others believe it may be in the Scottish lowlands, or somewhere else in northern England.

Scottish Arthurian place-names

Lewis Spence, writing in the April 1926 issue of *Scots Magazine*, said:

> It is sixty years since Stuart Glennie wrote his famous monograph on *The Arthurian Localities of Scotland,* and if his thesis that the Caledonian scene was the original stage of the Arthurian story be not altogether confirmed by subsequent research, it still retains sufficient authority to render it adequately clear that the Arthurian legend must have taken strong and early root in Scotland. It is entrenched in Perthshire and Forfarshire as well as at Edinburgh and Stirling. A stone known locally as the Stone of Arthur still stands in the parish of Coupar Angus, and such names as Arthurstone, Arthur's Fold, and Arthur's Seat are scattered over a considerable area...[48]

Glennie listed a gazeteer of place names in Scotland that are associated with Arthurian legends. For example, in the Edinburgh and Lothians area, he listed the Firth of Forth, Culross monastery,

Stirling Castle, Arthur's O'on, Stenhousemuir, the Carron, Camelon, near Falkirk, Bathgate, Linlithgow, the Avon, Lothian, Abercorn, Dalmeny, Cramond, Edinburgh Castle, Kirkliston, Arthur's Seat in Edinburgh, Trapain Law, Bass rock, Kilduff and Aberlady bay. In the Borders/Tweeddale area, he listed the Gala Water, Stowe, the river Tweed, Peebles, Caledonian Forest, Drummelzier, the Teviot, the Eildon Hills, Melrose, Abbotsford, Earlston, Kelso, Jedburgh and Berwick, among others.[49] Glennie listed other place names in other parts of Scotland as well, indicating that Arthurian legends and folklore must have taken a very early hold. W.J. Watson in his classic work *The Celtic Place-Names of Scotland* also lists places in the west of Scotland associated with Arthur, such as Arthur's Seat in Dumbarton, Loch Long, Arthur's Face, a rock on the west side of Glenkinglas, and Struarthour in Glassary, Argyll, for instance.[50]

As one can see, there are quite a number of places in Scotland that have been associated for centuries with Arthurian legends. As you may recall from chapter 4, one researcher even believes that Arthur may have been buried at Govan Old Parish Church, Glasgow, in the 6th C sarcophagus there, which experts attribute to St Constantine, the founder of Govan. This is controversial, of course, but as with all theories about an historical Arthur, no one can really say anything for certain, so speculation mounts. The Guinevere Monument, at Meigle in Perthshire, has long been associated with the Pictish queen Guinevere, possibly spelled as 'Guanhumara'. Today the museum at Meigle has a number of important Pictish stones, some of which are associated with Arthurian legends, especially those of Guinevere, which are centuries old in Scotland.

Scottish researcher Stuart McHardy has done a great deal of research on Scottish Arthurian place-names in Scotland. In particular, he points out the great importance of *oral transmission of the Arthurian tales at the time that Arthur lived*, something that is often forgotten, as the focus has usually been on manuscripts that were actually written much later. In general, literacy only became semi-universal in the last few centuries, he notes. The tremendous importance of oral traditions and storytelling in early Scotland is a known fact. McHardy clarifies this issue:

With stable social structures, the continuity of traditions such as storytelling... is preserved, and recent research from Australia shows that the oral tradition can carry specific information over tens of thousands of years. Our reliance on written records has blinded us to this for too long. Within societies reliant solely on oral transmission there is always the possibility of the merging of historical figures with mythological ones... in pre-Christian societies it is likely that such centralised structures... whether religious, military, or economic... were based within specifically tribal areas. Only after the advent of Christianity is there an out-side body of knowledge and belief to be referred to, and even then it was the general practice of the incoming Christians to absorb a certain amount of local belief...[51]

This is certainly worth noting, the overall importance of story-telling and oral traditions. He also believes that the Isle of May, in the Firth of Forth near Edinburgh, may be a possible Scottish can-didate for the isle of Avalon, as it has been shown to have been an important pre-Christian medieval Christian site, within the oral traditions of the P-Celtic speaking peoples of the Lothians and Forth area. Of course, not everyone agrees, but that is 'par for the course' with Arthurian theories and historical analysis – the spec-ulation is endless.

Arthur in Gaelic literature

The study of Arthur in Gaelic literature has also been exam-ined. Some scholars believe that many of the themes that occur in the stories about Arthur are also found in the Old Irish tales and can be traced back to them. J.E. Caerwyn Williams and Patrick Ford in *The Irish Literary Tradition* state:

...Schoepperle argues that the story about Grainne is but a variant of the Deirdre story... and represents a Celtic source of the story of Tristan and Isolt... it preserves many of the motifs that occur repeatedly in the French and German versions of the romance. Thurneysen believed that the tale of Cano mac Gartnain contains parallel themes, and that even the name of the old king in that tale, Marcan, was consistent with the French tradition...[52]

The story of the Grail is the only major continental Arthurian tale to be translated into Irish, as 'it was translated from a lost English version which seems to have been made in the 14th C. According to its editor, S. Falconer, the Irish translation was probably not made before the middle of the following century.' [53]

Esteemed scholar Dr Daithi O'hOgain of University College Dublin mentions two other possible Arthurian connections in the Irish tradition. One is the word *bolg* which was often easily confused with the ordinary word for a bag. The Fir Bolg, a people who occupied Ireland in ancient times, were later dubbed the 'men of the bags', as they were known to carry clay in bags. O'hOgain comments that '... since [the word] '*colg*' means a sword it was natural that *caladhcholg* should be substituted for the earlier form, so the typical weapon became a sword. In Welsh sources it is also a sword, though the original *bolgos* survived there in its aspirated form, viz. *caledvwlch* – hence Arthur's great 'Caliburnus' or 'Excalibur' in later romantic literature.' [54]

Some traces of a pre-Geoffrey of Monmouth Arthur survive as themes in earlier Gaelic literature, but the problem has always been how to interpret them.[55] Richard Barber in *The Figure of Arthur* took the view that that an Irish Artur [sic] was the original, absorbed into the Brittonic milieu at a later date, thereby explaining the relative absence of Arthur from certain genres such as saga poetry. Four of the more significant texts are the *Senchus Fe nAlban*, Adomnan's *Vita Columbae*, *De Causis Torche na nDessi*, and the *Acallam na Senorach*.

This last work, the *Accallam na Senorach* ('The Colloquy of the Ancient Men') was written in Ireland in the early 12th C, but it is known to contain many tales that were from a much earlier layer of oral tradition. It tells of St Patrick's encounters with the last remaining Fianna warriors. One episode is where the Fianna, Finn MacCumaill and his men, come by their horses, in which an Artur [sic], a son of the King of Britain, is humbled by the Fianna. According to authors Coe and Young, Professor William Gillies 'described the *Accallam* as seeming to antedate the possibility, or at least the likelihood, of acquaintance with the work of Geoffrey and the Romances.'[56]

An author comments: 'Another Artur [sic] is mentioned later on in the text as a member of Finn's 'first battalion', though this one plays a more minor role and drowns in Loch Lurgan.'[57] However, a number of scholars disagree about an Old Irish role, with one clearly commenting that 'Arthurian material in Irish is rare, late, and derivative... it is clear that there was no early, indigenous Irish Arthurian literature.'[58] Many Welsh scholars believe that some of the early Welsh poetry especially, such as that of the oldest Triads, provides a much earlier body of narratives that predate Geoffrey of Monmouth for the source of the Arthurian material. As this subject is clearly a very complex one, it is understandable that the debate will continue regarding the possible origins of the Arthurian material, for a long time to come.

Arthurian legends in Cornwall

Cornwall has a rich tradition relating to Arthur, most notably that King Arthur was born at Tintagel Castle on the north Cornish coast. This comes from Geoffrey of Monmouth's *Historia Regum Brittaniae* (History of the Kings of Britain), written in about 1135.

It mentions the birth of Arthur at Tintagel Castle, a scene which may be familiar to modern readers from the beginning of the well-known film 'Excalibur'. To summarize, at an Easter gathering, Uther Pendragon, the king: ... was seized with an obsessive lust for Ygerna, the beautiful wife of Gorlois, Duke of Cornwall. His advances to her were obvious. Gorlois withdrew from the court, taking his wife with him. The King treated this action as an insult. He sent Gorlois an ultimatum ordering him to return, and, when this was rejected, marched to Cornwall to ravage the ducal lands. Gorlois put Ygerna in Tintagel Castle, on a coastal headland which could only be approached along a narrow, easily guarded ridge. Having stowed her beyond Uther's presumed reach, he led a force to oppose the royal army, making his base at a fort some distance off. Uther surrounded Gorlois's weaker force and prevented its escape. Then, on a friend's advice, he sent for Merlin. The magician gave him a potion which turned him into an exact replica of Gorlois. Thus, effectively disguised, Uther passed the guards at Tintagel and found his way to Ygerna. Supposing him to be her husband, she caused no difficulties, and as a result of this encounter she conceived Arthur. Meanwhile, the real Gorlois had been killed in a sortie...[59]

Also according to Geoffrey, Arthur was badly wounded at the battle of Camlann, which he places somewhere in Cornwall. Geoffrey says that although Arthur succeeds in squelching the rebellion at Camlann, led by his nephew Modred, he is mortally wounded and is then taken to the isle of Avalon for his wounds to be tended. But he doesn't tell us anything more about what became of Arthur.

Tintagel has several important links to the Arthurian legend. 'Merlin's Cave' on the shore below the castle is where Merlin is said to have taken the baby boy Arthur from the sea. 'King Arthur's Footprint' is a hollow in the rock 'at the highest point of the Island's southern side. This is not entirely natural, having been shaped by human hands at some stage...'[60] 'King Arthur's Bed' is a long hollow in the rock, again cut by human hands 'and probably originally intended as a grave in medieval times. It is located by the chapel, not far from the footprint.'[61]

But until recently, scholars naturally tended to dismiss any Arthurian associations with Tintagel Castle, as it was built in the early 12th C for Reginald, Earl of Cornwall, long after the Dark Ages. It was assumed that Geoffrey named Tintagel to please Reginald, who was the wealthy brother of his patron, Robert, Earl of Gloucester. Excavations had concluded that there was a Celtic monastery on the site.

More recent excavations at Tintagel in 1990-91 tell a different story:

> ...the site was never a monastery, and was indeed used in the 5th and 6th centuries as a stronghold, possibly on a seasonal basis since it would be all but uninhabitable in winter storms. Moreover it is now clear that the medieval castle was not started until a century after Geoffrey was writing, so he had no reason at all to name Tintagel unless there was a tradition already in existence. [62]

Pottery was found that indicates that those who lived there had actually lived a rather luxurious lifestyle, perhaps as a holiday destination. More research and excavations are planned for the future to help clarify matters. But although there is still no definitive proof of a clear Arthurian connection, many believe that there is a lot of circumstantial evidence.

Originally the name Tintagel only referred to the Castle; the settlement nearby was called Trevena. This was changed to Tintagel following the opening in 1893 of the North Cornwall Railway to Camelford, which had obvious tourism implications for the area, as there is also a strong tradition that Arthur died at Slaughter Bridge near the river Camel. [63] The name Tintagel 'is derived from the Cornish Tyn-tagell. Tyn, or dyn, means fort, and tagell means constriction, which obviously relates to the neck of rock connecting the mainland with the 'island'... an alternative explanation for the origin of the name Tintagel is that the fortress was once known as *Tente d'Agel*, from the Norman-French meaning, 'stronghold of the Devil'.[64]

Another Cornish site associated with Arthurian legends is Dozmary Pool, famed for where Arthur's sword Excalibur was said to be thrown after he was mortally wounded in the Battle of Camlann. It is located out on Bodmin Moor.[65] King Arthur and nine kings are said to have pledged each other in the holy water from St Sennan's Well, after Arthur helped them slay the Danes near Land's End.[66] Robert Hunt, folklorist, writing in 1881, commented that 'not far from the Devil's Coit in St Columb, on the edge of the Gossmoor, there is a large stone, upon which are deeply-impressed marks... this is 'King Arthur's Stone', and these marks were made by the horse upon which the British king rode when he resided at Castle Denis, and hunted on these moors... King Arthur's bed, chairs, and caves, are frequently to be met with. The Giant's Coits... are probably monuments of the earliest types of rock mythology.'[67] There are also many other early Cornish traditions associated with Arthurian lore.

Arthurian legends and the arts

Arthurian tradition and chivalric ideals have also been carried on into more modern times, as exemplified by the great interest in and revival of Arthur by the Tudors, for example. Poets such as Tennyson, with his famous *Idylls of the King*, the Pre-Raphaelites such as Burne-Jones and Rossetti, and the composer Henry Purcell who wrote the music for an opera entitled *King Arthur or the British Worthy* (which was produced in March 1691 at London's

Dorset Garden Theatre with a libretto by John Dryden) also participated in the revival of Arthurian themes.

Novelists also reworked Arthurian themes, such as the 12-volume epic *King Arthur* by Lord Edward Bulwer-Lytton who was one of the most popular novelists of his time, the late 1840s. In this series, Arthur 'is located as a warrior-king of the Dark Ages who successfully leads the Cymrians – the Welsh or British – against the incursions of the Saxons, who are identified as Teutons. Arthur is both a national hero and a champion of Christianity, and is claimed by Bulwer-Lytton as the founder of the royal line that descends to Queen Victoria.'[68] Other visual artists, too, contributed to the Arthurian revival.

Even schools had paintings and murals depicting Arthur and his knights of the Round Table, to help instill chivalric ideals into their students. For example, between 1903 and 1910, Mrs M. Sargent-Florence, sister of Oakham School's headmaster,

> covered eight wall spaces in the Elizabethan Hall with frescoes illustrating *The Tale of Gareth*... details like Gareth's black armour and the dangling bodies of the Red Knight's victims show that Malory was also a source. The artist intended to present the patient, courteous, brave and humble hero as a suitable model for Oakham schoolboys. To this end she introduced the faces of students among the crowds. The castle hall of the hospitable Green Knight is the same hall that the frescoes decorate...[69]

Authors Barber and Pykitt in *Journey to Avalon* posit that a secret society called the Ancient Order of Prince Arthur was likely established by the Tudors:

> ... Many years after his death, [St] Edward received the title 'Patricius Arthurus' and it was sealed on his tomb. Those who did this must have had powerful authority behind them to have obtained the necessary permission. This shows that a Society of Knights must have existed, closely connected with the royal house... In the British Museum, there is a book titled The Ancient Order, Society, and Unity Laudable of Prince Arthur and Knightly Armoury of the Round Table, by Richard Robertson, printed by John Wolf, and published in London in 1583. It is dedicated to the chief custom official of the Port of London and to the Society of Archers. The book demonstrates that the Tudors established some kind of society, which, centered in England,

included in its membership men of other countries, some of them having been rulers of importance in Europe, as for example, the Holy Roman Emperor Maximillian I...[70]

So the legend of Arthur lives on. We have seen but a few of the key tales and theories, traditional or not, about King Arthur. This is a complex and fascinating subject which often has other powerful legends related to it. One of these is Merlin.

Merlin

Merlin is known as having many roles – wizard, bard, prophet, magician, advisor to King Arthur. But in nearly all accounts of him, he is portrayed as a 'man of the forest' or as a 'wild man of the woods':

> If he has occasion to move in established society, whether in an ancient kingdom... or in King Arthur's entourage, he does not make his home there. He is seen arriving at Arthur's court unexpectedly, coming from somewhere else. He is, in short, a marginal figure who designs to enter the social world only to give counsel, make prophecies, or perform a magic feat. As soon as he has accomplished his design he returns to his own domain. And this domain is the forest.[71]

His home is *the sanctuary of the forest*, harkening back to an earlier Celtic belief regarding the importance of groves of trees, as with the Druids, for example. Celtic scholar Jean Markale comments that although Merlin's behaviour in the Arthurian stories has also caused him to be labelled a 'wandering madman', perhaps he is actually to be considered as a wise man or sage:

> By taking refuge in the heart of the forest, or by agreeing to go to the invisible prison of the fairy Vivian, Merlin withdraws completely. He separates himself from the society of his time and affirms his discovery of a new reality, a new alliance. From this it is evident that Merlin, who is taken for a madman, is in fact a sage...[72]

Indeed, in our modern industrialized society we are often very cut off from nature. In these tales, Merlin seems to symbolize a powerful connection with nature, as well as more magical or spiritual types of knowledge. His home is the earth, and he is usually portrayed as a solitary figure living in the forest.

Professor A.O.H. Jarman in *The Merlin Legend and the Welsh Tradition of Prophecy* points out that the legend of Merlin and the Welsh prophetic tradition were originally separate and distinct from each other:

> ...despite the inclusion of the legend in the Arthurian complex in the 12th century, no such association existed at any earlier period. It was in his *Historia Regum Britanniae*, completed c. 1138, that Geoffrey of Monmouth transformed the legendary Welsh seer Myrddin into the internationally famous Merlin... who played a crucial role in bringing about the conception of Arthur and was prominent in later Arthurian story... both the Merlin legend and its associated prophecies may be divided into pre-Geoffrey and post-Geoffrey phases, with the proviso that manifestations of the first phase often continued after Geoffrey's lifetime and uninfluenced by him.[73]

And internationally famous did Merlin become!

Author E.M. Butler in *The Myth of the Magus* comments on the power of the legend of Merlin and includes him in a list of major historical mages, like a modern-day 'Who's Who'of magicians: '...none of these historically important magicians has contributed so signally to legend as Solomon, Cyprian, Theophilus, Virgil, Merlin, Bacon and Faust. In this category, and at this level, the latter is overshadowed by Solomon and Merlin...'[74] In other words, after detailed analysis of historically important mages and their legends, Merlin even over-shadowed Dr Faust, who was probably one of the most famous magicians in the history of western civilisation.

As a prophet, Merlin was said to have written prophecies, but scholars today point out that none of his early poems have survived, only descriptions of them by others, such as Geoffrey of Monmouth. This makes it nearly impossible to say for sure exactly what a historical Merlin may have said or written.

But the legends about his prophecies are well known to many of us through novels and films, many of which are based on Geoffrey's account:

> Confronted with Vortigern's magicians, the young Merlin... exposes their ignorance. Following his directions, an under-

ground lake is discovered beneath the foundations. Asked what is at the bottom of the lake, the magicians are again unable to answer. Merlin declares that they will find there two hollow stones, in each of which is a sleeping dragon. The lake is drained and the stones are found. The two dragons – one red and one white – emerge and start fighting each other. Merlin predicts the victory of the white dragon, which symbolises the Saxons; the red dragon's defeat means that the Britons will be enslaved until the Boar of Cornwall (Arthur) shall crush the invaders. Merlin also foretells Vortigern's end...[75]

But what of a possible historical Merlin? There is no doubt that he did exist, however, perhaps as a composite of several historical characters, as we shall soon see. Or, as others say, does it really matter, given the power of his enduring legend today? Either way you look at it, Merlin is important.

Merlin and St Kentigern

The sole historical reference we have to Merlin is connected with a 6th C battle. This is the battle of Arfderydd, now known as Artheret, near the Solway Firth, about 10 miles north of Carlisle between the rivers Esk and Liddel, on the border between Scotland and England. This battle is believed to have occurred in 573AD although not too many details about this particular battle are clear. It is implied that Merlin was present at this battle and 'went mad' from losing family, friends, and patron in it. He then fled to a forest. This fierce battle was fought between Gwenddolau, the King of the North and the patron of Merlin, and King Rhydderch Hael of Strathclyde, who defeated him in this battle.

From that point on, it is said, Merlin lived in the forest, only to emerge at certain points to prophesy or to advise Arthur. His whole legend grew from this experience. Strathclyde King Rydderch Hael was known to be a Christian, unlike Gwenddolau, and in this particular battle, his troops won. He then recalled St Kentigern from north Wales to his domain to help him re-evangelise the area.

Many legends about Merlin and St Kentigern have survived, mainly with a focus on how the wild, poetic man of the woods, the pagan Myrddin, was converted to Christianity by St Kentigern. According to local legend in the Stobo area of the Scottish Borders, Merlin was said to have met St Kentigern right before he died and was then converted to Christianity by St Kentigern. He is said to have finally died at Drumelzier, where the river Tweed meets the Powsail Burn. This place is called 'Merlin's Grave' today. Just upstream from there is a place called Merlindale.

Probably one of the most unusual aspects about the Merlin legend in this area is that the supposed location of his prophesied death at Drumelzier is precisely the same spot mentioned in a later prophecy by the 13th C Scottish seer Thomas of Ercildoune, also called 'Thomas the Rhymer'.

Interestingly, Stobo Kirk is one of the oldest churches in Scotland. Dating from Norman times, tradition says that it was built on an earlier site of a church founded by St Kentigern in the 6th C. An old persistent legend in the area is that Merlin was baptized by St Kentigern on the altar stone. Today, nearby Altarstone farm is close to Stobo Kirk, only a few miles away. The legend of Merlin and St Kentigern is also portrayed on a stained glass window in Stobo Kirk and can still be seen today. Clearly there is an old, persistent tradition in the Stobo and upper Tweeddale area about Merlin and St Kentigern – whatever the ultimate truth of the matter, 'the legend lives on'. The major Scottish sites associated with Merlin legends are: Dunragit, St Ninian's Cave, Mote of Mark (Rockcliffe), Sweetheart Abbey, Loch Arthur, Dumfries, Lochmaben, Hoddom, Burnswark, Caerlaverock Castle, Clochmabenstane, Hart Fell, Drumelzier, Altarstone, Stobo Kirk, Eildon Hills, Fast Castle, Greenan, Glasgow, Dumbarton, Loch Lomond, Stirling, Edinburgh and North Berwick.

Two historical Merlins

Many scholars believe that there were likely to have been *two historical Merlins*. One was Merlin Ambrosius, who lived in the mid-5th C. He is associated by Geoffrey of Monmouth with the

British leader Vortigern, and is portrayed as the Merlin of Uther Pendragon, Arthur's birth and childhood. He is believed to have been born in 450 and died about 536. He is named and described in Geoffrey's *Historia Regum Britanniae*, History of the Kings of Britain, in 1136.

Some years before that, Geoffrey had published a long series of prophecies attributed to Merlin, called the *Prophetiae Merlini*, which he incorporated in its entirety into his *Historia*. About 1150 he finished the *Vita Merlini*, a biography in which he delved further into Merlin's origins. With these three works, Geoffrey created a character which has fascinated novelists, poets, artists and scholars through the centuries.[76] The young Merlin was called Ambrosius in the 9th C work by Nennius called *Historia Brittonum*.

The other Merlin was known as Merlin Sylvestris (of the wood), Merlin Caledonius or Merlin the Wild. He is portrayed as having lived in the woods during the second half of the 6th C, after the time of Arthur's death, and is the Merlin described above at the battle of Arfderydd (Artheret).

His name is spelled 'Myrddin'. He is portrayed as a mad man who fled to the forest sanctuary, the location of which some writers believe was the upper Tweeddale area of the Scottish Borders, near Stobo. Count Nicolai Tolstoy, in his well-researched book *The Quest for Merlin*, believes that the location where the original Myrddin, or Merlin Sylvestris, had his forest sanctuary was the summit of Hart Fell, where a ridge nearby is also known as Arthur's Seat, near Stobo in the Scottish borders. Another possible location suggested is that of nearby Geddes's Well, near the top of Broad Law, in the same general area. Stobo is only about 15 miles from Hart Fell and 8 miles from Broad Law.[77]

After the battle of Arthuret, Merlin is described as having gone mad, living wild in the forest, eating fruits and berries, and having special knowledge of the language of the plants, birds and animals, especially that of wolves and deer. He prophesies and occasionally emerges from his forest sanctuary, but in general has withdrawn from society. Tolstoy also believes Merlin may be an incarnation of the mythic god Lugh in early Irish literature. The ancient

Celtic festival of Lughnasadh was held on the eve of August, to celebrate the harvest, often on a mountain top:

> ...so close a parallel between the legend of Merlin and the myth of Lug as to suggest either that they are identical or, as I argue, that Merlin was the incarnation of the god. In view of this and of the considerations already discussed, it is possible to suppose that the summit of Hart Fell was once the focus of a British Lughnasadh assembly.[78]

Although primarily a speculative work, Tolstoy also does an admirable job of dissecting much of early Welsh, Irish, and English folklore around the overall issue of Merlin and who he might have been, and where he may have fled to – again, ending up with a focus on the Scottish Borders area.

The 'threefold death' of Merlin

Tolstoy also notes similarities between the 'threefold deaths' of Merlin and Christ. In some manuscripts, Merlin is said to have predicted his own death; other accounts imply that the Lady of the Lake killed him. But he is also believed by some as having had a 'threefold death' as 1) He was stoned by the Christian shepherds of King Rhydderch Hael of Strathclyde; 2) He fell over a steep bank of the river Tweed by the foot of Dunmeller (Drumelzier); and 3) He fell into the river and impaled himself on a sharp stake, and so died from both impaling and drowning at the same time.

Tolstoy notes that this theme of a 'threefold death' occurs in other accounts of deaths in folklore and history. Christ is said by some to have had a 'threefold death' as 1) He was hanged on a tree; 2) His side was pierced with a spear; and 3) the sponge of vinegar was thought be to particularly lethal. Odin, the hero of Teutonic mythology, was said to have hung on Yggdrasil, the World Tree, for nine nights, and to have been wounded by a spear made by dwarfs. During this time he received the wisdom of the runes. Lugh, hero of early Irish mythology, was also said to have experienced a threefold death.[79] The number three often appears in folklore accounts and legends worldwide, and the stories about Merlin are no exception.

Jocelin's 12th C *Life of St Kentigern* gives surprising details about a certain Lailoken who lived in the middle of the forest and was also a prophet. This Lailoken appears to be the same figure as Merlin Sylvestris (of the woods) or Myrddin, discussed above. The Rev Dr Gordon Strachan of Edinburgh suggests that the name 'Merlin' may also be that of a title, and not simply a personal name:

> Yet the Scottish Merlin was probably the more historical and although he lived later, may even have been the prototype of the Arthurian Merlin, the legends about whom as we read them today, were largely the embellishments of later medieval romancers. Whatever may be the historical truth behind the mythology, it is probable that 'Merlin' was not a personal or family name, but a title... which was given to a Celtic wise man or seer. Whether recognised as or appointed as 'a Merlin' or 'the Merlin', the stories indicate that both Merlin Ambrosius and Merlin of the Woods held the rank of counsellor to princes and displayed gifts of prophecy, poetry and the praeternatural which were associated with the office of Chief Druid.[80]

One prominent Celtic scholar also points out just how universal it seems Merlin became in western Europe, as he was written about in Latin, Dutch, German, English, French, Icelandic, Italian, Portuguese, Provencal and Spanish.

Merlin as the 'Son of a Widow'

The French-language authors of the Middle Ages believed that Merlin's mother was a nun. He has also been called 'the son of a widow', or of a woman only, fatherless. 'The Cambridge 80 manuscript, detailing Merlin's military feats, will call him 'Only-Son-of-the-Nun', which in Welsh would sound like 'Merlin': *'un mab llian'*.'[81] Of course, the term 'son of a widow' shows up in Masonic legend as well, to be further discussed in chapter 8.

One major version of Merlin's birth comes from a medieval French clergyman named Robert de Boron, who wrote between 1188 and 1212. His Merlin comes on the scene about 50 years after the Latin account of Merlin by Geoffrey of Monmouth. In Geoffrey's account, Merlin's mother was Princess of Demetia, believed by some scholars to be Dyfed in south-west Wales. His father is an incubus, a spirit who seduced the princess by night while she slept, so Merlin is fatherless. In Geoffrey's account, Merlin is portrayed as the real power behind the throne of Arthur, and as a powerful prophet and counsellor.

Was Merlin 'framed'?

De Boron's account portrays Merlin as having a somewhat more suspicious character, with closer connections with evil spirits, but as being basically good overall, thanks to the intervention of a priest who blessed his mother. So he uses his powers for good in the end. De Boron says that Merlin's mother was a lovely virgin teenage girl of parents in difficulty, which is hardly the 'princess' of Geoffrey's account. Unfortunately, she forgot to say her prayers one fateful evening and was raped in the middle of the night by a demon, called an 'incubus' in medieval times. This tragic event was said to have resulted in Merlin's conception.

De Boron seems to deliberately taint the famous Merlin with further suspicions of black magic, horrible heresies and evil demons, which in medieval times was a way of conducting what we would now call a major 'smear campaign'. His account goes into more detail about how a group of devils plotted and planned to create an Antichrist who would be half-human and half-demon. This child was Merlin.

But a priest intervenes and the woman chosen to give birth to this creature is blessed. Merlin later repays this priest by telling him how Joseph of Arimathea brought the Holy Grail to Avalon. In de Boron's account, the infant Merlin seems to be portrayed as being more outside the pale of legitimacy, as an excommunicate with heretical qualities – clearly more so than in Geoffrey's account. 'Merlin was then subsequently condemned by the Church, and no wonder.'[82]

In de Boron's account, upon awakening after that fateful night, the poor girl knew that she was pregnant and this is what happens next:

...[she] keeps her head, however, and calls two friends and a servant to escort her as she consults her confessor. Unfortunately, 'sergeants' immediately arrest her for criminal sexuality punishable by death. She is shut up in a stone tower so that she can be isolated or quarantined from contaminating the public. Inside this tower she is sequestered and then walled up with two matrons, who will remain at her side to assist her until the child is delivered and nursed... soon her baby was to be 'taken from her'...[83]

But shortly after the baby is taken away, things seem to take a very unusual turn:

The two matrons shrieked when they saw the baby Merlin born, for he emerged as a swarthy male child completely covered with thick, black hair... the infant Merlin is from birth a prodigy and precocious beyond belief. At eighteen months, he consoled his condemned weeping mother, 'You will not be burned because of me.' Even the matrons heard him speaking clearly. Terrified, they abandoned both mother and child. The mother's death sentence... is to be carried out in forty days. She was also condemned by the judge for not naming the baby's father. Then the baby Merlin speaks again. He argues with the magistrate in terms that make us suspect he has already been studying Plato: 'I know whose son I am,' he cried... 'These enemies,' he goes on to explain, 'are called 'Incubes' (our Incubi)who are evil spirits and who have sexual relations with women in their beds at night. But God granted safety to my virtuous mother,' the baby cried, 'by granting me knowledge of the future.'[84]

Then, the baby Merlin talks directly to a rather astonished judge, continuing with a personal attack on him, which eventually causes the judge to disqualify himself. However, the trial ends well for Merlin's traumatized mother, who is then released in the custody of her confessor, Blaise. She then becomes a nun. This is the overall account of Merlin's mysterious birth as portrayed by de Boron.

One cannot help but notice some similarities here to the folklore motif of a 'talking baby' to the Celtic accounts of 'the changeling' – where the fairies are said to abduct one's good, healthy baby, and replace it with an ugly, demonic one of their own, as in certain Gaelic accounts. This frightening 'changeling' baby is often portrayed as talking just like an adult, or, as singing or playing an instrument like a piping chanter, just as an adult would.

In medieval times, when authors such as de Boron were writing, such a portrayal of a 'hairy, talking baby' would definitely imply a very dangerous 'demonic' connotation to a reader or listener of the tale of Merlin. This was something no one ever wanted to be associated with at the time, as one could be put to death for heresy. The message is that Merlin, even though his mother was blessed, *is still somehow dangerous, illegitimate, suspect, heretical* – clearly a change from his former glory as an esteemed wise man, mage or seer in the previous writings about him.

So some scholars believe that Merlin, whomever he may have been, seems to have been representative of a much earlier, pagan tradition of a 'wise man' or 'seer' that later Christian authors understandably wanted to downgrade or destroy, due to the changing times and circumstances of history. But here again, we have an example the power of a myth or legend in history, and how aspects of the story can change with the circumstances of history.

Merlin associated with nature, a 'man of the woods'

Merlin is also associated with nature, especially of having a special relationship to plants, trees, rocks and animals. He is described as having connections to a certain springs or fountains. Perhaps one of the most famous examples of this is when the Lady of the Lake arranged to meet Merlin at a fountain on Midsummer Eve. Author John Darrah says:

> In contrast to the relatively small number of references to rivers (except for river crossings) and lakes, the romances are full of accounts of events at 'fountains', as springs are always called in the French texts. In particular, springs are the staple of the 'challenge' theme. They were generally defended on behalf of a female supernatural being of some sort, a nymph or fee... springs were widely linked with this sort of local divine personage in popular thought... The origin of the challenge at the fountain is described in two ways. In one it is attributed to Merlin, who is said to have made a chapel over a small perron and to have provided a basin, and to have made a spell so that no knight errant could throw water from the basin without it producing thunder and lightening. In the other, Merlin himself says that it was Lunete who made it.[85]

Lunete is a name that is thought to represent the moon, implying a female guardian spirit of the spring, or the belief in one, a reflection of an earlier folk tradition. Many wells and springs, and even castles and caves with their buried treasures, were thought to be guarded by a female spirit. In early Celtic folklore, the theme of the 'White Lady' as guarding treasure and certain wells and springs is also found fairly frequently.

Merlin's connections with water: wells, springs and lakes

Merlin's connection with water also relates to his name. Professor A.O.H. Jarman, a prominent Welsh scholar, comments:

> ...we may here note two other derivations which have been proposed for the name Myrddin. Nikolai Tolstoy has given some qualified support to Rhys's suggestion that it could be based on *Moridunios*, meaning 'man of the sea-fort'... Professor Eric Hamp has explained the name as a reflex of British *Morifim*, (? meaning 'one of the sea'). Here again, assimilation to the place-name would probably have occurred. If either of these derivations is correct, however, the existence of the personal name could well have contributed to the creation of a... founder-figure of the town...[86]

Others hold the view that since it appears that Merlin's name means something like 'man of the sea', or a 'water man', that Merlin was actually St Dubricius, one of the early saints of Britain:

> The Latin ending '*icius*' means 'one connected with', and the Brythonic root '*Dubr*' means 'water'... water, however, also carries a profoundly religious significance in the context of early British Christianity on at least two counts. First, British ecclesiastics were especially associated with the rite of baptism... second, the pagan sacred wells had by no means died out with the Druids, and they were now maintained as holy sites by the early British Christians (for example, St Seiriol's Well in Mon). Furthermore, pagan rituals and beliefs regarding these wells were incorporated into Christian Welsh folklore, surviving until very recently.[87]

Merlin's connection with Viviane is also interesting in light of aquatic connotations. In some accounts, when she has put Merlin to sleep, or confined him, then she becomes the Lady of the Lake. She has a castle under the lake, and it is also in a lake where she helps Arthur get his sword; she takes it back from him in the same lake after the battle of Camlann, in which he was wounded. Jean Markale notes that 'we are told in the continental accounts that Vivian's father, a certain Dyonas, was the godson of Diana, and it is by the Lake of Diana that Vivian takes Merlin for a walk... we have come to see Vivian-Niniane as a kind of water divinity, or nymph... Diana is a divinity of forests as well as of springs...'[88]

As with Arthur, the debate continues as to how much of this material comes from the earlier pre-Christian tradition and how much of it relates to Christianity. As these manuscripts were written long after Arthur and Merlin supposedly lived, and many by Christian clerics who understandably had their own point of view, it is hard to say for sure what the original story may have been like. Even today, it seems that the Arthurian material and the Grail legends are claimed by *both* pagans and Christians. But ultimately, it seems the legends have a life of their own.

Merlin's legacy remains

Readers worldwide still enjoy many versions of these tales, finding meaning in them, with Arthur and Merlin having become archetypes who have lasted in human consciousness for 15 centuries. The Arthurian material is a treasure trove of tales, legends, history and folklore from a bygone era, whose memory continues, ageless and timeless.

Merlin as a prophet or seer has remained in the popular mind for generations, with one scholar commenting:

> Marvelous to the end, Merlin typifies the imposing miracle of a magical life, for he represents in his life a cultural force that people have always believed in and still believe in. His story constitutes a single, continuous, coherent master text containing all coded explanations, recommendations, symbols and their unvoiced solutions... Merlin... a wondrous prodigy...[89]

Perhaps Alfred Lord Tennyson summed it up best in his well-known poem *The Idylls of the King* about Merlin: that he was 'the great Enchanter of the Time'. Perhaps we might also add that Merlin is the archetypal Enchanter of All Time, who still exists in our memories today, the custodian of secrets.

Today we can recall the Arthurian and chivalric ideals of the Round Table. As John Morris said about Arthur in his seminal work *The Age of Arthur*: 'The tales that immortalised his name are more than a curiosity of Celtic legend. Their imagery illuminates an essential truth... The age of Arthur is the foundation of British history, and it lies in the mainstream of European experience.'[90] Let us all keep the flame of this ideal alive, as we embark on our own Quest.

We will now explore the legends of the Holy Grail and the knights of the Round Table.

Notes

[1] Doel, F & G, and Lloyd, T, *Worlds of Arthur: King Arthur in History, Legend, and Culture*, Tempus: Stroud, Gloucestershire, 1998, 51.

[2] Ibid, 52.

[3] Ibid.

[4] Goodrich, N, *King Arthur*, Harper & Row: New York, 1986, 8.

[5] Littleton, C S, & Malcor, L, *From Scythia to Camelot*, Garland, New York and London, 2000, 63.

[6] MacInnes, J, 'The Arthurian Legend', *World Mythology*, Ed. By R. Willis, Piatkus, London, 1997, 189.

[7] Green, M & Howell, R, *A Pocket Guide to Celtic Wales*, University of Wales Press, Cardiff, 2000, 117.

[8] Ibid, 111.

[9] Ibid, 114.

[10] Rees, A, & Rees, B, *Celtic Heritage: Ancient Tradition in Ireland and Wales*, Thames and Hudson, London, 1961, 178.

[11] Markale, J, *King of the Celts: Arthurian Legends and Celtic Tradition, Inner Traditions*: Rochester, VT, 1977, 181 [Engl. Transl.] Orig. Published as *Le Roi Arthur et la Societe Celtique*, by Payot, Paris, 1976.

[12] Roberts, B, 'Culhwch ac Olwen, the Triads, Saints' Lives', *The Arthur of the Welsh: the Arthurian Tradition in Medieval Welsh literature*,

Ed. By R Bromwich, A O H, Jarman, & B. Roberts, University of Wales Press, Cardiff, 1991, 90.

13 Ibid, 91.

14 Ibid.

15 Blake, S, & Lloyd, S, *The Keys to Avalon*, Element, Shaftsbury, 2000, 234-5.

16 Ibid, 235.

17 Ibid.

18 Ibid.

19 Ibid, 308.

20 Ibid, 39.

21 Carley, J, 'Arthur in English History', *The Arthur of the English*, Ed. By W.R.J. Barron, University of Wales Press, Cardiff, 1999, 47.

22 Ibid, 48.

23 Ibid, 48-9.

24 Ibid, 49.

25 Ashe, G, *The Discovery of King Arthur*, Henry Holt & Co., New York, 1985, 176.

26 Phillips, G, & Keatman, M, *King Arthur: The True Story*, Random House, London, 1992, 17.

27 Barber, R, *The Figure of Arthur*, Longman, London, 1972, 134.

28 Westwood, J, *Albion: A Guide to Legendary Britain*, Paladin Grafton Books, London, 1985, 24-5.

29 Cavendish, R, *King Arthur and the Grail*, Weidenfeld & Nicolson, London, 1978, 28.

30 Carley, op cit, 50.

31 *Adami de Domerham Historia de Rebus Gestis Glastoniensibus*, Ed. By T. Hearne, 2 volumes, Oxford, 1727, Vol. II, p. 587-9.

32 Carley, op cit, 51.

33 Ibid, 52.

34 Printed in *Anglo-Scottish Relations 1174-1328: Some Selected Documents*, ed, and transl. by E L G Stones (Edinburgh and London, 1965), no. 30.

35 See the Instructions and Processus of Baldred Bisset; printed in *Anglo-Scottish Relations*, ed, and transl. By E L G. Stones (Edinburgh and London, 1965), no. 31. On Scottish portrayals of Arthur see Flora Alexander, 'Late Medieval Scottish Attitudes to the figure of King Arthur: A Reassessment', *Anglia* 93 (1975), 17-34.

37 Lynch, Prof M, *Scotland: A New History*, Pimlico, London, 1991, 112.

38 Ibid, 113.

39 Carley, op cit, 52.

40 Davies, N, *The Isles: A History*, Macmillan, London, 1999, 194.

41 Ferguson, W, *The Identity of the Scottish Nation*, Edinburgh University Press, Edinburgh, 1998, 122.

42 Skene, W F, *Arthur and the Britons in Wales and Scotland*, Llanerch, Lampeter, 1988 reprint of 1868 original 'The Four Ancient Books of Wales', 16.

43 McNeill, F M, *The Silver Bough*, vol. 2, Wm. MacLellan, Glasgow, 1959, 81.

44 Ibid, 144.

45 McNeill, F M, *The Silver Bough*, vol. 4, 'The Local Festivals of Scotland', Stuart Titles Ltd, Glasgow, 1968, 192.

46 Moffat, A, *Arthur and the Lost Kingdoms*, Weidenfeld & Nicolson, London, 1999, 221.

47 Goodrich, op cit, 67.

48 Stoker, R, *The Legacy of Arthur's Chester*, Covenant, London, 1965, 1.

49 Spence, L, 'The Arthurian Tradition in Scotland', *Scots magazine*, Edinburgh and Glasgow: April 1926 issue, 17.

50 Glennie, J S, *Arthurian Localities*, Llarnerch Publishers, Lampeter, 1994 reprint of 1869 orig, 126.

51 Watson, W J, *The Celtic Placenames of Scotland*, Birlinn, Edinburgh, 1993 reprint of 1926 orig, 208.

52 McHardy, S, personal communication with Dr Karen Ralls-MacLeod, 1 March 2001.

53 Williams, J E C, and Ford, P, *The Irish Literary Tradition*, University of Wales Press, Cardiff, 1992, 136.

54 Ibid, 137.

55 O'hOgain, D, *Myth, Legend, and Romance: An Encyclopedia of the Irish Folk Tradition*, Prentice Hall, New York, 1991, 285.

56 Coe, J B, and Young, S, *The Celtic Sources for the Arthurian Legend*, Llarnerch Publishers, Lampeter, 1995, 156.

57 Gillies, W, 'Arthur in Gaelic Tradition, Part II: Romances and Learned Lore', *Cambridge Medieval Celtic Studies*, 3, summer 1982, Cambridge, 41-75.

[58] Coe and Young, op cit, 158.
[59] Lloyd-Morgan, C, 'The Celtic Tradition', *The Arthur of the English*, University of Wales Press, Cardiff, 1999, 1.
[60] Ashe, G, op cit, 9.
[61] Bord, J, and C, *The Enchanted Land*, Thorsons/Harper Collins, London, 1995, 133.
[62] Ibid.
[63] White, P, *King Arthur: Man or Myth?*, Bossiney Books, Lauceston, Cornwall, 2000, 11.
[64] Barber and Pykitt, op cit, 70.
[65] Ibid, 73.
[66] Filbee, M, *Celtic Cornwall*, Constable, London, 1996, 64.
[67] Hunt, R, *The Drolls, Traditions, and Superstitions of Old Cornwall*, 2nd series, [Ed.] Llarnerch Publishers, Lampeter, 1993 reprint of 1864 orig, 306.
[68] Hunt, R, *The Drolls, Traditions, and Superstitions of Old Cornwall*, 1st series, [Ed.], Llarnerch Publishers, Lampeter, 1993 reprint of 1881 orig, 186.
[69] Brooks, C, and Bryden, I, 'The Arthurian Legacy', *The Arthur of the English*, University of Wales Press, Cardiff, 1999, 253.
[70] Whitaker, M, *The Legends of King Arthur in Art*, D.S. Brewer, Cambridge, 1990, 310-1.
[71] Barber and Pykitt, op cit, 276-7.
[72] Markale, J, *Merlin,* Inner Traditions, Rochester, VT; 1995 (English translation of 1981 French orig, entitled *Merlin L'Enchanteur*), 113.
[73] Ibid, ix.
[74] Jarman, A O H, 'The Merlin Legend and the Welsh Tradition of Prophecy', *The Arthur of the Welsh*, Ed by Bromwich, R, Jarman, A O H, and Roberts B F, University of Wales Press, Cardiff, 1991, 117.
[75] Butler, E M, *The Myth of the Magus*, Cambridge University Press, Cambridge, 1948, 267.
[76] Gerritsen, W P, and van Melle, A.G, *A Dictionary of Medieval Heroes*, Boydell Press, Woodbridge, Suffolk, 1998 Engl. Translation of 1993 German orig, 178.
[77] Ibid.
[78] Tolstoy, N, *The Quest for Merlin*, Hodder and Stoughton, Sevenoaks, Kent, 1985, 87.
[79] Ibid, 183.

80 Strachan, G, *Merlin in Scotland*, Edinburgh Festival Fringe souvenir catalogue, Edinburgh, 1997, 1.

81 Goodrich, N, *Merlin*, Harper & Row, New York, 1988, 34.

82 Ibid, 46.

83 Ibid.

84 Ibid, 47.

85 Darrah, J, *Paganism in Arthurian Romance*, Boydell Press, Woodbridge, Suffolk, 1994, 93-4.

86 Jarman, A O H, op cit, 139.

87 Griffen, T D, *Names from the Dawn of British Legend*, Llarnerch Publishers, Lampeter, 1994, 74-5.

88 Markale, J, op cit, 84.

89 Goodrich, N, op cit, 326-7.

90 Morris, J, *The Age of Arthur: A History of the British Isles from 350 to 650*, Phoenix/Orion London, 1995 ed of 1973 orig, 510.

CHAPTER SEVEN

The Holy Grail

...as in a dream I seemed to climb
Forever: at the last I reached a door...
It gave, and throe' a stormy glare, a heat
As from a seventimes heated furnace...
And yet methought I saw the Holy Grail...[1]

In Tennyson's poem *Idylls of the King* the knight Lancelot on his search for the Grail follows 'a sweet voice singing in the topmost tower' and says he believes he saw the Grail there, amidst great heat and shining light.

The legend of the Holy Grail has probably gripped the western imagination more than any other. The idea of a Grail Quest is still seen by many today as being one of the greatest of all spiritual quests. The Grail tradition 'is the embodiment of a dream, an idea of such universal application that it appears in a hundred different places... Yet it remains elusive, a spark of light glimpsed at the end of a tunnel, or a reflection half-seen in a swiftly-passed mirror.'[2] There is something elusive yet compelling about it.

Although the Grail is usually thought of as a medieval idea, it is still highly relevant today. The word 'Grail' has even worked its way into our modern language, with one prominent geneticist recently declaring that he was hoping to find 'the Holy Grail of science' by decoding the DNA of humans with the huge Genome Project now underway. An unlikely comment from an unlikely source, it may seem, but the concept of the Grail continues to intrigue many today. But ultimately the Grail is a spiritual subject, and may never have been a physical object at all, as we will soon explore.

The Holy Grail, like the Ark of the Covenant, is portrayed as an awesome mystery. It can be dangerous, or even deadly, to certain people, and not without good reason, tradition asserts. When the Holy Grail appears in the Grail stories, some people see it, but others don't. Those who do see it, see it in different forms.

It is often shown being carried by a beautiful maiden, or in other instances it moves about by itself in mid-air. It represents many things, such as ultimate spiritual truth and the love of God.

Today the legend of the Grail lives on, from academic studies to films like *Indiana Jones and the Last Crusade* or *Monty Python and the Holy Grail*. But the real inner mystery of the Grail cannot be explained in words as it must be experienced; the Grail lives on in the heart and soul, beckoning many on their own spiritual journey today. We will now take a look at how these Grail stories came down to us centuries ago.

The Grail romances

The major Grail romances were written during the late 12th C and the 13th C. No one cohesive Holy Grail 'story' emerges, but a basic outline might be something like this:

> A mysterious vessel or object which sustains life and/or provides sustenance is guarded in a castle which is difficult to find. The owner of the castle is either lame or sick and often (but not always) the surrounding land is barren. The owner can only be restored if a knight finds the castle and, after seeing a mysterious procession, asks a certain question. If he fails in this task, everything will remain as before and the search must begin again. After wanderings and adventures (many of which relate to events which the young hero fails to understand the first time), the knight returns to the castle and asks the question which cures the king and restores the land. The hero knight succeeds the wounded king (usually called the Fisher King) as guardian of the castle and its contents.[3]

Perhaps you might remember such a legend from childhood stories or movies. But another way to summarize this Grail legend has been admirably done by Jungian analyst Ian Begg, who describes it as a series of stages:

One: Something has gone wrong. The world has run out of meaning and it is women who first sense this. The old king, standing for the established order, is impotent and the land is wasted...

Two: A youthful hero, typically an orphan, is destined to find the Grail, heal the old king and take his place. Two or three other chosen ones may share his vision and his quest. The Grail is glimpsed and then lost because a vital question has not been asked. This may be a failure of compassion in which the hero neglects to ask the old king what he is suffering; or, it may be a failure of understanding what the Grail is for and whom it serves.

Three: The Grail itself is active: something is operating in human lives that transcends conscious intentions. It names those who are to be its servants and leads them on their individual quest. It designates the high places where its presence will be commemorated and is the architect of the Grail castles and temples.

Four: There is a fellowship or family of the Grail who continue to further and protect its interests in the world.[4]

The whole Grail motif first appeared in *Perceval ou Le Conte du Graal,* by Chretien de Troyes in 1190. Chretien's patron was Count Philip of Flanders, a crusader knight. In this story, Perceval is portrayed as a guileless, rustic knight, the archetypal Fool, whose main character trait is innocence. In this romance, he sees the grail during a feast at:

A mysterious castle presided over by a lame man called the Fisher King... Chretien calls the object simply 'un graal', and its appearance is just one of the unusual events which take place during the feast... at this time, Perceval is also shown a broken sword which must be mended. The two objects together, sword and grail, are symbols of Perceval's development as a true knight.[5]

Unfortunately, Chretien died before he finished his story, and so other writers attempted to do so. These additional tales are called *The Continuations,* in which other Grail themes are brought in, such as a floating Grail on a platter in mid-air, the bleeding lance, the broken sword, and a very curious theme involving a Chapel of the Black Hand, where a mysterious hand snuffs out the candles in the chapel.

Other themes added later are a magic chess board, the broken sword again, the spear, the cup and the precious blood. Later, a lady offers Perceval a white stag's head and a dog, which he then loses and must find again, before he can return to the Grail castle. This whole adventure occurs at the mysterious Chapel of the Black

Hand. Once the sword is mended, Perceval 'as grail ruler heals the land. After seven years, he retires to a hermitage, and when he dies, the grail, lance and dish go with him.' [6] One more *Continuation* was done, this time adding in even more adventures he must experience before finding the Grail.

Then, between 1191 and 1200, Robert de Boron, a poet from Burgundy, wrote his Grail romances, also commissioned by a crusader patron, entitled *Joseph d'Arimathie* and *Merlin*, the two he is best known for. In his work he brings in a definitive Christian theme to the Grail story. In *Joseph d'Arimathie*, Pilate gives the cup used at the Last Supper and at the scene of the Crucifixion to Joseph of Arimathea, who is later imprisoned:

> Christ brings the grail to Joseph in prison where it sustains him and teaches him its secrets. Joseph is freed by the emperor Vespasian who has been cured by Veronica's veil (another mysterious relic associated with Christ's passion)... Joseph establishes a second table of the grail, and Bron catches a fish which is placed on the table and separates the just from the unjust. The object is called the Holy Grail... Alain, the leader of Bron's twelve sons, goes to Britain to await the 'third man' (Perceval?) who will be the permanent keeper of the grail.[7]

Bron then becomes the Fisher King and goes to Britain with the grail, and Joseph returns to Arimathea. Overall, with de Boron's Grail legends, the main issue is that the focus is on the knights undertaking the *quest* for the grail, rather than on the courtly knights who accomplished adventures for the love of a lady and the honour of the king.[8]

Wolfram von Eschenbach wrote his famous *Parzival*, also for a crusader patron, in about 1205. In his account, the Grail is a precious stone fallen from Heaven, and he brings in the subject of the Knights Templar as guardians of the Grail, although both men and women are mentioned. Prose versions of Robert de Boron's works began to link the Grail story more closely with Arthurian legend. A 13th C German romance called *Diu Krone* features Sir Gawain as the hero, while the *Queste del Saint Graal* has Galahad as its hero.

In *Queste del Saint Graal*, the quest for the Grail becomes a search for a mystical union with God. Only Galahad could actually look directly into the Grail and behold divine mysteries that cannot be explained in words. This work was heavily influenced by the teachings of the Cistercian Abbot St Bernard of Clairvaux, whose works describe the various states of grace that correlate with certain stages in man's rise toward perfection in the spiritual life. St Bernard of Clairvaux was also part of the group that were the founders of the medieval Knights Templar.

The *Queste del Saint Graal* also made Galahad the son of Lancelot, thus contrasting the story of chivalry inspired by human love, as with Lancelot and Guinevere, with that inspired by divine love, as with Galahad. This particular version has had great significance to the English-speaking world, as Sir Thomas Malory based his now famous late-15th C prose work *Le Morte D'Arthur* on it. This is the storyline most familiar to many today, as it was featured in the film *Excalibur* and the musical *Camelot*.

The Grail knights and their Quest

There are five major knights in the larger Grail story – Gawain, Galahad, Lancelot, Bors and Perceval. Of them, only three actually achieve the Quest, Galahad, Perceval and Bors. John Matthews summarizes:

> Of these, and of the many knights who set out from Camelot, only three are destined to achieve the Quest. Lancelot, the best knight in the world, fails because of his love for Arthur's queen. Gawain, a splendid figure may once have been the original Grail Knight, is shown... as being too worldly, though he comes close to the heart of the mystery... Galahad... is destined from the beginning to sit in the Perilous Seat and to achieve the Quest. Perceval, like Gawain originally a successful candidate, is partially ousted by Galahad, so that while he is permitted to see the Grail – and to use the Spear to heal the Wounded King – at the end of the Quest he returns to the Grail castle where he apparently becomes its new guardian... Bors, the last of the three knights to come in sight of the Mystery, to experience the Grail directly, is the humble, dogged, 'ordinary' man, who strives with all his being to reach towards the infinite, and who succeeds, voyaging with Galahad and Perceval to the Holy City of Sarras... Of the three, he alone returns to Camelot to tell of what has happened.[9]

So despite Galahad's success in seeing into the Grail – he dies then in a transcendent moment of Glory – the overall quest itself has been a failure. Bors, the sincere, ordinary man who also achieves the Grail, is the only one of the three to actually come home to Camelot to talk about his experiences. Perceval did not fully achieve the Grail like Galahad did, and still waits for its return.

Because once the Grail has been achieved and since it is fully achieved by one person only – Galahad – rather than the whole world for whom it is meant, the Grail is withdrawn – but not entirely, not forever. Perceval takes up residence again in the empty castle to await the return of the Grail, which will thereafter be once again available for all true seekers.[10]

So Perceval, the Grail knight, still waits for the Grail to return at some future time. Other variations on this theme have been the figure of the hermit St John, waiting in a cave, as the guardian of the Holy Grail, for example, or the related theme of a benevolent sleeping guardian who will awaken and return again one day to save the country or world, such as Merlin or King Arthur. This theme has also made its way into artwork, with the image of the Hermit in the tarot, or in the pre-Raphaelite Arthurian paintings of Byrne-Jones and Rossetti.

Gawain appears in the earliest Arthurian literature as a model of knightly perfection. In later versions of the story, he was no longer seen as ideal, as he was portrayed as too worldly, as a womaniser, as being unable to perceive the spiritual significance of the Grail, of relying too much on his own prowess, of refusing to seek divine help, and so as failing in the ultimate quest. He is illustrative of how someone's character can deteriorate, as shown further by his behaviour and attitudes in *Tristan* and Malory's *Le Morte D'Arthur*. Gawain's strength is portrayed as waxing and waning with the sun, leading some Celtic scholars to compare him to the solar deity of Celtic mythology, Gwalchmei. Others believe he may have a mythological connection to Lugh. While he was fighting Lancelot, Gawain's strength increased as the morning approached noon, but decreased as the sun declined, and later on he was conquered just before sunset.[11]

Gawain: a 'Son of the Goddess'?

Another battle story, the famous *Sir Gawain and the Green Knight*, features the much older theme of a beheading challenge. Here Gawain beheads the mysterious Green Knight, thought to symbolize the old year, at the winter solstice (21 December) and he has to submit to a similar fate the next year. Along with his brothers Gaheris, Gareth and Agravine, Gawain represents important symbolic aspects of the Celtic sacred year with its four quarters. All four were born of a Goddess named Margawse, Arthur's sister-wife, who also gave birth to the infamous Mordred, who eventually betrays and wounds Arthur at the battle of Camlann. Gawain is also symbolic of the son of the Mother, of Sovereignty, the spirit of the land. Clearly he is symbolic of some archaic remnants of ancient mythological themes from very early times, among them the Son of the Goddess. The portrayal in these Grail stories of Gawain and his subsequent 'deterioration' may also be symbolic of the gradual deterioration of the theme of the loyal man, or knight, of the Goddess from much earlier times, or perhaps as the deterioration of the light in springtime towards the darkness of winter.[12]

Galahad, portrayed as the pure knight and the son of Lancelot and Elaine, is the only knight who actually achieved the vision of God through the Grail, although he dies as a result of his transcendent vision. In the earlier romances of the Grail story, Perceval is the hero. But later, during the 13th C, a new, more spiritual and rather austere significance was given to the Grail.

Here the genealogy of Galahad is shown to be traced back to the House of David in the Old Testament. The story where Galahad features most prominently is the *Queste del Saint Graal* (The Quest for the Holy Grail) which forms part of what is called the Vulgate, or Prose Lancelot, cycle. As we saw before, the *Queste* has Cistercian influences and corresponds with the mystical teachings of St Bernard of Clairvaux. The emphasis with this version of the story is on the spiritual significance of the Grail and the overall quest for it.

In these Grail stories, each knight on the Quest has his own individual qualities and challenges that must be overcome. Every case is different. *The message is that every person's quest for the divine is unique, and often difficult and full of many trials, before the Grail can be achieved.* This is a different message from the idea that there is 'only one way' to God, as was promulgated by the church in medieval times.

Even today, the Grail material, although it seems to be Christian enough in many ways, is still viewed with suspicion by the church, although it is not actually condemned outright. Perhaps a real irony today is that more and more people are saying that they are actually finding genuine meaning in Christianity by studying and learning more about the Grail motifs and themes. Often in the Grail stories, few are found to have the qualities necessary to achieve the full mystery of the Grail. There are many trials and tests along the way. 'The Grail Quest above all promises that, as we are tested, so shall we achieve greater access to the mystery.'[13]

But perhaps equally important is that even if the Grail isn't achieved, a person is still ennobled and changed by the experience. In this sense, the Grail is for everyone. The idea is that what is ultimately important is someone's inner character, their spirituality and intentions, and not simply their family background, wealth, and so on. The stories teach many dimensions about the Grail.

What is the Grail?

In the romances, the Grail has been said to be many different things: a cup or chalice, a relic of the precious blood of Christ, a cauldron of plenty, a silver platter, a stone from Heaven, a dish, a sword, a spear, a fish, a dove with a communion Host in its beak, a bleeding white lance, a secret Book or Gospel, manna from Heaven, a blinding light, a severed head, a table, an Ark and so on. Many of these portrayals are allegorical and symbolic. In fact, the Grail is most likely not an earthly object at all, but something spiritual within every human being.

The search for the Grail is a personal quest and the Grail may manifest differently to each seeker:

> ...so the pointers to the Grail may only suggest a path to a beatific vision of its manifestations. Each finder discovers a unique insight into the divine... Through the control of the body and the

refining of the spirit, an understanding of self might be followed by a revelation of the divine. To attain the ever-changing Grail is to search deep within and so reach out to a personal path to God.[14]

A multi-faceted mystery, the Grail legend 'is indissolubly linked to the story of King Arthur and his knights, for whom the search for the Holy Grail was the ultimate quest. The Arthurian legends followed the same route of transmission as those of the Grail... Just as there was no single version of the Grail legend in the Middle Ages, so there is no single explanation of what the Grail was.'[15] One truth, many paths.

The Four Hallows of the Grail

The Four Hallows of the Grail – the cup, sword, dish, and lance – are shown as being either given directly to Perceval, or as being carried in the Grail procession that takes place in the Grail castle. As scholars have noted, these Four Hallows have some striking similarities to the four treasures of the *Tuatha de Danaan* in early Irish legend – the Sword of Nuada, the Lia Fail (a stone), the Cauldron of Dagda, and the Spear of Lugh. They also correspond in many ways to the four suits of the minor arcana in the tarot: the Swords, Cups, Pentacles, and Wands. These correlate with the sword, cup, dish and lance of the Four Hallows of the Grail. Clearly there is an ancient symbolism present here.

To take things a bit further into more modern times, these four tarot suits are very similar to the four suits in a deck of playing cards: the Spades (earlier a Blade), the Hearts (Cups), the Diamonds (Pentacle dish, a platter) and the Clubs (the 'rod of Jesse', symbolizing the continuing lineage of the House of David). No wonder the church greatly frowned on playing cards, when one considers the deeper symbolism they may have been seen to represent, especially the suit of Clubs, as it represented in medieval times the heretical concept of a possible continuing bloodline of Jesus. Margaret Starbird, Jessie L. Weston, Laurence Gardner and other contemporary authors have done good research about these lesser known connections with the symbols of the tarot and playing cards more widely known.

Yet in many of the Grail legends, the Grail seems to be a Christian talisman, a powerful relic and a mysterious manifestation of God. When the Grail does appear, it is often a rather fearful and awesome experience for the seeker. The idea is clear that anyone who tells its story falsely or for the wrong reasons will suffer for it. Storytellers in earlier times often told of the Grail in rather hushed voices; that they even took pains to be so careful may be reminiscent of an awareness of the power of the spoken Word, of memory, and of the possible 'evoking' of something by its telling:

> Its secret should never be revealed because, before the tale is fully told, something may be stirred up that is better left unaroused... these comments by medieval writers suggest that they were dealing with a mystery which they recognized as both profound and unorthodox. The Church, far from taking the Grail under its wing, treated the legends with cold reserve.[16]

This may seem quite surprising today, especially given that the Grail is usually thought of as a Christian symbol.

But following Pope Gregory IX's first Inquisition in 1231, 'Grail lore was condemned by the Church. It was not denounced outright as a heresy, but all material related to it was suppressed.'[17] This was because the idea of the Grail quest, which underlies many of the Grail stories, has as its focus the subject of an individual path to God, a view which was obviously seen as subversive to Church authority at the time. The sacred relic was referred to as the *san greal*, the Holy Grail, and which later, through an ingenious pun of the type often found in Old French literature, was turned into *Sang Real*, the Royal Blood, the blood of Christ.[18]

The cup or chalice

The usual Christian portrayals of the Grail are the cup or chalice of Christ, or the Precious Blood. The cup as the Grail was said to be the very cup used at the Last Supper. It was also said to be the cup which Joseph of Arimathea used to collect the actual blood of Christ while preparing his body for burial after the crucifixion.

Later legends say Joseph then brought the Grail to Britain via Gaul. It is also symbolised as a stone inside a chalice in some of the Grail stories.

The first portrayal of a cup in the Grail romances was called a *Graal*, a mysterious object about which we are told very little. Early prototypes of the Grail come from the cauldron of plenty in Celtic literature; later it became Christianised as the cup of Christ. The cup is believed to have certain special powers associated with it, including the ability to summon into its presence those who are worthy, of making one immortal and immune to evil. It is said to have restorative ability and to act as a 'cauldron of plenty' that can feed everyone present and never run out. The movie *Indiana Jones and the Last Crusade* is probably the best-known recent portrayal of the Grail as a cup.

Many believe that the chalice in Valencia Cathedral in Spain is the Grail, and it is the only one that has been declared to be authentic by the Vatican. Other prominent contenders are a wooden bowl found in Wales, a 'Grail' said to be hidden in the Apprentice Pillar of Rosslyn Chapel in Scotland, and the green glass chalice that was taken to Genoa. The Embriaci family, whose members played important roles in the Crusades in the Holy Land in the 11th and 12th centuries, were a powerful Genoese family. Guglielmo Embriaci brought back a green glass chalice that was captured from Caesarea and sent it to the cathedral of San Lorenzo in Genoa in 1102. It remained in Genoa until Napoleon took it to Paris, where it was scientifically examined. It was returned to Genoa in 1816 in ten pieces with one missing, which was retained by the Louvre. The Embriaci Tower, built in the 12th C, still stands in the old quarter of Genoa today.

The Grail as a dish from which Jesus and his disciples ate the Passover lamb at the Last Supper is also a Christian portrayal, as is the idea of the Grail as a reliquary that held the consecrated communion Hosts.

The Grail is often shown as a chalice surrounded by very bright, blinding light, or as a spear or sword appearing in mid-air, with blinding light all around it. Another theory is that the Grail could possibly be round balls of glass filled with water on a tripod that can light fire from sunlight, akin to the Jewish Urim and the Thummim, objects that were associated with the Ark of the Covenant.

The mysterious, blood-tipped lance that generally accompanied the Grail 'was said to be the weapon that pierced the hips of the Fisher King. It was identified with the Biblical spear of Longinus', the Roman centurion who pierced the side of Jesus on the cross.[19]

The Precious Blood

There are several sources for the relics of the Precious Blood in Christian tradition. One is the blood collected in a chalice at the crucifixion by Joseph of Arimathea, Nicodemus, Mary Magdalene or Longinus, depending on which version of the tradition you read. Especially in legends about Joseph of Arimathea and Mary Magdalene, the precious blood is often portrayed as being directly connected with the Holy Grail.

Some believe that the Grail is symbolic of a continuing bloodline of Jesus Christ, through his wife Mary Magdalene and children, an idea that has been around for many centuries, especially in France. Another source of the precious Blood is from miracles in which the blood and wine of the Eucharist were said to have turned spontaneously into the literal body and blood of Christ. Pilgrimage centres such as Bois-Seigneur-Isaac and Bolsena commemorate the Precious Blood today.

Another source of the Precious Blood was said to be particles 'of blood of unknown provenance', like that supposedly found in the tomb of St Philomena. There are a few miracles of liquefying blood belonging to various saints, the most famous being St Januarius of Naples, for whom the month of January is named.

The cult of the Precious Blood, which was very popular in earlier times, later changed its focus to the cult of the Sacred Heart of Jesus and the Immaculate Heart of Mary.[20] In some of the Grail legends, the symbols of the Grail and the heart are connected.

The Holy Lance or Spear

The Holy Lance is also interesting, as certain places of pilgrimage have grown around this legend. In the Grail stories, it often appears as a bleeding white lance, that which pierced the side of Christ, so it is believed to have very special powers. The Holy Lance was believed to have been made by 'Phineas, grandson of Aaron, according to a legend, admittedly transmitted by the Gnostic Ephrem the Syrian. Saul, in his madness, hurled it at David, and it was later used by Longinus to pierce the side of Christ and release blood and water into the Grail.'[21]

But the cult of the spear later became 'suspect' to the church, as the spear was believed to really symbolize the spear of Lugh, the pagan Celtic sun-god, or to be a symbol of the spear of death and victory of Wotan, a pre-Christian Teutonic god. So the cult of the spear was understandably frowned upon by the church in some districts.

That Hitler took an unhealthy interest in the Imperial spear in the Hofburg museum in Vienna is not widely known. But he (and others in the Third Reich) were very interested in certain relics. As with many of the relics attached to the Grail stories, they can be used either for light or for dark purposes.[22] The legend was that whosoever had this particular spear in his possession, that is the *very spear* that had pierced the side of Christ, would be victorious and rule the world. Strangely enough, many world leaders, most of them conquerors, have indeed possessed this Imperial spear in the past, ranging from Herod the Great in early times is the imperial spear the very spear to Otto the Great, Charles Martel, Charlemagne, Rudolph II, and into modern times, with Hitler in the 20th C. Through the ages, the lore about its legendary powers remained widely known and sought after.

Hitler sought the spear all for himself and it is known that Himmler kept an exact replica of it in his office:

> Some of the German Emperors of the Middle Ages had associated the legend with this very Spear... Napoleon... demanded it after the Battle of Austerlitz, before which it had been secretly smuggled out of Nuremberg and hidden in Vienna to keep it out of his tyrannical hands.[23]

Trevor Ravenscroft in *The Spear of Destiny* tells how at the end of World War II, on 30 April 1945, the Americans found this spear and other Imperial regalia in an underground bunker in the Oberen Schmied Gasse under Nuremberg Castle. The Allies had taken over Nuremberg Castle, under which they found many tunnels, and, finally, this particular bunker. General Patton later also saw the spear, along with other looted artwork and objects in the bunker, and he was apparently one of the few then who had heard of the legends about it and realized its significance. After their discovery by the Allies, both Austria and Germany adamantly sought the return of these and other treasured relics.

On 4 January 1946, General Dwight Eisenhower ordered that everything should be returned to Austria, from where the Imperial regalia were originally stolen by the Nazis. Today this spear is back in the Hofburg museum in Vienna, the same place where Hitler had first seen it as a young man. This may seem very strange or even laughable to many people today, but serious historians are now finally beginning to acknowledge what some of the actual beliefs of the inner Nazi circle may have been. At the Nuremberg Trials, for example, most of the 'occult' material and related evidence, which was known to be genuine *was deliberately left out of the public domain at the request of Sir Winston Churchill and others*, for understandable reasons at the time. Yet much of this type of material is now believed to have had a stronger influence on German policies of the time than many realised. Churchill also acknowledged this, and is known to have made the effort during the war to hire historian and scholar Walter Johannes Stein to assist him in trying to decipher this aspect of the Germans' behaviour and belief system.

Vienna and Nuremberg have since become pilgrimage centres of the Grail, with many people assuming that the city of Nuremberg was the centre of the Grail cult in Germany. However, Rudolf Steiner and his student Walter Johannes Stein felt that the Externsteine, rather than Nuremberg, was actually the centre of Germany's Grail cult. The Externsteine is an ancient group of large stones, rising above a lake in a clearing of the Teutoburger Wald, which has a special connection to the winter solstice. In early times, the Saxons' sacred tree, the Irminsul, stood close nearby, and was destroyed by the Christian armies of Charlemagne. Here is an unusual sculpture of the Descent from the Cross carved in the stone, which shows a sun and moon in mourning on either side of Jesus the Crucified. Joseph of Arimathea and Nicodemus are shown with Jesus, as are Mary and John. To the west, outside the main group of stones, is a 12th C replica of the Holy Sepulchre in Jerusalem (dated to about 1130) which contains a stone sarcophagus. There are runic carvings in the hermit's cell and also a grotto chapel on the site. Since very early times, it would appear this site has been considered sacred, to both pagans and Christians.

In many wars throughout history, the perceived powers of various relics were often believed by those in power to assist them in maintaining power, so in a sense this concept is not new. What *is* new is that professional historians are now recognising such matters and acknowledging their significance.

Another important spear, said to be the Spear of Longinus, surfaced at Antioch. A monk named Bartholomew had an important vision in 1098 during the First Crusade as to its whereabouts:

> It passed for a time into the hands of the Count of Toulouse. This was presumably the relic discovered by St Helena, mother of the Emperor Constantine, along with the True Cross and other instruments of the Passion. The Lance was for a time in the possession of the Emperor of the East in Constantinople, who pawned the head, later redeemed it and sent it to St Louis IX of France. The rest of the Lance remained in Constantinople until the fall of the city in 1453, when it passed to Sultan Mohammed II. His son, Bajazet, gave it to the Grand Master of the Knights of St John of Jerusalem in exchange for certain favours. The Grand Master, in turn, gave it to the Pope. It was received with rejoicing in Rome, in 1492 and placed in St Peter's...[24]

Probably the most famous of the other spears of destiny is that of St Maurice. The Abbey of St Maurice in Switzerland was founded in 515AD, by king Sigismund of Burgundy who had recently converted from the Arian heresy. In the late 3rd C, the whole Theban legion, which consisted of Egyptian Gnostic Christians under Maurice, who was their commander, refused the orders of the

Roman Emperor Maximian to sacrifice to the gods of Rome and to carry out ethnic cleansing operations against the local Celtic Christians. As a result, they were all slain by the Romans. But as previously mentioned in chapter 4, we also see here a connection (and great loyalty in this case) between the Egyptian Christians and the Celtic Christians.

A sanctuary to house these relics of the martyrs was built in the latter half of the 4th C by St Theodore the Just of Valais. Some of these relics are kept in magnificent caskets in the *tresor* of the Basilica there, and one of the most significant is a sardonyx cup made in Alexandria in the first or second century BC, which was donated to the Abbey by St Martin of Tours. As for the spear, it is said that the Emperor Maximian himself took it from the dying St Maurice.[25]

The grail as a Stone

The stone on which St Maurice knelt and was decapitated by the Romans is in the chapel of Beriolez nearby. It is described as a 'stone from Heaven', which is another portrayal of the Grail in many of the legends.

In *Parzival* by Wolfram von Eschenbach, the Grail is a stone and not a cup, as is often shown in other Grail legends. Wolfram, a German poet who is thought to have been from Bavaria, lived around the beginning of the 13th C and served Hermann of Thuringia, who died around the year 1217. He was the author 'of several unfinished works and one complete poem, *Parzival*, composed between 1197 and 1210, in which he undertook the tale of the quest of the hero brought to light by Chretien de Troyes.'[26] Interestingly, throughout *Parzival* Wolfram takes pains to flatter the powerful house of Anjou, a centre of the Plantagenet dynasty. He also implies that the medieval Knights Templar are the guardians of the Grail.

Wolfram says he got the essence of his Grail story from Kyot of Provence, who obtained it from Flegetanis, a mysterious source who was said to have known of the wisdom of the stars and who studied the great war in Heaven between the angels. According to

Wolfram, Flegetanis was of the line of Solomon and wrote in Arabic. In this great war, it was said that Lucifer, the Light-Bringer (not the Christian Devil, as he was later called) led one third of the Heavenly host in a revolt against God, but that he was defeated. As Lucifer was cast down out of Heaven, a large emerald fell from his crown, or forehead. This emerald is said to have been the very source of his power, and it fell to earth, thus becoming known as the 'Gral', i.e. 'the Grail'. Wolfram's idea of the Grail as a stone was called the *lapis exilis*, a stone 'which fell from Heaven'.

The colour green

That the colour green should figure so prominently here is quite interesting, as it comes up in other ways in relation to the Grail. Usually the specific shade of green is an emerald green, or a malachite green. In Genoa the *Sacro Catino* was also a green glass chalice, called the Holy Grail, and was:

> preserved in the cathedral there until it was shattered and proven false, i.e., not divine... Before Wolfram's day, one recalls the priestly, green robes and malachite eyes of Queen Guinevere herself, as she stood between malachite (copper) columns at the Grail Castle, and one also recalls verses from some Catharist troubadour...: 'la robe verte des saints' (the green robe of the saints).[27]

Of course, the Emerald Tablets of Hermes were green, as is the colour of the Celtic faeryland. Druidic neophytes were also known to have worn green robes. Green is also connected with Venus and the mystery of generation. Women described as 'fairies' with special powers in medieval ballads are always described as wearing green. Of course, in Ireland, modern-day celebrants of St Patrick's Day also wear green. In alchemical traditions, emerald green is also important, and many images of the Green Man adorn medieval chapels and cathedrals today.

Ironically like the Grail legends, the colour green itself also later became quite 'suspect' to the church, as it was associated with witches, fairies and the dead, and brought with it the familiar superstition that green is somehow 'unlucky'. An emerald sword appears as the very sword used to behead John the Baptist in certain versions; in *The High History of the Holy Grail*, it is the object quested for by Sir Gawain, the Green Knight. In Sufi tradition, there is El Khidr, the Green One, who wears a robe of shimmering green and is said to be the guardian of the source of the Waters of Immortality. El Khidr would often appear at the very moment when a person was most in need of help, and could take any form he wanted, the ultimate shape-shifter. Even in *The Wizard of Oz*, the wizard's home was in the Emerald City.

The Philosopher's stone

In *Parzival*, Wolfram tells us clearly that the Grail is a stone:

> A stone of the purest kind... called *lapsit exillas*... There never was human so ill that if he one day sees the stone, he cannot die within the week that follows... and though he should see the stone for two hundred years it [his appearance] will never change, save that perhaps his hair might turn grey.[28]

The hermit Trevrizent, Parzival's uncle, lectures to him about the Grail, telling him many things about it. He mentions that the Grail was on the Mount of Salvation (Munsalvaesche) in the Grail Castle, guarded by a race of royal Grail Kings, each of whom was called to the service of the Grail. At the Grail Castle on the Mount of Salvation, the hermit tells Parzival, live many brave Templars who live by virtue of a stone called *lapsit exillas*, the stone that burned the phoenix to death and resurrected it again from its ashes. This stone is the Holy Grail, he said, and it can give one eternal life, except for turning the hair grey.

Through the centuries other writers have felt that the Grail as a stone may be a reference to the Philosopher's Stone in alchemical writings. Otto Rahn, who conducted detailed research on the Grail for Hitler, was convinced that what he called 'the troops of Lucifer', i.e. the pope and the King of France, went after the Cathars with a vengeance because they wanted to 'recover the lost emerald, or Grail of his crown, which had fallen during Lucifer's expulsion from Heaven. His emerald was the Holy Grail'.[29] Rahn was absolutely convinced that the Cathars possessed the Grail, and that it was lost with them after the fall of Montsegur in 1244. It is known that Rahn was given support from the top echelons of the Third Reich initially, but, strangely enough, he is known to have supposedly 'disappeared' while on a trip in the Alps in circumstances that have never been fully explained.

French Celtic scholar Jean Markale further explains the many different possible connotations of the Grail as a stone:

> There is first of all an alchemical allusion, *lapis exillis* being quite close to *lapis elixir*, which is the term used by the Arabs to designate the Philosopher's Stone. Next the stone of the Grail guarded by angels irresistibly summons thoughts of the Ka'aba stone in Mecca... One is reminded in particular of the tradition that states that the Grail was carved into the form of a vessel from the gigantic emerald that fell from Lucifer's forehead... in addition, Wolfram's Grail/Stone bears a great resemblance to the Manichaean jewel, the Buddhist *padma mani*, the jewel found in the heart of the lotus that is the solar symbol of the Great Liberation and which can also be found in the Indian traditions concerning the Tree of Life.[30]

There are many legends worldwide about stones and their perceived power. We have already learned about the Scottish Stone of Destiny, and this is but one of many examples of special stones and the beliefs about them from other traditions.

Little is known of Wolfram's mysterious Kyot of Provence, the source for his Grail story. There was a historical Guiot de Provins, a troubadour, who was present at the knighting of Frederick Barbarossa's sons, including the future emperor Henry VI, at Mainz at Whitsun in 1184, before *Parzival* was written.[31] Many have supposed that he was a troubadour from Provence or the French Provins.

Another theory is that he may have been from Provence on Lake Neuchatel in Switzerland, giving things a more Merovingian twist, as the nearby town named Sion is thought by some to have really been the true home of Parzival. The Merovingians, of the Sicambrian Franks, were important early kings of France and have many associations with the Grail and also with the French monarchy. Another theory is that Wolfram's lady named Sigune was the daughter of a Duke Kyot of Catalonia, and was also Parzival's cousin.[32] No one can really say for sure, however.

The origins of the Grail

Varied in its many descriptions, the Grail is a universal theme. It has also been described as the Holy of Holies, the Water of Life, the source of life and immortality, the Philosopher's Stone, the cosmic centre, the womb of Life, and as a powerful fertility symbol through the ages. Its most popular portrayal as a cup or chalice is a theme also found in eastern folklore and mythology. 'It occupies the same place in western tradition as the vase in the East, or the sacrificial cup which contained the Vedic Soma, the Mazdean Haoma or the Greek Ambrosia and carries a eucharistic significance, and it is the symbolical source of physical and spiritual life.'[33]

The origins of the Grail have been sought in many traditions, among them Celtic, Christian, the classical mystery religions, Byzantine history, Persian, Jewish and Islamic religions, and the Nart sagas of the Sarmatians, an early Scythian tribe near the Black Sea. Clearly, there is no scholarly consensus on exactly where the material that forms the various Grail legends came from.

Generally, though, it has been agreed that early Celtic literature has much in it that later shows up in the Grail legends, as shown by R.S. Loomis, a leading Celtic scholar:

> The starting point of the Grail tradition was Ireland. The Irish derivation of several principal elements in the Tristan romance and of the Beheading Test or Game in *Gawain and the Green Knight* is now widely accepted... similarities between the Grail stories and the Irish sagas... are not merely illusory or accidental... Wales furnished also the names of a few persons most conspicuous in the Grail legends. Bran became Bron, Beli became Pelles... and [so on]... The Grail Castle was originally a Celtic Elysium, where old age and death were unknown...[34]

The early Welsh legend of *Peredur* was also quite important, many believe. One Welsh scholar believes that it is more in the legends of the Old North – parts of North Wales and lowland Scotland – that the Grail romances originate:

> The Grail romances probably owe more to British tradition, retained and related by the Welsh... than they do to Irish legend,

although it would be foolish to attempt to discount any Irish influence. The sovereignty legends of the Old North were the source of the material from which *Peredur* was created, and the now famous Grail scene is derived from the hero's visit to the Otherworld god... was moulded by the first author of *Peredur*. It was from a translated version of *Peredur* that Chretien derived his Perceval and that the *graal*, eventually becoming the dish of the Last Supper, entered continental literature.[35]

So the debate continues. Most scholars have tended to fall into either the 'Celtic' or the 'Christian' camp. One other theory, more unorthodox, was that of Dr Jessie L. Weston in the 1920s. She claimed that the Grail ritual and legend actually goes back to *much earlier* mystery cults, such as a primitive vegetation cult like that of Adonis or Tammuz, and maintains that this was only later shaped by Celtic and Christian lore. The universal myth of a vegetative or fertility cult was also discussed at length by Sir James Frazer in his classic *The Golden Bough*.

Weston also believed that Gnosticism had a lot to do with the formation of the Grail legend, and especially the philosophy of the Gnostic Christian group called the Naassenes, who were written about by the Church Father Hippolytus. But Weston firmly believed that the Grail legend primarily came from the vegetation ritual, stating '...the root origin of the whole...complex is to be found in the Vegetation Ritual, treated from the esoteric point of view as a Life-Cult, and in that alone. Christian legend, and traditional folk-tale, have undoubtedly contributed to... the corpus, but they are in truth... secondary features.'[36]

Obviously not everyone agrees as the origins of the Grail have been debated for a long time. The latest and more controversial theory is that the Grail material originally came from the Scythian Nart sagas of the Sarmatian peoples. In these sagas, themes like a sword coming out of a lake are present, for example, leading some scholars to consider them as a possible prototype for later Grail motifs. But the sheer power and beauty of the Grail stories themselves is what is really important in the long run, and many scholars, too, recognise this, no matter where the legends may have come from.

The Grail through history

The symbol of the Grail cup, vase, or chalice is also a feminine symbol, according to many. The loss of the Grail symbolizes a great unbalance, as with the Wasteland theme in the Grail legends. Only when the Grail is restored will the Wasteland be healed, an example of the resurrection of the vegetation ritual that the Grail legend seems to emphasize. Some researchers also believe that the Grail icon itself has gradually changed or evolved with the historical progression of western civilisation, roughly as follows, up to the Renaissance:[37]

Paleolithic and Mesolithic (200000-5000BC)	Skull, Rams Horn, Gourd, etc.
Neolithic (5000-2500BC)	Basin stone, Scallop shell
Bronze Age (2500-800BC)	Copper cauldron, Bell beaker
Iron Age and the Dark Age (800BC-800AD)	Chalice, the Baptismal font, and illuminated manuscripts
Middle Ages (900-1400AD)	Gothic Cathedrals, Knights Templar
Renaissance (1400AD on)	Alchemical symbolism

As we have seen, the Grail can be, and is, many different things to different people. It all depends on the time, the circumstances, and the seekers' intentions.

The Grail in Scotland

There have also been important Scottish traditions about the Grail. As the usual focus about the Grail has often been on England, Wales and France, with Scotland often being neglected. One key idea, as many believe today, is that *the land itself* is a type of Grail, involving Scottish sacred sites such as Iona, Scone, and so on. But the Grail is most likely not a material object at all, but nonetheless, many legends do exist which say that it is some kind of an object. A few of these refer to Scotland.

By far much of the speculation in recent times has centred on Rosslyn Chapel in Midlothian, near Edinburgh. Although we will learn about other aspects of Rosslyn Chapel in chapter 9, here we will see what has been said about it in terms of the Grail.

Rosslyn Chapel was founded in 1446 by Sir William St Clair, third and last St Clair Prince of Orkney. It is famed for its magnificent medieval stone carvings, featuring many biblical themes and a great variety of others relating to spirituality. There is a carving of a chalice, and also one of the Veil of Veronica, reminiscent of the Shroud of Christ, which some believe to be the Grail. There are many other Grail-related carvings and themes at Rosslyn Chapel, understandably leading many to call it 'the chapel of the Grail'. Even the roof itself is interesting regarding the Grail, in that it is the only large barrel-vaulted roof that has been built in solid stone in Scotland. It 'was literally a stone fallen from heaven – the *lapis exilis of Parzival* which was called the Grail.'[38] It is also important to note that the chapel is still a place of worship today and that it is part of the Scottish Episcopal Church.

The legend of the Apprentice Pillar and the Grail

Legend says that the Holy Grail is hidden in the Apprentice Pillar of Rosslyn Chapel. This is certainly one of the most persistent legends about the Grail at Rosslyn to have come down to modern times. Some say it is a silver platter, others that it is probably a chalice of some type. Many insist that this is simply just an old legend and nothing more. Still others aren't so sure.

The Apprentice Pillar, a beautiful, ornately-carved stone pillar, has a special legend of its own. In *An Account of the Chapel of Rosslyn*, written in 1774, Dr Forbes, Bishop of Caithness, describes the story:

> The Master Mason, having received from the Founder the model of a pillar of exquisite workmanship and design, hesitated to carry it out until he had been to Rome or some other foreign part and seen the original. He went abroad and in his absence an

apprentice, having dreamt that he had finished the pillar, at once set to work and carried out the design as it now stands, a perfect marvel of workmanship. The Master Mason on his return, seeing the pillar completed, instead of being delighted at the success of his pupil, was so stung with envy that he asked who had dared to do it in his absence. On being told that it was his apprentice, he was so inflamed with rage and passion that he struck him with his mallet, killed him on the spot and paid the penalty for his rash and cruel act.[39]

In addition to the Apprentice Pillar, there are also three carvings that relate to this story in the chapel – the head of the apprentice with a scar on his right temple, the head of his grieving, widowed mother, and the head of the master mason. This story is believed to be connected to important themes in Freemasonry, especially the legend of Hiram Abiff, which will be explored later in chapter 8.

However, although this particular legend about the Grail in the Apprentice Pillar persists, nothing has been found yet, so it remains just that – a legend. But some still believe that it may be true. As the old saying goes, it often doesn't matter whether something is necessarily true or not, it is whether people *believe* it to be true.

The well-known Grail researcher Trevor Ravenscroft claimed in 1962, after twenty-some years of research all over the world, that his Quest ended at Rosslyn Chapel. It is interesting to note that a number of years ago, his wife, so certain of the presence of the Grail in the pillar at Rosslyn, chained herself to it in 'a vain attempt to force the authorities to X-ray it and discover the Grail. Later radar researches, carried out by Tony Wood and Greg Mills, operating Groundscan radar equipment, have detected no metal object within.'[40] To our knowledge, the Pillar has not been X-rayed in more recent times, so the legend still remains today. Others point out that the object may not have been made of metal as many have assumed.

Rosslyn Chapel has been said to be the repository of many sacred objects, from the Ark of the Covenant and the sacred scrolls from the Temple of Jerusalem to the Holy Grail hidden within the Apprentice Pillar, to name but a few. Many books have been written about these various theories, from many different viewpoints. Even Sir Walter Scott in his poem *The Lay of the Last Minstrel* made reference to the Sinclair knights said to be buried in full armour in the vaults of Rosslyn Chapel, '... where Roslin's chiefs uncoffin'd lie, Each baron sheathed in his iron panoply...'[41] No one questions that Rosslyn Chapel is one of the finest examples of medieval architecture in Scotland, and that it has the largest number of Green Man carvings in Europe. It has become a focus for many legends throughout time, for better or for worse, and this includes legends about the Grail.

Andrew Sinclair, in his book *The Discovery of the Grail*, tells how the Nazis also showed a great interest in the Apprentice Pillar legend about Rosslyn Chapel, as they did in all Grail legends. They decided to investigate this legend and sent representatives to Scotland to see Rosslyn Chapel. In his book Sinclair makes reference to Lord Edward Bulwer-Lytton, who had been the head of the British Colonial Office and who wrote several books on esoteric themes. Bulwer-Lytton's biographer was a member of the Scottish Theosophical Society, which was visited by Dr Karl Hans Fuchs of the Thule Society in 1930. Dr Fuchs and a mysterious colleague visited Rosslyn Chapel:

> As that Holy Vessel was said to be concealed within the curious Apprentice Pillar of Rosslyn Chapel near Edinburgh, Fuchs inspected the place in 1930, accompanied by somebody who signed the visitors' book as D. Hamilton. Later, at the Theosophical Society in Edinburgh, Fuchs declared that Hess claimed to have Hamilton blood in his veins and was particularly interested in the 10th Duke, a close friend of Bulwer-Lytton, as well as in the contemporary duke, who graced the Nazi leaders with his presence at the Olympic Games in Berlin. Fuchs added that Hess was known as 'Parsifal' in the inner circles of the Third Reich, and that he believed Rosslyn was the Grail chapel 'where the black hand snuffed out the candle'...[42]

The mysterious 'Chapel of the Black Hand'

The Grail legend referred to earlier called the *First Continuation* was written anonymously after Chretien de Troyes died, as he was unable to complete his *Perceval ou Le Conte du Graal*. In this version of the Grail story, the author of the *First Continuation* mentions an unusual chapel called the Chapel of the Black Hand, in which a mysterious hand continues to snuff out the candles in the chapel. Strangely enough, it is known that the Italian secret society called the Carbonari claimed that *their origins were in Scotland* and that their symbol is a black hand with a flame in it. The Carbonari were also called the 'charcoal burners' and had several branches in other countries. But it is rather interesting that Rudolf Hess, according to Andrew Sinclair, was apparently quite convinced that Rosslyn Chapel in Scotland was the mysterious 'Chapel of the Black Hand', but it is not known on exactly what he based such convictions.

The wooden bowl at Rosslyn Chapel

Andrew Sinclair tells us in *The Secret Scroll* how he found a simple wooden oak bowl, a Grail, in the vaults of Rosslyn Chapel while assisting Niven Sinclair and his associates during the process of conducting various groundscans of the chapel:

> Evidence of lower chambers revealed by the process bore out ancient drawings and medieval tales of buried St Clair knights in vaults below the chapel floor. The radar pulses also detected reflectors, which indicated metal, probably the armour of the buried knights. Particularly exciting was a large reflector under the Lady Chapel, which suggested the presence of a metallic shrine there, perhaps that of the Black Virgin, which still marks so many holy places on the pilgrim route to Compostela, a sacred way that has one of its ending in Rosslyn Chapel...[43]

Next, he says the team had a problem, in that it was difficult to reach the vaults. He continues:

> The groundscan had shown two stairways leading beneath the slabs. Laboriously, one set of flagstones was lifted, rubble was cleared, and indeed, three steep stone steps were found to lead to

a vault below. I was the first to squirm into this secret chamber... Sifting through the debris below the broken coffins, I found human bones and the fragments of two skulls, two rusty Georgian coffin handles, a mason's whetstone, and a simple oak bowl, left there by a mason from his meal along with his flint for sharpening the tools of his craft.[44]

Sinclair then notes that such a simple wooden bowl 'is what the original Grail from the Last Supper would have been – a wooden platter passed by Jesus Christ in His divine simplicity to His poor Apostles... Such a simple workman's bowl, perhaps as old as the late Middle Ages when this chapel was designed as a Chapel of the Grail, was a Grail as good as any other, the container of God's bounty on earth.'[45] For that matter, any bowl, cup or chalice can be symbolic of 'the Grail', if one perceives it to be a material object in the shape of a cup.

Andrew Sinclair further tells us that in spite of the team's attempting to drill deeper into the vaults of the chapel, the drill bit jammed continuously, and much dust and debris kept blocking their way, leading him to conclude:

After a week of work, we were defeated. The vaults of this Chapel of the Grail would keep their secret shrine. The St Clair knights would not be disturbed in their tombs. Perhaps that is how it should be. They had been buried beyond the reach of intruders. They would only reappear on the Day of Judgment, when the stone slabs would crack open.[46]

So the mystery of what lies below Rosslyn Chapel remains unknown. It is possible that it could be something of great import for humanity, some experts now believe, while others remain sceptical. According to Andrew Sinclair, it is believed that something is there, as seems to be indicated by various scientific groundscans. But as to precisely what, no one knows for certain. It is believed by some members of the Sinclair family that in addition to the Sinclair knights in effigy buried in the vaults, there may also be the Holy Rood, of which the Sinclairs were once the custodians in Scotland, and possibly a Black Virgin. But until anything is known for sure, all must remain as speculation. But the belief that there may be important objects buried at Rosslyn Chapel remains in the public mind.

The meaning of the Grail: A Quest for all time

The Grail Quest is a universal quest and it has many meanings on many levels.

The Grail is often thought of by psychologists and scholars as a symbol of the missing, or neglected, divine Feminine in western culture.. The search for the Grail, the Grail Quest, is thought to be the search for a balance between polarities. In the legends, the story of the wounded Fisher King and the desolate wasteland around him is thought to be a metaphor of the lack of balance in our civilisation between the masculine and the feminine. Many writers, both male and female, have recognised that our modern western civilisation, especially with its increasing damage to the environment and continuing wars, is analogous to a spiritual wasteland.

Important female characters predominate in the Grail legends, with the Holy Grail often shown as only carried by a maiden, or a group of maidens. Women are portrayed as being the Grail bearers, men as the Grail guardians. Many times in the Grail legends, the hero, a knight, meets a female character at certain key junctures in the story, whether it is a maiden, the old hag Kundry, (also called the Loathly Damsel), Dindraine, the sister of the Grail winner, or Ragnell, an interesting archetype of the Loathly Damsel who later transforms into the Flower Bride. Ragnell, like some of the other female characters, represents Sovereignty, the feminine power that rules the Land. Ragnell's 'gift is sovereignty, which may be taken either in the conventional meaning of rulership of the land, or as the sovereign love of two hearts for each other... she must be recognised for the beauty which is inherent in her, though before this can happen she must suffer a long and wearisome period of despite.' [46]

The old, ill, maimed Fisher King is said to be symbolic of our patriarchal civilisation, as he is often shown as wounded in the thighs, groin or hips, for example. Jungian analysts Emma Jung and Marie-Louise von Franz in their classic work *The Grail Legend* point out that:

It is only in Robert de Boron that the King is infirm simply from old age; in most versions he has been wounded as well. In Chretien, the lamenting damsel, Perceval's cousin, tells him only that in battle the Fisher King had been hit in both hips by a javelin. In Wolfram, Anfortas was wounded by the poisoned spear of a heathen, who was likewise striving for the Grail. The King, however, was not at the time fighting in the service of the Grail but for the love of the beautiful Orgeluse. The arrogance and sinful worldliness of his opponent are there given as the true cause. The hermit who speaks to Parzival about this also admonishes him not to adopt a haughty deportment, recommending humility and modesty... The feminine symbol of the Grail, and its meaning, point to a compensation originating in the unconscious, by means of which the feminine and the soul of nature may once again achieve recognition.[47]

Restoring the Wasteland

As 'the king and the land are one', when the king is maimed, the land, and Sovereignty, also suffer. So it seems that the Grail legends may be telling us, according to Jungian analysts, that the restoration of the feminine in our collective consciousness is an important goal for everyone in western civilisation today – men and women alike. In a nutshell, this means we all must learn to cooperate more rather than compete, for example, and listen more to others instead of insisting on only our own viewpoint, akin to a personal inner resurrection.

In referring to Wolfram's *Parzival*, the well-known scholar, the late Professor Joseph Campbell, commented:

> The Grail is housed not in a church but in a castle; its guardian is not a priest but a king. It is carried not by an assortment of males but by twenty-five young women, whose virtue must be unsullied, and the knight who achieves the quest, and so restores the Wasteland to bounty, succeeds through integrity of character, in the service of a singly focussed love, amor.[48]

It is this higher ideal, of a higher love, *amor*, that is a key to a better understanding of the troubadours and chivalry.

We have all inherited an unbalanced worldview in modern

western culture, and as part of our individual journey, and perhaps the very survival of humanity, we must make an effort to find the proper balance within ourselves, or the whole earth suffers. Even major figures of the 18th C Enlightenment saw the definite need for balance and criticised the excesses of their time, which led in turn to new extremes. However, as a number of social theorists and scholars now believe, the pendulum is now starting to swing the other way in an attempt to correct existing imbalances yet again.

Many people now recognise the need for a new paradigm for humanity, especially that we have now entered a new millennium. In spite of war, environmental damage, and other uncertainties of our time, we must ask: can we restore the Wasteland, or is it too late?

Perhaps this is our collective question, as important as the one Parzival needed to ask the wounded king, in order to compassionately restore the Wasteland as a fertile garden: 'What ails thee, uncle?' In other versions of the tale, the key question is 'For whom does the Grail serve?' Indeed, whom does the Grail serve? Of course, it can serve everyone.

But will we restore the Wasteland?

Notes

1. Tennyson, Lord Alfred, *Idylls of the King*, (1859-91), Penguin, London, 1988, 2: 829-44.
2. Matthews, J, *Elements of the Grail Tradition*, Element, Shaftesbury, 1990, 1.
3. Wood, J, 'The Holy Grail: From Romance Motif to Modern Genre', *Folklore*, Vol. 111, No. 2, London, Oct. 2000, 170.
4. Begg, I, and Begg, D, *In Search of the Holy Grail and the Precious Blood*, HarperCollins, London, 1995, ix-x.
5. Wood, op cit, 171.
6. Ibid.
7. Ibid, 172.
8. Ibid.
9. Matthews, J, op cit, 5.
10. Ibid.
11. Matthews, J, *The Mystic Grail: The Challenge of the Arthurian Quest*, Sterling Publishing, New York, 1997, 55.
12. Matthews, J, *Gawain*, HarperCollins, London, 1990, 22.

[13] Matthews, J, & C, *Ladies of the Lake*, HarperCollins, London, 1992, 158.

[14] Sinclair, A, *The Discovery of the Grail*, Random House, London, 1998, 124.

[15] Lively, P, & Kerven, R, *The Mythical Quest*, The British Library, London, 1996, 83.

[16] Cavendish, R, *King Arthur and the Grail*, Weidenfeld & Nicolson, London, 1978, 126.

[17] Gardner, L, *Bloodline of the Holy Grail*, Element, Shaftesbury, 1996, 250.

[18] Cavendish, op cit, 127.

[19] Gardner, op cit, 250.

[20] Begg, I, and Begg, D, *In Search of the Holy Grail and the Precious Blood*, HarperCollins, London, 1995, xvi.

[21] Ibid.

[22] Cooper, J C, *An Illustrated Encyclopedia of Traditional Symbols*, Thames and Hudson, London, 1978, 76.

[23] Ravenscroft, T, *The Spear of Destiny*, Samuel Weiser, ME, 1973, 8.

[24] Begg, I, op cit, xvii.

[25] Ibid, 206.

[26] Markale, J, *The Grail*, Inner Traditions, Rochester, VT, 1999 Engl. ed. of 1982 French orig, 133.

[27] Goodrich, N, *The Holy Grail*, HarperCollins, New York, 1992, 272.

[28] Matthews, J, Elements, op cit, 52-3.

[29] Goodrich, N, op cit, 271.

[30] Markale, J, op cit, 133-4.

[31] Barber, R, *The Knight and Chivalry*, Boydell & Brewer, Woodbridge, Suffolk, 1995 rev. ed. of 1970 orig, 97.

[32] Goodrich, N, op cit, 226.

[33] Markale, op cit, 134.

[34] Loomis, R S, *The Grail: From Celtic Myth to Christian Symbol*, Princeton University Press, Princeton, NJ, 1991 edition of 1963 orig, 272-3.

[35] Goetinck, G, *Peredur: A Study of Welsh Tradition in the Grail Legends*, Univ. Of Wales Press, Cardiff, 1975, 275.

[36] Weston, J L, *From Ritual to Romance*, Princeton University Press, Princeton, NJ, 1993 edition of 1920 orig, 163.

[37] Harrison, H, *The Cauldron and the Grail,* Archives Press, Los Altos, CA, *1992, 204.*

[38] Sinclair, A, *The Secret Scroll,* Sinclair-Stevenson, London, 2001, 155.

[39] Earl of Rosslyn, *Rosslyn Chapel,* Official Guidebook, Rosslyn Chapel Trust, Roslin, Midlothian, 1997, 27.

[40] Begg, I, op cit, 23.

[41] Earl of Rosslyn, op cit, 37.

[42] Sinclair, A, *Discovery of the Grail,* op cit, 310.

[43] Sinclair, A, *Secret Scroll,* op cit, 155-6.

[44] Ibid.

[45] Ibid.

[46] Matthews, C & J, *Ladies of the Lake,* op cit, 204.

[47] Jung, E, & von Franz, M-L, *The Grail Legend,* Princeton University Press, Princeton, NJ, 2nd edition, 1970 Engl. Transl, by C.G. Jung Foundation, of 1960 German orig, 199-205.

[48] Campbell, J, *The Flight of the Wild Gander,* HarperCollins, New York, 1969, 219.

CHAPTER EIGHT

Masonic and Medieval Guild Traditions in Scotland

SURPRISINGLY, FREEMASONRY AND ITS philosophical impact in western society has been largely under-researched by professional historians in general until quite recent times. This has also tended to be the case regarding the study of other related philosophies, such as the history of the early Guilds, chivalric Orders, Hermetic philosophy and so on. Nearly ten years ago, when a University of Edinburgh Religious Historian and Celtic scholar (Ralls-MacLeod) met a knowledgeable local Scottish Masonic researcher (Robertson), research findings were compared. Then, as now, we were both surprised to consistently find a number of overlapping areas of interest in our respective fields, and even more so during the overall process of writing this book.

As a result, the approach taken here is intended to be neither 'for' nor 'against' Freemasonry *per se*, and may even raise a few eyebrows here and there in either camp by occasionally challenging certain conventions. The overall approach taken is simply that of an historical enquiry and investigation regarding Freemasonry as a philosophy and belief system, especially regarding the history of Scotland. Contrary to popular belief, it is allowable to be a Freemason, for example, and to write about it and not end up 'hanged under Blackfriars Bridge' in London as some of the more sensational writers on the subject would have one believe. Similarly, the same can be said for membership in related organisations. It is hoped that this chapter may encourage those who may want to learn more about these subjects to do further in-depth study of their own as well. Of course, Masonic scholars themselves also continue to research, analyse and debate such matters today.

Freemasonry: a rather speculative subject

Firstly it must be stated that the study of Freemasonry and the medieval Guilds, which influenced its development, is a rather speculative subject for a number of reasons. Initially, we have to determine what is actually meant by the term 'Freemason', which is not really as straightforward as it may seem. The first generally known use of the word 'Freemason' was in 1376, however it cannot be proven that this necessarily bears any resemblance to the modern usage of the term.[1]

Another reason for difficulties is that the earliest Masonic ceremonies were based on *oral transmission* of its teachings, a practice that is thought by many to have been adopted from the trade guilds. This practice still continues today in Freemasonry, within certain parts of the ceremonies and rituals, to ensure that initiates only are privy to 'the secrets'. Based on very ancient customs, Freemasons practice initiatory rites that provide them with various modes of recognition. The signs, handshakes and tokens given to members constitute their 'secrets', although, as one modern-day Mason pointed out recently, much of this is actually no longer 'secret' as it can be readily found in books available in public libraries.

'A society with secrets'

But a policy of secrecy has been in place because in the past it allowed Masons to establish whether or not strangers who tried to enter their lodges were in fact Freemasons, and therefore eligible to join in their ceremonies, as members would have been properly initiated into an understanding of what takes place. This is understandable, because of the very real fear of persecution in past centuries, when 'secret societies' of many types were actually outlawed. Masons today assert that Freemasonry is not a 'secret society', but 'a society with secrets'. In 1986, the Duke of Kent declared that ancient references to such extreme-sounding physical penalties as 'having one's tongue cut out and his throat slit' if he breaks his oaths would be removed from the candidate's obligations in the

United Grand Lodge of England, a significant step to counter some of the negative publicity regarding such matters.

But the practice of allowing admission to 'members only', however, has certainly not been restricted to Freemasonry. The Knights of Columbus, for example, is a Roman Catholic society that also has initiation rites that restrict membership; in Britain, there is the 'old school tie' of the public school that forms an exclusive group. There are exclusive golf clubs, college fraternities and so on. Membership of other clubs and professional bodies can be viewed in a similar way, and one could argue that there have been many groups throughout history which have restricted their information to those 'in the know' for various reasons. All of these groups may be just as easily be accused of favouritism, for instance, as the Freemasons. In recent times, it seems that Freemasonry in particular has been unfairly singled out and mis-understood, perhaps because of media publicity about its so-called 'secrets'. But recently, to their credit, Masonic lodges have made more efforts to be inclusive, but this generally has pertained only to men, although there are some separate women's Masonic bodies in existence. There also exist, for example, the Order of the Eastern Star and Co-Masonry, which are open to both men and women. So there are *many different types of worldwide Masonic bodies* in existence today, something that doesn't seem to be widely understood by the general public. This is also true of modern neo-chivalric orders, of which there are also a great variety.

However, the 'real secret' of Freemasonry may be the fact that its earliest beginnings are still largely shrouded in mystery. Masonic scholars themselves are still uncertain about the exact origins and influences that their ceremonies are based on. The teachings and history of the Craft are normally investigated by other Freemasons with their findings largely remaining 'in house', being published in prestigious Masonic journals for members only, such as the *Ars Quatuor Coronatorum*. Even with all that has been researched and written by members, however, so many dif-fering views have been presented through the years that in some ways the situation has actually been hindered rather than helped.

But one must also consider that many academic historians

have, until quite recently, seldom considered to study Freemasonry, let alone include any mention of it and its cultural influence in their books and papers, thus ignoring its significance, which has often resulted in an incomplete view of western history. For example, it may be argued that certain periods in history actually cannot be properly analysed or studied *without* including a serious study of the influence of Freemasonry (and related organisations) at the time, i.e. the Enlightenment, the French Revolution, or the American Revolution. The 18th C itself has been called 'The Age of Freemasonry', for instance, and at the very least Freemasonry was certainly known to have been an important philosophical, cultural and social phenomenon of the time and profoundly influenced the leading philosophers of the day. For example, it is known that James Hogg, James Boswell, Jean Desaguliers, Charles de Montesquieu, Francois Voltaire, Andrew Michael Ramsay, Robert Burns, Jonathan Swift and George Washington were prominent Freemasons. A recent book sums up this situation quite succinctly, when discussing the principles of the 18th C Enlightenment:

> Without eighteenth-century Freemasonry, the principles at the very heart of the conflict – liberty, equality, brotherhood, tolerance, the 'rights of man' – would not have had the currency they did. True, those principles owed much to Locke, Hume, Adam Smith and *les philosophes* in France. But most, if not all, of those thinkers were either Freemasons themselves, moved in Freemasonic circles or were influenced by Freemasonry.[2]

Freemasonry helped provide a milieu for new ideas. That large numbers of prominent men were known, active members of Freemasonry, yet this fact is rarely mentioned in many conventional histories, is interesting to note. One has to ask: why? You do see mention of their membership in various churches or, for example, in certain Scottish clubs of the time such as the Gentlemen's Club of Spalding, the Bannatyne Club or the Maitland Club, yet, often, many of the same members were also known to have been Freemasons. But this is rarely even investigated, let alone mentioned, and ironically this tendency has seemed to be strongest with those who purport to be 'scientific' in their research methodology. If prominent members of such movements as those listed above were Freemasons, and therefore met regularly to discuss ideas, then isn't this important regarding a proper study of that period in history?

As many would argue, absolutely. Concepts like 'liberty, equality, fraternity' and the rights of man in society had been well-known Masonic concepts for years, for example, and these ideas have clearly influenced many in western history. Similar concepts were also present in the medieval Guilds, certain chivalric Orders, the Rosicrucian fraternities and so on. So various Medieval, Renaissance, Masonic, and Enlightenment ideals all combined together to create a new, progressive spirit of the time, emphasizing the ideals of brotherhood, equality, liberty, and reason.

Detailed Masonic records are available for study, yet few academics in the past have consulted them, Freemason or not. But fortunately this situation seems to be greatly changing in recent years, especially given the fact that highly respected universities and colleges in Europe and the USA are now said to be among the largest purchasers of rare and antiquarian Masonic (and related) books and papers, according to university librarians and key antiquarian book dealers in London and New York. This is because they have correctly foreseen that a new era is now emerging regarding such previously neglected areas of historical study, and given the keen competition for grants and so on, leading universities are now taking notice of these largely untapped research areas and sources in western history. Perhaps contrary to popular belief, Masonic librarians and curators *are* open to receiving visitors and answering questions, and in fact, they largely see it as their duty to do so. In London, at the United Grand Lodge of England, for example, public tours are conducted daily and the museum and library are open to the public during business hours. The Grand Lodge of Scotland also has an informative website, and an interesting library and museum with its very knowledgeable curator, Mr Robert Cooper, in addition to being the location of an important Georgian building regarding the history of the city of Edinburgh.

Sir Isaac Newton: a case in point

So times are changing, with many scholars now being more open-minded about such cultural influences in history than in the past. As we saw before, it is now more widely known that Sir Isaac Newton, the genius mathematician and physicist, also seriously studied alchemy much of the time, and that this clearly had an influence on his life's work and research. We have all heard about his part-time job at the Royal Mint, yet are rarely told about the hundreds of thousands of pages of Newton's work involving subjects like alchemy *that scholars know to be genuine*. It may also not be so widely known, for example, that Newton adhered to the Arian heresy and did not believe in the Trinity. In previous years, however, this information was understandably not generally shared with the public, given the climate of the times. In recent years academic books have addressed the alchemy issue in greater detail and have been getting good reviews, and more detailed research is also being done by others. One recent important academic study notes:

> The academic study of these developments is a comparatively recent phenomenon. Most literature about the various aspects of 'western esotericism' has traditionally been of an apologetic or polemic nature: a debate, basically, among believers and their opponents. Academic researchers generally tended to avoid an area of cultural expression that was widely regarded as inherently suspect; openly to express interest in these traditions might too easily endanger a scholar's prestige among colleagues. During the last few decades, the realization has been growing that this attitude has little to commend it from a scholarly point of view, and may on the contrary have blinded us to important aspects of our cultural past. Even more importantly, it has become increasingly clear that the scholarly recovery of 'esoteric' traditions may eventually force us to question the basic received opinions about the foundations of our present culture.[3]

From a sociological point of view, too, Freemasonry's impact has been immense, as has that of other similar groups. Taking Scotland, for example, one would find it difficult to point to a town on a map and not find a Masonic lodge there, or perhaps even the previous location of a medieval Knights Templar preceptory, or a former hospital and sanctuary of the early Knights of St Lazarus or Knights Hospitaller, all of which were also present in medieval Scotland. Even the national Bard, Robert Burns, was a Freemason, and a number of his poems are known to have Masonic references in them. The Church of Scotland has also debated the issue, not withstanding the fact that some of its past Moderators have also been Freemasons, and the subject is still discussed today by many people with different viewpoints. But the purpose of this chapter is to offer the general reader an insight into the traditions and legends of Freemasonry that may be pertinent to Scotland's past in some way.

Debate on Freemasonry's origins: Anderson's 'Constitutions'

Freemasonry as it is structured today traces its origins back to the establishment of the first Grand Lodge of Freemasons, set up by four Lodges in London in 1717. Many Masonic writers refer to this event as a revival rather than an actual beginning because the traditions and legends associated with the Craft are known to be much, much older. Today there are many Grand Lodges all over the world, although many, but not all, follow similar practices.

In Scotland, the Grand Lodge and its daughter lodges work in similar ways to those of England, Ireland and some other Masonic constitutions around the world. However – and this is very important to note – *its history and lore are totally unique among Masonic traditions around the world*. Ancient traditions and legends lie at the heart of Scottish Freemasonry and its degrees, and some of these make reference to events from significant periods in Scottish history. In fact, little has actually been published about the very early Scottish Masonic rituals and some of the rituals may be in private archives.

The first written origins of modern Freemasonry appeared soon after the foundation of the premier Grand Lodge (1717). Written by Scottish Presbyterian minister James Anderson in 1723, this work was entitled *Book of Constitutions of the Antient and Honourable Fraternity of Free and Accepted Masons*, simply called 'Anderson's Constitutions' by many today. This was the first truly Masonic book in the modern sense, and it started the debate about what was and what wasn't Masonic 'history', and it laid down some of the important principles of Masonry. The *Constitutions* stated the loyalty of the Freemasons to the House of Hanover, but they also *forbade political and religious discussions in the lodge, and the declaration of one's political allegiances*. It is still debated as to whether, and to what extent, Anderson's *Constitutions* actually advocated deism; they certainly seem to have come quite close to doing so, as Masonic lodges were to be open to anyone who believed in God or a Supreme Being, regardless of their personal religious beliefs. Anderson referred to the Supreme Being as 'the Great Architect of the Universe'. The duty of obedience to the King and his government was mentioned in addition to emphasis that all men were equal, regardless of class, political or religious affiliations – something rather unusual up to that time, and a concept which would continue to gain momentum throughout the 18th C.

The *Constitutions* also contained in its pages a semi-mythical account referred to as a 'traditional history' of the craft, which was derived from medieval manuscripts that had previously been used by the medieval Guilds of operative stone masons. Because of this, many Masons seemed to feel more comfortable with taking 1717 as a starting point for official Freemasonry, a situation that still exists today. The specific details of Anderson's traditional history will be discussed later in this chapter.

Following Anderson's *Constitutions*, virtually thousands of books were written, by Masonic and non-Masonic writers alike, putting forward hundreds of theories as to the possible origins of Freemasonry and the nature of its teachings. Some, usually disgruntled ex-members, allege all sorts of bizarre practices, while the majority promote the highest principles and ideals, so there is definitely a very wide range of material available.

Many theories exist

Long before the increasing interest in such matters today, Freemasons had become adept at producing many ingenious theories as to where they and their system may have first taken root. Early rather fantastic suggestions include the Craft starting in the Garden of Eden with Adam, or with the mysteries and rites originated by the builders of the Pyramids in Egypt. Other legendary claims include theories that perhaps the builders of the Tower of Babel or those of King Solomon's Temple originated the rites. Freemasons use symbolism derived from builders, so it is obvious why ancient religious edifices have often been cited in Masonic writings. King Solomon's temple in Jerusalem is considered to be the first temple of the Judeo-Christian faith, so it is unquestionably significant throughout European and western history.

Not just builders of temples, but *all workers in stone for religious purposes* have been held in esteem by Freemasons. In chapter 1, we learned about the significance of special stones to the early Hebrews, and of the importance of the centre stone of Solomon's temple as the pillar that Jacob was said to have rested his head on, that is 'Jacob's Pillow'. Regarding the early Scots, we also learned how this legend has played an important role in the coronation rites of their kings.

Further speculation as to where Masonic practices may have come from have been the mystery schools of Egypt, early Greece and Rome and, especially, the rites of Mithras. Mithraism at one time was a serious challenge to Christianity as the number one faith of the Roman Empire. As history has shown, Christianity triumphed under Constantine the Great in the 4th C; ironically, however, he still maintained the feast days of Apollo and Mithras, both of which were also on 25 December, Christmas Day. The theme of a god who died and rose again was something that the ancient world had already been familiar with, albeit in many guises. The mysteries of the Essenes are also believed by some to have had great influence on Freemasonry. The Essenes were an important Jewish sect that produced the Dead Sea Scrolls, and of which some argue that Jesus himself may have been a member.

The founder of The Philosophical Research Society, Manly P. Hall, was one of the leading 20th C Masonic scholars. He believed that the various influences on Freemasonry were quite numerous and that they evolved over a long period of time into the various rites and systems now termed 'Masonic':

> Freemasonry is a world-wide university, teaching the liberal arts and sciences of the soul to all who will hearken to its words. Its chairs are seats of learning and its pillars uphold an arch of universal education. Its trestleboards are inscribed with the eternal verities of all ages and upon those who comprehend its sacred depths has dawned the realisation that within the Freemasonic Mysteries lie hidden the lost arcana sought by all peoples since the genesis of human reason. The philosophical power of Freemasonry lies in its symbols – its priceless heritage from the mystery schools of antiquity.[4]

Importance of allegory, drama and symbol

Before proceeding it is important to make a distinction between the search for ancient historical origins, which is nearly impossible to establish for certain, and the speculative enquiry into Freemasonry's most probable influences. Various books try, and often fail, to find an ancient historical lineage for Freemasonry. Instead, a search for the origins of *influences* that inspired Masonic philosophies proves to be much more fruitful. Within the limited space available here, our present enquiry does not claim to be anything other than only one more insight into this vast topic.

Freemasonry as it is known and practised today was officially established as a result of the first Grand Lodge of 1717. At that time, an organised craft was given a public persona that had previously not been actively promoted. We know that members of this group met then, as they do now, behind closed doors in buildings known as lodges. In those earlier times, lodges were held in gentlemen's clubs and taverns, long before modern-day Masonic temples were built. Rites of initiation were practised involving secret signs, handshakes and words of recognition, to be used exclusively by members to identify their fellow Freemasons.

Included in the ceremonies were *allegorical stories* used as a vehicle to impress upon the candidate virtuous principles and moral lessons. Allegory is a word used to describe ways of using stories to reveal hidden meanings. These are certain dramas that are acted out where the initiate himself is a key player. They are believed to have performed the same function as many of the ancient mystery schools of antiquity and of the medieval miracle and passion plays of Christian Europe, many of which were sponsored by the Guilds.

Freemasonry under this Grand Lodge method then spread out from Britain, and on to the Continent, the Americas, and later throughout the British Commonwealth and the rest of the world, mainly, at first, via military lodges – lodges of Freemasons within various army regiments, especially in the 18th C. So the principles of Freemasonry were being applied around the globe in a relatively short space of time. Unfortunately, as is often the case in such situations, some of the original rituals and principles were sometimes changed or corrupted with the passage of time. As with many other philosophies and belief systems, new innovations later appeared, not all of which remained exactly true to the original principles. The many developments and innovations in Freemasonry over the last three centuries has resulted in a situation where, globally, there are hundreds of degrees (Masonic ceremonies) and probably thousands of Masonic and quasi-Masonic bodies in existence.

Freemasonry not a single organisation

Before proceeding with an investigation into the Scottish Craft specifically, we need to establish one important fact. Scottish Lodges, or indeed those of any other constitution, do not belong to one single worldwide organisation called 'Freemasonry'. Many writers, particularly those who are hostile to Freemasonry, make the erroneous assumption that Freemasonry is simply one large, organised worldwide body, involved in all sorts of bizarre organised conspiratorial activities, but this is not likely to be the case. Of course, every organisation has its 'bad apples', so to speak, but one cannot then simply generalise about the entire organisation from the behaviour of a few errant individuals. There are, in truth, many different kinds of Masonic bodies in existence, and not all of whom even officially recognise each other. This is very similar to the many different denominations of the Christian church, not all of whom necessarily get along with or agree with one another, even today. So, put directly, one simply cannot 'lump' all Masonic lodges together and then generalise about them as a whole.

The Grand Lodge of Scotland and its member lodges are different to those of Ireland and England and have, in some cases, different rituals and practices. The general objectives of many Grand Lodges are not at variance with one another and are largely involved in supporting their lodges in charitable works to benefit the community at large. Many Grand Lodges throughout the world do acknowledge each other and their members may visit each others lodges. However, others are deemed to be 'irregular' lodges and so no reciprocity is acknowledged or permitted. The term 'Freemasonry' is also sometimes wrongly attributed to groups which, just because they carry out initiation ceremonies of some type, are then automatically wrongly labelled as 'Masonic' organisations.

'Liberty, Equality, Fraternity'

The great appeal of Freemasonry as it first started to rapidly spread around the globe was largely due to its fraternal nature, with liberty, equality, brotherhood and camaraderie being essential aspects of its philosophy. At the time of its initial growth under a Grand Lodge network, such philosophies were very similar to, and had a profound influence on, the Enlightenment thinking of the 18th C which was occurring at the same time, so each clearly influenced the other. Freemasonry also attracted many aristocrats and influential gentlemen of the time.

In France, the motto of the Republic, *Liberty, Equality, Fraternity*, summed up many of the ideals of Freemasonry. France gave America the Statue of Liberty and supported the ideals and principles of the American Revolution. This new way of thinking at the time was having a profound effect on philosophy and politics, something that is acknowledged by historians today. The overall tide of political, philosophical and religious thinking was rapidly changing in Europe and north America, creating a movement against oppression and for greater freedom of thought and speech. Masonic lodges were very conducive to this thinking, as many influential people from all quarters of society were actively involved in bringing about these changes, and it so happens that a number were also Freemasons. In the 16th and 17th centuries, for example, Masonic lodges were one of the few places where one could safely read the Bible or discuss emerging 'heretical' scientific ideas, and this freedom also attracted many influential gentlemen to lodges. These disparate groups all worked together to bring about these new changes in society. Not everyone agreed, however: in 1738, a papal bull was issued condemning Freemasonry.

In 18th C England, many lodges were being created, ready to accept into their ranks thinking men of the day. In Scotland, the situation was slightly different, in that all the earliest Lodges of the new styled 'Freemasons' were in fact merely a development of lodges that had previously been in existence, probably as trade Guilds of operative masons. There is evidence in Scotland that development of Operative and Speculative (philosophical) masons both met together in the same lodges, and that this had been taking place throughout the 17th C, and likely even earlier. Some English Masonic scholars also say that there were earlier lodges in existence there too, which is also possible, and more research is being done in all these areas today.

Old pre-existing Scottish lodges

The claim of many of these old Scottish Lodges, even today, is that they were *already ancient* when the Guild Masons Craft was reorganised by William Schaw on the feast day of St John the Evangelist in 1598. The most widely accepted patron saint of the mason craft was St John, and even in the 17th C, for example, Scottish lodges held their major meeting of the year on 27 December, the Feast Day of St John the Evangelist, and others on 24 June, the Feast Day of St John the Baptist.

According to Professor David Stevenson, the earliest known pre-1710 references to lodges in Scotland are: Aitchison's Haven (9 January 1599), Edinburgh (31 July 1599), St Andrews (27 November 1599), Kilwinning (28 December 1599), Stirling (28 December 1599), Haddington (1599), Dunfermline (1600-1), Glasgow (31 December 1613), Dundee (1627-8), Linlithgow (2 March 1654), Scone [Perth] (24 December 1658), Aberdeen (1670?), Melrose (28 December 1674), Canongate Kilwinning (20 December 1677), Inverness (27 December 1678), Dumfries (20 May 1687), Canongate and Leith (29 May 1688), Kirkcudbright (1691?), Hamilton (25 March 1695), Dunblane (April 1695), Kelso (2 June 1701), Haughfoot (22 December 1702), Banff (1703), Kilmolymock [Elgin] (27 December 1704) and Edinburgh Journeymen (1707-12).[5]

Indeed, when the Grand Lodge of Scotland was formed in 1736, it had approximately 100 lodges to deal with, which were already in existence. Not all of them even wanted to join the Grand Lodge; in fact, as the official website of the Grand Lodge of Scotland states, only 33 of these lodges were represented at the foundation meeting, leaving around 67% of them who apparently felt that a centralised Grand Lodge wasn't really necessary at the time, as some of them had already been in existence for 140 years prior to then. So the point here is that many of these very early Scottish lodges have disappeared in the course of time, yet, this whole situation clearly did affect the way the Grand Lodge of Scotland was founded, as there were so many pre-existing lodges at that time.

According to the official website of the Grand Lodge of Scotland, regarding these early lodges:

> ...very little is known of them. Indeed many are only known by their village or town name. It can be seen, therefore, that the Grand Lodge of Scotland began as a 'bottom-up' organisation – that is, with many Lodges pre-existing Grand Lodge. Other Grand Lodges were formed at a time when there were relatively few Lodges and began from a 'top-down' position. This historical difference in the early organisation of Grand Lodges gives Scottish Freemasonry a distinct and unique character... Scottish Lodges have the right to choose the colours of the Lodge regalia... there is no such thing as a 'standard' ritual for Scottish

Lodges. Each Lodge has had the right to devise its own, within reason, and many do so... the connection between the craft of stone masonry and modern Free-masonry can only be established in Scotland. This direct connection can be traced from existing written records...[6]

Of course, resistance to the imposition of a centralised authority is not particularly new to Scotland: the Church of Scotland even today, for example, does not have Bishops, preferring a less hierarchical approach. Even back in the days of the Declaration of Arbroath, as we learned in chapter 1, the 'Community of the Realm' concept about the role of the monarch and the people was a much more community-orientated, 'bottom-up' approach to what was the standard policy of the time. In later years, of course, came the now-famous lyrics of Robert Burns, *A Man's A Man for A' That*. So, by the time of the formation of the Grand Lodge of Scotland in 1736, we also see a similar tendency, which isn't really all that surprising.

Schaw, the Master of Works to King James VI of Scotland, is regarded as a learned Renaissance man of the time, who injected hermetic philosophy into the Scottish craft. In some ways he can be considered to have been the founding father of modern Freemasonry in Scotland. An excellent study of Schaw's involvement within Scottish operative masonry and in 17th C Freemasonry in Scotland in general can be found in Professor David Stevenson's well-researched book *The Origins of Freemasonry, Scotland's Century 1590-1710*, as referred to above. A Professor of History at St Andrews University, although not a Freemason himself, Stevenson presents an important study of the impact of Freemasonry in Scotland during this period, which later led up to the Enlightenment of the 18th C. He approached various Scottish lodges while undertaking this monumental work and was given open access to some important minute books and lodge histories, a vast amount of which was not previously available to the general public. His work is still quoted and debated by academics and Masonic scholars today.

The ancient traditions of many old Scottish lodges state that they date back to at least the time when stonemasons were building the great abbeys and cathedrals throughout the country. Mr Roy Lauchlan MBE JP, a dedicated local historian in Kilwinning, states:

> ...the artisans of those days lived in a feudal society, and as such were slaves to the system. They could not work, nor move out with their own local community, without permission from their superiors... During the eleventh century, the Church of Rome became concerned about the condition of their European monasteries... To meet this challenge the Vatican took the unprecedented decision to allow freedom of travel, without restriction, to certain groups of masons and architects engaged on the building and renovation of monasteries... This new-found freedom resulted in those masons being referred to as Freemasons.[7]

Mr Laughlan further claims that some of these Freemasons were responsible for building Kilwinning Abbey c.1188 (others say 1140) and for creating a lodge within the area that has remained there up to the present day. Kilwinning Abbey was dedicated to the Virgin Mary and also to the 6th C St Winnin, from whom it takes its name. Kilwinning literally means 'the cell of Winnin'. Kilwinning has argued the claim for centuries to being the oldest Masonic Lodge in Scotland and even the world. The Lodge of Edinburgh, Mary's Chapel No. 1, also promotes itself as being the most ancient in Scotland, partly based on a tradition that its foundation dates back to the time of King David 1 and the building of Holyrood Abbey in Edinburgh. But Kilwinning is still called 'Mother Kilwinning'.

Early record of masons' work at St Giles Church in Edinburgh

From the Bannatyne Club archives, a record of a 1387 builders' contract exists, of work to be done at St Giles Church in Edinburgh by three stone masons:

> *1387 Edinburgh, St Giles' Church*: Three masons undertake to build five chapels in the south aisle, with vaults [based] on the design of the vault of St Stephen's Chapel, Holyrood. Four chapels shall have a three-light window and the fifth a door like that at the west end of the church. They shall have stone roofs,

with gutters between them. They are to have 600 marks Scots –
£40 in advance – and are to set 1,200 of ashlar and coigns and
to guarantee the work weatherproff.[8]

Early history of St Giles Cathedral: the Aisle of St John

In terms of documentable evidence, a number of Masonic
writers have suggested that the Seal of Cause issued to the Trades
of Edinburgh in 1475 can be used to authenticate the lodge's early
beginnings, although a specific lodge is not mentioned by name.
The Seal of Cause was granted to the Wrights and Masons of
Edinburgh, and it established that religious ordinances and certain
customs were to be observed by the trades within Edinburgh. In
the charter of 1475, the Wrights and Masons are instructed to
worship Almighty God, the Virgin Mary, and the patron of the
church they were meeting in, St Giles. St Giles Cathedral is now
known as the High Kirk of the (Presbyterian) Church of Scotland,
and is also a popular tourist destination today.

The charter outlines some of the religious expectations of the
Craft, stating that the Masons and Wrights were to supply:

> ...a divine service daily to be done at the Alter of Sanct Jhone the
> Evangelist, foundit in the College Kirk of St Geile of Edinburgh,
> and for reparatioun beilding and polecy to be maid in honour of
> the said sanct of Sanct Jhone, and of the glorious sanct Sanct
> Jhone the Baptist, to have consentit and assignit, and be thir our
> present lettres consentis and assignis, to our lovit nychtbouris the
> hale Craftismen of the Masonis and of the Wrichtis within the said
> burgh, the Ile and Chapell of Sanct Jhone...[9]

The Edinburgh Seal of Cause clearly illustrates that *the
masons and wrights of Edinburgh were using the Aisle of St
John(s) in the Church of St Giles to conduct a daily service in honour of St John(s) and were also bound to carry out certain respon-
sibilities for the maintenance and repair of the altar.* This connection to both St Johns features significantly throughout Scottish
Freemasonry and could also suggest a link to some early influences
that helped to shape the modern craft, as will be discussed later.

According to the Grand Lodge of Scotland's informative booklet *Historical Sketch of the Grand Lodge of Antient Free & Accepted Masons of Scotland 1736-1986*:

> The earliest reference to a Lodge in Edinburgh is to be found in the Statute 'anent the government of the Master Masons of St Giles, 1491' which is to be found in the Burgh records. It lays down the conditions of employment of those engaged on the work and it can be compared with the ordinances of York Minster dated 1370, for the Edinburgh Statute declares that the Masons are to 'get a recreation in the Common Lodge'... The word 'Lodge' was used in this sense by the specialist builders, particularly engaged on cathedrals and castles or the major contracts of the day, but the builders in Scotland, unlike their English counterparts, found there was little demand for building after Bannockburn and were forced to amalgamate with the craft associations...[10]

And, as further stated by the Grand Lodge of Scotland:

> It would appear that in the early Lodge the Apprentice received the secret of the Masons Word and the Fellow of the Craft was subjected to a practical test. With the increasing presence of the Speculative Mason there was an advance in ritual and there have been found a number of manuscripts... It was an Englishman, the late Brotherhood Harry Carr, who said that 'Masonry is indebted to the Scots for the oldest Lodge Minutes in the world, the oldest codes of official regulations for the management of operative Lodges and the oldest complete ritual texts with descriptions of the admission ceremonies of their day. It is no exaggeration to say that the clearest light on our beginnings in operative Masonry is drawn from these priceless relics...'[11]

Kilwinning Lodge No. 0: 'Mother Kilwinning'

Kilwinning Lodge in Ayrshire holds the position of being Lodge No. 0 on the Roll of the Grand Lodge of Scotland whilst Mary's Chapel in Edinburgh is listed as No. 1. This unusual situation came about as a result of the creation of the Grand Lodge of Scotland which was founded in 1736. A few years after its inception, Grand Lodge decided that lodges were to be given numbers and ranked in accordance to their antiquity. In many cases, as oral traditions went back much further than the earliest written documentation of many of the old lodges, this situation was unsatisfactory for Lodge Kilwinning, which claimed a very ancient history.

So Lodge Kilwinning withdrew from Grand Lodge in 1744 and remained independent until 1807. In that year, a compromise was reached, whereby Kilwinning would appear at the top of the list, but without a number, and Mary's Chapel would remain as number 1. Mary's Chapel was previously appointed No. 1 because its earliest minute book dates from 1599. This book, along with all other minutes up to the present day, designates this Edinburgh Lodge as the oldest in the world that can prove a continuous existence over 400 years. Mary's Chapel No. 1 still meets in Edinburgh on a regular basis in Hill Street. At some point, Kilwinning began to be referred to as No. 0, and this unusual situation has continued to the present day.

The 'Kilwinning lodges'

'Kilwinning lodges' were a product of Lodge Mother Kilwinning, and issued charters to new lodges, all of whom included Kilwinning in their names, as in Dalkeith Kilwinning and Peebles Kilwinning. Kilwinning, as we have seen, means the cell of St Winnin (or Finnan) and has around 45 lodges indirectly associated with his name.

Numerous suggested influences that may have contributed to the overall philosophy and origin of the teachings of Freemasonry have already been briefly mentioned. Examining nearly all the evidence available to us regarding to the origins of Freemasonry, Britain is the location from where Freemasonry spread its principles throughout the world. Within Britain, much of the earliest documentary evidence for Freemasonry seems to be predominately found in Scotland. Of course, some Masonic scholars from other areas disagree, but many others continue to believe that Scotland has the earliest evidence to date. This matter is still being researched and debated by Masonic scholars today.

Some theorists have put forth past origin theories about Freemasonry suggesting that it may have ultimately originated from early Scottish customs, or perhaps also from certain Celtic church communities, which are believed by some eminent scholars to have received their practices from the Eastern Christian Church of St John, the Johannine church. This particular area of study has tended to be vastly under-researched, and is therefore given only a passing mention in many works, and is a very complex topic.

Masonic historian R.F. Gould also writes about similar early Indo-European and Indian beliefs to those of Freemasonry:

> ...the religion of Abraham's descendants was that of Ras; that Masonry in that country is called Raj or Mystery; that we have also found the Colida and most other of these matters on the Jumma, a thousand miles distant in North India... it is clear that one must have borrowed from the other, let him determine the question: Did York and Scotland borrow from the Jumna and Carnatic, or the Juma and Carnatic from them?'[12]

Gould also mentions that in another work, Mr Godfrey Higgins says that the Culdees were the last remains of the Druids, who had been converted to Christianity before the Roman Church got any footing in Britain. 'They were Pythagoreans, Druidical monks, probably Essenes, and this accounts for their easily embracing Christianity; for the Essenes were as nearly Christian as possible'.[13]

Of course, many Celtic scholars would not agree with the above, as just as it is with Freemasonry with its great emphasis on *oral transmission*, the Druidic methods of teaching were also purely done by oral transmission, and so no written records are available to prove, or disprove, any theories about a possible 'Celtic' or 'Druidic' origin to Freemasonry. There are no existing written records, so all one can do is speculate, and even then, with very great caution. Also, parts of Higgins' work have been questioned by scholars. But we have opted to include such accounts as they are important nonetheless in analysing the historical mythic accounts and legends about Freemasonry.

The first Three Degrees of Freemasonry

There are still those who debate whether Freemasonry and Christianity are compatible because of the lack of overt references to Christ personally in Masonic ritual. The setting for the first degrees and ceremonies of Freemasonry are based on Old Testament stories and teachings. These first three degrees are given names that correspond to craft terms: Apprentice, Fellow-craft and Master Mason.

The lessons of the first three degrees are given an Old Testament setting and the biblical stories are used in an allegorical way to exemplify certain moral principles that are actually contained in all the major faiths. In symbolic terms, the various elements of Masonic degrees represent the highest principles of the Christian faith as much as they represent that which is best in all religions and philosophical systems. There are many different Masonic orders, some of which are open *only* to those that profess a belief in the Christian faith; so, many church members are also Freemasons.

In Germany, during WWII, Freemasonry was suppressed by the Nazis mainly because of its apparent 'Jewishness' (as was believed by Hitler), and as a result, many Freemasons were persecuted and sent to the concentration camps. Many assumptions about Freemasonry exist because of a fundamental lack of understanding of the subject, but, admittedly, this situation has not been helped by Masons themselves over the years who have appeared very aloof or evasive when faced with genuine inquiries by the public, which only adds to the problem in how they are perceived in general.

'St Johns' Masonry': Saints John the Evangelist and John the Baptist

Among many old documents pertaining to the Guilds of operative masons, there are many references to the Christian saints John the Evangelist and John the Baptist. Scottish Freemasonry in particular has always been termed '*St John's Masonry*', a tradition that pre-dates the first Grand Lodge of 1717.

By and large, however, 'St Johns Masonry' has more generally been understood to refer to the institution as a whole, rather than to unaffiliated lodges only. In Scotland, specifically, we find St John connected in an official manner with masonry by an enactment of 1799, when it was resolved by the Grand Lodge 'that they sanction the *Three Great Orders of Masonry*, and these alone, of APPRENTICE, FELLOW CRAFT, and MASTER MASON, being the ancient order of SAINT JOHN.' Similarly, in a letter from the Grand Secretary of the Royal Order of Scotland to an applicant, the former tries to explain the distinction between the 'Royal Order of Scotch Masonry', of which he was the Secretary, and 'the Holy Lodge of St John', over which the Grand Master of Scotland presided.[14]

Dr George Oliver (1782-1867), a prominent English Freemason, introduced the term 'Johannite Masonry' to describe Masonry according to St John (or the two St Johns) as practiced in Scotland, Ireland and in some parts of the United States. Oliver firmly believed that Freemasonry was Christian, although not overtly so, and believed that it contained within its rituals the remains of early Christian doctrine. Oliver, a doctor of Divinity, was also a prolific writer. His interests were numerous, and included the ancient Britons, church history, archaeology, and many of his writings discussed Masonic antiquities, with at least one major work on the Johannite Masons.

However, the importance of St John regarding the early Scottish Masonic lodges is interesting to note, as it is known that St John(s) was quite important to the Celtic Christian communities, the Culdees, and also to these early Scottish Lodges. The Celtic tonsure was referred to by those on the Continent as the 'St John's tonsure', and it is especially noteworthy that *Scottish Freemasonry has always been called 'St Johns Freemasonry'*, and that St John(s) is still important in worldwide Freemasonry today. The medieval Knights Templar and other chivalric Orders also highly revered St John(s). Also – and this is important to note – *both Catholics and Protestants in Scotland* have highly revered St John through the centuries, so this is not necessarily the sectarian issue that it may first seem. The medieval Guilds were Catholic, of course, but they especially valued St John, as did the later

Protestants in Scotland and the early Masonic lodges. So St John(s), it seems, has always been highly esteemed in Scotland. Could the concept of 'the Word' possibly have something to do with this?

Exactly when the term 'St John's Masonry' was first established is not known, but it is thought to go back to at least early medieval times. In Scotland, so great was the veneration of St John that nearly all of the old lodges took for a distinctive name that of St John. Curiously, 69 Scottish Lodges, representing in many cases some of the very oldest ones, contain the name St John in their title. Both St Johns are still highly esteemed by Masons today, apparently based on the fact that one St John baptised the Lord and the other spread his 'Word', that is 'the latter completed by his learning that which the former began with his zeal'.[15]

Both St Johns were important to the medieval Knights Templar, especially John the Baptist. The Battle of Bannockburn, for example, was fought on the 24 June 1314, the Feast Day of St John the Baptist, and even today many churches and Masonic lodges in Scotland are dedicated to either St John the Baptist or St John the Evangelist. Certain branches of the early Celtic church, and later the Culdees, were also known to have had special reverence for both St Johns. The Celtic tonsure was once called the 'St John's tonsure', as referred to in chapter 5.

Another explanation of the great emphasis on both St Johns in Masonic tradition may refer to the survival of earlier pre-Christian religious practices that were adopted by the early Church as it tried to established itself in Britain, having, according to some, a possible astronomical basis:

> It is most probable, however, that the custom of dedicating Lodges to these saints arose from astronomical reasons. The Sun enters Cancer on or about the 21st day of June, and the 24th is dedicated to St John the Baptist and reaches Capricorn on 22nd December, the 27th being dedicated to St John the Evangelist. These two important heliacal periods being so close to the festival days of the two St Johns, in the course of time caused their adoption as patrons.[16]

Another Masonic writer acknowledges the great importance of the feasts of both St Johns as being of Masonic significance, but seems unsure as to why, so he alludes to a connection with the summer and winter solstices:

> Masons must not overlook the fact that for some apparently inexplicable reason these two saints are always associated with Freemasonry, despite the fact that the real patron of the masons of the Middle Ages was S. Thomas. There is nothing in Holy Scripture to warrant this association and yet, even as late as the time of the formation of Grand Lodge, the association was so strong that Anderson is careful to say that the famous meeting was held 'on S. John the Baptist's Day.' Even still, Craft Masonry in Scotland and also in many other parts of the world is always called 'St John's Masonry'. S. John in Summer and S. John in Winter really represent the old Fertility Festivals of the Summer and Winter Solstice, and when the Church found that she could not stop the pagan feasts she fixed the feasts of the two S. Johns at the same period and so changed these festivals into nominally Christian ones. For all that, it is difficult to see why people should jump through the fire on S. John's Day in summer, seeing that the saint was not burnt, but beheaded.[17]

An additional insight on this is in chapter 9, about Rosslyn Chapel and the mystery plays that continued to be performed in medieval times in the glen there in Midsummer, one of which was entitled *Robin Hood and Little John*.

St John and 'The Word'

St John the Evangelist and his association with 'The Word' is also linked with Freemasonry. The symbol of St John in biblical terms is the eagle. He, and 'the Word', are also linked to certain communities of the Celtic Church, where St John was known to be highly regarded. Freemasonry teaches of a 'Mason Word' to describe the highest principles that man can hope to attain. And, as we know, the beginning of the Fourth gospel, that of St John, starts with 'In the beginning, was the Word...' This reference to 'the Word' does *not* mean something written down – it refers to an oral tradition and, ultimately, is an inexplicable mystery of God.

In cryptic terms, Masonic teachings also suggest that 'the true Word has been lost' and that until it is found we must console our-selves with substituted secrets. The Word, or Logos as it is referred to in Greek, means 'word', 'speech' or 'reason'; in John's Gospel, the Logos is neither a rational principle nor an intermediary agent, but God's *pre-existing Word* who formed creation and became flesh in Jesus Christ. (John 1:1-14) The Logos has also been thought of as the primal divine sound of the universe as well. It was used in Christian theology to mean the Second Person of the Trinity, the Son:

> The term was known both in pagan and Jewish antiquity. In the Old Testament, God's word was not only the medium of his com-munication with men; what God said had creative power, and by the time of the Prophets the Word of the Lord was regarded as having an almost independent existence. In Hellenistic Judaism, the concept of the Logos as an independent hypostasis was fur-ther developed. In the New Testament the term in its technical sense is confined to Johannine writings. In the Prologue to St John's Gospel, the Logos is described as God from eternity, the Creative Word, who became incarnate in the man Jesus of Nazareth. Though it is clear that the author was influenced by the same background as Philo, his identification of the Logos with the Messiah was new. In Patristic theology, the Johannine teaching about the Logos was taken up by St Ignatius and devel-oped by the Apologists of the 2nd C, who saw it as a means of making the Christian teachings compatible with Hellenistic phi-losophy.[18]

The 'Lost Word' of Freemasonry: the Mason's Word

In Freemasonry, the 'Masons Word' can be a rather confusing term. It is sometimes used in the same way that the Logos is used, referring to Jesus and/or the Word of Life. It is also used to describe a secret that was known only to the three Grand Masters of the first Temple of Jerusalem. In Masonic tradition, the 'Word' of the Master Mason is lost to us because of the untimely death of the principal architect, implying, perhaps, that the true secrets of

Freemasonry may not even be known in their entirety within the Craft.

Speculating, it may also refer to the lost teachings of the second person of the Trinity, the Son, as some believe. The problem is that Freemasonry uses *allegory* and *symbolism* in everything that it does, so one can only speculate on the meanings as there is no way of proving for certain the original intention behind the ceremonies. An esoteric explanation of 'The Word of Life' is given by Christian author and Freemason A.E. Waite:

> Explicitly or implicitly, it stands always for a Word of Life. It may act on those who can receive it as an awakening of the soul's consciousness in the direction of things that are Divine and in the first participation of human in Divine Nature. Here is the sense in which man is saved by the power of the Name YEHESHUAH; this is the abiding presence signified by that of IMMANUEL, the grace from everlasting to everlasting in the mystic cipher I:.N:.R:.I:, and the eternal mercy which is JEHOVAH. But in the Lodges of Mount Sinai and the Chapters of Holy Sanctuary, the Words and Names are recited as things spoken with the lips and received into physical ears: except to the very few they do not stand for life. There is no translation of symbols so that allegories testify full meaning from within and that pageants move not only in ordered sequence but in the Grace of God and His power. It comes about therefore that the Word is lost even in its recovery. Peace has departed from the Tabernacles and light out of the Holy Places, the Sacred Cities remain unfinished, and the Sanctuary can be erected only in the heart of the elect because the word of Life is Lost.[19]

First mention of a 'Mason's Word' in Scotland

The first written mention of a 'Masons Word' in Scotland appears in a very unusual poem entitled *Muses Threnodie*, written by Henry Adamson of Perth and published in Edinburgh in 1638:

> For what we do presage is not in grosse,
> For we be brethren of the Rosie Crosse:
> We have the Masons Word and second sight,
> Things for to come we can fortell aright...[20]

This extract from Adamson's full and lengthy poem apparently only came into the public domain because 'his friend Drummond of Hawthornden induced him to print it'.[21] Along with this reference to the Mason's Word, the poem also states that the *brethren of the Rosie Crosse* have the gift of second sight, a point that is normally overlooked in favour of descriptions of the Rosy Cross.

> Second sight is also an old Highland tradition and it is described as: ... a revelation, in fact, to certain gifted individuals of a world different from, and beyond, the world of sense... The shepherds of the Hebrides Isles are usually credited with the largest possession of the gift, but the doctrine was well known over the whole Highlands, and as firmly believed in Ross-shire and the highlands of Perthshire as in the remotest Hebrides... It is a Celtic belief...[22]

The 'all-seeing eye of God'

In many Masonic lodges the '*all-seeing eye of God*' is depicted on lodge walls, an old symbol which many have thought may have had its origins in ancient Egypt. Contrary to popular belief, this single, all-seeing eye of God is *not* always shown as being within a triangle in Masonic lodges as it is often portrayed on its own. Some Masons also theorise that it may have had an origin in certain very early Celtic and/or Christian beliefs as a type of protective talisman to safeguard the membership against the evil eye, implying that there has also always been a uniquely 'Scottish version' of this ancient, universal symbol. The so-called evil eye was believed to damage or injure anything – or anyone – it looked upon, so it may not be surprising that a single protective eye to counteract this negative effect is mentioned in early Scottish folk-lore accounts. Of course, this universal belief is also found in many other early societies.

An old charm used in the Scottish Highlands against the evil eye, for example, ends by making a reference to 'the eye of the Son of God' as a protective measure:

> Talkative are folk over thee,
> Christ has taken away their likeness,
> Twelve eyes before every eye,
> Strong is the eye of the Son of God,
> Weak is the eye of the unjust.[23]

The interpretation of these lines is believed by some to mean that the elemental forces of nature (fairies, devas and so on) which are here called 'folk', were made invisible to mortals by God and are portrayed as speaking among themselves over the affected person. In this charm, the succour of the twelve apostles and of Christ is seen as being more powerful than the injustice of man. Notice, though, that the power of the charm is based on *the one eye of the Son of God*. Other variations of the charm replace the title Son of God with the King of the Elements, God of Grace and yet others, with the Trinity.[24]

This image of a single protective eye of God, present today in buildings where Masonic lodge meetings are held, is interesting in that Masonic custom, even today, makes it very clear when the ritual is read out about this 'eye of God' – that 'no one who is at variance with the other' may be present together in the room.

The Rosy Cross

The mention of the 'Rosie Crosse' in Scotland in 1638, per Adamson's poem above, is also interesting and is a matter that has been much speculated upon. Rosicrucianism had been sweeping Europe especially since 1614, and its teachings – which have been variously described as mystical Christian, Protestant, Alchemical and/or Hermetic in nature – all point to more hidden philosophical traditions at the time. Kabbala, the secret teachings of the Jews, was said to be restricted only to the rabbis and never taught to the uninitiated; some believe that it may have also influenced Rosicrucianism.

The famous 19th C French historian and mystic Eliphas Levi comments on the history of magic through the centuries, and how the knowledge of 'the lost Word' was transmitted:

> Magic was the science of Abraham and Orpheus, of Confucius and Zoroster, and it was the magical doctrines which were graven on tablets of stone by Enoch and by Trismegistus. Moses purified and re-veiled them – this being the sense of the word 'reveal'. The new disguise which he gave them was that of the Holy Kabbalah – that exclusive heritage of Israel and inviolable secrets of its priests. Jerusalem... ended by losing in its turn the

Sacred Word, when a Saviour, declared to the magi by the holy star of initiation, came to rend the threadbare veil of the old temple, to endow the Church with a new network of legends and symbols – ever concealing from the profane and always preserving for the elect that truth which is the same forever... the memory of this doctrine summarized in a word, of this word alternately lost and recovered, which transmitted to the elect of all antique initiations. ...it was this same memory handed on to secret associations of Rosicrucians, Illuminati and Freemasons which gave a meaning to their strange rites, to their less or more conventional signs.[25]

Rosicrucianism appeared at just about the same general period in history as when Lutheranism and Calvinism were sweeping Europe, challenging the power, authority and practices of the Church of Rome, taking on what were seen at the time to be excess corruptions and abuse of power. Professor Stevenson of St Andrews University comments on Freemasonry in Scotland at that time:

Just 15 years before the Rosicrucian explosion of 1614 William Schaw had reworked the remnants of older Masonic organisation in Scotland into a lodge system of secret societies, and had to a greater or lesser extent injected into these lodges Hermetic influences. Other aspects of Renaissance thought led to the conclusion that the mason craft was far superior to all others, with a central place in the advancement of knowledge – and of course knowledge and spiritual enlightenment were inextricably linked.[26]

King James VI/I

At the time of William Schaw, King James VI of Scotland was the reigning monarch. James VI/I was a Protestant king in a volatile Europe, where one's faith could quite literally cost one his life in the wrong circumstances. Schaw, a man with a great love for architecture and the trusted advisor and Master of Works to the King, also travelled abroad extensively. Schaw, as a practising Roman Catholic in a Protestant court, may have been 'flexible in religion', as Stevenson puts it, not unlike other notable men of the time, like Lord Seton.[27] If we are to believe that Schaw was steeped in Hermetic philosophy, as many learned men at the time were, his relationship with the King is an interesting one and thus may be seen in a new light.

King James VI/I is portrayed in history as being a very superstitious man in many ways. In 1597 he wrote a short, infamous book entitled *Daemonoloie* that was Calvinistic in nature and strongly denounced Witchcraft. He is also acknowledged as being responsible for the Authorised, or King James Version, of the Bible which was printed in 1611.

According to Masonic tradition held by the Ancient Masonic Lodge of Scoon and Perth No. 3, King James VI/I also became a Freemason. Their history states that 'In 1601... King James VI was by his own desire entered a Freemason and Fellowcraft.'[28] Intriguing as this may be, like many of the earlier Scottish Masonic traditions, there is no contemporary evidence other than Scottish oral traditions to back this up, so it must therefore remain as mere speculation only.

Considering Schaw's close relationship with the Royal court in Scotland, however, this type of seemingly outrageous claim may not actually be as fantastic to contemplate as it may seem. It is far more likely that James VI/I had Rosicrucian connections on the Continent, or at least had some tendencies in that direction. But, as is well known, James VI/I was a Protestant king, and the Rosicrucian tracts certainly were known to have advocated similar beliefs. Sir Robert Moray, a Scot, was a founder of the Royal Society and a Freemason and also had significant links with the Rosicrucians. He was also a friend and patron of Thomas Vaughan, the Welsh Rosicrucian, who published the English translation of the first Rosicrucian manuscript, the *Fama Fraternitatis*, in 1652.

In 1614, the same year that the *Fama* initially appeared in Germany, the esteemed German Rosicrucian and Hermetic philosopher Michael Maier sent a rather cryptic manuscript to King James VI in Scotland. The document, now in Edinburgh at the Scottish Record Office, contains the enigmatic phrase 'Greetings to James, for a long time King of Great Britain. By your true protection may the rose be joyful.' [29] The rose, of course, is the Rosy Cross, the primary symbol of Rosicrucianism. It is obvious that the highly regarded scholar Michael Maier would not have sent something to King James VI if he did not think that he would know of its meaning. Unfortunately, to date, this unusual letter and pictorial diagram to the king and its enigmatic contents has yet to be properly explained, if it is mentioned it at all. But, as it is addressed to a king, it seems to be rather hard to simply ignore or minimise its importance.

St John tradition(s) in Scotland

The prolific references to the two St Johns in Scottish Masonry may point to the 'lost' influences of the Craft and also to certain communities of early Celtic Christianity in which St John was revered. It is known that it was influenced by the teachings of St John the Evangelist, who, along with the other apostles, was promoting a 'purer form of faith', in their eyes, than that which was being eroded. The author Geoffrey Ashe writes that the Apostle John (emphasis ours):

> ...is said, in certain quarters, to have founded a Church-within-the-Church, that works in secret till God chooses to reveal it. The source of the notion is the last chapter of his gospel. This records a conversation that puzzled the early Christians themselves. Three times Jesus says to Peter, 'Dost thou love me?' Peter was deeply moved when he asked a third time, 'Dost thou love me?' And said unto him, 'Lord, thou knowest all things; thou canst tell that I love thee'. Jesus said to him, 'Feed my sheep'... Peter turned, and saw the disciple whom Jesus loved, following him... Seeing him, Peter asked Jesus, 'And what of this man Lord'? Jesus said to him, *'If it is my will that he should wait till I come, what is it to thee? Do thou follow me'. Here Christ entrusts his flock to Peter, yet he seems to reserve John for some other task.* Several... writers hint at the continuance of a Johannine succession within the framework of the Petrine succession, preserving doctrines and sacramental principles for which the world is not ready. Conceivably the Celts imagined their Church to contain a Johannine element, which had to be safeguarded, but could not be discussed.[30]

So we still have the ancient image, even used recently in popular films about the Holy Grail, of the devout hermit St John, in his cave, waiting... and waiting...

In making reference to a neglected heritage in Britain, one

author stated 'In all debates between the early Churches, those of Gaul and Britain were acknowledged by Rome to be products of the Eastern Church, which followed the teachings of John'.[31]

In another work, a more specific oral account of how 'the Word' was originally brought to Scotland by followers of St John is discussed:

> The early dissemination of Christianity will not be difficult to understand if we consider the condition of the primitive church as planted by Christ and his Apostles. The peculiarity of the early Church was that it prescribed no dogmatic creed, but only required assent to certain events as expressions of Divine grace, and pledges of a Divine promise and purpose. Very little is known of the first introduction of Christianity into Pictland; but a tradition resting, however, on no very solid basis, existed to the following effect, that during the reign of Domitian (AD81) some disciples of the Apostle John visited Caledonia, and there preached the Word of Life.[32]

The statement that this early church prescribed *no dogmatic* creed is also something that modern Freemasonry practises. Scottish Masonic lodges accept among their members men of all faiths, the only provisions being that they must be upstanding, moral individuals and hold a belief in a Supreme Being. For this to be assured, they must be proposed and seconded by members of the Lodge after which a ballot is conducted by the brethren of the lodge. But, it must be emphasized, that in order to become a Mason, one *must* believe in a Supreme Being, however one defines it for oneself.

Thomas Innes, a Roman Catholic bishop writing in 1735, quotes the 16th C Scottish historian George Buchanan. As a Roman Catholic, Innes certainly did not always agree with Buchanan, whom he reports was 'a product of the Reformation', however, as a historian, he does include an account by Buchanan, which stated: *'the ancient Britons received Christianity from St John's disciples by learned and pious monks of that age.'*[33] This was widely believed to be true by many at the time. Innes further cites another author, David Buchanan, who in the 17th C also subscribed to the belief that the followers of St John travelled to Scotland early on. He wrote that:

'... those who came into our northern parts', to wit, into Scotland, 'and first made known unto our fathers the mysteries of heaven, were the disciples of S. John the Apostle.' He repeats again that the Scots had received 'their tenents and rights,' that is, the doctrine and discipline of Christianity, 'from their first apostles, disciples of S. John,' according to 'the church of the East.'[34]

An Edinburgh minister writing in 1811 also believed that Johannine Christianity, with its emphasis on St John, came to Britain in early times. He further states that according to him, this teaching formed the basis of the faith of certain Culdee communities:

> For Tertullian, who flourished in this age (close of the 2nd C), asserts that the gospel had not only been propagated in Britain, but had reached those parts of the island into which the Roman arms had never penetrated. This perfectly agrees with the defence, made by the Culdees, of their peculiar modes of worship. For they affirmed, that they had received these from the disciples of John the Apostle.[35]

According to biblical tradition, St John the Beloved was the disciple to whom Jesus gave special revelation, took on special occasions and with whom he prayed before his death. He also outlived all of the original apostles and disciples, and is thought to have possibly lived to the advanced age of 101 years; Irenaeus refers to him as still living in 98 AD, and Jerome dates his death as 68 years after the Crucifixion. So, if he lived that long, no doubt his own disciples may have travelled far and wide after his death.

Scottish Lodges and ceremonies regarding St John: Melrose

The oldest named St John's lodge of Freemasons in Scotland is the *Lodge of Melrose, St John no 1(2)*. Scottish Freemasonry has a peculiar numbering system that accommodates a number 0, a number 1, a number 1(2), and a number 1(3), all of whose origins are acknowledged to be ancient by the Grand Lodge of Scotland. The Melrose lodge is known to have existed from before 1598, having been one of the early lodges organised by William Schaw.

This particular old lodge still holds true to its ancient custom of installing its office bearers on the feast day of St John the Evangelist, 27 December, each year.

An early Masonic paper entitled *A Masons Confession* dated about 1727, claims to discuss the workings of a Scottish operative lodge of Masons, and describes a yearly imposing of '*oaths throughout the land on St John's day as it is termed, being the 27 December.*'[36] At Melrose, even today, an evening ceremony is held on the Feast Day of St John the Evangelist in which the new Master is led out of the lodge into the night air. Ceremoniously, he is escorted around the ruins of Melrose Abbey in a torchlight procession before returning to the Lodge rooms to complete his installation into the 'Chair of King Solomon' as it is phrased, to become the Master of the Lodge.

No contemporary sources have survived that relate to the ancient foundation of the lodge at Melrose, proclaimed as 1136 AD, the same time that the Abbey was being built. On a Master Mason diploma issued in 1874 there are written the words '... *the Ancient St Johns lodge Melrose AD 1136 as appears from Authentic Documents in the hands of the Master and Office Bearers of the said lodge*'.[37]

However, if evidence did exist in 1874, it has sadly now been lost. In the lodge's own history, an entry from a minute book says:

> At a meeting on 28 December 1812, Bro John Smith reported that he had had a visit from Bro Alexander Deuchar, Master of St Mary's Chapel Lodge, Edinburgh, (now the Lodge of Edinburgh, Mary's Chapel No. 1) who in the presence of the office-bearers perused the books and papers of the Lodge. Bro. Deuchar, 'a very Skilful Antiquary', declared himself satisfied that, 'with the single exception of St Mary's Chapel, no Lodge in Scotland could produce documents having a claim to equal Antiquity'.[38]

The Abbey at Melrose is also famously known in Scottish history for having within its grounds the buried heart of King Robert the Bruce, as previously noted. The duty of taking the deceased King's heart to Jerusalem was given to Sir James Douglas, Sir William St Clair and Sir Robert Logan of Restalrig, among others. The future heirs of Sir William St Clair of Roslin were to become the hereditary Grand Masters of the Masons in Scotland, according to Masonic traditions, apparently having the honour bestowed on them by King James II in the year 1441. Researchers Knight and Lomas go as far as to suggest that it was at this time Freemasonry was actually founded, although no contemporary evidence yet exists to substantiate their claim.[39]

Melrose Abbey was established by the Cistercians, or 'White Monks', in 1136, as discussed in chapter 4. The monks built their house near – but not exactly on – the site of Old Melrose, which is described by an official Melrose Abbey guide book as being 'hallowed in the annals of the Celtic or Culdee Church...'.[40]

It is notable that the great Abbeys and Cathedrals of the late 11th and 12th centuries were being built for new monastic orders that were being introduced into Scotland. Queen Margaret, later canonised as St Margaret, and her son King David I were largely responsible for the introduction of other orders into Scotland, in what was as much a political as a religious development. However, this process does appear to have expedited the decline of the Culdees, as other influences with the weight of the continental church behind them began to proliferate. If, as some Scottish Masonic lodges state, their inception was during this period, then the theory of a possible 'Culdee influence' may arise from this period. After all, one of the main doctrines of the Middle Ages, based on Church precepts and teachings, was that of *the just price and the just wage – 'a fair day's wages for a fair day's work'*. So, it is not inconceivable that some of the Christian communities would have felt a kindred bond, so to speak, with some of the early lodges and craft guilds then in existence, as after all, *somebody* had to build their churches, abbeys, and cathedrals. This is, of course, speculation; however, another subsequent reason for Masonic secrecy – if this theory is true – would have been because these 'Celtic' practices were now no longer acceptable in Scotland, or to the Continental Orthodoxy, and so a policy of more secrecy would have been prudent in the circumstances.

In 1147, Pope Eugenius III greatly increased the power of the Augustinian Monks in Scotland. *He not only gave them a title to elect their own superior, but enacted that on the decease of*

Culdees canons, regulars should be appointed in their place. [41] In other words, when a Culdee canon died, an Augustinian should be appointed in their place. This was known to be a difficult time for the remaining Culdee communities in Scotland. In 1150, David I endorsed this policy and when he sent his authoritative letters to the last main centres of Culdee influence in Scotland, those of Loch Leven and St Andrews, the final 'death knell' for the Culdees was sounded, and their decline was quite rapid from then on, as we saw in chapter 5. [42]

Another important Order was introduced into Scotland by David I, which was later officially suppressed by the Church in 1312, after the initial 1307 arrests in France. This famous monastic military crusading Order that still inspires many today was the 'Poor Fellow Soldiers of Christ and of the Temple of Solomon', or, as it is more commonly known today, the medieval Knights Templar. They had their Scottish headquarters at Balantradoch, now called the village of Temple in Midlothian, the lands of which were granted to Hughes de Payen on 21 June 1128 by David I, which was later confirmed at the Council of Troyes. The Knights Templar have a long history in Scotland, and today, there are several neo-chivalric Templar orders in Scotland.

Scottish Masonic lodge dedications: 69 to St John(s)

In the present day, Scottish Freemasonry is unique in its abundance of Lodges dedicated to Christian saints. The vast majority of these saints are Celtic, or, at the very least, seem to be attached to various Celtic areas and traditions. But of all of them, *St John is the clear winner in terms of Scottish lodge dedications.*

St John has some *69 Scottish lodges* dedicated to him, either as St John the Baptist or St John the Evangelist, quite a high number overall.

St Andrew, the Apostle and patron saint of Scotland, is quite popular, having at least 48 lodges named after him within the Scottish Constitution. He has even more lodges associated to him in North America and around the rest of the world.

St James' lodges account for 14 Scottish lodges, however precisely which St James is not clear in every case.

It is also interesting that of the four leaders of the church after Christ's death, three of them – St John, St Andrew and St James – have the largest number of Scottish Masonic lodges named after them. The fourth church leader, St Peter, has two lodges named after him in Scotland.

Scottish lodges: others saints' dedications

Other saints who have lodges named after them in Scottish Masonry include: St Ninian, St Columba, St Colm, St Ronan, St Serf or Servanus, St Kentigern or Mungo, St Fillan, St Adrian, St Cuthbert, St Bride or Bryde, St Baldred, St Congan, St Coval, St David, St Donan, St Ebbe, St Duthus, St Enoch, St Fergus, St Kessac (Kessog), St Nathalan of Tullich-in-Mar, St Patrick, St Mirren, St Machar, St Modan, St Monan, St Marnock, St Munn, St Molios, St Ronan, St Regulus and St Vigean. There are others named after saints, however these constitute the predominant ones and are all generally thought of as 'Celtic' saints or as those who did much missionary work in Celtic areas.

Although this is interesting in itself, any attempt to suggest that this was merely a premeditated choice of names by later Freemasons to link themselves to the early Celtic Church would seem to be erroneous. For the most part, the names are connected to old existing local churches in the vicinity of Masonic lodges, some of which were already ancient themselves, and other lodges were built in the vicinity of early church foundations in the area. Freemasonry celebrates the builders of the Old Testament temples, so it is reasonable to conclude that Masons would naturally associate themselves with churches built by their own ancient forebears within their local areas. However, it is mainly the form of faith and religious practice of the saints of these early sites that is the subject of this line of enquiry, and not necessarily the builders of the later churches on these sites.

A recent publication on Celtic saints says:

The Celtic Church of the 5th and 6th centuries was not an identifiable organisation with a central leadership. Led by monastic abbots rather than diocean bishops, it was marked out by its ethos, a philosophy markedly different from the Church of Rome. No other Christian community has lived so closely with the Jewish Law.[43]

Jewish traditions in Freemasonry and early Judaic, Essene, or Eastern church ties to the Celtic church make the names of the above-mentioned Scottish lodges interesting to note and an area in need of further research. In early Ireland, for example, it is known that some of the early Christian communities were even accused of being 'too Jewish' in their calendar and customs.

Legends of 'Judaic refugees' coming to Britain

Traditions of 'Jewish refugees' supposedly coming to Britain in early times are quoted by a great variety of authors. Isabel Hill Elder quotes a statement made by an ancient writer named Freculuphus, 'that certain friends and disciples of Our Lord, in the persecution that followed His Ascension, found refuge in Britain in AD37'.[44] The followers of Jesus were in fact considered by many to be Jews and were not universally called Christians per se in certain areas until about 42AD.[45]

Numerous legendary accounts abound in Britain of the remaining Druids, early on, without violence or resistance, accepting the Christian faith, or at least practising a form of it. They were monotheists and believed in a trinity concept, the Awen, as was previously mentioned in chapter 5, so the remaining Druids obviously would have felt a type of kinship with some of the early Christians. One Masonic writer, A.G. MacKay, comments about the Druids:

> ...the constitution of the Order was in many respects like that of the Freemasons. In every country there was an Arch-Druid in whom all authority was placed... There was an annual assembly for the administration of justice and the working of laws, and, besides four quarterly meetings, which took place on the days when the sun reached his equinoctial and solstitial points. The latter two would very nearly correspond at this time with the festivals of St John the Baptist and St John the Evangelist. It was not

lawful to commit their ceremonies or doctrine to writings, and Caesar says (Bell. Gall., vi, 14) that they used the Greek letters, which was of course, as a cipher. The doctrines of the Druids were the same as those entertained by Pythagoras. They being taught the existence of one Supreme Being; a future state of rewards and punishments; the immortality of the Soul, and metempsychosis; the object of their mystic rites was to communicate these doctrines in symbolic language, an object and a method common alike to Druidism, to the Ancient Mysteries and to modern Freemasonry.[46]

The Arch Druid is said to have worn a breastplate during important rituals that was similar to that worn by the High Priest of the Jews. In Judaism, the breast plate is inlaid with twelve stones representing the twelve tribes of Israel; in some legendary accounts of the Druids, as the above author believes, there are said to be a corresponding number of stones worn on the Arch Druids breast plate. In some Masonic rituals, there are similar descriptions given of the regalia worn by the High Priest at Jerusalem while officiating in the Holy of Holies on the most sacred days as described in Old Testament Scripture. As a result of the wisdom of the Druidic philosophy, young men from all over Gaul travelled to ancient Britain to receive their teachings. The Scots, as with the Gauls, have gone down in the annals of both nations as being highly patriotic people. Eliphas Levi, former priest and well-known 19th C historian, suggests that '... for the Gauls, patriotism itself was a religion; women and even children carried arms, if necessary, to withstand invasion. Joan of Arc and Jeanne Hachette of Beauvais only carried on the traditions of those noble daughters of the Gauls'.[47]

The following account comes from MacKay's *Encyclopaedia of Freemasonry*, critically acknowledged in its day (1920) as one of the more reliable works on the subject. It is a summary of some of the various legends about the Druids and the Culdees:

> When St Augustine came over in the beginning of the sixth century, to Britain, for the purpose of converting the natives to Christianity he found a body of priests and their disciples, who were distinguished for their pure and simple apostolic religion which they professed. These were Culdees... . The chief seat of

the Culdees was the island of Iona... At Avernethy (Abernethy), the capitol of the Kingdom of the Picts, they founded another in the year 600, and subsequently other principal seats at Dunkeld, St Andrews, Brechin, Dunblane, Dunfermline, Kirkcaldy, Melrose, and many other places in Scotland. A writer in the London Freemasons Quarterly Review (1842, p. 36) says they were little solicitous to raise architectural structures, but sought chiefly to civilise and socialise mankind by imparting to them the knowledge of those pure principles which they taught in their Lodges... It is however undeniable, that Masonic writers have always claimed that there was a connection – it might be only a mythical one – between these apostolic Christians and the early Masonry of Ireland and Scotland. The Culdees were opposed and persecuted by the adherents of St Augustine, and were eventually extinguished in Scotland.[48]

Another Masonic historian, Kenneth MacKenzie, writing in 1877, said of the Culdees that they were 'an order which had at one time established itself all over England, Scotland, and Ireland... They were much persecuted, and lived in as retired a manner as possible. A society of them settled at York, and were found there by King Athelstan on his return from Scotland, in 936'.[49] MacKenzie's book is interesting in light of some of the more unusual Masonic traditions, both British and Continental, although some of it is hotly debated today, like many of these early sources are.

Within Freemasonry there are two notable rites, the *York Rite* and the *Scottish Rite*. Debates as to how old these rites actually are is still a minefield, but the fact remains that there is a universal acceptance of these traditions within Freemasonry around the world. Historically, both of these are believed to have had some type of connections with certain Culdee communities, although it is obvious that more detailed research needs to be done in this area. The precise designation of 'Scottish', 'Scotch' or 'Scots' as they are applied to ancient Masonic traditions and rites still awaits a clear definition from Masonic researchers. The truth is, even Masonic scholars aren't exactly certain what the origins of these rites are.

The terms 'Scotch', 'Scottish' and 'Scots' in Masonic writings

One distinguished Masonic encyclopaedia proclaims that Masonic references to the terms 'Scottish', 'Scotch' and 'Scots' rites and practices are probably 'amongst the most troublesome words in Masonic writing'. [50] The rise in the usage of Masonic titles using Scots (or the French term Ecossais) as related to degrees and rites grew in predominance on the continent of Europe and in America from the 1740s. A belief made public at the time stated that an ancient tradition existed to the effect that 'Knight-Masons from Scotland' were involved in excavating the ruins of Solomon's temple *prior* to the building of the Second, or Zerubbabel's, Temple. During these excavations it is said that the Knight-Masons from Scotland discovered the Ineffable name and the true secret of Freemasonry. Some other traditions come forward in time and have Scottish Masons in Jerusalem at the time of the Crusades. The debate continues on this matter yet today.

Numerous writers, including Masonic historians, have suggested that the influence of Scottish Masonry abroad was merely the result of exiled Scots trying to promote the Jacobite cause. The term 'Jacobite' was given to the followers of James the VII and his heirs, claimants to the Scottish throne who were forced to live in exile. In Protestant Hanoverian Britain, the Jacobites and the Stuart cause were exiled in favour of the royal family from the house of Hanover in Germany. As one might imagine, this period in history has caused many problems within Masonic history, trying to clarify details.

Some of the earliest Masonic practices did find their way abroad with the Jacobite exiles, and indeed the foundation of the Grand Lodge System of government for the craft has been viewed by some researchers as a Hanoverian device to regulate the practices of the Craft and to make them more conducive to Hanoverian beliefs. There are also some instances of exiled Jacobites using Masonic meetings to promote their cause:

> Scots Jacobites had been consciously trying to rise above denominational divisions for some time, using Freemason's lodges as

one of their means of doing so... Though not popular with the papacy, freemasonry was countenanced by the great Roman Catholic monarchies, and many Scottish Freemasons were catholic and Jacobite... one of the themes of contemporary Freemasonry was that religion was too important to be left to priests, and that true religion should unite, not divide men... the lay elite of Scottish Jacobitism was consciously trying, with some success, to rise above... sectarianism.[51]

'Jacobitism' is another title and term that has often been misunderstood by many, and an in-depth study far beyond the scope of this book is would be required to fully understand it in relation to Freemasonry. Suffice it to say here that it was a movement that was seen as pro-Scottish, but not necessarily as exclusively Catholic or Protestant, as it represented the culture and traditions of a people more than a particular religion per se. Of course, the Stuarts were very important at the time regarding Scottish traditions. It is strongly argued that the Scottish and Ecossais degrees that appeared during this period were not necessarily mere inventions but the revealing of traditions previously held as secret. But the debate on the details of this continues with Masonic researchers today.

Andrew Michael Ramsay: 'Chevalier Ramsay'

One key person who introduced Scottish influences of Freemasonry to the Continent in a way that had not taken place before was Andrew Michael Ramsay. A particularly close friend of David Hume, Ramsay would also have been known to the Scottish Masons, as he had been born at Ayr near Kilwinning on 9 June 1686. He studied at the Universities of Edinburgh and Leyden and received his law degree at Oxford. In 1719, he was invested as a knight in Paris into the neo-chivalric Order of the Knights of St Lazarus by the French regent Philippe d'Orleans and was thereafter called 'Chevalier de Ramsay'. Also in 1719 in Paris, and very likely read by Ramsay, there appeared the last volume of Heylot's monumental *Histoires des Ordres Monastique Religieux et Militaires*. Ramsay is also known in Scottish history as having been the tutor of the young Charles Edward Stuart, or 'Bonnie Prince Charlie'.

As a young man, he joined a quasi-'Rosicrucian' society called the 'Philadelphians', and studied with a close friend of Isaac Newton. He was later to be associated with other friends of Newton, including John Desaguliers. He was also a particularly close friend of David Hume, and they exercised a reciprocal influence on each other... In 1729, despite his Jacobite connections, Ramsay returned to England... he was promptly admitted to the Royal Society. He also became a member of another prestigious organisation, the fashionable 'Gentlemen's Club of Spalding', which included the Duke of Montague, the Earl of Abercorn, the Earl of Dalkeith, Desaguliers, Pope, Newton and Francois de Lorraine. By 1730, he was back in France and increasingly active on behalf of Freemasonry, and increasingly associated with Charles Radclyffe.[52]

Ramsay is often referred to as a convert to Roman Catholicism, but in fact, according to some, it is much more likely that he actually belonged to the *Gallican* Church in France.[53] Gallicanism, especially in France, acted in freedom from the ecclesiastical authority of the Papacy and the Gallican Rite, a non-Roman form of liturgy found in western Europe between the 4th and 8th centuries, is described as follows:

> The term is used with three meanings: 1) for the liturgical forms used in Gaul before the adoption of the Roman rite under Charlemagne; 2) loosely, for all non-Roman rites in the early Western Church; and 3) for the 'neo-Gallican' liturgies of the 17th and 18th centuries... It is not known why the rites of No. Italy, Gaul, Spain, and the Celtic Church in early times differed from that of Rome; (however) various suggestions have been made.[54]

An *Encyclopaedia of Catholicism* states:

> Gallicanism, an ecclesiology, with roots already in the 13th C, that claimed for France the right to resist all but very restricted forms of papal intervention within its jurisdiction. The French kings had controlled the papacy in Avignon from 1303 to 1377... [later] under Louis XIV... four articles of the 'Declaration of 1682' of the Assembly of France: 1) rejection of the extreme parliamentary position that denied any papal intervention in temporal matters; 2) admission of papal authority but only subject to conciliar supremacy; 3) demand that popes respect the

ancient canons and customs of the French church; 4) admission of papal primacy in matters of faith but denial of papal infallibility apart from the consent of the universal church... [Yet] Gallicanism never proposed schism from the Roman see. Gallicanism became obsolete with the French Revolution, but the restoration of the monarchy in France in the 19th C revived its influence...[55]

In 1729, he was elected a Fellow of the Royal Society. Ramsay was also a Freemason, being Grand Chancellor of the Paris Grand Lodge. In Masonic histories, Chevalier de Ramsay was famous for an especially influential pamphlet that was circulated around Paris in 1737. This work has come to be commonly known as *Ramsay's Oration* and it has been one of Freemasonry's most influential documents.

The full English translation of his lecture is presented here – which is rarely done – in which Ramsey promotes the worthy and venerable principles of the order, along with his suggested origins of the Craft. Essentially, *Ramsay's Oration* emphasized three major points, among others:

The *first* places the origin of Masonic Ritual 'at the time of the last Crusades' and associates them with the Knights of St John of Jerusalem... and the esoteric traditions of other medieval Christian Orders. The *second* asserts that after the suppression of the Templars [*note*: Ramsay doesn't actually mention them by name] in the beginning of the 14th C and the decline of the other Orders, their esoteric traditions were originally grafted onto, or found shelter among, some Scottish Masonic lodges, e.g. the Mother Lodge of Kilwinning. And the *third* maintains that those Scottish Traditions (or Orders), which are Christian by definition, though not specifically Catholic (due to their pre-Reformation origin) were still continuing in Scottish Masonry, and that he himself represented them in France as well as England.[56]

It is presented here, along with relevant material in bold for our purposes:

The noble ardour which you, gentlemen, evince to enter into the most noble and very illustrious Order of Freemasons, is a certain proof that you already possess all the qualities necessary to become members, that is, humanity, pure morals, inviolable secrecy, and a taste for fine arts.
Lycurgus, Solon, Numa, and all political legislators have failed to make

their institutions lasting. However wise their laws may have been, they have not been able to spread through all countries and ages. as they only kept in view victories and conquests, military violence, and the elevation of one people at the expense of another, they have not had the power to become universal, nor to make themselves acceptable to the taste, spirit, and interest of all nations. Philanthropy was not their basis. Patriotism badly understood and pushed to excess, often destroyed in these warrior republics love and humility in general. Mankind is not essentially distinguished by the tongues spoken, the clothes worn, the lands occupied, or the dignities with which it is invested. The world is nothing but a huge republic, of which every nation is a family, and every individual a child. Our Society was at the outset established to revive and spread these essential maxims borrowed from the nature of man.

We desire to reunite all men of enlightened minds, gentle manners, and agreeable wit, not only by a love for the fine arts, but much more by the grand principles of virtue, science, and religion, where the interests of the Fraternity shall become those of the whole human race, whence all nations shall be enabled to draw useful knowledge, and where the subjects of all kingdoms shall learn to cherish one another without renouncing their own country. **Our ancestors, the Crusaders, gathered together from all parts of Christendom in the Holy Land, desired thus to reunite into one sole Fraternity the Individuals of all nations.** What obligations do we not owe to these superior men who, without gross selfish interests, without even listening to the inborn tendency to dominate, imagined such an institution, the sole aim of which is to unite minds and hearts in order to make them better, and form in the course of ages a spiritual empire where without derogating from the various duties which different States exact, a new people shall be created, which, composed of many nations, shall in some sort cement them all into one by the tie of virtue and science.

The second requisite of our Society is sound morals. The religious orders were established to make perfect Christians, military orders to inspire a love of true glory, and the Order of Freemasons, to make men loveable men, good citizens, good subjects, inviolable in their promises, faithful adorers of the God of Love, lovers rather of virtue than of reward.

Nevertheless, we do not confine ourselves to purely civic virtues. We have amongst us three kinds of brothers: Novices or Apprentices, Fellows or Professional Brothers, masters or perfected Brothers. To the first are explained the moral virtues; to the second the heroic virtues; to the last the Christian virtues; so that our institution embraces the whole philosophy of sentiment and the complete theology of the heart. This is why one of our worshipful brothers has said –

Freemason, illustrious Grand Master,
Receive my first transports,
In my heart the Order has given them birth,
Happy I, if noble efforts
Cause me to merit your esteem
By elevating me to the sublime,
The primeval Truth,
To the Essence pure and divine,
the celestial origin of the soul,
The source of life and love.

Because a sad, savage, and misanthropic philosophy disgusts virtuous men, our ancestors, the Crusaders, wished to render it loveable by the attractions of innocent pleasures, agreeable music, pure joy, and moderate gaiety. Our festivals are not what the profane world and the ignorant vulgar imagine. All the vices of heart and soul are banished there, and irreligion, libertinage, incredulity, and debauch are proscribed. Our banquets resemble those virtuous symposia of Horace, where the conversation only touched what could enlighten the soul, discipline the heart, and inspire a taste for the true, the good, and the beautiful...

Thus the obligations imposed upon you by the Order, are to protect your brothers by your authority, to enlighten them by your knowledge, to edify them by your virtues, to succour them in their necessities, to sacrifice all personal resentment, and to strive after all that may contribute to the peace and unity of society.

We have secrets; they are figurative signs and sacred words, composing a language sometimes mute, sometimes very eloquent, in order to communicate with one another at the greatest distance, and to recognise our brothers of whatsoever tongue. These were the words of war which the Crusaders gave each other in order to guarantee them from the surprises of the Saracens, who often crept in amongst them to kill them. These signs and words recall the remembrance either of some part of our science, or of some moral virtue, or of some mystery of the faith. That has happened to us which never befell any former Society, our Lodges have been established, and are spread in all civilised nations, and, nevertheless, among this numerous multitude of men never has a brother betrayed our secrets.

Those natures most trivial, most indiscreet, least schooled to silence, learn this great art on entering our Society. Such is the power over all natures of the idea of a fraternal bond! This inviolable secret contributes powerfully to unite the subjects of all nations, and to render the communication of benefits easy and mutual between us. We have many examples in the annals of our Order. Our brothers, travelling in diverse lands, have only needed to make themselves known in our Lodges in order to be there immediately overwhelmed by all kinds of succour, even in time of the most bloody wars, and illustrious prisoners have found brothers where they only expected to meet enemies.

Should any fail in the solemn promises that build us, you know, gentlemen, that the penalties which we impose upon him are remorse of conscience, shame at his perfidy, and exclusion from our Society.

Yes, sirs, the famous festivals of Ceres at Eleusis, of Isis in Egypt, of Minerva at Athens, of Urania amongst the Phoenicians, and of Diana in Scythia were connected with ours. In those places mysteries were celebrated which concealed many vestiges of the ancient religion of Noah and the Patriarchs. They concluded with banquets and libations, and neither that intemperance nor excess were known into which they gradually fell. The source of these infamies were the admission to the nocturnal assemblies of persons of both sexes in contravention of the primitive usages. It is in order to prevent similar abuses that women are excluded from our Order. We are not so unjust as to regard the fair sex as incapable of keeping a secret. But their presence might insensibly corrupt the purity of our maxims and manners.

The fourth quality required for our Order is the taste for useful sciences and the liberal arts. Thus, the Order exacts of each of you to contribute, by his protection, liberality, or labour, to a vast work for which no academy can suffice, because all these societies being composed of a very small number of men, their work cannot embrace an object so extended. All the Grand Masters in Germany, England, Italy, and elsewhere, exhort all the learned men and all the artisans of the Fraternity to unite to furnish the materials for a Universal Dictionary of the liberal arts and useful sciences, **excepting only theology and politics.**

The work has already been commenced in London, and by means of the union of our brothers it may be carried to a conclusion in a few years. Not only are technical words and their etymology explained, but the history of each art and science, its principles and operations, are described. By this means the lights of all nations will be united in one single work, which will be a universal library of all that is beautiful, great, luminous, solid, and useful in all sciences and in all noble arts. This work will augment in each century, according to the increase of knowledge, and it will spread everywhere emulation and the taste for things of beauty and utility.

The word Freemason must therefore not be taken in a literal, gross, and material sense, as if our founders had been simple workers in stone, or merely curious geniuses who wished to perfect the arts. They were not only skilful architects, desirous of consecrating their talents and goods to the construction of material temples; but also religious and warrior

princes who designed to enlighten, edify, and protect the living Temples of the Most High. This I will demonstrate by developing the history or rather renewal of the Order.

Every family, every Republic, every Empire, of which the origin is lost in obscure antiquity, has its fable and its truth, its legend and its history. Some ascribe our institution to Solomon, some to Moses, some to Abraham, some to Noah, some to Enoch, who built the first city, or even to Adam. Without pretence of denying these origins, I pass on to matters less ancient. This, then, is a part of what I have gathered from the annals of great Britain, in the Acts of Parliament, which speak of our privileges, and in the living traditions of the English people, which has been the centre of our Society since the eleventh century.

At the time of the Crusades in Palestine many princes, lords, and citizens associated themselves, and vowed to restore the Temple to the Christians in the Holy Land, and to employ themselves in bringing back their architecture to its first institution. They agreed upon several ancient signs and symbolic words drawn from the well of religion in order to recognise themselves amongst the heathen and Saracens. These signs and words were only communicated to those who promised solemnly, and even sometimes at the foot of the altar, never to reveal them. This sacred promise was therefore not an execrable oath, as it has been called, but a respectful bond to unite Christians of all nationalities in one confraternity. Some time afterwards our Order formed an intimate union with the Knights of St John of Jerusalem. From that time our Lodges took the name of Lodges of St John. This union was made after the example set by the Israelites when they erected the second Temple, who whilst they handled the trowel and mortar with one hand, in the other held the sword and buckler.

Our Order therefore must not be considered a revival of the Bacchanals, but as an order founded in remote antiquity, and renewed in the Holy Land by our ancestors in order to recall the memory of the most sublime truths amidst the pleasures of society. The kings, princes, and lords returned from Palestine to their own lands, and there established divers Lodges. At the time of the last Crusades many Lodges were already erected in Germany, Italy, Spain, France, and from thence in Scotland, because of the close alliance between the French and the Scotch. James, Lord Steward of Scotland, was Grand Master of a Lodge established at Kilwinning, in the West of Scotland, MCCLXXXVI, shortly after the death of Alexander III, King of Scotland, and one year before John Baliol mounted the throne. This lord received as Freemasons into his Lodge the Earls of Gloucester and Ulster, the one English, the other Irish.

By degrees our Lodges and our rites were neglected in most places.

this is why of so many historians only those of Great Britain speak of our Order. **Nevertheless it preserved its splendour among those Scotsmen to whom the Kings of France confided during many centuries the safeguard of their royal persons.** [note: a reference to the Scots Guard]

After deplorable mishaps in the Crusades, the perishing Christian armies, and the triumph of Bendocdar, Sultan of Egypt, during the eighth and last Crusade, that great Prince Edward, son of Henry III, King of England, seeing there was no longer any safety for his brethren in the Holy Land, from whence the Christian troops were retiring, brought them all back, and this colony of brothers was established in England. As this prince was endowed with all heroic qualities, he loved the fine arts, declared himself protector of the Order, conceded to it new privileges, and then the members of this fraternity took the name of Freemasons, after the example set by their ancestors.

Since that time Great Britain became the seat of our Order, the conservator of our laws, and the depository of our secrets. The fatal religious discords which embarrassed and tore Europe in the sixteenth century caused our Order to degenerate from the nobility of its origin. Many of our rites and usages which were contrary to the prejudices of the times were changed, disguised, suppressed. Thus it was that many of our brothers forgot, like the ancient Jews, the spirit of our laws, and only retained the letter and the shell. The beginnings of a remedy have already been made. it is only necessary to continue, and to at last bring everything back to its original institution. This work cannot be difficult in a State where religion and the Government can only be favourable to our laws.

From the British Isles the Royal Art is now repassing into France, under the reign of the most amiable of Kings, whose humility animates all his virtues, and under the ministry of a Mentor, who has realised all that could be imagined most fabulous. In this happy age when love of peace has become the virtue of heroes, this nation [France] one of the most spiritual of Europe, will become the centre of the Order. She will clothe our work, our statutes, and our customs with grace, delicacy, and good taste, essential qualities of the order, of which the basis is the wisdom, strength, and beauty of genius. It is in future in our Lodges, as it were in public schools, that Frenchmen shall learn, without travelling, the characters of all nations, and that strangers shall experience that France is the home of all peoples. Patria gentis humanae.[57]

Aftermath of Ramsay's Oration

At the time that Ramsay produced this important pamphlet, Europe was a far different place than it is today. The French Revolution and the American War of Independence had not yet taken place. In Britain, the crisis of 1745 had not yet happened, but the seeds had already been sown. The union of the crowns and the creation of Great Britain had happened the century before, and it was only 30 years on from the union of the parliaments in Britain. Throughout Europe religious tensions were still being felt as a consequence of the Reformation. And with all this in mind, *Ramsay's Oration* seems to have purposely tried to balance various tensions and different issues by presenting a diplomatic paper with 'something for everyone' in it. However, of course, not everyone agreed with this – then or now.

He states that it was in Palestine that the princes of Christendom, with a common purpose, united with the builders to re-establish old traditions that had been eroded, and that the order had then flourished all over Europe, especially in Scotland, but that it had again declined. A point of special note is that Ramsay speaks of the Crusaders in a general sense *and does not specifically mention the Templars by name.* Ironically, this is nearly always misunderstood even today. The only Crusading order that he actually mentions by name is the Order of St John of Jerusalem, which some had previously thought he may have been a member of;[58] however, it is now known for certain that he was inducted into the Order of St Lazarus in Paris.[59]

After *Ramsay's Oration* there was a great deal of debate about Freemasonry being a possible further development of the medieval Knights Templar or other medieval Crusading bodies. Masonic historians generally dismiss Masonic connections with the Crusades, stating that no evidence for Freemasonry exists until later, so they attribute Ramsay himself with this invention. In a controversial yet informative Masonic essay, we find the following explanation of a Knight Templar/St John the Evangelist connection and the practices of the earliest Christian faith:

...Jesus conferred on his disciples the evangelical initiation, caused his spirit to descend upon them, divided them into different orders, according to the custom of the Egyptian priests and Hebrew priests, and placed them under the authority of St John, his beloved disciple, and whom he had made supreme pontiff and patriarch. John never quitted the East; his doctrine, always pure, was not altered by the admixture of any other doctrine...

Down to 1118, the mysteries and the hierarchical order of the Egyptian initiation, transmitted to the Jews through Jesus Christ, were religiously preserved by the successors of the apostle John. These mysteries and these initiations regenerated through the evangelical initiation of baptism formed a sacred deposit which, thanks to the simplicity of primitive customs from which the brothers of the East never departed, never underwent the slightest alteration.

The Christians of the East, persecuted by the infidels, appreciating the courage and piety of those valiant crusaders who, sword in one hand and cross in the other, flew to the defence of the holy places; doing justice above all, to the virtues and the ardent charity of Hugh of Payens (Grand Master of the Knights Templar at their inception), considered it their duty to entrust to hands so pure the treasures of knowledge acquired during so many centuries, and sanctified by the cross, the teachings and the ethics of the Man-God.

Hugh was then invested with the patriarchal apostic power, and placed in the legitimate line of successors of the Apostle or Evangelist. Such is the origin and foundation of the Templars, and of the introduction amongst them of the different modes of initiation of the Christians of the East, designated by the primitive or Johannite Christians. It is to this initiation that belong the various degrees consecrated by the rules of the Temple, and which were so much called in question in the famous but terrible action brought against this august Order.[60]

Such legendary accounts about possible Templar, or Crusader, connections with Freemasonry are as frequently debated now as they were in Ramsay's time. Also debated is whether, and to what extent, Ramsay may have been responsible for introducing the Royal Arch degree. A year after *Ramsay's Oration*, a papal bull was issued condemning Freemasonry.

Other legendary accounts of a possible Templar survival and/or various connections with Masonic history include the Strict

Observance Rite, promulgated by an influential 18th C Freemason named Baron Karl von Hund, and also the Larmenius Charter, which purports to date from 1324 and was first brought to public attention in 1804 by Bernard-Raymond Fabre-Palaprat, although many today believe that it was circulated in France well before then. Other questions about both the Larmenius Charter and von Hund remain, so the details of both of these matters continue to be debated today.[61]

Looking at another of these legends, the German Masonic writer Roessler states:

> ...Scotch Templars were occupied in excavating a place at Jerusalem in order to build a temple there, and precisely on the spot where the temple of Solomon – or at least that part of it called the Holy of Holies – had stood. During their work they found three stones which were the corner stones of the Solomon temple itself. The monumental form of these excited their attention; this excitement became all the more intense when they found the name of Jehova engraved in the elliptical spaces between the stones – this which was also a type of the mysteries of the Copt – the sacred word which, by the murder of the Master Builder, had been lost, and which, according to the legend of the first degree, Hiram had had engraved on the foundation stone of Solomon's temple. After such a discovery the Scotch Knights took this costly memorial with them, and, in order eternally to preserve their esteem for it, they employed these as the corner stones of their first temple at Edinburgh.[62]

This tale about a possible connection between Scottish Crusaders and/or so-called 'Scotch Knights', the Holy Land, and Masonic traditions is intriguing enough, yet many allege it is merely a fabricated story influenced by Ramsay's Oration, which is, of course, possible. However, strangely enough, it also seems to relate to a particular Scottish craft Guild tradition that predates Ramsay, notably those traditions surrounding the origins of the Blue Blanket or Craftsmen's Banner of the medieval Guilds of Edinburgh.

The Blue Blanket of Edinburgh

This account, which describes a Scottish tradition connected to the craft Guilds of Edinburgh and also to Jerusalem, predates *The book of Constitutions of the Freemasons* written by Anderson in 1723.

In this description, written in 1722, Mr Alexander Pennecuik, a '*burgess and guild brother*' presented an historical account of the legend of the Blue Blanket to the Convenor of the fourteen Incorporations of Edinburgh. The account was inspected by antiquarians for its historical accuracy and was believed to be authentic at the time. Pennecuik wrote the following account of a blue standard that had been especially prized for centuries by Scottish medieval trade guilds:

> It is generally agreed upon, that it (Edinburgh) was made a Burgh Royal by King William I in whose reign a fervour of devotion, encouraged by Pope Urban II, seized the spirits of the princes and cavaliers of Europe, under the command of Godfrey of Bouillion, to rescue Palestine, and the city of Jerusalem out of the hands of Saladin... Vast numbers of Scots mechanics having followed this holy war, taking with them a Banner, bearing this inscription out of the Ii. Psalm, *In bona voluntate tua edificenter muri Jerusalem.* Upon their returning home, and glorying that they were amongst the fortunate who placed the Christian standard of the cross in the place that Jesus Christ had consecrated with his blood, they dedicated this Banner, which they stiled The Banner of the Holy Ghost, to St Eloi's altar in St Giles's church in Edinburgh; which, from its colour, was called The Blue Blanket.

> Tho' none of our Historians mention the Original Institution of the Blue Blanket, nor is there any Vouchers for it, saving old imperfect Manuscripts; yet 'tis highly probable, it had its Rise from the Croisade, or Holy War: For Monsieur Chevereau, in his *History of the World*, tells us, that Scotland was engaged in that War, and sold or mortgaged their Estates for that Expedition; and that she was amongst the most forward Nations in it. Pére Maimbourg, *Histoire des Croisades*, informs us, That the Knights of St Lazarus, an Order of Men educate to the holy War, were numerous everywhere, but especially in Scotland and

France; as appears by the Charters and Grants of Princes in their
Favours; and the distinctive Crosses they wore, evince, that the
Scots were as forward, gallant, and zealous in the Service, as any
of their Neighbours.[63]

This account seems to say that some early guild brothers
('Scots mechanics') of Edinburgh had taken their blue standard to
the Holy Land during the time of the Crusades, and once there,
took it to the blessed Holy Sepulchre in Jerusalem, and then
brought it back to Edinburgh to St Eloi's altar in St Giles Church.
It also seems to illustrate a Scottish-French connection prior to the
'Auld Alliance', which was officially established by treaty during
the Scottish wars of independence against England and remained
in effect until the death of Mary Queen of Scots and the political
transformation that the Reformation brought about.

St Eloi and St Giles

St Giles and St Eloi were saints imported as a result of the
Crusades. The earliest church dedicated to St Giles on its site was
built during the reign of David I and was the responsibility of the
medieval chivalric Order of the Knights of St Lazarus, who held St
Giles as a patron. St Giles was born in Athens towards the close
of the 8th C. He is said to have travelled to France to seek solitude
and became a hermit near what is now called Saint-Gilles in
France near Arles. It is said that amongst St Giles's many disciples
was the illustrious Charlemagne, the first emperor of the Holy
Roman Empire.

Eloi is the French form of Eligius, the patron saint of metalworkers. In France he lived during the reigns of King Chlotar II
and Clovis II, where he was the treasurer. It is said that he gave
away his wealth to the poor.

The responsibility for the upkeep of the altar dedicated to St
Eloi in the church of St Giles in Edinburgh was the responsibility
of the Guild of Hammermen, as they were metalworkers:

> The Crafts of Edinburgh, having this order of the Blanket to
> glory in, may justly take upon them the title of the Knights of the
> Blanket, or, Chevaliers of arms: For, as the learned Skene, De

Verborum Significatione, in his title, Banrents observes, that Banrents are called Chevaliers of Arms, or Knights, who, obtaining great honours and dignities, have power and priviliges granted to them by the King, to raise and lift up a banner, with a company of men of weir (war), either horse or foot; which cannot be done by any save baronets, without the King's special licence... and Dr Smith, in his Treatise of the Commonwealth of England... informs us, that Knights Banrents are allowed to display their arms on a Banner in the King's host. As the Knights of St George have their meeting at Windsor Castle, and those of the Thistle in the royal palace of Holyrood-house, so the Knights of the Blanket have theirs at St Eloi, who was a French Bishop and their guardian, his altar, to which they mortify considerable sums for the maintenance of a chaplain, and reparation of the ornaments of the chapel; as appears from the Craftsmens seal of cause...[64]

From this account we see that the author Pennecuik felt that the Scottish craft guilds were, upon their return from the Crusades, rightfully deemed to be Knights of the Blanket in recognition of this duty. During the time of the First Crusade in 1099, when Jerusalem was first taken, the Blue Blanket according to this tradition was said to be the first Standard to be flown from the newly captured walls of Jerusalem which thereafter was dedicated to the 'Hally Guist'.[65]

The Blue Blanket appears again in Scottish history during the reign of James III, who had been imprisoned by some of his barons for nine months at Edinburgh Castle. His release came about when:

William Bertram, provost, displayed the Blue Blanket to the Corporation of Trades, who thereupon stormed the said Castle, and delivered the King for which deed was granted them a patent of many high privileges, which they called their Golden Charter. The craftsmen in commemoration, renewed their banner, and the Queen with her own hands, painted on it a St Andrews Cross, a thistle, a crown, and a hammer, with the following enscription: Fear God, and honour the King, with a long lyffe and prosperous reign: and we shall ever pray to be faithfulle for the defence of his sacred Majesty's Royal persone till death.[66]

The Blue Blanket is also said to have made a gallant appearance at Flodden Field.[67]

The foundation stone of the Grand Lodge of Scotland

The London *Illustrated Times*, dated 10 July 1858, reported the laying of the foundation stone of the Grand Lodge of Scotland in Edinburgh. On that occasion, a great Masonic procession took place, led by the Lodge of Journeymen Masons of Edinburgh, carrying the Blue Blanket. The paper reported:

> Perhaps the most interesting feature in the recent grand Masonic pageant at Edinburgh, was the appearance of the venerable old banner, dear to all Scotland, and especially to Edinburgh, as the most ancient ensign of the country, under which almost all of the high privileges of the citizens have been won.[68]

The Blue Blanket still exists in Edinburgh, and in spite of its seemingly illustrious history in Scotland, it is rarely, if ever, mentioned in Scottish history books. It does occasionally appear in books on local Edinburgh customs, if at all. This is yet another aspect of history that is vastly under-researched; however, in 2002 the National Museum of Scotland is to have an exhibition in which this Blue Blanket be on display, the same one that tradition states that James III gifted to the Scottish craft guilds.

The Royal Order of Scotland

One of the most acknowledged Lodge histories in Scotland is Murray Lyon's *History of the Lodge of Edinburgh (Mary's Chapel) No.1*, 1873. Lyon is critical of anything that does not have contemporary written evidence, however he still includes what has been handed down as tradition. He describes the legendary beginnings of the Royal Order of Scotland, one of the most prestigious Masonic orders:

> The Royal Order... is composed of two degrees –viz, that of 'Heredom of Kilwinning,' alleged to have originated in the reign of David 1, King of Scotland; and the 'Rosy Cross,' affirmed to have been instituted by Robert the Bruce, which monarch is also represented as having in 1314 revived the former and incorporated it with the latter under the title of The Royal Order of

Scotland. The ritual of this rite embraces what may be termed a spiritualisation of the supposed symbols and ceremonies of the Christian architects and builders of primitive times, and also closely associates the sword with the trowel as to lead to the second degree being denominated an order of Masonic knighthood, which its recipients are asked to believe was first conferred on the field of Bannockburn as a reward for the valour that had been displayed by a body of Templars who aided Bruce in that memorable victory; and that afterwards a Grand Lodge of the Order was established by the King at Kilwinning, with the reservation of the office of Grand Master to him and his successors on the Scottish throne.[69]

Legendary claims about a possible contingent of Templars who assisted Bruce at Bannockburn have not been proven, however. But, as those who remain sceptical of the orthodox 'noble camp followers' theory ask, why exactly did Edward II and his 500 best knights supposedly flee from Scottish peasants banging pots and pans on the battlefield, costing them the entire battle? Why did one of the English Templars, when questioned at his trial in England, supposedly claim that the English had heard rumours that there might be some Templar assistance to Robert the Bruce and to be 'on the lookout' for possible reinforcements? So could it be, as some have speculated, that the English *thought* that there may well have been some Templars in the camp followers' group. Of course, no one can say anything for sure about this contentious matter, because no documentation is known to exist publicly. But it is acknowledged that after the official suppression of the Order in 1312, any remaining Templars in Scotland – if there were any – would have certainly been 'out of work', so to speak, by 1314, the year of Bannockburn. As some speculate, as they were famed warrior knights with proven skills in battle, they would have obviously been highly desirable mercenaries at the time, to both sides.

Of course, it is also known that neither Bruce nor the Templars at the time had a particular liking for the papacy, so, if any Templars did manage to survive, Bruce would probably be someone they would logically contact, as the English may have believed. So, even as laughable as such a scenario may seem today, perhaps it may not be totally impossible that they may have, iron-ically, ended up fighting on both sides. One thing seems certain, however: if any Templars *did* manage to somehow survive such horrific circumstances after 1312, they certainly would not have necessarily wanted to appear as Templars, as they were still 'hunted men' for heresey, so they wouldn't likely be wearing their trade-mark mantles and red cross!

Until more hard evidence is forthcoming, nothing can really be said about this matter and its many accompanying legends through the centuries. But, here again, 'the myth lives on'...

Regarding the Royal Order of Scotland, even today a vacant seat is left for a future Scottish monarch to fill, however symbolic. The first degree of Kilwinning is believed to have been based back in the 12th C, the time of David 1, and it predates most modern Masonic degrees and is Christian in emphasis. 'Heredom' was said to be a Scottish mountain, and it is known that a charter in 1315 makes reference to a 'Halidom' in the Kilwinning area. It is also interesting to note that the second degree of the Royal Order is said to have been instituted by Robert the Bruce 'to sort out irreg-ularities that had crept into the Craft'. This enigmatic statement makes one wonder if the term 'Craft' might perhaps have referred to some kind of an earlier existing Scottish Masonic, craft Guild, or knightly tradition, or, that it could conceivably be thought of as the word 'faith'. If this is the case, as some researchers believe, then could it be that Robert the Bruce was attempting to re-establish some form of an early ('Celtic'-orientated?) Scottish tradition, perhaps one also relating to Christianity, in the tradition of St John and 'the Word'?

Some old accounts in the Kilwinning, Argyll and the Dumfries and Galloway areas, that are in or near 'Bruce country', also have early and strong connections to the Celtic church in Scotland, and also to various early Masonic and chivalric traditions.

But there also seem to have been *two* coronation ceremonies for Robert the Bruce:

> ...there were, in fact, two separate coronations. The first, of which few details survive, seems to have been more or less con-ventional and to have taken place on 25 March 1306, in the

Abbey Church at Scone... The second coronation took place two days later, and involved Bruce being placed upon the throne of Scone in accordance with ancient Celtic custom. Traditionally, he should have been ushered on to the royal seat by the country's premier peer, the Earl of Fife, who had for centuries played this role in the crowing of Scottish kings. At the time, however, the Earl of Fife had only just come of age, and was wholly in the power of Edward of England. In consequence, the boy's function was discharged by his sister Isobel, wife of the Earl of Buchan, one of Comyn's cousins, who rode north from her estates in England especially to perform the ceremony. In the past, historians have tended to regard Bruce's career, and his campaign for Scottish independence, as essentially political, rather than cultural. In consequence, the Celtic element has been largely ignored... Now, in fact, it becomes apparent that the contribution of Celtic Scotland was crucial. As a specifically Celtic leader, intent on restoring an ancient Celtic kingdom, Bruce's campaign was not just political, but cultural and ethnic as well.[70]

This does make one wonder about the cultural element possibly having had a much greater influence than has previously been thought.

Further details of Anderson's Constitutions

Looking to more modern times, *Anderson's Constitutions* were written for the Grand Lodge of England six years after its inception. Dr James Anderson, who is referred to as the 'Father of Masonic History'[71] gleaned from old manuscripts the rules and regulations of the operative brethren from medieval times, to be used by the Freemasons. He also included a version of the operative masons *Traditional History of the Craft*, as mentioned earlier.

Anderson was a Presbyterian minister born and educated in Aberdeen. In 1710 he arrived in London's Piccadilly to take up the ministry of a church in Swallow Street. His father was known to have been a member of the Aberdeen Lodge in 1670, at which time three-quarters of its members were non-operative masons, that is 'speculative' or philosophical masons, but it is not known when or where James himself became a Mason. Coil's *Masonic Encyclopaedia* states that it was 'probably in Aberdeen Lodge, particularly, as we find him later adhering to several Scotch Masonic terms and substituting them for the corresponding English'[72].

The manuscripts Dr Anderson used are now referred to as the 'Old Charges' or the 'Gothic Constitutions'. It is not clear what manuscripts were consulted by him because he makes no mention of specific documents, only that he extracted the necessary information from 'The ancient Records of Lodges beyond the Sea, and those in England, Scotland and Ireland'.[73] It is known today that about 113 of these documents exist, the oldest being the Regius Poem, or 'Halliwell' manuscript now in the British Museum, dated to around 1390. The 'Cooke' manuscript, also in the British Museum, was written around 1425. These earliest documents are of English origin and later Scottish charges contain similar information. If any early Scottish charges existed at some point they are unfortunately lost to us now.

Interestingly, these documents all basically say the same thing, i.e. that the Mason swears to be an upright citizen and follow the moral law, that he be a true man to God and the Holy Church and be faithful to the King. This Mason swears upon a book (the Bible if the candidate was a Christian) to uphold this charge. The purpose of the traditional history seems to have been to impress upon the craftsman the mystery and importance of the undertaking he was entering into and also the great observance that he was thereafter charged to uphold. It may also be a veiled message as to the teachings of the Christians of the early church. It also had many Hermetic allusions in it.

Seven liberal arts and sciences: Geometry supreme

The Traditional History begins by explaining the importance of the seven liberal arts and sciences, which are Grammar, Rhetoric, Logic, Arithmetic, Geometry, Music and Astronomy. It is stressed that of all these sciences, Geometry is the most important and is the foundation of all the others. Freemasons themselves declare that Geometry and Masonry are actually synonymous terms.

The history goes on to say that before Noah's flood, Lamech had four children who began all of the crafts in the world. The eldest son, Jabel, founded Geometry and created the first building. His brother, Jubal, founded the craft of Music, song of tongue, harp and organ. The third brother, Tubal Cain, became the first worker in metals, and his sister, Naamah, founded the craft of weaving. Knowing that God was about to destroy the sinful by either fire or water they wrote their sciences on two pillars of stone. A statue of Tubal Cain, sponsored by the Guild of Hammermen, still stands in Nicolson Square in Edinburgh today. The Guild of Hammermen in Edinburgh also have important early connections to the Magdalen Chapel in the Grassmarket, a place which has an important connection to the National Covenant and later, the Reformation.)

Anderson's history continues: One pillar was made of marble so that it would not burn and the other was made of *laternus*, a material that would not drown in water. After the flood, these pillars were discovered by Hermarines (Hermes) the great grandson of Noah. Hermes then becomes the teacher of the Seven Liberal arts and sciences. Some manuscripts say that one pillar is found by Hermes and that the other is found by Pythagoras. Joseph Fort Newton states, 'Surely this is all fantastic enough, but the blending of the name Hermes, the 'father of wisdom,' who is so supreme a figure in the Egyptian Mysteries, and Pythagoras, who used numbers as spiritual emblems, with old Hebrew history, is significant.'[74]

The manuscripts continue, saying that Nimrod, who was a mason, erected the Tower of Babel and the city of Nineveh along with other cities of the East. After these great building feats, he charges the masons thereafter to abide by the rules that he lays down for them. These charges state, amongst other things, that they should be true to one another, and that they should serve the lord truly for their pay, and it further states that this was the first time ever that any Mason had any charge of his Craft.

Next to be mentioned are Abraham and Sara, who are said to go to Egypt to teach the seven sciences to the Egyptians. Abraham's worthiest pupil, we are told, is Euclid. Throughout this description there is again great emphasis placed on the charges, being true to God and the King, and the carrying out of the Lord's work.

The next account refers to the children of Israel when they settled in the land that they called Jerusalem. King David plans to build a Great Temple for Yahweh, but this task is left to his wise son Solomon to carry out. Solomon builds the temple with the help of a neighbouring king, Hiram, King of Tyre. Masons are employed from many lands and Solomon reiterates the charges that his father David had given to the Masons. One of the craftsmen named Naymus Grecus takes his craft to France where he teaches it to a man of royal blood named Charles Martel. Charles becomes the King of France and a great patron of the Masons. He grants a charter to the Masons allowing them to hold annual Assemblies.

England, we are further told, was void of any charge of Masonry until the time of St Alban. St Alban, a worthy Knight, brings Masonry to England and obtains from the King a charter for the masons to hold a general council. Soon after St Albans' martyrdom, the good rule of Masonry was destroyed by wars until the time of King Athelstan. Athelstan's son Edwin was a great practitioner of Geometry and he teaches the Masons the Craft. Edwin obtains from his father a charter for the masons to hold an annual assembly at York. At this York assembly, Edwin tells all the masons to gather together all the writings that they can find relating to the charges. The writings collected include some in French, Greek, English and other languages. The noble intent in them all being the same, Edwin laid down the format that became the Old Charges.

This concludes the legendary Traditional History that the medieval stone masons are believed to have received upon admission into their craft.

Some inaccuracies found

Anderson's traditional history, fascinating as it is, has been found to have various inaccuracies and anomalies, for example, King Athelstan did not have a son called Edwin. Athelstan ascended the Anglo-Saxon throne in 924 where he reigned until his death in 940 and the Edwin being mentioned is more likely to be '... Edwin, King of Northumbria, whose residence was at Auldby, near York, in 626, and who assisted in building a stone church at York – St Peter's – after his baptism in 627.'[75] This Edwin was the first King of Northumbria to become a Christian, and was the king who took Edinburgh from the Goddodin in 638. After Edwin's death, a cult grew up around him with its centre at Whitby.

Another example of historical inaccuracy is regarding Abraham, who is believed to have lived about 2000 BC, yet is claimed here to have taught the sciences to Euclid, who lived about 300 AD. This history cannot be taken as a factual account of events, however, it may be looked upon as an important reference to the practices that the Masons promoted, incorporating various Hermetic, Pythagorean and Old Testament traditions in a *highly allegorical way*. Hermes is particularly interesting in that this name can refer to a number of things. Coil's *Masonic Encyclopaedia* describes Hermes or Hermes Trismegistus in the following way:

> There were two identifiable characters called Hermes. One was the Roman god Mercury or the Messenger, represented with winged feet. The other was supposedly an Egyptian savant, philosopher, scientist, priest, or lawgiver who lived about 1300 BC It was claimed that he wrote many books, taught hieroglyphics to the Egyptians and, according to the Alchemists, founded their art, hence the name Trismegistus, meaning thrice great, and hence the terms, Hermetic and Hermeticism, as applied to alchemical, magical, and occult studies. It was, therefore, to Hermes, the scholar, and not to the Roman Mercury, that the scribes of the Gothic Constitutions referred and they undoubtedly gained their information from Higden's Polycronycon printed in 1482 by Claxton at London. There is a third theory that Hermes Trismegistus was not a person or a god, but a book or collection of writings protesting against the destruction of Learning, the burning of libraries and against the inevitable illiteracy that was to overtake the world and lend its name to a large part of the middle ages. And, so some think that Hermes Trismegistus was a storehouse of learning to prevent its loss, just as the Antediluvians had hoped to preserve the Seven Liberal Sciences by carving them on two pillars. Under that theory, we would conclude that Hermes Trismegistus was the first Encyclopaedia and that the Polycronycon was the second.[76]

Many Scottish records and books lost in the course of history

Scotland, like many countries, has suffered a series of attempts by many to destroy its books and libraries. Scottish history has many examples of the persecution and destruction of records, and we hear of this from many disparate sources. Two thousand years ago, the Roman Empire systematically set out to eradicate the wisdom of Druidic philosophy from Britain. Later, early Irish chronicles and some old legends claimed that St Patrick and his monks may have destroyed a body of important Druidic knowledge on Iona, but, of course, this can never be proven for certain. But it is known that many so-called 'Druidic books' were destroyed. The Vikings, in turn, were responsible for the destruction of many Christian libraries and artefacts. Pictish monasteries and libraries were destroyed, with almost no Pictish manuscripts left at all. Next, we find the Roman Church in Scotland being blamed for the suppression and destruction of early material relating to the Celtic Church. Then, later, Edward I purposely removed Scottish records from the religious houses around the country in an attempt to destroy national identity. Centuries later, the Reformers destroyed Roman Catholic works with equal zeal, and also smashed the relics of saints, many of whom were Celtic. Many ancient churches were destroyed. The Hanoverians suppressed Jacobite material and forced their traditions to go overseas. During the 'Anglicisation' of the Highlands and lowlands of Scotland following the 1745 uprising, there was a deliberate move to erode Scottish culture even further, as historical hindsight has shown. So, the list goes on and on, of all of the efforts by many different parties, to destroy various Scottish records, libraries, and artefacts. But clearly, no one 'culprit' exists – there are many. Frankly, in retrospect, it is rather amazing that anything has survived at all!

So, one may speculate that if certain ancient Scottish traditions were actively being preserved, they would have had to have been preserved *in an unassuming manner in order to avoid persecution.* If this was the case, then Scottish Freemasonry may well have been, ironically, a perfect vehicle, through its use of *allegory* and *veiled symbolism*, to preserve certain ancient truths for posterity. And, it might also be argued, so were certain craft guilds and some of the medieval chivalric Orders.

If this has indeed been the case over the centuries, then we can conclude that perhaps the real 'secret' of Freemasonry may lie in the ingenious, creative way that it has reinvented itself through the ages to preserve this ancient lore. We will now take a look at one of the chapels that, fortunately, *did* survive: Rosslyn Chapel.

Notes

[1]   *The Year Book of the Grand Lodge of Antient Free and Accepted Masons of Scotland*, Edinburgh, 1991, 46.

[2]   Baigent, M and Leigh, R, *The Temple and the Lodge*, Little Brown & Co, New York, 1989, 252.

[3]   van den Broek, R, and Hanegraaff, W J, [Ed.], *Gnosis and Hermeticism: From Antiquity to Modern Times*, State University of New York, Albany, 1998, viii.

[4]   Hall, M P, *The Secret Teachings of All Ages, an Encyclopaedic Outline of Masonic, Hermetic, Qabbalistic and Rosicrucian Symbolical Philosophy*, The Philosophical Research Society, Los Angeles, 1928, CLXXVI, reprinted 1977.

[5]   Stevenson, Prof D, *The Origins of Freemasonry, Scotland's Century 1590-1710*, Cambridge University Press, Cambridge, 1988, Appendix.

[6]   Grand Lodge of Scotland Official Website, www.grandlodgeofscotland.com.

[7]   Laughlan, Roy, MBE JP, *The Kilwinning No. 0 Masonic Lodge in old picture postcards*, European Library, Zaltbommel/Netherlands, 1994, 1.

[8]   Salzman, L F, *Building in England Down to 1540*, Oxford University Press, Oxford, 1952, 466.

[9]   Colston, J, *The Incorporated Trades of Edinburgh*, Edinburgh, 1891, 66.

[10] Grand Lodge of Scotland, *Historical Sketch of the Grand Lodge of Antient Free & Accepted Mason of Scotland 1736-1986*, Grand Lodge of Scotland, George St, Edinburgh, 3.

[11] Ibid, 7, 10.

[12] Gould, R F, *The History of Freemasonry*, Vol. 1, London, 1887, 54.

[13] Ibid, 54.

[14] Horne, Bro A, 'The Saints John in the Masonic Tradition',

Transactions of the Quatuor Coronati Lodge No. 2076, London, 1962, 81.

15   Wells, R, Understanding Freemasonry, (audio) Tape 10, Recorded Talks, Q.C.C.C, London, 1989.

16   MacKenzie, K, *The Royal Masonic Cyclopaedia*, The Aquarian Press, London, 1877, reprinted in 1987, 148 - 149.

17   Ward J S M, *Who was Hiram Abiff?* Lewis Masonic, Plymouth, 1992 147.

18   Livingstone, E A, [Ed.], *The Concise Oxford Dictionary of the Christian Church*, Oxford University Press, London, 1977, 307.

19   Waite, A E, *A New Encyclopaedia of Freemasonry*, Reprint of 1926 original, Wing Books, New York 1996 vol.ii 469 - 470.

20   Brydon, R, *Rosslyn: A History of the Guilds, the Masons, and the Rosy Cross*, Rosslyn Chapel Trust, Roslin, Midlothian, 1994, no page number listed.

21   Crawford Smith, D, *History of the Ancient Lodge of Scoon and Perth No.3*, Edinburgh, 1898, 18.

22   Campbell, J G, *Witchcraft and Second Sight in the Highlands and Island of Scotland*, Tales and traditions collected entirely from Oral Sources, Glasgow, 1902, 120 - 121.

23   Ibid, 65.

24   Ibid.

25   Levi, E, *The History of Magic*, (English transl of 1862 French orig. by A.E.Waite), London, 1913, 30 - 32.

26   Stevenson, D, *The Origins of Freemasonry, Scotland's Century 1590 - 1710*, Cambridge University Pess, Cambridge, 1988, 98.

27   Ibid, 28.

28   Crawford Smith, D, op cit, 18.

29   McIntosh, C, *The Rosy Cross Unveiled*, The Aquarian Press Ltd, Northamptonshire, 1980, 55.

30   Ashe, G, *King Arthur's Avalon: The Story of Glastonbury*, London, 1974, 126.

31   Taylor, G, *Our Neglected Heritage*, Vol. I, The Early Church, London, 1969, 47.

32   Wise, T A, *History of Paganism in Caledonia*, London, 1884, 201.

33   Innes, T, *The Civil and Ecclesiastical History of Scotland*, Spalding Club, Aberdeen, 1853, 10/11.

34   Ibid.

35 Jamieson, J, *A Historical Account of the Ancient Culdees of Iona*, 1811, (popular edition, reprinted 1890), 17.

36 Wells, R, op cit, cassette tape.

37 Drummond, W. A, *The Lodge of Melrose St. John No. 12*, Privately printed, Melrose, 1986, 3.

38 Ibid.

39 Knight, C and Lomas, R, *The Hiram Key*, Century, London, 1996, 366

40 Richardson, J S, *Melrose Abbey, Official Guide*, HMSO, Edinburgh, 1949, 1.

41 MacEwan, A R, *A History of the Church in Scotland*, London, 1913, 189.

42 Donaldson, Prof G, *Scottish Historical Documents*, Glasgow, 1974, 23.

43 Delap, D, *Celtic Saints*, Pitkin, Great Britain, 1998, 2.

44 Elder, I H, *Celt, Druid, and Culdee*, London, 1944, 88.

45 Taylor, G, op cit, 47.

46 McKay, A G, *An Encyclopaedia of Freemasonry*, New York and London, 1920, 221.

47 Levi, E, op cit, 184.

48 McKay, A G, op cit, 191.

49 MacKenzie, K, op cit, 143.

50 Coil, H W, *Coil's Masonic Encyclopaedia*, Macoy Publishing and Masonic Supply Company, New York, 1961, 595.

51 Murray Lyon, D, *History of the Lodge of Edinburgh (Mary's Chapel) No.1*, Edinburgh, 1873, 6.

52 Baigent, M, and Leigh, R, op cit, 187.

53 Gould, R F, *The History of Freemasonry*, Vol. 5, London, 1887, 80.

54 Livingstone, E A, op cit, 206.

55 *Encyclopaedia of Catholicism*, [R P McBrien, Gen. Ed.], HarperCollins, New York, 1995, 553

56 Piatigorsky, Prof A, *Freemasonry*, Harvill Press, London, 1999, 116-7.

57 Gould, R F, op cit, 84.

58 Ibid.

59 Waite, A E, op cit, 315. [See also Baigent, M & Leigh, R, p 187; Pick, F L & Knight, G N, *The Pocket History of Freemasonry*, [Ed by Smyth, F], Hutchinson, London, 8th ed, rev, 1992, 230; and Ridley, J, *The Freemasons*, Constable, London, 1999, 70.

60 Cooper-Oakley, I, *Traces of a Hidden Tradition in Masonry and Mediaeval Mysticism*, London, 1900, 98 - 100.

61   Baigent, M, and Leigh, R, op cit, 74-5.
62   Cooper-Oakley, I, op cit, 95.
63   Pennecuik, A, *A Descriptive Account of the Blue Blanket*, Edinburgh, 1780.
64   Ibid.
65   Illustrated Times, London, 1858, 21.
66   Ibid.
67   Ibid.
68   Ibid.
69   Murray Lyon, D, op cit, 306.
70   Baigent, M, and Leigh, R, op cit, 31.
71   Coil, H W, op cit, 49.
72   Ibid, 49.
73   McLeod, W, 'The Old Charges', ARS Quatuor Coronatorum, *Transactions of Quatuor Coronati Lodge No. 2076*, Vol. 99, The Garden City Press, Hertfordshire, 1987, 120.
74   Newton, J F, *The Builders*, Unwin Brothers Ltd, Woking, 1934, 86.
75   MacKenzie, K, op cit, 180.
76   Coil, H W, op cit, 305.

CHAPTER NINE

Rosslyn Chapel: An Archetypal 'King Solomon's Temple'?

JUST SIX MILES SOUTH of Edinburgh, the capital of Scotland, is a special place known as Rosslyn Chapel. Perhaps you may have visited Rosslyn Chapel before, seen it in TV documentaries, or have heard of it from books like *Holy Blood and the Holy Grail* or *The Hiram Key*. Once known as 'the Chapel amidst the woods', it is officially known as the Collegiate Chapel of St Matthew and remains an active Scottish Episcopal church today.[1] It stands on College Hill as part of the beautiful scenery of Roslin Glen, the North Esk river below, and the nearby Pentland Hills.

Many have passed through its wondrous doors. Lewis Spence, in one of his many works on early Scottish traditions, referred to Rosslyn Chapel as the Chapel of the Grail, saying 'Nothing can shake my conviction that Rosslyn was built according to the pattern of the Chapel of the Grail as pictured in Norman romance, and that William St Clair had in his poet's mind a vision of the Chapel Perilous when he set hand to the work.'[2] In the past, William and Dorothy Wordsworth, Sir Walter Scott, Dr Samuel Johnson, James Boswell, Robert Burns and other luminaries are known to have visited Rosslyn Chapel and its environs. Indeed, Rosslyn Chapel continues to inspire and intrigue, remaining a place of worship, pilgrimage and exploration for many today.

So much so that Rosslyn Chapel has been thought to be the repository for everything from the Ark of the Covenant, the mummified head of Christ, the Holy Grail, the lost scrolls of the Temple of Jerusalem excavated by the Knights Templar, the Holy Rood, etc, hidden deep within its vaults. For centuries, many have speculated about what, if anything, may have been hidden at Rosslyn, who put it there, and why. Others understandably remain sceptical, saying that until the vaults are actually excavated no one can say anything for certain. Many best-selling books in recent years have put forth various theories about the chapel and what secrets it may hold. It seems that – for better or worse – history, myths, legends and facts are all intertwined when dealing with a subject as complex as Rosslyn.

But on our journey here, let us begin with some of the known facts about Rosslyn Chapel, as stated by The Earl of Rosslyn in his recent guidebook *Rosslyn Chapel*. Work on this magnificent stone chapel began in 1446, an extraordinary effort directed by the founder himself, Sir William St Clair, the third and last St Clair Prince of Orkney. Historian Walter Bower updated Fordun's *Chronicle of the Scottish Nation* in his new *Scotichronicon* (1447), saying that '*Willelmus de Sancto-Claro est in fabricado sumptuosam structuram apud Roslyn*', which, translated, says that Sir William St Clair is erecting an elegant structure at Rosslyn.[3]

Rosslyn Chapel is actually only part of what was intended to be a much larger cruciform building with a tower at its centre. It took 40 years to build, and the learned Sir William oversaw the entire building process, personally inspecting each carving in wood before he allowed it to be carved in stone. That such loving care was taken is amazing in and of itself, and assures us that nothing in Rosslyn Chapel is there by accident, as the founder himself inspected each and every carving.[4]

One of the best sources and manuscripts about Rosslyn Chapel and the St Clair family was written in 1700, about 216 years after the chapel was completed. This extensive work was written by Father Richard Augustine Hay, Canon of St Genevieve in Paris and Prior of St Piermont:

> He examined historical records and charters of the St Clairs and completed a three-volume study in 1700, parts of which were published in 1835 as *A Genealogie of the Saintclaires of Rosslyn*. His research was timely, since the original documents subsequently disappeared.[5]

In this important work, Father Hay also described founder Sir William's great dedication to the building process:

> Prince William, his age creeping up on him, came to consider... how he was to spend his remaining days. Therefore, to the end, that he might not seem altogether unthankful to God for the

benefices he received from Him, it came into his mind to build a house for God's service, of most curious work... he cause artificers to be brought from other regions and foreign kingdoms and caused daily to be abundance of all kinds of workmen present as masons, carpenters, smiths, barrowmen, quarriers... first he caused draughts [plans] to be drawn upon eastland boards [imported Baltic timber] and he made the carpenters carve them according to the draughts [plans], and he gave them for patterns to the masons...[6]

But exactly where these 'other regions' and 'foreign kingdoms' that the builders came from is still debated. From this excerpt, it seems clear that Sir William personally inspected and approved the draft plans for each design before it was given to the masons to carve in stone. His family motto was 'Commit thy Work to God', and indeed he did, in a most extraordinary way.

Order of the Golden Fleece

The principle architect and founder, Sir William St Clair, was a very cultured, erudite, learned man, certainly one of the most knowledgeable of his time. He was also a member of the Knights of Santiago and the Order of the Golden Fleece. Ironically, he was not a Templar or a Freemason, contrary to what is commonly assumed today.

The Order of the Golden Fleece is also a title that is familiar to Freemasons today. At the initiation of all newly created Freemasons, they are told that their badge of office is more ancient than the Golden Fleece, more honourable than the Garter, or any other Order in existence. Some believe that this reference in modern Masonic ritual may have found its way there because of Sir William St Clair's association with these medieval chivalric orders, combined with the claim of his being the hereditary patron and protector of Masons. The Order of the Garter was the most prestigious Order in England.

The Order of the Golden Fleece was established in 1430 to uphold the Christian faith and was dedicated to the Blessed Virgin and St Andrew. Founded by Philip the Good, Duke of Burgundy, the original Order consisted of a Grand Master (the sovereign

Duke) and 23 Knights. The membership was later increased to 31 and then to 51[7] and was 'perhaps in its time, the most prestigious Order of Knighthood in Europe...'[8]

The Order of the Cockle mentioned by Father Hay is likely to have been an error, and instead should be regarded as the Order of the Couquille St Jaques:

> The 'Clamshell' in France, where Hay was educated, is called the 'Couquille St Jaques' and alludes to the 'Order of San Jago di Compostella', better known as 'The Knights of Santiago', founded with strong Templar connection in the 12th century. At the time that Sir William belonged, novices were obliged to spend six months aboard ship! After the Templar suppression of 1307, many fugitive Templars joined this particular Order. A Scottish membership of this body would certainly suggest that the incumbent had completed the pilgrimage to Santiago de Compostella. Like so many other Scots of that time![9]

The church of St James at Santiago is said to have been built over the relics of the apostle and is famous for the pilgrims who still travel there. Dr Walter Johannes Stein states:

> St James is the patron of all pilgrims who make their pilgrimage by land or sea. When Portuguese travellers and heroes of discovery went to India, St James was their patron... We find the pilgrimage of St James leading as far south as India, and also to the north, to a chapel situated near Edinburgh... Rosslyn Chapel.[10]

The emblem of St James was the scallop shell, which pilgrims carried with them to deposit at their place of pilgrimage. Stein suggests that these shells were used in the mortar of Rosslyn Chapel when it was being built. Stein, in his opinion, has further suggestions about possible links of Rosslyn Chapel to the Grail:

> There are two spiritual traditions which found each other and united in Rosslyn Chapel. These two traditions appear also in the history of the Holy Grail... The microcosmic aspect follows the story of Joseph of Arimathea who took away with him the saviour's blood. Whenever the Holy Blood is worshipped, this microcosmic tradition is found... The other, the macrocosmic tradition, was used as the source for another story of the Holy Grail by Wolfram of Eschenbach, who shows the connection of the Holy Grail with astrology... That these two traditions have

united in Rosslyn Chapel can be seen in the symbols there used, which indicate both paths: how man can strive to become Divine, and how the Divine became flesh. Christ as the cornerstone of cosmic and human evolution is shown in the chapel. Statues in this chapel are situated in such a way that those portraying certain events of the Old Testament are placed opposite to statues portraying events in the New Testament... the master who built the chapel has conveyed many secrets of evolution to those who study, not only what is portrayed, but how it is portrayed.[11]

The chapel was generously endowed by the founder Sir William, and by his grandson (also Sir William) in 1523, with land for dwelling houses and gardens. But as the Reformation took hold in Scotland, this change had a devastating effect on Rosslyn Chapel. The Sinclair family remained Catholic, and many churches and their altars and furnishings were deemed to be 'idolatrous' and 'Popish' at the time:

> ...Oliver St Clair was repeatedly warned to destroy the altars in the chapel and in 1592 was summoned to appear before the General Assembly and threatened with excommunication if the altars remained standing after August 17, 1592. On August 31st... 'the altars of Roslene were haille demolishit'. From that time the Chapel ceased to be used as a house of prayer, and soon fell into disrepair.[12]

Then, in 1650, Cromwell's troops under General Monk attacked Rosslyn Castle and his horses were stabled in the chapel. Given the exquisite beauty of the chapel, it is rather hard to believe that horses were once stabled there. But, as some believe, perhaps using the chapel as a stable may actually have helped to save the building from even further damage at the time. Others have claimed that because Cromwell was a Freemason and would have known about certain Masonic-related carvings in the chapel, that this was the reason the chapel was spared, but there appears to be no evidence of this to date. As to General Monk, we do not know...

Later, on the evening of 11 December 1688, a Protestant mob from Edinburgh and villagers from Roslin damaged the Chapel. It remained abandoned until 1736, when James St Clair glazed the windows for the first time, repaired the roof, and re-laid the floor with flagstones. Sir John Clerk of Penicuik was instrumental in encouraging St Clair to make these 18th C renovations. It is also interesting to note that 1736 is the same year as the founding of the Grand Lodge of Scotland and that Clerk was also a Freemason.

So, given this turbulent history, we are very fortunate indeed to have Rosslyn Chapel in all of its glory still available for us to see today.

In a Chapel guide book written in the 1930s, the author refers to Rosslyn Chapel as resembling the Temple of Jerusalem and a Bible in stone, adding:

> Like Solomon's Temple, for which David, his father, made such ample provision, the 'Collegiate Church of St Matthew' was intended to be 'exceedingly magnificent, of fame and glory throughout all countries' (1 Chron. 22, 5) and such it has proved to be through the centuries.[13]

This is a passing reference to King Solomon's Temple, which we will learn more about later. The *arcanum in stone* that Rosslyn was designed to be also contains some imagery that is not Christian, although many biblical scenes are depicted. However, it is known that many of the symbols of the earlier pagan wisdom traditions were adopted by Christians and the Church Fathers and were then re-explained in a Christian context. So it is not surprising to find such a wide variety of symbolism prevalent in many medieval Gothic cathedrals and chapels like Rosslyn.

The Green Man and Roslin Glen

One example of such a symbol is the archetypal Green Man, of which Rosslyn Chapel has more carvings of than any other medieval chapel in Europe. There are known to be at least 103 carved images of the Green man inside Rosslyn Chapel alone, and this total does not include those on the outside of the chapel or on the roof. The Green Man is usually portrayed as a head with profuse foliage growing from the mouth, which also represents fertility. The many faces of the Rosslyn Green Men appear in various guises, some full and beaming with health, others looking decidedly skeletal, with the rest falling somewhere in between. Some believe they may collectively symbolise the four seasons of nature. The Green Man symbol in a Christian context is often said to represent death and resurrection, similar to earlier traditions of vegetation gods who died and rose again, like Tammuz or Osiris, for example. Generally, it wasn't until around the 6th C that the Green Man motif made its way into western Christian church carvings.

Although the Green Man is usually assumed to be an overwhelmingly Celtic motif, this is actually *not* the case, as the Green Man is also found carved in ancient eastern temples, something which unfortunately doesn't seem to have been widely acknowledged in the west. Ancient images of the Green Man can still be seen in the Apo Kayan area of Borneo, where he is perceived as the Lord God of the Forest, in the chapels of Dhankar Gompa, high in the Indian Himalayas, in the temples of Kathmandu, Nepal and the Jain temples of Ranakpur, among others.

Clearly, the Green Man is a universal symbol that has been around for quite some time:

> Heads from the Lebanon and Iraq can be dated to the 2nd century AD, and there are early Romanesque heads in 11th century Templar churches in Jerusalem. From the 12th to 15th centuries heads appeared in cathedrals and churches across Europe...[14]

British Folklore Society scholar Jeremy Harte comments that 'for all their differences in mood, these carvings give a common impression of something – someone – alive among the green buds of summer or the brown leaves of autumn. Green Men can vary from the comic to the beautiful, although often the most beautiful ones are the most sinister.'[15] Or, perhaps as with a few of the Rosslyn ones, downright impish!

But in the context of a late medieval Scottish chapel, no doubt the founder Sir William was also acknowledging the Celtic traditions of the area, and also the very setting of the chapel itself, 'amidst the woods', glen and all of nature's bounty. Indeed, it may well be said that the chapel is placed there *because of* the surrounding glen and natural environment. Some gifted dowsers have said that it was probably built there because several important 'ley lines' intersect at that point, making it a very important location in geomantic terms. If this is true, then the prolific symbols of the Green Man may also be acknowledging the 'aliveness' of the earth, as well as the processes of nature, a not-too-surprising image to find in such a location. Of course, el Khidr is also portrayed as a green man of wisdom in Sufi traditions, as referred to in chapter 7, and Osiris was often portrayed as a green man in Egyptian tradition.

Other pagan customs have also found their way into Christian festivals, including Easter egg hunts and Easter bunnies, obvious representations of fertility that are now inseparable from many children's Easter celebrations, or, the Yuletide tree, now included in nearly all Christian celebrations of Christmas. The Green Man at Rosslyn Chapel is also said to be representative of Robin Goodfellow, 'Jack o the Green', and/or Robin Hood.

Scottish Templar Historian Mr Robert Brydon, FSA Scot, is the owner of the Rosslyn Chapel museum exhibition now on display. He told us that in May and June of each year until the time of the Reformation, there was an annual festival held in Roslin Glen by the Gypsies, where they performed their annual May Plays. The Castle of the Sinclairs at Rosslyn had two towers, one named Robin Hood and the other Little John. The founder of the chapel, Sir William, would have grown up with this tradition.

A short summary of the overall situation:

> Legislation against gypsies in Scotland had always been harsh, and during the Reformation it became more so. In 1574, the Scottish Parliament decreed that all gypsies apprehended should be whipped, branded on the cheek or ear, or have the right ear cut off. Further, even more severe, legislation was introduced in 1616. By the end of the 17th century, gypsies were being deported *en masse* to Virginia, Barbados, and Jamaica. In 1559, however, Sir William Sinclair was Lord Justice General of Scotland under Queen Mary. Although his efforts do not appear to have been notably successful, he nevertheless opposed the measures then being implemented against gypsies. Availing himself of his judicial status, he is said to have intervened on one critical occasion and saved a particular gypsy from the scaffold. From then on, the gypsies became annual visitors to the Sinclair estates, which offered them a welcome refuge. Every May and June, they would

congregate in the fields below Rosslyn Castle, where they would perform their plays...[16]

So even after the earlier decree by the Scottish Parliament on 20 June 1555 which legally banned the specific play entitled *Robin Hood and Little John*, Scotland's Chief Justice was sponsoring them, on his estates, in defiance of this ban! As he obviously felt they were important, the plays continued to be performed in Roslin Glen, as stated to us by Mr Robert Brydon.

The 1894 work *Scottish Gypsies under the Stewarts* remarks that

> ...it is surely more than coincidence that the towers were assigned to them (on their visits) were known as 'Robin Hood' and 'Little John'. It seems equally significant that their performances took place every year in May and June. Because 'Robin Hood and Little John' was one of the most famous of the May-tide plays in Scotland, during the fifteenth and sixteenth centuries.[17]

The details of these plays are largely lost to us as a result of the act passed by the Scottish Parliament in 1555. The names of the plays were mentioned in the act when it 'ordained that in all time coming no manner of person be chosen Robert Hude, nor Little John, Abbot of Unreason, Queenis of Maij, nor otherwise, under various severe pains and penalties.'[18] Indeed, such was the popularity of these 'pagan plays' with the people that the church understandably felt threatened and took necessary action to stop them, often going to the extreme. Most of these plays had the 'King of the May' as their focus. In England, too, such plays, often sponsored by the Guilds, were also under heavy attack.

But the 'King of the May' in Scotland was very likely to have been Robin Hood, and many May celebrations were held, following older Beltane customs that were already indigenous to Scotland. Although normally thought of as exclusively an English hero, the fact is that the name of Robin Hood was also well known in Scotland by the early years of the 15th C:

> But to whatever source he owed his origin, to minstrelsy, mythology, or history, the name of Robin Hood was well known in Scotland by the early years of the 15th century. It seems therefore perfectly natural that this hero, whose deeds were on the lips not

only of the professional minstrel but of the folk, should be adopted as the lord of the May feast At any rate, it is noteworthy that the Scottish records have so far revealed no trace of Maid Marian, who, says Sir Edmund Chambers, is inseparable from Robin Hood in the English May game... We do find a few references to the Queen of the May... from at least 1492 onwards, the Edinburgh Guildry gave financial support to 'Robertus Hud', who, by 1500, if not earlier, was joined by his associate Little John...[19]

This, of course, was the play that was performed in Roslin Glen, *Robin Hood and Little John*. We also learn from the above excerpt that *from at least 1492, the Edinburgh Guilds were giving financial support to 'Robin Hood' plays*. It is highly likely that this was occurring even earlier as well.

The Romany Gypsies had been in Scotland for quite some time, and the head of the noted Gypsy family of Faa found protection under the hand and seal of James v 'as 'our lovit Johnne Faa, Lord and Earle of Littil Egipt'. This singular write was renewed thirteen years after, during the minority of Queen Mary.'[20]

As Mr Brydon also told us, there were many families of Gypsies in the Midlothian area around Edinburgh in those days. The Faa family and the Gypsy royalty of Scotland were centred in the Kirk Yetholm area, near Kelso; the last crowning of the Scottish Gypsy king occurred there many decades ago, with 10,000 people present for the event.

The Scottish Gypsy clans of the Bailleys, the Wilsons, and the Browns were centred on two special 'villages of refuge' – Middleton and Temple, some ten or twelve miles south of Edinburgh. Temple is the modern village name for Balantradoch, which was also the location of the headquarters of the Scottish medieval Knights Templar.

Tim Wallace-Murphy and Marilyn Hopkins in *Rex Deus* offer an interesting summary of the real significance of such Mayday celebrations in Roslin Glen:

Behind the official record there lies 'the hidden hand of history' which records the experience of the underdogs, the beliefs of the hidden schools of philosophy and spirituality, and the hidden tensions within society that have formed and moulded it. The imprint of the hidden hand of history is recorded in the stories, song, dance, drama and ritual of the folklore tradition. In many cases the disguise that surrounds this subversive story was effective, for the rituals were accepted as an everyday part of normal life. For example, the carvings of the green man that decorate so many medieval church buildings and the dances celebrating the rites of Mayday, were deemed harmless; yet both of these are visual expressions of a 'spiritual resurrection' that plays a central role in... heretical religious beliefs... In other cases the true import of the celebration was seen for what it was, a means of transmission of heresy...[21]

In time nearly all of the skills of the Gypsies, as gifted craftsmen, artisans, musicians, metal workers, horn-carvers, etc, were either no longer valued or outlawed, many had to turn to other activities to survive. In earlier times, the Gypsies, the tinkers, and the travellers were highly valued for their skills in certain areas and also for their legendary storytelling skills.

But there were also *other 'strolling players', and 'minstrels' around at the time*, as well as Romany Gypsies, so it is actually quite likely that the performers at the Sinclair plays were also drawn from several of these groups. Mr Brydon states that with regard to the old artisan Guilds and fraternities 'there lay a ritual symbolism involving a search for something remote, hidden or lost... Bards, troubadours, Meistersingers, and strolling gypsy players, by way of song, sonnet and pageant, carried onwards just such an esoteric doctrine.'[22] So by the method of acting out pageants, singing songs, reciting poetry and playing instruments, this ritual symbolism was preserved. It should also be pointed out that the Gypsies have always had much lore around Christian themes, such as *The Legend of the Three Nails* of the crucifixion, for example, as Mr Brydon explained to us.

In the museum exhibition at Rosslyn Chapel, there is a head of St Sara that was carved in Santiago and made from jet. St Sara is the patron saint of the Gypsies and is still celebrated today, especially in southern France. Icons and holy pictures of St Sara often occur along with images of the Black Virgin, also called the Black Madonna.

The origins of St Sara are mysterious, but especially in

Provençal tradition, there is still a strong Catholic practice of worshipping the Black Madonna today. The most famous pilgrimage site is Les Saintes Maries de la Mer, where there is a special cult of St Sara. In Catholic tradition, Sara was said to be the black assistant who accompanied the three Marys from the Holy Land to France – Mary, the sister of the Virgin, Mary the mother of James and John, and Mary Magdelene. In Gypsy tradition, Sara was a Gypsy woman (some say 'Egyptian') who helped the three Marys land safely in southern France after the crucifixion. The pilgrims keep vigil there before a statue of St Sara in the crypt.

This, like the whole Black Virgin tradition, tends to make orthodox Catholic priests rather uncomfortable, however. When asked recently in France by visitors why these special Madonnas were always black, the usual reply was 'it's from centuries of candle soot and smoke'. This is highly doubtful, as a number of them were originally carved from materials like jet, for example. The Black Madonna has been shown to have been derived from earlier goddess traditions, especially Isis holding her son Horus, for instance, so it is understandable why this may make more orthodox priests uncomfortable, notwithstanding the fact that a black lady has a prominent role in the Old Testament wisdom tradition, Song of Songs.

Some believe that in earlier times, a special statue of a Black Virgin may have been at Rosslyn Chapel. Niven Sinclair has personally stated that he believes it is quite possible that a Black Virgin, among other objects, may still be hidden in the vaults of Rosslyn Chapel today. It is also quite interesting to note that in 1584, on Corpus Christi Day, a number of Gypsies sought refuge with the Knights of St James of Santiago, fleeing arrest as heretics. The Knights accepted and protected them, as they were convinced of their Christian convictions. Even today, Compostela is a major pilgrimage centre. At Rosslyn, scallop shells have been found, symbols of St James, left there by medieval pilgrims who had come all the way from Spain to Scotland. The founder of Rosslyn Chapel, Sir William St Clair, was a member of the Order of the Knights of Santiago.

Regarding other traditions and the May rites, an ancient poem about *Robin Hood and the Widow's Three Sons*, starts with the lines:

> There are twelve months in all the year, As I hear many say, But the merriest month of all the year, Is the merry month of May.[23]

As a rather curious and humorous aside, one Masonic writer named Cleland suggested in 1766 that Masons may have derived their rites and their name from the practices of the Druids:

> Considering that the May [May-pole] was eminently the great sign of Druidism, as the Cross was of Christianity; is there anything forced or far-fetched in the conjecture that the adherents to Druidism should take the name of Men of the May, or, the 'May-sons'?[24]

In a footnote on the same page, it further states that 'Both the May pole and the German Christbaum have a pagan origin, the type of each being the ash, Yggdrasil'[25] The mention of the tree Yggdrasil from Norse mythology is interesting, in that some believe that the base design of the Apprentice Pillar is based upon this theme.

Apprentice Pillar

The famous Apprentice Pillar at Rosslyn Chapel has many legends about it, some of which we learned about in chapter 7. Judy Fisken, the former Curator of Rosslyn Chapel, has done extraordinary work on researching all aspects of Rosslyn, including the Apprentice Pillar, and has extensive knowledge of related subjects as well. Many books and articles have appeared through the years about the famed pillar at Rosslyn, which still intrigues many today, including churchmen, Freemasons, members of chivalric orders like the Knights Templar, the Rosicrucians and others.

The Apprentice Pillar is a beautiful, ornately carved stone pillar that has one unique legend all its own, that of 'The Murdered Apprentice'. Briefly:

> The Master Mason, having received from the Founder the model of a pillar of exquisite workmanship and design, hesitated to carry it out until he had been to Rome... and seen the original.

He went abroad and in his absence an apprentice, having dreamt that he had finished the pillar, at once set to work and carried out the design as it now stands, a perfect marvel of workmanship. The Master Mason on his return, seeing the pillar completed, instead of being delighted at the success of his pupil, was so stung with envy that he asked who had dared to do it in his absence. On being told that it was his apprentice, he was so inflamed with rage and passion that he struck him with his mallet, killed him on the spot and paid the penalty...[26]

This tale has been told from at least the 17th C, but some believe it may have originated from the time of the actual building of the Chapel. An early telling of the tale is given by a Yorkshire man, Thomas Kirk, in his travels through Scotland in 1671. After a brief stop at St Catherine's well on the outskirts of Edinburgh, Kirk writes of his first encounter with the Chapel:

Two miles further we saw Roslen Chapel, a very pretty design, but was never finished, the choir only and a little vault. The roof is all stone, with good imagery work; there is a better man at exact descriptions of the stories than he at Westminster Abbey: this story he told us that the master builder went abroad to see good patterns, but before his return his apprentice had built one pillar which exceeded all that ever he could do or had seen, therefore he slew him; and he showed us the head of the apprentice on the wall with a gash in the forehead and his masters head opposite to him.[27]

However, it must be pointed out that *this story of a builder being killed at the erection of a holy edifice is not unique to Rosslyn*. At Rouen in France there is a similar tale attributed to a Rose window, where the murderer is said to have been pardoned by the Vatican to allow the building work to be completed. In penance, he then had to spend the rest of his life in a holy order carrying out good works.

A similar tale is also familiar to Freemasons, who have the legend of the murder of Hiram Abiff, King Solomon's Master of Works, regarding the building of the Temple. Hiram Abiff was murdered by three jealous masons who attempted to extort from him the secrets of a Master mason; when Hiram would not reveal them, they treacherously murdered him. The theme of an unfinished temple being brought about as a result of the murder of a builder is also a theme present in other traditions. In Rouen, we find the papacy stepping in to ensure that the building was finished. In the Bible, the death of the builder, or, more precisely, 'the principal architect', is not even mentioned specifically, nor is the issue of the temple being left incomplete.

Around the bottom of the Apprentice Pillar there are carved eight serpents, or dragon-like beasts, who are portrayed gnawing at the roots of a tree. Gleaned from Scandinavian tradition, where the eight dragons of Neifelheim were said to lie at the base of Yggdrasil, the great ash tree which bound together heaven, earth, and hell, the serpent-dragons are said to keep the fruit of knowledge from growing on the tree of life. The idea of divine knowledge being suppressed or kept from man by his own ignorance – which the serpent-dragons likely represent – is a recurring theme in many western philosophical traditions, of which Rosicrucianism, Hermeticism, Alchemy and Freemasonry are a part. In Christian terms, it also signifies the constant conflict between good and evil, and the divine interplay of this process through the ages.

At the top of the pillar is a scene carved from the biblical story of Abraham and his son Isaac, whom he is shown preparing to kill, because of his strong faith. This biblical story is highly allegorical and can be read on many levels. Rosslyn Chapel, in many ways, is about the interplay between the divine and the everyday in our lives, of life and death, and of the presence of God in creation. 'God is everywhere around us', the chapel seems to say.

Why was the 'Apprentice' carving 'altered'?

The Rosslyn Chapel 'murdered Apprentice' story has certainly been popular for several centuries, but it seems that the murdered apprentice carving may not have actually been the original design at all, as it appears that the original carving was deliberately 'altered' at some time in the past. Researcher Keith Laidler brought up this rather unusual point:

> Robert Brydon, whom I was fortunate to meet, was again able to
> offer confirmation of this identification. He told me that the face

of the Apprentice is not what it seems to be. An American Templar, on a visit to Rosslyn, had examined the face of the 'Apprentice' in detail. The carving has been very carefully altered: it originally possessed a beard and moustache, but these have been painstakingly removed (I was able to confirm this myself later, with the aid of high-power binoculars). This was a highly significant discovery. In medieval times, an apprentice stone mason was not allowed to sport a full beard and moustache. Facial hair was reserved for those who had completed their initiation into the mysteries of the craft. In other words, the head on the plinth at Rosslyn was not the head of the Apprentice, but the head of the Master.[28]

Surprising as it may seem, others through the years have also noticed this. Did someone deliberately 'alter' a few of the carvings at Rosslyn at some time in the past, carefully chiselling away some of their features? And if so, *why*?

If they did, this would clearly alter the meaning of the carvings as they were originally created by the founder, Sir William St Clair. Who, one might rightly ask, would have had the audacity to tamper with his vision? And perhaps more important, what really was the founder's *original* vision?

Perhaps the carving and its legend may have been more unusual than we now realise, as if it was in fact altered then obviously its message upset someone enough in the past to go to such lengths to change it. Who, when, and why?

There are other carved faces in the vicinity near the usual three that are always mentioned – the apprentice, his grieving mother, and the master – yet they are rarely, if ever, described. Who are they meant to represent certain saints, perhaps? Or do they just not 'fit in' with the 'story' of the murdered apprentice, and are therefore conveniently ignored?

Perhaps no one knows for sure, of course, but it does seem rather strange that the 'spin' on what these carvings supposedly mean does not seem to correlate with, or include, all of what is actually there. No doubt this 'spin' was decided some centuries ago, by someone for a specific reason, and since then many people have therefore just automatically 'assumed' that it is true, which may seem understandable. But is it?

One is thus left to wonder at the strange anomaly of the murdered 'apprentice' carving at Rosslyn Chapel having once had a beard and a moustache *yet now he does not*. Why? So who, then, was this carving originally supposed to represent?

It may not have ever been a carving of an 'apprentice' at all, as only Master masons were allowed to sport a full beard. Hiram Abiff, who features in the Masonic legend, had a beard and was King Solomon's Master of Works; when he refused to divulge the Master mason's secrets to the three jealous masons who kept badgering him about them, they murdered him. As has been speculated, could the 'apprentice' at Rosslyn Chapel have originally really signified the Master? If so, then there is a connection to the Masonic legend of Hiram Abiff, but the question still remains as to why someone would want to chisel off the beard and moustache, *to appear to 'demote' the Master down to the rank of a mere apprentice*.

This may seem strange enough, but what has also happened in this instance is that the bearded Master (who was treacherously murdered himself by three jealous masons) *has now been turned into a murdered apprentice*, as he is said to have been killed by his jealous Master upon his return to Rosslyn from Rome. In short, it is obvious that the Master has been 'demoted' and that the original vision of Sir William St Clair has been 'doctored', to use modern-day terminology. It seems that one legend has been deliberately altered to appear to be another, i.e. the gifted bearded Master who was murdered by three jealous apprentices has now become the talented apprentice who was murdered by his jealous Master.

Or if this carving wasn't altered, which could be possible, of course, why does it so obviously *appear* to have been? Clearly, something has been done to it. Its current condition, according to some, is not merely the result of efforts to clean or paint the carvings, which was known to have occurred in Victorian times.

Perhaps in the future more will become known about this fascinating carving. As we are not experts in medieval stone preservation, we must leave this issue for those more qualified to answer. Perhaps some day, we will find out why.

We are not, of course, putting responsibility for this on anyone specifically, as this must have happened a long, long time ago. We are only asking that the actual facts be known and the true vision of the founder be clarified. It may be that the *real* story of the carving and its legend are even more intriguing than the story that now exists. But if the 'apprentice' carving definitely once had a beard and a moustache – which means he was a Master – and it doesn't now, then this should certainly be taken into account, as should the other carvings in the area.

Another carving open to question by some is that dubbed 'The Veil of Veronica'. The Veil of Veronica represents the well-known story of the lady Veronica, and how she compassionately wiped the face of Christ as he was carrying his heavy cross in agony, and as a reward for her kindness, a miraculous image of his face remained on the cloth. This relic became known as 'The Veil of Veronica', not to be confused with the Shroud of Turin.

This carving is present at Rosslyn Chapel, but is quite damaged, as the actual image of the person holding the cloth is not clearly discernible. However, the cloth, or towel, clearly shows the head of Christ on it (emphasis ours):

> With 'the Veronica' carving, two aspects immediately stand out. The image of the person holding the cloth has been badly damaged. The head has been removed and it is impossible to know whether the image represents St Veronica, or even if it is female. Robert Brydon, the Templar archivist and one of the most knowledgeable of all Rosslyn researchers, has examined the chapel in detail... He told me that he is convinced *the damage in the chapel is 'very specific, not done by accident... Someone has deliberately damaged parts of it for a reason'*. This puts a new slant on the removal of the head of 'St Veronica'. Everyone assumes that the head of the person holding the towel is female; however, if the head of the person holding the towel was that of a man, this would change the meaning of the image utterly...[29]

But who, then, would this be, and what would it mean? This would obviously change the meaning of the carving. It has not been contested that the image on the cloth is that of Christ; what is under the microscope, so to speak, is who was originally portrayed as holding the cloth. Fascination with Rosslyn seems to go on and on but admittedly the issue of the possible deliberate alteration of certain carvings 'for a reason' is most intriguing, *if* it is at all true. Perhaps in the future more will also become known about this enigmatic carving.

Another carving that has been questioned is that of the supposed 'Death mask of Robert the Bruce'. Mr Robert Cooper, Curator of the Grand Lodge of Scotland Museum and Library, in an article entitled 'Rosslyn Chapel: The Faces of Robert the Bruce', points out that this carving obviously appears to be that of a young face, rather than that of an old man. He states that it does not seem to look like what the face of Robert the Bruce would have been like in medieval times. He says:

> Dr Ian MacLeod, a consultant at the Edinburgh Dental Institute, assisted by Dr Richard Neave, one of Britain's foremost forensic medical artists, produced a 'warts an' all' reconstruction of Bruce's head at the time of his death. This reconstruction took account of the obvious scarring, i.e., a sword wound to the head, a broken cheek-bone, a distended eye socket and upper jaw damage. Drs. MacLeod and Neave were sure that Robert I suffered from leprosy and this too is reflected in the reconstruction...[30]

Indeed, it is believed that Robert the Bruce suffered from leprosy, and towards the end of his life it is known that he painfully made a pilgrimage to Whithorn in 1329, as we saw in chapter 4. Cooper then asks the obvious, vexing question:

> Does the carved face in Rosslyn Chapel fit any of these reconstructions? Sadly, for me, the answer must be no. The carving is that of a young face rather than that of an old man. It is supposed to be a copy of the death mask of Bruce but shows none of the marks of time, none of the scarring, none of the 'wear and tear' of 55 years. But compare them for yourself and draw your own conclusions.[31]

However, one may be also compelled to ask: perhaps it *was* meant to be that of Robert the Bruce, but of a younger Bruce, a mask of his likeness but not that of an actual 'death mask' Who decided it was to be specifically called a 'death mask'? Another question would be: if it isn't that of Robert the Bruce, then *whose is it*? Mr Cooper does not say specifically here, and no one else seems to know for certain about this issue, so it remains unresolved today.

Another Masonic author comments on an interesting carving of a depiction of Christ with both arms raised above his head and on either side of him are seven prostrate Kings of Europe:

> On closer inspection, it can be seen that the Kings on either side of Christ are both facing away from him while all the others are facing him. Could there be hidden meaning to this? On the architrave to the right and facing south there is a depiction of the Old Testament hero Samson...[32]

A very interesting point indeed. Samson was known for his long hair in the Bible, and as one may also note, this may imply a Merovingian issue, in that these early Visigothic kings of France also were renown for their wisdom and are known to have believed that life resided in their long hair. The legacy of the Merovingians, certain royal families of Europe, and their fascinating history regarding the Rex Deus theory and a possible connection to Rosslyn Chapel, have been expounded on by other authors.

There are many other exquisite carvings in Rosslyn Chapel, many of which have obvious biblical and Old Testament themes. Some of the more enigmatic carvings include an image of Moses with horns, the Templar seal of the Agnus Dei, or Lamb of God, Christ with his right hand raised in blessing, an angel holding a scroll, a devil with a kneeling couple beside him, an angel with the engrailed (Sinclair) cross, musician angels with various instruments, a fox dressed as a priest, portrayed as preaching to a flock of geese, and so on. Templar, Masonic, Rosicrucian and Christian symbolism and iconography are woven throughout Rosslyn Chapel in a fascinating tapestry of stone.

Also contained in various carvings all over the chapel are the wonders of life and death. Specific carvings include the seven deadly sins, the seven virtues, and the popular medieval theme of The Dance of Death. This implies that Death is all around us, every day, so awareness of this fact and how we live our lives each day is what really matters. Again, we see the constant interplay of opposites in Rosslyn: light and dark, male and female, life and death and so on.

On the outside of the building on the east wall, near the southeast corner, is what appears to be a carving of a head with wings. It is too worn to be certain, but many experts believe it may be a portrayal of the winged god Hermes. Some say that the Masonic Hiram Abiff is actually a corruption of Mercury, who was also called Hermes in some earlier writings. An excerpt from *Coil's Masonic Encyclopaedia* says that Hermes can be three things: a god, a philosopher, or a body of knowledge opposed to the destruction of learning. No doubt Sir William St Clair, the founder of Rosslyn Chapel, was understandably concerned about the destruction of learning and the burning of books at the time. So, he would want to build something that would last forever for posterity.

A chapel made of stone can also be viewed as the codification in stone, for posterity, of a perennial wisdom tradition that also involves Christianity. Many have been drawn to Rosslyn and its unique symbolism for centuries. As Robert Brydon sums up in *Rosslyn: A History*:

> Over the years the Guilds, the Templars, the Rosicrucians, and the Masons have all recognised something of their own mystery teaching in the complex allegory presented by Rosslyn Chapel. An arcanum, a book in stone...[33]

It seems that history has shown that the founder, Sir William, was right – yes, there were various attempts to destroy Rosslyn Chapel. Yet, it still survives today, an arcanum in stone.

Zerubabbel's Temple

In the south east corner of Rosslyn Chapel, there are inscribed the only words originally carved in Rosslyn Chapel, '*Forte est Vinu(m) Fortior est Rex Fortiores Sunt Muliers Sup(er) Om(nia) vincit veritas*', which mean:

Wine is Strong,
the King is stronger,
Women are stronger,
but above all, Truth conquers.

These words were obviously approved by the founder, Sir William St Clair, and so one should certainly take note of them.

This particular phrase is also familiar to many Freemasons as it appears in many Masonic degrees, including those of the Royal Arch, The Royal Order of Scotland and the Ancient and Accepted Scottish Rite, for example.

The phrase itself comes from one of the apocryphal books of the Bible called 1st Esdras. The Apocryphal books are those which, for one reason or another, did not make it into the orthodox canon that we now call 'the Bible'. These decisions were made at various church councils in the first few centuries of Christianity, and were often made for political as well as doctrinal reasons. Some of the apocryphal books are now recognised by respected biblical scholars as being as authentic as, if not more so, some of those in the orthodox canon, the Gospel of Thomas being only one example. The editors of the Apocrypha for the Revised Standard Version of the Bible say, 'Some have suggested that the books were 'hidden' or withdrawn because they were deemed to contain mysterious or esoteric lore.'[34] Biblical scholars also now admit that some of them were likely excluded for such reasons at the time.

The apocryphal book of 1st Esdras, chapter 3, relates to the time that the first Temple had been destroyed in Jerusalem and the Jews were suffering in exile in Babylon. King Darius of Persia invaded Babylon and captured it from Nebuchadnezzar, the king of Babylon and enemy of the Jews. These Jewish exiles and their descendants had been held captive in Babylon for at least 60 years, after the destruction of Jerusalem in 590BC

At this time he takes on amongst his most trusted guards one of the exiled Jews, a man named Zerubbabel. Zerubbabel is of the Royal House of David, a 'Prince of Judah', and was born in exile. The king poses a question to three of his guards, one of whom is Zerubbabel. He wants to find out who is the wisest, and asks them: 'What is the strongest?' The first guard answers wine, the second answers the King, and Zerubbabel answers with 'Women are the strongest, but above all things, Truth bearest the victory' (1st Esdras, chapter 3, verse 12).

On hearing this, the King decides to allow Zerubbabel to lead his people to their freedom and gives them back their temple treasures. They return to the Holy Land to rebuild the city of

Jerusalem and rebuild the Second Temple, which is referred to as 'The House of the Lord'. This is important, as the first book of Esdras, from which the words carved in stone in Rosslyn Chapel originate, does not give any dimensions or measurements for the Second Temple, and does not specifically claim that this 'Temple of the Lord' was a copy of the original design of King Solomon's temple. These verses are to be found in 1st Esdras, chapters 5 and 7. It took 18 years to build this Second Temple, according to this account.

So at Rosslyn Chapel, it appears that the founder, Sir William St Clair, may have identified with Prince Zerubabbel as the master architect and builder of the chapel (as the 'Temple of the Lord') which probably explains why the only words there are those from 1st Esdras. But the question of whether or not Rosslyn Chapel is a 'King Solomon's Temple', or a spiritual interpretation of Herod's Temple, has been put forth by other authors, notably Knight and Lomas.

Their book *The Hiram Key* propelled many to wonder if – and when – the vaults at Rosslyn Chapel will be excavated, and if so, what may be found there. Knight and Lomas believe that Rosslyn Chapel is a spiritual interpretation of Herod's Temple and claim that the sacred scrolls from the Temple of Jerusalem are hidden under the floor of the chapel, having been excavated in the Holy Land by the Knights Templar in the 12th C, and then brought back to Europe. They say:

> ... Rosslyn is the Scroll Shrine. The question to be asked is: are the scrolls still there? The answer is almost certainly yes, they are. There is no evidence, historical or physical, of any tampering with the foundations of the building, despite the wars and battles that have raged on the turf around it. Ultrasound ground-scans have already established that there are cavities under the floor of Rosslyn and we intend to use our new evidence as powerfully as we can to gain the authority to excavate below the building and recover the scrolls...[35]

Not everyone agrees with their theory, of course, but many have been intrigued by such questions through the centuries. Sir Walter Scott wrote in his famous poem, *The Lay of the Last Minstrel* about 20 barons of Roslin buried in full knightly armour, beneath Rosslyn Chapel:

... Seem'd all on fire that chapel proud,
Where Roslin's chiefs uncoffin'd lie,
Each Baron, for a sable shroud,
Sheathed in his iron panoply...
There are twenty of Roslin's barons bold
Lie buried within that proud chapelle...
And each St Clair was buried there
With candle, with book and with knell...[36]

In 1693 John Slezer, in an old account of the chapel, says of the barons: 'The last lay in a vault so dry that their bodies have been found intire after Fourscore Years, and as fresh as when they were first buried. There goes a tradition, that before the death of any of the family of Roslin, this Chapel appears all in Fire.'[37]

The Bishop of Caithness, Dr Robert Forbes, in *An Account of the Chapel of Roslin* (1774) does make reference to ten barons of Roslin buried in the vaults of the chapel, but doesn't mention any treasure. Critics understandably contend that if there was any treasure, then it should have been mentioned, a fair enough point; yet others point out that it may be that the treasure and/or scrolls were stored elsewhere, or that there may be other vaults in or around the chapel area that were not seen by Forbes at the time. This could also be a possibility, but who knows? Until the vaults are actually excavated, no one can say anything for certain, so unfortunately, the question still remains unresolved today.

There have been many theories about what may be hidden at Rosslyn Chapel. It has now become a modern-day 'myth in the making', with an impetus all its own, making it difficult to sort out the truth from fiction. It is also possible, as some contend, that there may be nothing there. But many people still want to know what mysteries Rosslyn Chapel may hold today, which begs the question: Will the vaults of Rosslyn Chapel ever be excavated? Or, should they ever be excavated at all? Perhaps they are best left alone. Others are adamant that if there is something there that has great import for humanity, something as important as the scrolls from the Temple of Jerusalem, for example, then people have a right to know about it.

On the other hand, one would think that this decision, under-standably, should be up to the Earl and his family for obvious reasons. In an effort to find some answers to these questions, the Director of Rosslyn Chapel Trust, Mr Stuart Beattie was asked about the excavation issue, and explained:

> Due to the Scottish law of the 'Right of Sepulchre', a rather lengthy legal procedure would have to be followed, in order to secure the necessary permission to dig on the church grounds by the authorities. Meanwhile, the focus is on preservation of the building, and not on excavation, at this time.[38]

This basically means that as there are important existing gravestones around the chapel, one cannot simply start digging up graves, so to speak. This is why there is a law of the 'Right of Sepulchre', so that graves and kirkyards will not be disturbed. Much work needs to be done on the chapel itself at the present time in order to save it from further damage and also to preserve it for posterity, Mr Beattie says, adding that this obviously must be the priority of Rosslyn Chapel Trust. He further says that perhaps at some future point, they *may* put forth a challenge to the legal hurdle of the 'Right of Sepulchre' in order to obtain the proper legal permission that would be needed to begin a professional excavation. But this is clearly not likely to be anytime soon, Mr Beattie believes, as the emphasis is necessarily on preservation of the building.[39]

So speculation will undoubtedly continue, as no immediate plans for excavation exist.

Rosslyn Castle as a medieval scriptorium

Rosslyn Castle was also a medieval scriptorium, which does not seem to be widely acknowledged or understood today, as most of the focus has been on the chapel itself. A scriptorium is where medieval manuscripts were manufactured with great care and this process took much time, skill and attention.

Five St Clair manuscripts are in the National Library of Scotland and each one bears one or more St Clair signatures. The booklet *Rosslyn: A History*, by Robert Brydon, explains this situation:

> One of these is a giant compendium mostly written by James Mangnet in 1488. Commissioned by William St Clair (for his inscription appears as that of first owner), the 1,000 hand-written pages contain significantly: GUILD LAWS, FOREST LAWS, and 'THE LAWIS AND CUSTUMIS OF YE SCHIPPIS'. Legalities all vital to the Scottish Operative Guilds! A work also necessary for the legal guidance of their hereditary Patrons, Protectors and Arbitrators; the St Clairs of Rosslyn.[40]

In addition to the Guild, Forest and Shipping Laws, this manuscript – the Rosslyn-Hay manuscript – also contains a section entitled *The Buk of the Order of Knighthede* (The Book of the Order of Knighthood). *The Rosslyn-Hay manuscript is the earliest extant work in Scottish prose.*[41]

He further informs the reader in greater detail about the scriptorium at Rosslyn Castle, and about the Rosslyn-Hay manuscript:

> ...according to its inscription, Gilbert Hay, knight, carried out the translation and produced the three part folio on the instructions of William Sanctclare of Rosslyn. A small panel (PATRICUS LOWES ME LIGAVIT), integral to the leather binding, indicates that the binder was Patrick de Lowis, a burgher of Rosslyn who died in 1466. The heavily worked leather binding is recognised as the most important example of its kind in the British Isles.[42]

Obviously the Rosslyn scriptorium was very important. But this is only one of the many manuscripts now have been be associated with Rosslyn. In recent years, for example, another medieval manuscript in the Bodleian Library at Oxford University was found to have been made at Rosslyn Castle.

Mr Brydon continues about the Rosslyn scriptorium:

> Paper-makers, translators, and scribes, such as the recently iden-
> tified James Gray, were certainly part of the manuscript manu-
> factory attached to the great library at Rosslyn Castle which was
> looted in the 17th century. It is now understood that in the trans-
> lation and reproduction of important manuscripts, Rosslyn
> could be compared with Anjou in France. (Some of the works
> produced at Rosslyn are known to have originated at Anjou).[43]

This indicates that Rosslyn had connections on the Continent
as well, and with the illustrious house of Anjou, another fascinating
subject in its own right.

One local tale about Rosslyn Castle tells of a great fire which
gutted the castle in 1441, after a premonition. Sir William was
said to have been beside himself thinking that his precious books
and scrolls had been destroyed, but, as the account relates, the
trustworthy chaplain had lowered a trunk full of manuscripts
from the window thus saving them for posterity, much to the relief
of Sir William. Father Hay tell us:

> The news of this fire coming to the Prince's ears, through the
> lamentable cries of the ladies and gentlewomen, and the sight
> thereof coming to his view... upon the College Hill (the site of
> the chapel) he was sorry for nothing but the loss of his Charters
> and other writings; but when the Chaplain, who had saved him-
> self by coming down the bell-rope tied to a beam, declared how
> his Charters and writs were all saved, he became cheerful, and
> went to recomfort his princess and the ladies... and rewarded his
> chaplain very richly. Yet all this stayed him not from the build-
> ing... neither his liberality to the poor, but was more liberal to
> them than before, applying the safety of his Charters and writ-
> ings to God's particular Providence.[44]

Many writers speculate that the purpose of the Chapel was to
house this knowledge, but whether there are scrolls or manuscripts under the chapel remains to be seen.

Speculation about Rosslyn does not stop with the chapel or the
castle, however. Regarding possible biblical parallels with Roslin,
there are features of the landscape in and around Rosslyn that are
metaphorical and that parallel the biblical Valley of Kidron.
Strangely enough, from a mythical landscape standpoint, there do

seem to be a few parallels to the Old Testament Valley of Kidron with the topography of the land around Rosslyn. Authors Knight and Lomas mention this and go even further, actually declaring that 'we found that the area appeared to have been selected because it reflected the topology of Jerusalem. To the east lies Scotland's own Kidron Valley and in the south runs the Valley of Hinnon.'[45] It is also true that Rosslyn Chapel has a fair amount of Old Testament imagery in it.

The Valley of Kidron is mentioned in the Bible, and is located to the south and east of Jerusalem. It is also called the Valley of Joshoshaphat. The river Esk at Roslin is situated not unlike the river Kidron. It was here, near a stream of water, that the Israelites defeated the Ephrimites, in the Valley of Joshoshaphat. As some have pointed out, at Roslin during the Scottish wars of independence, the Scots defeated the English in a single day at the Battle of Roslin (1302/3) and it was said that the Esk 'ran red for days', a battle metaphor.

At Kidron, there is the Temple on top of the hill, just like the Chapel is situated at the top of the hill at Roslin. These are the more verifiable parallels, mythic as they are, yet, although they may seem strange to us today, they are interesting to note, given that much of Rosslyn Chapel is about metaphor, allegory and symbolism. This is especially true when attempting to better understand the founder of Rosslyn Chapel and his vision.

More about Freemasonry and 'King Solomon's Temple'

Scottish Masonic traditions hold the St Clairs as the hereditary masters and patrons of the craft. Archibald D. Orr Ewing, Grand Master Mason, Grand Lodge of Scotland, states in a recent publication:

> Scottish Freemasonry has a long, well documented history from as early as 1598. The connection of Scottish masons with the St Clairs of Roslin began, at least, from c.1601 when the masons of Scotland petitioned William, Earl of Roslin (c.1580-c.1628) to again become their 'patron and protector'. This, known as the

'First St Clair Charter', implies that there was an earlier association with the Scottish masons and the St Clair family. It can only be speculation that this commenced c.1446 with the building of Rosslyn Chapel. c.1628, the Scottish masons petitioned the Earl's son, also William (?-1650) and this 'Second St Clair Charter' is a similar appeal. Both of these precious documents are the property of the Grand Lodge of Scotland and are held in the Library at Freemason's Hall, 96 George Street, Edinburgh. After a gap of over 100 years, the connection with the family was re-established in 1736 when yet another William St Clair of Roslin (1700-1778) became the first Grand Master Mason of the newly created Grand Lodge...[46]

The St Clair (Sinclair) family clearly has a long history regarding Freemasonry in Scotland. At Kilwinning, it is said that in the past, once a year, an assembly was held where William St Clair sat in judgement of the craftsmen and any disputes were resolved as in the manner of the wise King Solomon.

The First St Clair Charter, attributed to Schaw and dated about 1601/2, links the St Clairs of Roslin to the Scottish Craft, and acknowledges the St Clairs of Roslin as the hereditary patrons and protectors of the Scottish Craft, having been so 'from adge to adge'.[47] This letter from the 'freemen of masons'[48] of 1602 was sent to the Sir William St Clair of that day, and was then followed up by another to his son, also Sir William, in 1628. In this letter of 1628, there is mention of an original charter that was granted to the founder of the chapel. The document suggests that the original, said to have been destroyed in a fire, was granted to Sir William St Clair, the founder of Rosslyn Chapel. As protector and patron of the Crafts in Scotland, Sir William's extraordinary chapel epitomises the St Clair family motto: 'Commit thy Work to God', and as a tribute to the medieval craftsmen who built it.

The Second St Clair Charter reads as follows:

... as from adge to adge, it has been observed amongst us and our predecessors, that the Lairds of Roslin has ever been patrons and protectors of us and our privileges, likeas our predecessors has obeyed, reverenced, and acknowledged them as patrons and protectors, whereof they had letters of protection and other rights granted be his Majestie's most noble progenitors of worthy, whilk with sundrie uthir of the Lairds of Roslins, his wreats, being consumed in ane flame of fire, within the castle of Roslin, anno... the consumation and burning thereof being clerly known to us and our predecessors...[49]

Although the actual date was not recorded on this 1628 document itself, it is known that it refers to the time of James II and to Sir William St Clair. The point here is rather obvious – that the St Clairs of Roslin had been the hereditary heads of the Masons in Scotland since the 15th C. Of course, as stated above, this is speculation, as the original was destroyed in a fire. But this was a time when the trade incorporations were beginning to flourish under the Stuarts and they were granted many royal privileges. If the earlier original charter actually existed, it means that William Schaw in 1598 reorganised a network that had already been established for at least a century and a half under the St Clairs of Rosslyn.

One of the oldest Masonic lodges in Scotland, if not the oldest, is Lodge Kilwinning, as we learned about in chapter 8. It holds to the tradition that:

> ...when James II was crowned King of Scotland in 1437 he passed over the office of Grand Master, in perpetuity, to Sir William St Clair, Earl of Orkney and Caithness, and Baron of Roslin, and to his successors, to the Barony of Roslin. For close on 300 years, the Barons of Roslin held the Office of Grand Master of the Scottish Lodges and in this time, they regularly assembled their Grand Lodges in Kilwinning.[50]

These important Charters provided the Grand Lodge of Scotland with an early tradition that the premier Grand Lodge of England did not possess. But, of course, Masonic scholars around the world are still debating these matters today. Some Masons believe, however, that the Scottish Craft at the time may not have actually known of the *full* tradition, and that maybe not all of the tradition actually got passed down, even to the Sinclairs. The William Sinclair who became Grand Master Mason of Scotland in 1736 found Rosslyn Chapel in bad condition at the time, and from then on, saw to it that necessary repairs were made to the building. It was another wise and learned man in the tradition of King Solomon that helped preserve what we have today.

Hiram Abiff story

The Hiram Abiff story in Freemasonry is believed to have parallels with the tale of the 'murdered Apprentice' carving at Rosslyn Chapel. Lewis Spence suggests that Hiram Abiff, the principal architect of Solomon's Temple, is the blueprint for the 'apprentice story' at Rosslyn, stating:

> ...the legend of the pillar bears a certain resemblence to that, so familiar to Freemasons, which tells of the assassination of Hiram Abiff, the architect of the Temple of Solomon, who was slain by his jealous underlings because of his superior skill in the builder's art. He also was done to death by a mallet, and was probably the artificer of the two marvellous pillars Jachin and Boaz, which stood at the entrance to the Temple. It seems not improbable that the Hebrew story came to be attached in some manner by the men of the mason's craft to the church at Roslin.[51]

The theme of sacrifice is clearly evident here. Hiram, in a show of unshaken fidelity as he will not reveal his builder's secrets to the uninitiated, is murdered, but he can also be seen to have nobly sacrificed his own life, rather than disclose them. Reminiscent of the biblical story of Abraham and Isaac, such allegorical tales about sacrifice contain profound spiritual truths and teach of a spiritual life which we all potentially possess, but which is much greater than mundane, everyday life.

What is rather intriguing about this link is the fact that the Hiramic legend is supposed to have been first associated with Freemasonry in Anderson's *Constitutions* (1723) and the legend that became associated with the third degree of Freemasonry was a development thought to have first appeared in Scotland in the year 1726.[52] It would appear that the story, if genuine, of the 'murdered Apprentice' at Rosslyn predates this, as some believe.

Or perhaps even more accurately, the original carving – that of a bearded Master and not an apprentice – at Rosslyn Chapel would definitely have predated this, as Rosslyn was built beginning in 1446.

In another unusual link, the Masonic/Hebrew legend states that the Temple was left incomplete because of the death of the principal architect. In 1484, Sir William St Clair, founder of Rosslyn Chapel, died, leaving his work incomplete. His son did not complete his father's work, but did finish off the Choir area that had taken nearly 40 years to build. We cannot tell for certain whether he was not particularly interested in completing the building, which would have been of enormous cost to the family, or, whether the secret of the completed design died with Sir William, the founder. If it was built to his specification alone, as has been suggested, then this may have been the case.

Could this all be 'life imitating art', as some believe, as the story of Sir William St Clair may have been somehow incorporated into an allegorical tale that had meaning to the Masons? There is certainly no mention in the orthodox versions of the biblical story of the Temple being left incomplete. If there is any foundation to this line of inquiry regarding Sir William, then Rosslyn Chapel may well represent – or have been made to look like – an allegorical 'King Solomon's Temple'.

From English Masonic lectures describing King Solomon, the following statement could, some believe, equally be applied to Sir William St Clair:

> ...he being the first Prince who excelled in Masonry, and under whose royal patronage many of our Masonic mysteries obtained their first sanction.[53]

King Solomon was described as the wisest of men in his time, which seems to also describe Sir William St Clair. Also, Sir William was a Prince of Orkney who excelled in Masonry.

Importance of allegory

Rosslyn Chapel was originally planned to be five times as large. It is interesting to note that Glasgow Cathedral's choir area has a similar construction and layout to the building at Rosslyn. We know that King Solomon's Temple was certainly not a place of worship as we understand it today, but was built as the House of YAHWEH, the House of the Lord, a House of 'the Word'. And also the place where the precious scrolls and other ritual objects would be stored. The Holy of Holies in Solomon's Temple was not entered by anyone except the High Priest and even then, only once a year.

Freemasonry by its own definition is '… a peculiar system of morality, veiled in allegory and illustrated by symbols'.[54] 'Peculiar' in its usage here means particular or specific. The symbolic use of Biblical edifices, events, peoples and places, are employed alongside the working tools of the stonemasons to illustrate moral principles.[55] The term 'allegory' is something that holds a deeper or more significant meaning beyond the literal meaning, so by its very nature, allegory is complex and multi-levelled and cannot be taken at face value alone. Nearly all profound religious and spiritual works seem to present themselves this way. For instance, Christianity uses the symbol of a cross to mean *far more* than simply a wooden cross, which is what may appear initially to the eye at face value.

Freemasonry also uses allegory as its greatest educational tool. Joseph Fort Newton in his Masonic book *The Builders* describes Masonry as:

> …a science which is engaged in the search after divine truth… Of no one age, Masonry belongs to all ages; of no one religion, it finds great truth in all religions. Indeed, it holds that truth which is common to all elevating and benign religions, and is the basis of each; that faith that underlies all sects and overarches all creeds… masonry was not made to divide men, but to unite them, leaving each man free to think his own thought and fashion his own system of ultimate truth.[56]

Today, we might think of such concepts as quite ecumenical in nature. Other western philosophical traditions, such as Rosicrucianism, Hermeticism, Alchemy and some of the medieval guilds and chivalric Orders, also valued a more ecumenical approach and used allegorical teaching methods.

The *arcanum in stone* that Rosslyn Chapel is, contains much imagery that is not purely Christian, in common with many other medieval churches. It is interesting to note that in medieval building traditions, it is *the northeast stone* that is laid first and which is considered to be the foundation stone for the structure. The 'laying of the foundation stone' is a very important allegorical concept in the Old Testament, Freemasonry, and the medieval Knights Templar.

Son of the Widow theme

In the Hiram Abiff legend, the master builder Hiram is referred to as the 'son of a widow'. Among the carvings in Rosslyn Chapel, traditional guidebook descriptions point out the head of the 'Apprentice', the head of the 'Master' who is said to have killed him, and the head of the 'grieving Mother' of the Apprentice. The Apprentice himself, like Hiram Abiff, is called the 'son of a widow'.

> Freemasons refer to themselves as Sons of the Widow, a term used in Masonic traditions as a title that was attributed to Hiram, the principal architect at the building of Solomon's Temple. 'It is perhaps curious to note that the mother of Jesus is traditionally reported to have comported herself as a widow after the miraculous conception.'[57]

The implication is that Christ is also a 'Son of the Widow'. In Egyptian mythology, Horus is also described in a similar fashion, and many peoples from all over the world also have this motif in their mythologies. Even Merlin was called 'a Son of the Widow' in some of the Arthurian stories, as we saw in chapter 6. JS Ward, a Masonic author, writes about other links to the 'Son of the Widow' theme:

> The title survived not only among Masons, but in the Graal legends where Perceval is called the 'Son of the Widow Lady', and it would be possible to compile quite a list of 'Questing Heroes', who are similarly called 'Sons of the Widow.'[58]

This 'Son of the Widow' theme is clearly of a universal nature and goes back many centuries. It is also interesting to note that Rosslyn Chapel was built beginning in 1446. This is approximately 134 years after the official dissolution of one Order by papal bull, the medieval Knights Templar (1312) and about 290 years before the official formation of the other, the Grand Lodge of Scotland, in 1736. So, this has added to the speculation by some that Rosslyn Chapel may have been built with one or both of these traditions in mind.

'Treasure' is spiritual

The St Clairs of Rosslyn also appear to have had a relationship with certain medieval Guilds in Edinburgh and also with certain Orders of Knighthood. Mr Robert Brydon asks, regarding the Rosslyn-Hay manuscript and *The Buk of the Order of Knighthede* it contains:

> As hereditary judges, or 'Grand Masters' administering Guild Laws, did the hereditary St Clair mandate extend over other Orders or fraternities such as those of Knighthood? This has always remained an unanswered question.[59]

Like many issues regarding Rosslyn, there continue to be many unanswered and unresolved questions such as this one. Experts do not always agree, and it seems that there will always be room for even more speculation, for better or worse, until the vaults are excavated and the truth is known for certain. But perhaps the 'treasure' isn't a material one at all? We believe that the 'treasure' – real or not – is and always was ultimately spiritual, in any case.

As Tim Wallace-Murphy and Marilyn Hopkins point out in *Rosslyn*:

> Many medieval castles are rumoured to contain buried treasure and Roslin is no exception. A persistent local legend speaks of an enormous treasure whose hiding place will not be revealed until the day when a trumpet blast shall awaken from her long sleep 'a certain Lady of the ancient house of St Clair'. Yet one man with a profound knowledge of Templarism, Michael Bentine, when interviewed at Rosslyn in 1994 was dismissive of tales of treasure. In his view, the real treasure of Rosslyn was the spirituality that can be felt there. He was convinced that the Templars had access to great secrets and that the eventual opening of the vaults of Rosslyn would disclose important documentation.[60]

So in addition to Christians, the modern-day Freemasons, Templars, and Rosicrucians have also found Rosslyn Chapel to be an important place for a variety of reasons, as do many others. The point is that it is the *spiritual* search that is important, not material objects per se. And even if any material objects are eventually found, such as the Holy Rood or scrolls, for instance, an important question would also be: what is their relevance in spiritual terms?

The New World and Prince Henry Sinclair

The search for the New World was begun in very early times, with the Vikings and others. Even before Rosslyn Chapel itself was built, the Sinclairs were involved in the search for the New World. Prince Henry Sinclair, Earl of Orkney, set off on a voyage of discovery for a great new country and dropped anchor in Guysborough Harbour, Nova Scotia, on 2 June 1398. From there, he is believed to have also gone on to Massachusetts – 94 years *before* Columbus was said to have discovered the New World. Andrew Sinclair in *The Discovery of the Grail* comments about Prince Henry and his voyage:

> ... he was also the Lord of Orkney and the Shetlands, the axis of transatlantic trade... in 1398, Prince Henry St Clair set out with a large expedition of soldiers and monks to establish two colonies in the New World; one at Louisburg in Nova Scotia... and another at Newport, Rhode Island. The notorious round tower on a hill there, with its 8 arches in the manner of the original Church of the Holy Sepulchre...[61]

Also, at Westford, Massachusetts, is a worn carving of what is believed by experts to be a medieval knight in effigy, dated to the latter half of the 14th C. These matters are still being studied today, and more information about this research can be obtained from books and the Clan Sinclair website. Frederick Pohl in *Prince Henry Sinclair* tells us a bit more about the Westford knight carving:

> The long sword with large wheel pommel is of a late fourteenth-century type. It is a Scottish claymore of 1350-1400... Armorial scholars say that the basinet is of a form that was in fashion for only twenty-five years, from 1375 to 1400...[62]

So as the late 14th C is obviously *before* the time of Columbus, one is inclined to ask: what, then, is it doing in Massachusetts? And who might it represent?

Also in Rosslyn Chapel there are specific carvings that are known to be representations of New World plants, such as aloe and maize. As Rosslyn was built beginning in 1446, again, this would be before Columbus is said to have discovered – or, perhaps more accurately, 're-discovered' – America.

Many intriguing questions remain, of course, and more research is still being done on these issues. Also of interest is the theory that other 'heretical' groups fleeing persecution in Europe, such as the Cathars or the Rosicrucians, may have also possibly left their mark in the New World in some way. Pennsylvania, for example, has several early communities that claim German Rosicrucian origin.

Rosslyn took 40 years to build, so it was not completed as we know it today until 1486. But two years earlier, in 1484, two illustrious people were said to have died: one, is the founder of Rosslyn Chapel, Sir William St Clair, and the other, is the mythical Christian Rosencreutz.

Christian Rosencreutz, the Rosicrucians, and the year 1484

The Rosicrucian traditions of medieval times adapted, spread, and grew in accordance with the interest in Hermetic subjects, all of which greatly flourished amongst the learned in the 17th and 18th centuries. The alchemical schools of Europe used the symbol of the Rosy Cross (or Rose Croix) and 'evolved a complex philosophical symbolism which incorporated elements of the old Operative Craft Guild mystery traditions.'[63]

The Rosicrucian movement first officially surfaced in 1614 in Kassel, Germany, with the publication of *Fama Fraternitatis, des Löblichen Ordens des Rosenkreutzes* (The Declaration of the Worthy Order of the Rosy Cross). The *Fama* revealed the existence of a fraternity said to have been founded by one Christian Rosencreutz. He was believed to have lived in the 14th and 15th centuries and to have travelled extensively in the East, returning to Europe with this new inspiring wisdom and knowledge. Members of the Rosicrucian movement were secretive, i.e. incognito, and were said to travel about healing the sick, and inspiring others with their special knowledge.

Upon the death of the founder, Christian Rosencreutz, in 1484, his place of burial was kept a secret. But recently, said the *Fama*, the burial vault of Christian Rosencreutz had been found by the new brotherhood of Rosicrucians, and that this symbolised the beginning of a New Age for humanity. Naturally, this unusual publication stimulated much discussion and debate at the time, the early 17th C.

Often simplistically thought of as a 'Protestant movement', as it advocated freedom of thought and speech at the time, the Rosicrucian manifestos actually only had a few Catholic adversaries once they were published, the bulk of them being other Protestants! But nonetheless, the manifestos were certainly the talk of Europe at the time. The author of the *Fama* and other important Rosicrucian tracts is reputed to have been Johann Valentin Andreae (1586-1654) a learned, influential German Protestant pastor from Tübingen.

Christian Rosencreutz, according to the *Fama*, is buried in a vault with perpetual lamps in his tomb and a mysterious book, M, is also buried with him. His tomb is rediscovered after 120 years by the Rosicrucians, and when the vault is opened, it is all ablaze with the light from the ever burning lamps. Researcher Christopher McIntosh, an expert on the Rosicrucians, says that 'in Rosicrucian legend, it is the Brotherhood which reawakens, while its founder, although ostensibly dead, remains undecayed as a symbol of his undecaying influence through his followers'.[64] So, the opening of his tomb was symbolic of the beginning of a New Age for all.

Sir William St Clair, of course, was a very cultured intellectual and an initiate of the Order of the Golden Fleece. It is interesting to note that this order, the most prestigious Order of Knighthood in Europe at the time, was founded on 10 January 1429, only 17 years before the foundation of Rosslyn Chapel. It was started by the Duke of Burgundy.

In 1604, Rosicrucian traditions say that the vault was opened and the uncorruptable body of the founder, Christian Rosencreutz, was said to be preserved intact and the book of wisdom still with him. Some Rosicrucian traditions also state that:

> At some far distant time, Rozenkreuz, wearing a white linen coat, girded crosswise with a broad red band and four red roses in his hat, made his way to a strange castle. On arrival he wit-

nessed a Royal marriage and was invested with '*The Order of the Golden Fleece*'. His curiosity led him to a secret chamber where he found Venus asleep on a bed, and, in the Castle library, the '*King's secret books of wisdom*', which he obtained.[65]

Rosslyn parallels with Rosicrucian legends

Rosslyn mythic parallels with the Rosicrucian legends are interesting, given that Sir William St Clair, the principal architect of Rosslyn Chapel, also died in 1484, the same year as the mythical Christian Rosencreutz is said to have died. After St Clair's death, work on Rosslyn Chapel was left unfinished, as his son does not appear to have wished to spend the tremendous amount of money it would have taken to complete it at the time. But other possible mythic or legendary parallels, although purely speculative of course, are interesting in this case.

To clarify these legends even further: *Christian Rosencreutz* died in 1484 and was said to have travelled afar and had been involved in various esoteric traditions. He was said to have been an initiate of the Order of the Golden Fleece, and was buried with the mysterious book 'M', in a tomb all ablaze with ever-burning lamps. The Rosicrucian legend speaks of secrets hidden in his tomb which are to be released to the world 120 years after his death, i.e. in about 1604. When his tomb is opened, the body was said to be in perfect condition, and there is also a tale about Venus and a great library.

Sir William St Clair died in 1484, was said to have travelled afar and was deeply versed in many Knightly and philosophical traditions. He was also an initiate of the Order of the Golden Fleece, was said to have been buried with a candle, a book and with knell, (Sir Walter Scott) and there was already an existing Sinclair tradition of the chapel being all ablaze or glowing when a St Clair died (Slezer). Freemasonry, arguably, is established in Scotland under Schaw who acknowledges the St Clairs of Rosslyn as their hereditary patrons (St Clair Charters), it is said, and this occurred around 1601-3. An historical statement by Slezer (1693) reports that after fourscore years, the bodies of the Barons of

Rosslyn lay as fresh as when they were first buried. Rosslyn Castle also has a persistent local legend about a ghostly white lady and the great library of Rosslyn.

Possible links, if any, between Masonic philosophy and Rosicrucianism have long been debated, so this example is but one of many. It may also be worthy of note that one of the more recent Earls of Rosslyn had railings placed in the interior of the chapel. Although seemingly a small detail, and perhaps a coincidence, some have nonetheless noticed that these railings are pointed and have the St Clair engrailed cross on them, with a rose placed in the middle of the cross, a very similar emblem to the Rosy Cross of the Rosicrucian tradition.

Sir John Clerk of Penicuik

Near the village of Roslin there are also other important places, such as the villages of Penicuik, Temple, Cranston, etc. Sir John Clerk of Penicuik was also a very learned and cultured man. Like many educated men of his time, the 18th C, he was very gifted in many fields, including law, agriculture, music, poetry and scholarship of all kinds. Regarded as the most knowledgeable authority on ancient Roman archaeology in his time, much of his collection can still be seen today in the National Museum of Scotland in Edinburgh.

Although not always included in the conventional accounts of his life, he was especially known to have been very knowledgeable about certain esoteric matters at the time. He was a Freemason prior to the official beginning of the Grand Lodge of Scotland (1736), as he had joined St Mary's Chapel No. 1 in 1710, and he was also one of the architects of the 1707 Treaty of Union. Sir John also a member of the Society of Antiquaries, the Royal Society and the Gentlemen's Club of Spalding.

Sir John lived in the elegant Penicuik House, not far from Rosslyn Chapel. During the summer of 1739, he had a visitor named Mr Gale; the following account describes how Sir John Clerk persuaded Lord Sinclair to completely restore the chapel:

Baron Clerk and the Restoration of Rosslyn Chapel:

...Gale visited Scotland in the autumn of 1739... In [his] letter to Maurice Johnston, dated... 18 Aug. 1739, he mentions that he was at Penicuik House, and twice at Mavisbank; and he further gives such particulars as enable us to add to the list of the Baron's good deeds the preservation of Rosslyn Chapel, that richest example of Gothic Scotland.

Gale writes: 'We were twice at Mavisbank, four miles to the south of Edenborough, built by Sir John Clerk, in true Palladio style, one of the most elegant I ever saw, for situation, wood, and water, though the house is small. We went four miles farther to another seat of Sir John's that is called Pennycuick (*Mons cuculi*), built in the ancient style, but not without its natural beauties, particularly a vast pond or lake, with two islands in it, and full of fish.

In the way to it we saw Roslin-chapel, a most noble Gothic structure, exceeded by few: founded, as appears by an inscription cut the whole length of the windows, by Sir William Sinclair, Earl of Orkney and Zetland, AD 1453. It has laid open to the weather ever since the Reformation, but has withstood all its effects, by the goodness of the materials, and the excellency of its work to a miracle; however, the rain now penetrating through the roof, which is vaulted with stone, would have in a few years have dissolved it entirely, had not that true lover of antiquities and all the liberal arts, Sir John Clerk, persuaded the present Lord Sinclair to put it to complete repair. The workmen have been upon it all this summer, and as Sir John has the whole direction of it, in a year more it will not be only secured from ruin, but be made as beautiful and stately as most of that sort of edifices in the kingdom.[66]

This excerpt also gives us a bit of an impression of life involving Penicuik House at the time, the 18th C.

Sir John Clerk was also the great-grandson of William Drummond of Hawthornden, who is highly regarded for his literary pursuits and who was a personal friend of Ben Jonson, the Poet Laureate of England in Shakespeare's time. Drummond was also mentioned in the last chapter for prompting Henry Adamson of Perth to print his unusual poem, the *Muses Threnodie*, in 1636, which was the first mention of the 'Mason's Word'.

Three years after Sir John Clerk assisted Lord Sinclair in the renovation of Rosslyn Chapel, he also built some unusual features in Penicuik House and a most unusual cave on his estate. 'Hurley's Cove', as it is called, is a small tunnel hewed out of the sandstone through the side of a small hill, and contains a small room halfway down its length. The room, which was known to have been used for ritualistic purposes involving astronomical calculations, has, among other things, a very peculiar inscription carved on the wall. In his memoirs, Sir John Clerk says, 'This year I made the antique cave at Hurley where I had made a large pond... this rural scheme... adds a good deal of beauty to the enclosures of Penicuik House, as it resembles the Grotto of Pausilipo at Naples.'[67] The Grotto of Pausilipo at Naples is thought to have been the work of Virgil, whose tomb is not far away.

John Slezer in his *Theatrum Scotiae* (1693) also wrote of Rosslyn Chapel, and this is one of the earliest accounts of Rosslyn in existence today:

This Chapel lies in Midlothian, four miles from Edinburgh, and is one of the most curious Pieces of Workman-ship in Europe. The Foundation of this rare Building was laid Anno 1440 by William St Clair, Prince of Orkney, Duke of Holdenburgh...

A Man as considerable for the public Works which he erected, as for the Lands which he possess'd, and the Honours which were conferred upon him by several of the greatest Princes of Europe. It is remarkable that in all this Work there are not two Cuts of one sort. The most curious Part of the Building is the Vault of the Quire, and that which is called the Prince's Pillar so much talk'd of. This Chapel was possess'd by a Provost, and Seven Canons Regular, who were endued with Several considerable Revenues through the Liberality of the Lairds of Roslin.

Here lies buried George Earl of Caithness, who lived about the Beginning of the Reformation, Alexander Earl of Sutherland, great Grand-Child of King Robert de Bruce, Three Earls of Orkney, and Nine Barons of Roslin.

The last lay in a Vault, so dry that their bodies have been found intire after Fourscore Years, and as fresh as when they were first buried. There goes a Tradition, that before the Death of any of the Family of Roslin, this Chapel appears all in Fire.[68]

This excerpt is also interesting, in that it mentions nine Barons of Roslin, plus five Earls, buried at Rosslyn Chapel, and the 'Prince's Pillar', known to us today as the Apprentice Pillar.

Many authors, then and now, have been interested in visiting and writing about Rosslyn Chapel. From the 17th C, we also have the accounts of Thomas Kirk and Ralph Thoresby, from their 'Tours in Scotland 1677 and 1681'. St Catherine of Alexandria is the patron saint of the Sinclair family. In the summer of 1677, Thomas Kirk wrote about his visit to St Catherine's Well, near Rosslyn Chapel:

> On Friday 27th (July 1677) we... came to Edinburgh by Lough Levin (Lochleven) and Queen's-ferry. Here we rested ourselves till 12th August... we rode out of town two miles to St Catherine's Well, which has an oil swimming upon it, and they often dry it, and find much bituminous oil at the bottom of it, which they use for anointing little children's joints for the rickets... They say that St Catherine travelling this way with her cruise of oil, fell here and broke it, and ever since it has run with oil.[69]

Then they go on to see Rosslyn Chapel, and describe its many wonders, including the Apprentice Pillar. They say that the guide there told them about the story of the 'murdered Apprentice', and they say they saw this carving, and comment on the gash on his forehead. This occurred in 1677.

St Catherine's Balm Well is in the Liberton area of Edinburgh, and although padlocked, is still a place of pilgrimage today. Dedicated to St Catherine of Alexandria, in earlier times it was believed to be a healing well that was especially effective for skin conditions and leprosy. The water comes through oil shale and a black tarry residue floats on the surface. James IV made an offering there in 1504, and James VI refurbished it in 1617, but Cromwell's troops destroyed it in 1650. St Margaret also was known to have shown an interest in the well.

It is evident that many different groups and individuals have had their own theories about Rosslyn Chapel through the centuries, and this continues into modern times. A recent *Scotsman* newspaper article, commenting on the growing number of unusual theories in recent years, sums up how ludicrous it can all seem at times:

It has been said variously to house the mummified head of Jesus Christ, a lost gospel, the other Stone of Destiny and even the mothership. If every theory about what lies under Rosslyn Chapel in Midlothian were true, the church would sit on a mound of earth at least 150ft high.[70]

But this state of affairs is largely because of the unfortunate emphasis put by many on the material at the expense of the spiritual, and the fact that no major excavation has been done to satisfy the public one way or the other, thus leaving a gap wide open for wild speculation of all types.

Niven Sinclair, devoted patron and scholar of Rosslyn, has also wisely pointed out that it is unfortunate that humans have consistently sought only the printed word for historical 'evidence', stating that:

History can more accurately be found:

in the face of the land,
in the faces of the people we meet,
in the language(s) we speak,
in our customs, traditions, and superstitions,
in our genes because that which is born
in the bone can never be driven out of the blood.[71]

The hidden meaning of medieval symbolism, especially the exquisite carvings of Rosslyn Chapel, Chartres Cathedral, or Notre Dame, for example, is found mainly in an allegorical, *visual* way, so it does not rely only on printed interpretations. In fact, in medieval times, only a privileged few could even read or write, yet many people were able to contemplate art and symbolism, which is timeless and universal.

Much of this, in a symbolic sense, represents the true spiritual nature and potential of humanity and the quest that each of us may undergo to find this Truth. The skilled craftsmen who built these amazing edifices and those learned ones who sponsored and assisted them, have left us a silent, spiritual message to decipher. Books can be burned, paper and wood can be destroyed, but stone tends to last much longer. The complex allegory presented by Rosslyn Chapel is:

An Arcanum, a book in stone. An unfinished labour of love that lasts forever.[72]

And this is something that can never be taken away – the true spiritual meaning of Rosslyn Chapel.

But this may also be said to apply to genuine Truth itself, the real key of the Quest, perhaps best summed up by Alfred Lord Tennyson in his poem *Locksley Hall*,[73]

Knowledge comes, but Wisdom lingers…

Notes

[1] Forbes, R, *Account of Roslin Chapel*, Edinburgh, 1774, 1.

[2] Spence, L, *Mystical Roslin*, Scotland's SMT Magazine, May, 1952, 29.

[3] *Proceedings of the Society of Antiquaries*, xii, Edinburgh, 1877-8, 223.

[4] Earl of Rosslyn, *Rosslyn Chapel*, Official Guidebook, Rosslyn Chapel Trust, Roslin, Midlothian, 1997, 2.

[5] Ibid.

[6] Ibid.

[7] Encyclopedia Britannica CD 98, CD Rom, 1998.

[8] Brydon, R, op cit, 9.

[9] Ibid.

[10] Stein, W J, *The British, their Psychology and Destiny*, Temple Lodge Press, London, 1990, 28.

[11] Ibid, 29-30.

[12] Earl of Rosslyn, op cit. 2.

[13] Grant, W, *Rosslyn: Its Chapel, Castle, and Scenic Lore*, Edinburgh, 1936, 37.

[14] Harding, M, *A Little Book of the Green Man*, Aurum Press, London, 1998, 58.

[15] Harte, J, *The Green Man*, Pitkin Unichrome Ltd, Andover, Hampshire, 2001, 1.

[16] Baigent, M, and Leigh, R, *The Temple and the Lodge*, Little Brown, New York, 1989, 118.

[17] MacRitchie, D, *Scottish Gypsies Under the Stewarts*, Edinburgh, 1894, 57.

[18] Ibid, 58.

[19] Mill, A J, *Medieval Plays in Scotland*, St. Andrews University publ.'s, No. xxiv, Wm. Blackwood & Sons Ltd, Edinburgh and London, 1927, 23-5.

[20] Murray, R, *The Gypsies of the Border*, T.F. Brockie, Galashiels, 1875, 1.

21 Hopkins, M, Simmans, G, and Wallace-Murphy, T, *Rex Deus*, Element Books, Shaftesbury, 2000, 240-1.
22 Brydon, R, *Rosslyn: A History of the Guilds, the Masons, and the Rosy Cross*, Rosslyn Chapel Trust, Roslin, 1994, 2.
23 Armstrong, R, *Old Ballads of England and Scotland*, London, 1909, 125.
24 Gould, R F, *The History of Freemasonry*, vol. I, London, 1887, 6.
25 Ibid.
26 Earl of Rosslyn, op cit, 27.
27 Kirk, T, & Thoresby, R, *Tours in Scotland 1677 and 1681*, [Ed.] P. Hume Brown, Edinburgh, 1892, 41-2.
28 Laidler, K, *The Head of God*, Weidenfeld & Nicolson, London, 1998, 276.
29 Ibid, 263.
30 Cooper, R, 'Rosslyn Chapel: The Faces of Robert the Bruce', *The Ashlar*, Issue 11, Circle publications, Helensburgh, 2000, 39.
31 Ibid, 40.
32 Munro, J, 'Rosslyn Chapel: Part 4: Inside and Around', *The Ashlar*, Issue 4, Circle publications, Helensburgh, 1998, 22.
33 Brydon, R, op cit, back page.
34 Pelikan, J, [Ed.], *Sacred Writings, Christianity: The Apocrypha and the New Testament*, Quality paperback Book Club, NY, 1992, xi.
35 Knight, C, and Lomas, R, *The Hiram Key*, Century, London, 1996, 321.
36 Earl of Rosslyn, op cit, 37.
37 Slezer, J, *Theatrum Scotiae*, London, 1693, 63.
38 personal communication by Rosslyn Chapel Trust Director Mr Stuart Beattie to author Dr Karen Ralls-Macleod, FSA Scot, Nov. 2000.
39 Ibid.
40 Brydon, R, op cit, 5.
41 Ibid.
42 Ibid.
43 Ibid.
44 Hay, R A, *Genealogy of the Sinclairs of Roslin*, Edinburgh, 1835, 27-8.
45 Knight and Lomas, op cit, 324.
46 Orr Ewing, A D, Grand Master Mason, 'Preface', in *An Account of the Chapel of Roslin 1778*, [Ed by Bro R L D Cooper], Grand Lodge of Scotland, Edinburgh, 2000, iii.
47 Hay, op cit, 157.
48 Ibid.
49 Ibid, 159.

50 Laughlan, Roy, MBE, JP, *The Kilwinning No. 0 Masonic Lodge in old picture postcards*, European Library, Zaltbommel/Netherlands, 1994, 2.

51 Spence, op cit, 28.

52 *The Year Book of the Grand Lodge of Antient Free and Accepted Masons of Scotland*, Edinburgh, 1991, 46.

53 *The Lectures in Craft Masonry*, Emulation working, London, 1919, 4.

54 Wells, R, *Understanding Freemasonry*, (audiotape 10), Recorded Talks, Q.C.C.C, London, 1989.

55 The United Grand Lodge of England, *The Freemasons*, VHS video, Aspen Spafax Television, 1987.

56 Newton, J F, *The Builders*, Unwin Brothers Ltd, Woking, 1934, 173.

57 MacKenzie, K, *Royal Masonic Cyclopaedia*, Aquarian, Wellingborough, 1987 ed of 877 orig.), 682.

58 Ward, J S M, *Who Was Hiram Abiff?*, Lewis Masonic publications, Plymouth, 1992, 235.

59 Brydon, R, op cit, 18.

60 Wallace-Murphy, T, and Hopkins, M, *Rosslyn*, Element Books, Shaftesbury, 1999, 198.

61 Sinclair, A, *The Discovery of the Grail*, Random House, London, 1998, 247.

62 Pohl, F J, *Prince Henry Sinclair: His Expedition to the New World* in 1398, Nimbus, Halifax, N.S, no year listed, reprint of 1969 orig, 163.

63 Brydon, R, op cit, 18.

64 McIntosh, C, *The Rosicrucians*, Thorsons, Wellingborough, 1987 rev. ed of 1980 orig, 33.

65 Brydon, R, op cit, 18.

66 Sir John Clerk, *Memoirs of Sir John Clerk of Penicuik*, Edinburgh, 1893, 250.

67 Ibid.

68 Slezer, J, *Theatrum Scotiae*, London, 1693, 63.

69 Kirk, T, and Thoresby, R, *Tours in Scotland 1677 and 1681*, [Ed by Hume Brown, P], Edinburgh, 1892, 41-2.

70 Hannan, M, *Scotsman* newspaper, Edinburgh, 14 September 1998.

71 Personal communication by Niven Sinclair to author Dr Karen Ralls-MacLeod, Dec. 1999.

72 Brydon, R, op cit, back page.

73 Flower, D A, *The Shores of Wisdom: The Story of the Ancient Library of Alexandria*, Pharos Publications, Ramsey, Isle of Man, 1999, 9.

Bibliography

Adam, J, [Ed], *The Declaration of Arbroath*, Herald Press, Arbroath, 1993

Aitchison, N, *Scotland's Stone of Destiny*, Tempus, Stroud, 2000

Alcock, L, *The Neighbours of the Picts: Angles, Britons, and Scots at war and at home*, Dornoch, 1993

Allen, P M, and Allen, J, *Fingal's Cave*, the poems of Ossian and Celtic Christianity, Continuum, New York, 1999

Anderson, A O, *Scottish Annals from English Chroniclers, AD500-1286*, Edinburgh, 1908

Anderson, M O, 'Lothian and the Early Scottish Kings', *The Scottish Historical Review*, Vol. XXXIX, Thomas Nelson & Sons, Edinburgh, 1960

Anderson, M O, *Kings and Kingship in Early Scotland*, Edinburgh, 1980

Anderson, M O, [Ed], *A Scottish Chronicle known as the Chronicle of Holyrood*, with add. Notes by Anderson, A O, Scottish History Society, Edinburgh, 1938

Armit, I, *Celtic Scotland*, Historic Scotland, B T Batsford, London, 1997

Armit, I, *Scotland's Hidden History*, Tempus, Stroud, 1998

Armstrong, R, *Old Ballads of England and Scotland*, London, 1909

Ashe, G, *The Discovery of King Arthur*, Henry Holt & Co, New York, 1985

Ashe, G, *King Arthur's Avalon: The Story of Glastonbury*, London, 1974

Baigent, M and Leigh, R, *The Temple and the Lodge*, Little Brown & Co, New York, 1989

Bannerman, J, 'The Scottish takeover of Pictland and the relics of Columba', *Spec Scotorum: Hope of Scots*, Ed by D. Broun & T. Clancy, T & T Clark, Edinburgh, 1999

Barber, E, *The Mummies of Urumchi*, Macmillan, London, 1999

Barber, R, *The Figure of Arthur*, Longman, London, 1972

Barber, R, *The Knight and Chivalry*, Boydell & Brewer, Woodbridge, Suffolk, 1995 rev. ed. Of 1970 orig.

Barbour, J, *The Bruce*, Edinburgh, 1997

Barnett, T R, *Scottish Pilgrimage*, John Grant, Edinburgh, 1942

Barrow, G W S, *Robert Bruce*, 3rd ed., Edinburgh, 1988

Barrow, G W S, 'The Clergy in the War of Independence', *The Kingdom of the Scots: Gov't., Church, and Society from the 11th to the 14th century*, London, 1973

Barrow, G W S, *The Anglo-Norman Era in Scottish History*, Oxford Univ Press, Oxford, 1980

Begg, I, and D, *In Search of the Holy Grail and the Precious Blood*, HarperCollins, London, 1995

Bennett, M, *Scottish Customs from the Cradle to the Grave*, Edinburgh Univ Press, Edinburgh, 1992

Bertoldi, V, 'Problems of Etymology', *Zeitscrift fur Romanische Philologie*, vol. 56, London, 1936

Boece, H, *Scotorum Historiae*, Ed by J. Bellenden, 1531

Bonwick, J, *Irish Druids & Old Irish Religions*, London, 1894

Bord, J and C, *The Enchanted Land*, HarperCollins, London, 1995

Bourke, C, [Ed], *Studies in the cult of St. Columba*, Four Courts Press, Dublin, 1997

Bradley, I, *Celtic Christianity*, Edinburgh University Press, Edinburgh, 1999

Bradley, I, *The Celtic Way*, London, 1993

Bradley, R, and Thomas, J, 'Some new information on the henge monument at Maumbury Rings, Dorchester', *Proceedings of the Dorset Natural History and Archaeological Society* 106, 1985, 132-4

Bradley, R, *Altering the Earth: The Origins of Monuments in Britain and Continental Europe*, Society of Antiquaries of Scotland, Edinburgh, 1993

Bradley, R, *The Significance of Monuments*: On the Shaping of Human Experience in Neolithic and Bronze Age Europe, Routledge, London, 1998

Bradley, R, 'Deaths and Entrances: a contextual analysis of megalithic art', *Current Anthropology*, 30, 1989, 68-75

Breeze, D, *Roman Scotland: Frontier Country*, Historic Scotland, B T Batsford, London, 1996

Brooke, D, *Wild Men and Holy Places: St. Ninian, Whithorn, and the Medieval Realm of Galloway*, Canongate, Edinburgh, 1994

Brooks, C, and Bryden, I, 'The Arthurian Legacy', *The Arthur of the English*, University of Wales Press, Cardiff, 1999

Broun, D, 'Pictish Kings 761-839: Integration with Dal Riata or Separate Development?', in *The St. Andrews Sarcophagus*, Ed by S. Foster, Four Courts Press, Dublin, 1998.

Broun, D, 'The church of St. Andrews and its foundation legend in the early 12th Century: recovering the full text of version A of the foundation legend', *Kings, Clerics and Chronicles in Scotland, 500-1297*, [Ed] Simon Taylor, Four Courts Press, Dublin, 2000

Broun, D, 'The Seven Kingdoms in De situ Albanie: A record of Pictish political Geography or imaginary Map of ancient Alba?', *Alba: Celtic Scotland in the Medieval Era*, [Ed by Cowan, E J, & McDonald, R A] Tuckwell Press, East Linton, 2000

Broun, D, 'The Birth of Scottish History', *Scottish Historical Review*

Bruce-Gardyne, T, 'Tartan Truths', *Caledonia*, Edinburgh, April 2000

Bruford, A, 'What happened to the Caledonians?', *Alba: Celtic Scotland in the Medieval Era*, [Ed by E J Cowan and R Andrew McDonald], Tuckwell Press, East Linton, 2000

Brydon, R, *Rosslyn: A History of the Guilds, the Masons, and the Rosy Cross*, Rosslyn Chapel Trust, Roslin, Midlothian, 1994

Butler, E M, *The Myth of the Magus*, Cambridge University Press, Cambridge, 1948

Campbell, Rev D M, *The Campbell Collection of Gaelic Proverbs and Proverbial Sayings*, [Ed] Donald Meek, Inverness, 1978

Campbell, J G, *Superstitions of the Highlands and Islands of Scotland*, Glasgow, 1900

Campbell, J G, *Witchcraft and Second Sight in the Highlands and Island of Scotland*, Tales and traditions collected entirely from Oral Sources, Glasgow, 1902

Carley, J, 'Arthur in English History', *The Arthur of the English*, Ed by W R J Barron, University of Wales Press, Cardiff, 1999

Carmichael, A, *Carmina Gadelica*, 6 vols., Edinburgh, 1900, 1928, 1940, 1941, 1954, & 1971

Cavalli-Sforza, L L, *Genes, People, and Languages*, Penguin, Harmondsworth, 2000

Cavendish, R, *King Arthur and the Grail*, Weidenfeld & Nicolson, London, 1978

Chadwick, N, *The Age of the Saints in the Early Celtic Church*, Oxford University Press, Oxford, 1961

Chambers, R, *Domestic Annals of Scotland*, Edinburgh, 1858

Chambers, R, *Traditions of Edinburgh*, Edinburgh, 1847

Charles-Edwards, T, 'Early Medieval Kingships in the British Isles', in S Bassett [Ed] *The Origins of Anglo-Saxon Kingdoms*, Leicester, 1989

Charles-Edwards, T, 'Food, Drink and Clothing in the Laws of Court', in *The Welsh King and His Court*, [Ed by Charles-Edwards, T, Owen, M E & Russell, P], Univ of Wales Press, Cardiff, 2000

Clancy, T, and Markus, G, *Iona: The Earliest Poetry of a Celtic Monastery*, Edinburgh University Press, Edinburgh, 1995

Clancy, T O, 'Columba, Adomnan, and the cult of Saints in Scotland', *Spec Scotorum: Hope of the Scots*, [Ed by D. Broun and T. O. Clancy], T&T Clark, Edinburgh, 1999

Coe, J B And Young, S, *The Celtic Sources for the Arthurian Legend*, Llarnerch Publishers, Lampeter, 1995

Coil, H W, *Coil's Masonic Encyclopaedia*, Macoy Publishing and Masonic Supply Company, New York, 1961

Colston, J, *The Incorporated Trades of Edinburgh*, Edinburgh, 1891

Cooper, J C, *An Illustrated Encyclopedia of Traditional Symbols*, Thames and Hudson, London, 1978

Cowan, E J, 'Identity, Freedom, and the Declaration of Arbroath', in *Image and Identity: The Making and Re-making of Scotland through the Ages*, [Ed] by Broun, D, Finlay, R J, & Lynch, M, John Donald, Edinburgh, 1998

Cowan, E J, 'The Invention of Celtic Scotland', *Alba: Celtic Scotland in the Medieval Era*, [Ed by Cowan, E J and McDonald, R Andrew], Tuckwell Press, East Linton, 2000

Cowan, Prof E J, *Scotland's Story*, Vol. 1, First Press Publishing, Glasgow, 1999

Crawford, B E, [Ed], *Scotland in Dark Age Europe*, St. Andrews, 1994

Crawford, B E, [Ed], *Scotland in Dark Age Britain*, St. Andrews, 1996

Crawford Smith, D, *History of the Ancient Lodge of Scoon and Perth No.3*, Edinburgh, 1898

Cruickshank, G D R, 'The Battle of Dunnichen and the Aberlemno Battle-Scene', *Alba: Celtic Scotland in the Medieval Era*, [Ed by Cowan, E J & McDonald, R Andrew], Tuckwell Press, East Linton, 2000

Cunliffe, B, *The Ancient Celts*, Oxford University Press, Oxford, 1997

Curtis, R & M, *Callanish: Stones, Moon and Sacred Landscape*, self-published, Callanish, 1994

Dames, M, *The Avebury Cycle*, Thames & Hudson, London, 1977

Darrah, J, *Paganism in Arthurian Romance*, Boydell Press, Woodbridge, Suffolk, 1994

Dawkins, P, *Arcadia*, Francis Bacon Research Trust, Upper Tysoe, 1988

Davies, N, *The Isles: A History*, Macmillan, London, 1999

Delap, D, *Celtic Saints*, Pitkin, Great Britain, 1998

de Santillana, G, and von Dechend, H, *Hamlet's Mill*: An Essay investigating the origins of human knowledge and its transmission, David R Godine, Boston, 1969

Doel, F, & G, and Lloyd, T, *Worlds of Arthur: King Arthur in History, Legend, and Culture*, Tempus, Stroud, Gloucestershire, 1998

Donaldson, Prof G, *Scottish Historical Documents,* Glasgow, 1974

Drummond, W A, *The Lodge of Melrose St. John No. 12*, Privately printed, Melrose, 1986

Dunbavin, P, *Picts and Ancient Britons: An Exploration of Pictish Origins*, Third Millennium Publishing, Nottingham, 1998

Dunford, B, *The Holy Land of Scotland*, Brigadoon, Aberfeldy, 1996

Dunning Community Council, *Historic Dunning: A Brief History of an Old Perthshire Village*, Dunning Community Council, Dunning

Earl of Rosslyn, *Rosslyn Chapel*, Official Guidebook, Rosslyn Chapel Trust, Roslin, Midlothian, 1997

Edington, C, 'Paragons and Patriots: National Identity and the Chivalric Ideal in Late-Medieval Scotland', in *Image and Identity*, [Ed] by Broun, D, Finlay, R J, & Lynch, M, John Donald, Edinburgh, 1998

Elder, I H, *Celt, Druid, and Culdee*, London, 1947

Ellis, P B, *The Druids*, Constable, London, 1994

Encyclopaedia of Catholicism, [R P McBrien, Gen Ed], HarperCollins, New York, 1995

Farmer, D H, *The Oxford Dictionary of Saints,* Second Edition, Oxford University Press, Oxford, 1987

Fawcett, R, *Dunkeld Cathedral*: A Short History and Guide, The Society of Friends of Dunkeld Cathedral, with Historic Scotland, 1990

Fawcett, R, *Scottish Abbeys and Priories*, Historic Scotland, B T Batsford, London, 1994

Feehan, F, 'Suggested Links Between Eastern and Celtic Music', *The Celtic Consciousness*, [Ed R. O'Driscoll], Celtic Arts Board of Canada, George Braziller Inc., New York, 1981

Ferguson, F, *The Identity of the Scottish Nation*, Edinburgh University Press, Edinburgh, 1998

Filbee, M, *Celtic Cornwall*, Constable, London, 1996

Finlay, R J, 'Caledonia or North Britain? Scottish Identity in the 18th Century', *Image and Identity, The Making and Re-Making of Scotland through the ages*, [Ed by Broun, D, Finlay, R J, and Lynch, M.] John Donald, Edinburgh, 1998

Flower, D A, *The Shores of Wisdom: The Story of the Ancient Library of Alexandria*, Pharos Publications, Ramsey, Isle of Man, 1999

Forbes, R, *Account of Roslin Chapel*, Edinburgh, 1774

Forsyth, K, 'Language in Pictland, spoken and written', in *Nations, Nationalism and Patriotism in the European Past*, [Ed by Bjorn, C, Grant, A, & Stringer, K J], Copenhagen, 1994

Forsyth, K, 'Some thoughts on Pictish symbols as a formal Writing System', in *The Worm, the Germ, and the Thorn: Pictish and related studies presented to Isabel Henderson*, Pinkfoot Press, Balgavies, Angus, 1997

Foster, S, 'The Picts: Quite the Darkest of Peoples in Dark Age Britain', *The Worm, The Germ, and The Thorn*, Ed by Henry, David, Pinkfoot Press, Balgavies, Angus, 1997

Foster, S, [Ed], *The St. Andrews Sarcophagus*, Four Courts Press, Dublin, 1998

Foster, S, *Picts, Gaels, and Scots*, Historic Scotland, B T Batsford, London, 1996

Gardner, L, *Bloodline of the Holy Grail*, Element, Shaftesbury, 1996

Gawler, J C, *Our Sycthian Ancestors*, Commonwealth Publishing, Utah, 1994 reprint of 1875 orig.

Gerber, P, *Stone of Destiny*, Canongate, Edinburgh, 1997

Gerritsen, W P, and van Melle, A G, *A Dictionary of Medieval Heroes*, Boydell Press, Woodbridge, Suffolk, 1998 [Engl. Transl.] From German orig., 1993

Gillies, W, 'Arthur in Gaelic Tradition, Part II: Romances and Learned Lore', *Cambridge Medieval Celtic Studies*, 3, summer 1982, Cambridge

Glennie, J S, *Arthurian Localities*, Llarnerch Publishers, Lampeter, 1994 reprint of 1869 orig.

Goetinck, G, *Peredur: A Study of Welsh Tradition in the Grail Legends*, Univ of Wales Press, Cardiff, 1975

Goodrich, N, *King Arthur*, Harper & Row, New York, 1986

Goodrich, N, *Merlin*, Harper & Row, New York, 1988

Goodrich, N, *The Holy Grail*, HarperCollins, New York, 1992

Gould, R F, *The History of Freemasonry*, 5 vols, London, 1887

Grand Lodge of Scotland, *Historical Sketch of the Grand Lodge of Antient Free & Accepted Mason of Scotland 1736-1986*, Grand Lodge of Scotland, George St., Edinburgh

Grand Lodge of Scotland, *The Year Book of the Grand Lodge of Antient Free and Accepted Masons of Scotland*, Edinburgh, 1991

Grant, A, 'The Middle Ages: the defence of independence', in Mitchison, R, [Ed], *Why Scottish History Matters*, 2nd ed., Edinburgh, 1997

Grant, W, *Rosslyn: Its Chapel, Castle, and Scenic Lore*, Edinburgh, 1936

Green, M, & Howell, R, *A Pocket Guide to Celtic Wales*, University of Wales Press, Cardiff, 2000

Green, M, *Celtic Goddesses*, British Museum Press, London, 1995

Green, M, *The World of the Druids*, Thames & Hudson, London, 1997

Griffen, T D, *Names from the Dawn of British Legend*, Llarnerch Publishers, Lampeter, 1994

Hall, M P, *The Secret Teachings of All Ages*, Philosophical Research Society, Los Angeles, 1977 ed. (of 1928 orig.)

Hall M P, *The Secret Teachings of All Ages*, an Encyclopaedic Outline of Masonic, Hermetic, Qabbalistic and Rosicrucian Symbolical Philosophy, The Philosophical Research Society, Los Angeles, 1928, CLXXVI, reprinted 1977

Hannan, M, *Scotsman* newspaper, Edinburgh, 14 September 1998

Hanson, R P C, *Saint Patrick: His origins and Career*, Oxford University Press, Oxford, 1968

Harding, M, *A Little Book of the Green Man*, Aurum Press, London, 1998

Harrison, H, *The Cauldron and the Grail*, Archives Press, Los Altos, CA, 1992

Harte, J, *The Green Man*, Pitkin Unichrome Ltd., Andover, Hampshire, 2001

Hay, R A, *Genealogy of the Sinclairs of Roslin*, Edinburgh, 1835

Hearne, T, [Ed], *Adami de Domerham Historia de Rebus Gestis Glastoniensibus*, 2 volumes, Oxford, 1727, Vol. II

Henderson, I, 'Primus Inter Pares', in *The St. Andrews Sarcophagus*, Ed by Foster, Sally, Four Courts Press, Dublin, 1998

Henebry, R, *The Life of Columbcille*, ZCP III, London, 1901

Her Majesty's Stationery Office, HMSO, *The Declaration of Arbroath-1320*, 1980.

Hodges, R C, *Exploits, Curious Anecdotes and Sketches of the most Remarkable Scottish Gypsies*, Galashiels, 1983 reprint of 1823 orig.

Horne, Bro A, 'The Saints John in the Masonic Tradition', *Transactions of the Quatuor Coronati Lodge No. 2076*, London, 1962

Howe, Linda M, Evidence of 7000-year-old Flood and Human Habitation Discovered Beneath the Black Sea, www.earthfiles.com, Nov. 2, 2000

Hughes, K, and Hamlin, A, *Celtic Monasticism*, Seabury Press, New York, 1981

Hunt, R, [Ed], *The Drolls, Traditions, and Superstitions of Old Cornwall*, 2nd series, Llarnerch Publishers, Lampeter, 1993 reprint of 1864 orig., 306.

Hutton, R, *The Stations of the Sun*, Oxford University Press, Oxford, 1996

Hutton, R, *The Triumph of the Moon*, Oxford University Press, Oxford, 1999

Innes, T, *The Civil and Ecclesiastical History of Scotland*, Spalding Club, Aberdeen, 1853

Jackson, J, *Tales of Roslin Castle*, Edinburgh, 1836.

Jacob, M C, *Living the Enlightenment: Freemasonry and Politics in 18th Century Europe*, Oxford University Press, Oxford, 1991

Jamieson, J, *A Historical Account of the Ancient Culdees of Iona*, 1811, (popular edition, reprinted 1890)

Jarman, A O H, 'The Merlin Legend and the Welsh Tradition of Prophecy', *The Arthur of the Welsh*, Ed by Bromwich, R, Jarman, A O H, and Roberts, B F, University of Wales Press, Cardiff, 1991

Jefferson, Thomas, *Declaration of Independence*, (as orig. written by Thomas Jefferson), USA, 1776, ME 1:29, Papers 1:315.

Jones, P, & Pennick, N, *A History of Pagan Europe*, Routledge, London, 1995

Jowett, G F, *The Drama of the Lost Disciples*, Covenant, London, 1996 ed., of 1961 orig.

Jung, E, & von Franz, M-L, *The Grail Legend*, Princeton University Press, Princeton, NJ, 2nd edition, 1970 [Engl. Transl. by C G Jung Foundation] From German orig., 1960

Kirk, T, & Thoresby, R, *Tours in Scotland 1677 and 1681*, Ed by Hume Brown, P, Edinburgh, 1892

Knight, C, and Lomas, R, *The Hiram Key*, Century, London, 1996

Laidler, K, *The Head of God*, Weidenfeld & Nicolson, London, 1998

Laughlan, Roy, MBE, JP, *The Kilwinning No. o Masonic Lodge in old picture postcards*, European Library, Zaltbommel/Netherlands, 1994

de Lettenhove, le Baron Kervyn, [Ed] *Le Livre de Chevalerie par Geoffroi de Charny*, in Oeuvres de Froissant, 26 vols, Brussels, 1867-77

Lectures in Craft Masonry (The), Emulation working, London, 1919

Levi, E, *The History of Magic*, [Engl. Transl. by Waite, A E] London, 1913, From French orig., 1862

Lines, M, *Sacred Stones, Sacred Places*, St. Andrew Press, Edinburgh, 1992

Littleton, C S, & Malcor, L, *From Scythia to Camelot*, Garland, New York and London, 2000

Lively, P, & Kerven, R, *The Mythical Quest*, The British Library, London, 1996

Livingston, William, *Vindication of the Celtic Character*, Greenock, 1850

Livingstone, E A, [Ed], *The Concise Oxford Dictionary of the Christian Church*, Oxford University Press, London, 1977

Lloyd-Morgan, C, 'The Celtic Tradition', *The Arthur of the English*, University of Wales Press, Cardiff, 1999

Loomis, R S, *The Grail: From Celtic Myth to Christian Symbol*, Princeton University Press, Princeton, NJ, 1991 edition of 1963 orig.

Low, M, *Celtic Christianity and Nature*, Edinburgh University Press, Edinburgh, 1996

Lyall, R J, 'The Lost Literature of Medieval Scotland', in *Brycht Lanternis: Essays on the Language and Literature of Medieval and Renaissance Scotland*, [Ed by McClure, J D & Spiller, R R G], Aberdeen, 1989

Lynch, Prof M, *Scotland: A New History*, Pimlico, London, 1991

Lynch, Prof M, 'A Nation Born Again? Scottish Identity in the 16th and 17th Centuries', *Image and Identity: The Making and Re-Making of Scotland through the ages*, [Ed by Broun, D, Finlay, R J, & Lynch, M], John Donald, Edinburgh, 1998

MacEwan, A R, *A History of the Church in Scotland*, London, 1913

Macinlay, J, *Folklore of Scottish Lochs and Springs*, Wm. Hodge & Co., Glasgow, 1893

MacInnes, J, 'The Arthurian Legend', *World Mythology*, Ed by Willis, R, Piatkus, London, 1993

Mack, A, *Field Guide to the Pictish Symbol Stones*, Pinkfoot Press, Balgavies, Angus, 1997

Mackey, J, [Ed], *An Introduction to Celtic Christianity*, T&T Clark, Edinburgh, 1989

MacKenzie, K, *The Royal Masonic Cyclopaedia*, The Aquarian Press, London, 1877, reprinted in 1987

MacKinley, J M, *Folklore of Scottish Lochs and Springs*, Wm. Hodge & Co., Glasgow, 1893

MacLagan, R C, *Our Ancestors, Scots, Picts, and Cymry*, Foulis, Edinburgh, 1913

MacNeill, F M, *The Silver Bough, "The Local Festivals of Scotland"*, Volume 4, Stuart Titles Ltd, Glasgow, 1968

MacNeill, F M, *The Silver Bough, Vol. I, Scottish Folklore and Folk-Belief*, MacLellan, Wm, Glasgow, 1977 ed. of 1957 orig.

Macquarrie, A, *Scotland and the Crusades*, John Donald, Edinburgh, 1997

Macquarrie, A, *The Saints of Scotland*, John Donald, Edinburgh, 1997

MacRitchie, D, *Scottish Gypsies Under the Stewarts*, Edinburgh, 1894

Mallory, J P, and Mair, V, *The Tarim Mummies*, Thames & Hudson, London, 2000

Markale, J, *King of the Celts: Arthurian Legends and Celtic Tradition*, Inner Traditions, Rochester, VT, 1977, 181 [Engl. Transl.] From French orig. *Le Roi Arthur et la Societe Celtique*, Payot, Paris, 1976.

Markale, J, *Merlin*, Inner Traditions, Rochester, VT, 1995 [Engl. Transl.] From French orig. *Merlin L'Enchanteur*, 1981

Markale, J, *The Grail*, Inner Traditions, Rochester, VT, 1999 [Engl. Transl.] From French orig., 1982

Markale, Prof J, *The Druids*, Inner Traditions, VT, 1999 [Engl. Transl.] From French orig. *Le Druidisme, Traditions et dieux des Celtes*, 1985

Martin, M, *A Description of the Western Isles of Scotland circa 1690*, Edinburgh, 1716 & 1934

Matthews, J, & C, *Ladies of the Lake*, HarperCollins, London, 1992

Matthews, J, (Ed), *The Druid Source Book*, Blandford, London, 1996

Matthews, J, *Elements of the Grail Tradition*, Element, Shaftesbury, 1990

Matthews, J, *Gawain*, Harper Collins, London, 1990

Matthews, J, *The Mystic Grail: The Challenge of the Arthurian Quest*, Sterling Publishing, New York, 1997

McCone, K, *Pagan Past and Christian Present in Early Irish Literature*, Maynooth, 1991

McHardy, S, 'The Wee Dark Fowk o' Scotland: The role of oral transmission in Pictish studies', *The Worm, the Germ, and the Thorn*, [Ed by D. Henry], Pinkfoot Press, Balgavie, 1997

McHardy, S, *Scotland: Myth, Legend and Folklore*, Luath Press, Edinburgh, 1999

McIntosh, C, *The Rosicrucians*, Thorsons, Wellingborough, 1987 rev. ed of 1980 orig.

McIntosh, C, *The Rosy Cross Unveiled*, The Aquarian Press Ltd, Northamptonshire, 1980

McKay, A G, *An Encyclopaedia of Freemasonry*, New York and London, 1920

McKerracher, A, *Perthshire in History and Legend*, John Donald, Edinburgh, 1988, rev. ed. 2000

McLeod, W, 'The Old Charges', *ARS Quatuor Coronatorum, Transactions of Quatuor Coronati Lodge No. 2076*, Vol. 99, The Garden City Press, Hertfordshire, 1987

McNeill, F M, *The Silver Bough, vol. 2*, Wm. MacLellan, Glasgow, 1959

McNeill, F M, *The Silver Bough, vol. 4*, 'The Local Festivals of Scotland', Stuart Titles Ltd, Glasgow, 1968

Mill, A J, *Medieval Plays in Scotland*, St. Andrews University publ.'s, No. XXIV, Wm. Blackwood & Sons Ltd., Edinburgh and London, 1927

Moffat, A, *Arthur and the Lost Kingdoms*, Weidenfeld & Nicolson, London, 1999

Moorman, J R, *A History of the Church in England*, A & C Black, London, 1980

Morgan, R W, *St. Paul in Britain*, Marshall Bros., London, 1922

Morris, J, *The Age of Arthur: A History of the British Isles from 350 to 650*, Phoenix/Orion London, 1995 ed., of 1973 orig.

Mowat, F, *The Alban Quest*, Weidenfeld & Nicolson, London, 1999

Munro, J, 'Rosslyn Chapel: Part 4: Inside and Around', *The Ashlar*, Issue 4, Circle publications, Helensburgh, 1998

Murphy, A C Rev, *The Declaration of Arbroath – 1320*, (booklet), Midlothian privately printed, 1999

Murray Lyon, D, *History of the Lodge of Edinburgh (Mary's Chapel) No.1*, Edinburgh, 1873

Murray, R, *The Gypsies of the Border*, T F Brockie, Galashiels, 1875

Newton, J F, *The Builders,* Unwin Brothers Ltd, Woking, 1934

Nicolson, A, [Ed] *Gaelic Proverbs*, Birlinn, Edinburgh, 1996, 3rd ed., orig 1881

Nicolson, R, *Scotland, The Later Middle Ages, 4 vols.*, Edinburgh, 1974

O'hOgain, D, *Myth, Legend, and Romance: An Encyclopedia of the Irish Folk Tradition*, Prentice Hall, New York, 1991

Orr Ewing, A D, Grand Master Mason, 'Preface', in *An Account of the Chapel of Roslin 1778*, [Ed by Bro R L D Cooper], Grand Lodge of Scotland, Edinburgh, 2000

Owen, A L, *The Famous Druids: A Survey of three centuries of English literature on the Druids*, Oxford University Press, Oxford, 1962

Pelikan, J, [Ed], *Sacred Writings, Christianity: The Apocrypha and the New Testament*, Quality paperback Book Club, NY, 1992

Pennant, T, *A Tour in Scotland & Voyage to the Hebrides*, Vol. 2, Chester, 1774

Pennecuik, A, *A Descriptive Account of the Blue Blanket*, Edinburgh, 1780

Phillips, G, & Keatman, M, *King Arthur: The True Story*, Random House, London, 1992

Piatigorsky, Prof A, *Freemasonry*, Harvill Press, London, 1999

Piggott, S, *Scotland Before History*, Polygon, Edinburgh, 1982

Piggott, S, *The Druids*, Thames & Hudson, London, 1968

Pitts, M, *Hengeworld,* Century, London, 2000

Pohl, F J, *Prince Henry Sinclair*: His Expedition to the New World in 1398, Nimbus, Halifax, NS, no year listed, reprint of 1969 orig.

Ponting, G & M, *The Stones Around Callanish*, self-published, Callanish, 1984 (rev. In 1993)

Proceedings of the Society of Antiquaries, XII, Edinburgh, 1877-8

Purser, J, *Scotland's Music*, Mainstream, Edinburgh, 1992

Ralls-MacLeod, K, *Music and the Celtic Otherworld*, Edinburgh University Press, Edinburgh, 2000

Ralls-MacLeod, K, [Ed] *Indigenous Religious Musics in the Contemporary World*, with Dr Graham Harvey [Ed], Ashgate Academic Press, London, 2001, with CD

Ralls-MacLeod, K, *The Templars and the Grail*, Quest Books, Chicago, forthcoming, 2003

Reid, N, [Ed], *Scotland in the Reign of Alexander III*, Edinburgh, 1990

Raoult, M, 'The Druid Revival in Brittany, France and Europe', in *The Druid Renaissance*, (Ed) P. Carr-Gomm, Thorsons, London, 1996

Ravenscroft, T, *The Spear of Destiny*, Samuel Weiser, York Beach, ME, 1973

Reade, W Winwood, *The Veil of Isis or the Mysteries of the Druids*, C J Skeet, London, 1861

Rees, A, & Rees, B, *Celtic Heritage: Ancient Tradition in Ireland and Wales*, Thames and Hudson, London, 1961

Reeves, Wm, *The Culdees of the British Islands as they appear in History*, Royal Irish Academy, M H Gill, Dublin, 1864 orig., reprint 1994 by LLarnerch Publishers, Felinfach, Wales

Richardson, J S, *Melrose Abbey*, Official Guide, HMSO, Edinburgh, 1949

Rigby, G, *On Earth as it is in Heaven*, Rhaedus, Guernsey, 1996

Ritchie, A, *Govan and its Carved Stones*, Pinkfoot Press, Balgavie, 1999

Ritchie, A, *Picts*, HMSO, Edinburgh, 1989

Ritchie, A, *Scotland BC*, Historic Buildings and Monuments, HMSO, Edinburgh, 1988

Ritchie, J N Graham, 'Recording Early Christian Monuments in Scotland', in *The Worm, the Germ, and the Thorn: Pictish and related studies presented to Isabel Henderson*, Pinkfoot, Balgavies, Angus, 1997

Roberts, B, 'Culhwch ac Olwen, the Triads, Saints' Lives', *The Arthur of the Welsh: the Arthurian Tradition in Medieval Welsh literature*, Ed by R. Bromwich, A O H Jarman, & B Roberts, University of Wales Press, Cardiff, 1991

Ross, A, *The Druids*, Tempus, Stroud, 1999

Ross, A, *The Folklore of the Scottish Highlands*, Batsford, London, 1976

Salzman, L F, *Building in England Down to 1540*, Oxford University Press, Oxford, 1952

Scott, A B, *The Pictish Nation*, T N Foulis, Edinburgh and London, 1918

Scott, T, *Tales of Sir William Wallace: Guardian of Scotland*, Gordon Wright Publishing, Edinburgh, 1981 [Adapted from The Wallas of Blin Hary]

Scott, Sir W, *Letters on Demonology and Witchcraft*, London, 1831, 1868, et al.

Sinclair, A, *The Discovery of the Grail*, Random House, London, 1998

Sinclair, A, *The Secret Scroll,* Sinclair-Stevenson, London, 2001

Sir John Clerk, *Memoirs of Sir John Clerk of Penecuik*, Edinburgh, 1893

Skene, W F, *Arthur and the Britons in Wales and Scotland*, Llanerch, Lampeter, 1988 reprint of 1868 original 'The Four Ancient Books of Wales'

Skene, W F, *Celtic Scotland: A History of Ancient Alba*, Vol II, David Douglas, Edinburgh, 1877

Slezer, J, *Theatrum Scotiae*, London, 1693

Smith, D, *Celtic Travellers: Scotland in the Age of Saints*, HMSO, Edinburgh, 1997

Spence, L, 'The Arthurian Tradition in Scotland', *Scots magazine*, Edinburgh and Glasgow, April 1926 issue

Spence, L, *The History & Origins of Druidism*, Rider & Co., London, 1947

Spottiswoode, J, *The History of the Church of Scotland*, R. Norton, London, 1666

Stein, W J, *The British, their Psychology and Destiny*, Temple Lodge Press, London, 1990

Stringer, K J, 'Reform Monasticism and Celtic Scotland: Galloway c.1140-c.1240', *Alba: Celtic Scotland in the Medieval Era*, [Ed by Cowan, E J & McDonald, R Andrew], Tuckwell Press, East Linton, 2000

Stevenson, Prof D, *The Origins of Freemasonry, Scotland's Century 1590-1710*, Cambridge University Press, Cambridge, 1988, Appendix.

Stevenson, Prof D, *The First Freemasons,* Aberdeen University Press, Aberdeen, 1988

Stewart, HRH MJ, *The Forgotten Monarchy of Scotland*, Element, Shaftesbury, 1998

Stewart-Smith, D, *Life Experience Petition*, Vermont College, August 1990

Stoker, R, *The Legacy of Arthur's Chester*, Covenant, London, 1965

Strachan, G, *Jesus the Mystery Builder, Druid Mysteries and the Dawn of Christianity*, Floris Books, Edinburgh, 1998

Taylor, S, 'The Coming of the Augustinians to St. Andrews and version B of the St. Andrews foundation legend', *Kings, Clerics, and Chronicles in Scotland, 500-1297*, [Ed] Simon Taylor, Four Courts Press, Dublin, 2000

Taylor, S, 'Seventh-Century Iona abbots in Scottish place-names', *Spes Scotorum: Hope of Scots*, T&T Clark, Edinburgh, 1999

Taylor, G, *Our Neglected Heritage, Vol. 1, The Early Church*, London, 1969

Tennyson, Lord Alfred, *Idylls of the King*, (1859-91), Penguin, London, 1988

Thiede, C P, & D'Ancona, M, *The Quest for the True Cross*, Orion Books, London, 2000

Thurneysen, R, *A Grammar of Old Irish*, Dublin Institute of Advanced Studies, (D.I.A.S.) Dublin, 1980

Tolstoy, N, *The Quest for Merlin*, Hodder and Stoughton, Sevenoaks, Kent, 1985

Toulson, S, *Celtic Journeys*, Hutchinson & Co., London, 1985

Trevarthen, D, 'Illuminating the Monuments: Observation and Speculation on the Structure and Function of the Cairns at Balnuaran of Clava', *Cambridge Archaeological Journal*, Vol 10, No 2, October 2000, 295-315

Turnbull, A, *St. Andrew: Scotland's Myth and Identity*, St. Andrew Press, Edinburgh, 1997

United Grand Lodge of England (The), *The Freemasons*, VHS video, Aspen Spafax Television, 1987

van den Broek, R, and Hanegraaff, W J, [Ed], *Gnosis and Hermeticism: From Antiquity to Modern Times*, State University of New York, Albany, 1998

Vantoura, Haik, *The Music of the Bible Revealed*, [Ed by J. Wheeler], Babel Press, San Francisco, 1991

Waite, A. E, *A New Encyclopaedia of Freemasonry*, Reprint of 1926 original, Wing Books, New York, 1996, vol. II

Wallace-Murphy, T, and Hopkins, M, *Rosslyn*, Element Books, Shaftesbury, 1999

Ward, J S M, *Who was Hiram Abiff?* Lewis Masonic, Plymouth, 1992

Watson, F, 'The Enigmatic Lion: Scotland, Kingship and National Identity in the Wars of Independence', *Image and Identity: The Making and Re-Making of Scotland through the Ages*, [Ed by Broun, D, Finlay, R J, & Lynch, M] John Donald, Edinburgh, 1998

Watson, W J, *The Celtic Placenames of Scotland*, Birlinn, Edinburgh, 1993 reprint of 1926 orig.

Wells, R, *Understanding Freemasonry*, (audiotape 10), Recorded Talks, Q.C.C.C., London, 1989

Weston, J L, *From Ritual to Romance*, Princeton University Press, Princeton, NJ, 1993 edition of 1920 orig.

Westwood, J, *Albion: A Guide to Legendary Britain*, Paladin Grafton Books, London, 1985

Whitaker, M, *The Legends of King Arthur in Art*, D S Brewer, Cambridge, 1990

White, P, *King Arthur: Man or Myth?*, Bossiney Books, Lauceston, Cornwall, 2000

Williams, J E C And Ford, P, *The Irish Literary Tradition*, University of Wales Press, Cardiff, 1992

Wise, T A, *History of Paganism in Caledonia*, London, 1884

Wood, J, 'The Holy Grail: From Romance Motif to Modern Genre', *Folklore*, Vol. 111, No. 2, London, Oct. 2000

Wright, D, *Druidism: The Ancient Faith of Britain*, Ed J. Burrow & Co., London, 1924

Yeoman, L, *Reportage Scotland*, Luath Press, Edinburgh, 2000

Yeoman, P, *Pilgrimage in Medieval Scotland*, Historic Scotland/B T Batsford, London, 1999

Territories of the Celtic Saints

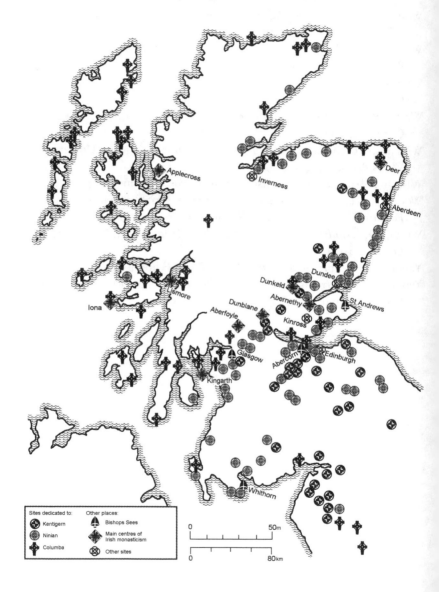

Applecross
Inverness
Deer
Aberdeen
Dunkeld
Dundee
Abernethy
St Andrews
Lismore
Dunblane
Iona
Aberfoyle
Kinross
Glasgow
Abercorn
Edinburgh
Kingarth
Whithorn

Sites dedicated to:
Kentigern
Ninian
Columba

Other places:
Bishops Sees
Main centres of Irish monasticism
Other sites

0   50m

0   80km

Design © 2001

Index

ANCIENT QUEST

Ancient Quest is an historical research organisation based in Oxford, England, dedicated to the exploration of the Celtic and western philosophical and spiritual traditions, especially those of the Medieval and Renaissance periods.

Founded in 1999, by author, lecturer and researcher Dr. Karen Ralls-MacLeod, Ancient Quest makes the academic accessible and develops a key idea present in many of these traditions — that of a Search, or Quest.

Manifest your Quest!

To invite Karen to speak at a conference, to be interviewed for a film/TV project or to present a workshop, please contact

www.ancientquest.com

"Knowledge comes, but Wisdom lingers"
Alfred Lord Tennyson

THE QUEST FOR

The Quest for Arthur
Stuart McHardy
ISBN 1 84282 012 5 HBK £16.99

King Arthur of Camelot and the Knights of the Round Table are enduring romantic figures. A national hero for the Bretons, the Welsh and the English alike Arthur is a potent figure for many. This quest leads to a radical new interpretation of the ancient myth.

Historian, storyteller and folklorist Stuart McHardy believes he has uncovered the origins of this inspirational figure, the true Arthur. He incorporates knowledge of folklore and placename studies with an archaeological understanding of the 6th century.

Combining knowledge of the earliest records and histories of Arthur with an awareness of the importance of oral traditions, this quest leads to the discovery that the enigmatic origins of Arthur lie not in Brittany or England or Wales. Instead they lie in that magic land the ancient Welsh called Y Gogledd, the North; the North of Britain which we now call Scotland.

The Quest for the Nine Maidens
Stuart McHardy
ISBN 0 946487 66 9 HBK £16.99

When Arthur was conveyed to Avalon they were there. When Odin summoned warriors to Valhalla they were there. When the Greek god Apollo was worshipped on mountain tops they were there. When Brendan came to the Island of Women they were there. Cerridwen's cauldron of inspiration was tended by them and Peredur received his arms from them. They are found in Pictland, Wales, Ireland, Iceland, Gaul, Greece, Africa and possibly as far as field as South America and Oceania.

They are the Nine Maidens, pagan priestesses involved in the worship of the Mother Goddess. From Stone Age rituals to the 20th century, the Nine Maidens come in many forms. Muses, Maenads, valkyries and druidesses all associated with a single male. Weather-workers, shape-shifters, diviners and healers, the Nine Maidens are linked to the Old Religion over much of our planet. In this book Stuart McHardy has traced similar groups of Nine Maidens, throughout the ancient Celtic and Germanic world and far beyond, from Christian and pagan sources. In his search he begins to uncover one of the most ancient and widespread institutions of human society.

ON THE TRAIL OF

On the Trail of Robert Burns
John Cairney
ISBN 0 946487 51 0 PBK £7.99

Is there anything new to say about Robert Burns?

John Cairney says it's time to trash Burns the Brand and come on the trail of the real Robert Burns. He is the best of travelling companions on this convivial, entertaining journey to the heart of the Burns story.

Internationally known as 'the face of Robert Burns', John Cairney believes that the traditional Burns tourist trail urgently needs to find a new direction. In an acting career spanning forty years he has often lived and breathed Robert Burns on stage. *On the Trail of Robert Burns* shows just how well he can get under the skin of a character. This fascinating journey around Scotland is a rediscovery of Scotland's national bard as a flesh and blood genius.

On the Trail of Robert Burns outlines five tours, mainly in Scotland. Key sites include:

Alloway - Burns' birthplace. 'Tam O' Shanter' draws on the witch-stories about Alloway Kirk first heard by Burns in his childhood.
Mossgiel - between 1784 and 1786 in a phenomenal burst of creativity Burns wrote some of his most memorable poems including 'Holy Willie's Prayer' and 'To a Mouse.'
Kilmarnock - the famous Kilmarnock edition of *Poems Chiefly in the Scottish Dialect* published in 1786.
Edinburgh - fame and Clarinda (among others) embraced him.
Dumfries - Burns died at the age of 37. The trail ends at the Burns mausoleum in St Michael's churchyard.

'*For me an aim I never fash I rhyme for fun*'.
ROBERT BURNS

'*My love affair on stage with Burns started in London in 1959. It was consumated on stage at the Traverse Theatre in Edinburgh in 1965 and has continued happily ever since*'. JOHN CAIRNEY

'*The trail is expertly, touchingly and amusingly followed*'. THE HERALD

On the Trail of William Wallace
David R. Ross
ISBN 0 946487 47 2 PBK £7.99

How close to reality was *Braveheart*?

Where was Wallace actually born?

What was the relationship between Wallace and Bruce?

Are there any surviving eye-witness accounts of Wallace?

How does Wallace influence the psyche of today's Scots?

On the Trail of William Wallace offers a refreshing insight into the life and heritage of the great Scots hero whose proud story is at the very heart of what it means to be Scottish. Not concentrating simply on the hard historical facts of Wallace's life, the book also takes into account the real significance of Wallace and his effect on the ordinary Scot through the ages, manifested in the many sites where his memory is marked.

In trying to piece together the jigsaw of the reality of Wallace's life, David Ross weaves a subtle flow of new information with his own observations. His engaging, thoughtful and at times amusing narrative reads with the ease of a historical novel, complete with all the intrigue, treachery and romance required to hold the attention of the casual reader and still entice the more knowledgable historian.

74 places to visit in Scotland and the north of England

One general map and 3 location maps

Stirling and Falkirk battle plans

Wallace's route through London

Chapter on Wallace connections in North America and elsewhere

Reproductions of rarely seen illustrations

On the Trail of William Wallace will be enjoyed by anyone with an interest in Scotland, from the passing tourist to the most fervent nationalist. It is an encyclopaedia-cum-guide book, literally stuffed with fascinating titbits not usually on offer in the conventional history book.

David Ross is organiser of and historical adviser to the Society of William Wallace.

'Historians seem to think all there is to be known about Wallace has already been uncovered. Mr Ross has proved that Wallace studies are in fact in their infancy.' ELSPETH KING, Director the the Stirling Smith Art Museum & Gallery, who annotated and introduced the recent Luath edition of *Blind Harry's Wallace.*

'Better the pen than the sword!'

RANDALL WALLACE, author of *Braveheart,* when asked by David Ross how it felt to be partly responsible for the freedom of a nation following the Devolution Referendum.

On the Trail of Robert the Bruce

David R. Ross

ISBN 0 946487 52 9 PBK £7.99

On the Trail of Robert the Bruce charts the story of Scotland's hero-king from his boyhood, through his days of indecision as Scotland suffered under the English yoke, to his assumption of the crown exactly six months after the death of William Wallace. Here is the astonishing blow by blow account of how, against fearful odds, Bruce led the Scots to win their greatest ever victory. Bannockburn was not the end of the story. The war against English oppression lasted another fourteen years. Bruce lived just long enough to see his dreams of an independent Scotland come to fruition in 1328 with the signing of the Treaty of Edinburgh. The trail takes us to Bruce sites in Scotland, many of the little known and forgotten battle sites in northern England, and as far afield as the Bruce monuments in Andalusia and Jerusalem.

67 places to visit in Scotland and elsewhere.

One general map, 3 location maps and a map of Bruce-connected sites in Ireland.

Bannockburn battle plan.

Drawings and reproductions of rarely seen illustrations.

On the Trail of Robert the Bruce is not all blood and gore. It brings out the love and laughter, pain and passion of one of the great eras of Scottish history. Read it and you will understand why David Ross has never knowingly killed a spider in his life. Once again, he proves himself a master of the popular brand of hands-on history that made *On the Trail of William Wallace* so popular.

'David R. Ross is a proud patriot and unashamed romantic.' SCOTLAND ON SUNDAY

'Robert the Bruce knew Scotland, knew every class of her people, as no man who ruled her before or since has done. It was he who asked of her a miracle - and she accomplished it.'

AGNES MUIR MACKENZIE

On the Trail of Mary Queen of Scots

J. Keith Cheetham

ISBN 0 946487 50 2 PBK £7.99

Life dealt Mary Queen of Scots love, intrigue, betrayal and tragedy in generous measure.

On the Trail of Mary Queen of Scots traces the major events in the turbulent life of the beautiful, enigmatic queen whose romantic reign and tragic destiny exerts an undimmed fascination over 400 years after her execution.

Places of interest to visit – 99 in Scotland, 35 in England and 29 in France.

One general map and 6 location maps.

Line drawings and illustrations.

Simplified family tree of the royal houses of Tudor and Stuart.

Key sites include:

Linlithgow Palace – Mary's birthplace, now a magnificent ruin

Stirling Castle – where, only nine months old, Mary was crowned Queen of Scotland

Notre Dame Cathedral – where, aged fifteen, she married the future king of France

The Palace of Holyroodhouse – Rizzio, one of

Mary's closest advisers, was murdered here and some say his blood still stains the spot where he was stabbed to death

Sheffield Castle – where for fourteen years she languished as prisoner of her cousin, Queen Elizabeth I

Fotheringhay – here Mary finally met her death on the executioner's block.

On the Trail of Mary Queen of Scots is for everyone interested in the life of perhaps the most romantic figure in Scotland's history; a thorough guide to places connected with Mary, it is also a guide to the complexities of her personal and public life.

'In my end is my beginning'
MARY QUEEN OF SCOTS

'...the woman behaves like the Whore of Babylon'
JOHN KNOX

On the Trail of Robert Service

GW Lockhart
ISBN 0 946487 24 3 PBK £7.99

Robert Service is famed world-wide for his eye-witness verse-pictures of the Klondike goldrush. As a war poet, his work outsold Owen and Sassoon, and he went on to become the world's first million selling poet. In search of adventure and new experiences, he emigrated from Scotland to Canada in 1890 where he was caught up in the aftermath of the raging gold fever. His vivid dramatic verse bring to life the wild, larger than life characters of the gold rush Yukon, their bar-room brawls, their lust for gold, their trigger-happy gambles with life and love. 'The Shooting of Dan McGrew' is perhaps his most famous poem:

> A bunch of the boys were whooping it up in the Malamute saloon;
> The kid that handles the music box was hitting a ragtime tune;
> Back of the bar in a solo game, sat Dangerous Dan McGrew,
> And watching his luck was his light o'love, the lady that's known as Lou.

His storytelling powers have brought Robert Service enduring fame, particularly in North America and Scotland where he is something of a cult figure.

Starting in Scotland, *On the Trail of Robert Service* follows Service as he wanders through British Columbia, Oregon, California, Mexico, Cuba, Tahiti, Russia, Turkey and the Balkans, finally 'settling' in France.

This revised edition includes an expanded selection of illustrations of scenes from the Klondike as well as several photographs from the family of Robert Service on his travels around the world.

Wallace Lockhart, an expert on Scottish traditional folk music and dance, is the author of *Highland Balls & Village Halls* and *Fiddles & Folk*. His relish for a well-told tale in popular vernacular led him to fall in love with the verse of Robert Service and write his biography.

'A fitting tribute to a remarkable man - a bank clerk who wanted to become a cowboy. It is hard to imagine a bank clerk writing such lines as:
> A bunch of boys were whooping it up...
The income from his writing actually exceeded his bank salary by a factor of five and he resigned to pursue a full time writing career.' Charles Munn,
THE SCOTTISH BANKER

'Robert Service claimed he wrote for those who wouldnit be seen dead reading poetry. His was an almost unbelievably mobile life... Lockhart hangs on breathlessly, enthusiastically unearthing clues to the poet's life.' Ruth Thomas,
SCOTTISH BOOK COLLECTOR

'This enthralling biography will delight Service lovers in both the Old World and the New.' Marilyn Wright, SCOTS INDEPENDENT

On the Trail of John Muir

Cherry Good
ISBN 0 946487 62 6 PBK £7.99

Follow the man who made the US go green. Confidant of presidents, father of American National Parks, trailblazer of world conservation and voted a Man of the Millennium in the US, John Muir's life and work is of continuing relevance. A man ahead of his time who saw the wilderness he loved threatened by industrialisation and determined to protect it, a crusade in which he was largely successful. His love of the wilderness began at an early age and he was filled with wanderlust all his life.

Only by going in silence, without baggage, can on truly get into the heart of the wilderness. All other travel is mere dust and hotels and baggage and chatter. JOHN MUIR

Braving mosquitoes and black bears Cherry Good set herself on his trail – Dunbar, Scotland; Fountain Lake and Hickory Hill, Wisconsin; Yosemite Valley and the Sierra Nevada, California; the Grand Canyon, Arizona; Alaska; and Canada – to tell his story. John Muir was himself a prolific writer, and Good draws on his books, articles, letters and diaries to produce an account that is lively, intimate, humorous and anecdotal, and that provides refreshing new insights into the hero of world conservation.

> John Muir chronology
> General map plus 10 detailed maps covering the US, Canada and Scotland
> Original colour photographs
> Afterword advises on how to get involved
> Conservation websites and addresses

Muir's importance has long been acknowledged in the US with over 200 sites of scenic beauty named after him. He was a Founder of The Sierra Club which now has over ½ million members. Due to the movement he started some 360 million acres of wilderness are now protected. This is a book which shows Muir not simply as a hero but as likeable humorous and self-effacing man of extraordinary vision.

'I do hope that those who read this book will burn with the same enthusiasm for John Muir which the author shows.'
WEST HIGHLAND FREE PRESS

HISTORY

Reportage Scotland: History in the Making

Louise Yeoman

Foreword by Professor David Stevenson

ISBN 0 946487 61 8 PBK £9.99

Events – both major and minor – as seen and recorded by Scots throughout history.

Which king was murdered in a sewer?
What was Dr Fian's love magic?
Who was the half-roasted abbot?
Which cardinal was salted and put in a barrel?
Why did Lord Kitchener's niece try to blow up Burns's cottage?

The answers can all be found in this eclectic mix covering nearly 2000 years of Scottish history. Historian Louise Yeoman's rummage through the manuscript, book and newspaper archives of the National Library of Scotland has yielded an astonishing range of material from a letter to the king of the Picts to in Mary Queen of Scots' own account of the murder of David Riccio; from the execution of William Wallace to accounts of anti-poll tax actions and the opening of the new Scottish Parliament. The book takes pieces from the original French, Latin, Gaelic and Scots and makes them accessible to the general reader, often for the first time.

The result is compelling reading for anyone interested in the history that has made Scotland what it is today.

'Marvellously illuminating and wonderfully readable'.
Angus Calder, SCOTLAND ON SUNDAY

'A monumental achievement in drawing together such a rich historical harvest'
Chris Holme, THE HERALD

Blind Harry's Wallace

William Hamilton of Gilbertfield

Introduced by Elspeth King

ISBN 0 946487 43 X HBK £15.00
ISBN 0 946487 33 2 PBK £8.99

The original story of the real braveheart, Sir William Wallace. Racy, blood on every page, violently anglophobic, grossly embellished, vulgar and disgusting, clumsy and stilted, a literary failure, a great epic.

Whatever the verdict on

BLIND HARRY, this is the book which has done more than any other to frame the notion of Scotland's national identity. Despite its numerous 'historical inaccuracies', it remains the principal source for what we now know about the life of Wallace.

The novel and film *Braveheart* were based on the 1722 Hamilton edition of this epic poem. Burns, Wordsworth, Byron and others were greatly influenced by this version 'wherein the old obsolete words are rendered more intelligible', which is said to be the book, next to the Bible, most commonly found in Scottish households in the eighteenth century. Burns even admits to having 'borrowed... a couplet worthy of Homer' directly from Hamilton's version of BLIND HARRY to include in *'Scots wha hae'*.

Elspeth King, in her introduction to this, the first accessible edition of BLIND HARRY in verse form since 1859, draws parallels between the situation in Scotland at the time of Wallace and that in Bosnia and Chechnya in the 1990s. Seven hundred years to the day after the Battle of Stirling Bridge, the 'Settled Will of the Scottish People' was expressed in the devolution referendum of 11 September 1997. She describes this as a landmark opportunity for mature reflection on how the nation has been shaped, and sees BLIND HARRY'S WALLACE as an essential and compelling text for this purpose.

'A true bard of the people'.
TOM SCOTT, THE PENGUIN BOOK OF SCOTTISH VERSE, on Blind Harry.

'A more inventive writer than Shakespeare'.
RANDALL WALLACE

'The story of Wallace poured a Scottish prejudice in my veins which will boil along until the floodgates of life shut in eternal rest'. ROBERT BURNS

'Hamilton's couplets are not the best poetry you will ever read, but they rattle along at a fair pace. In re-issuing this work, the publishers have re-opened the spring from which most of our conceptions of the Wallace legend come'.
SCOTLAND ON SUNDAY

'The return of Blind Harry's Wallace, a man who makes Mel look like a wimp'. THE SCOTSMAN

Old Scotland New Scotland

Jeff Fallow

ISBN 0 946487 40 5 PBK £6.99

'Together we can build a new Scotland based on Labour's values.' DONALD DEWAR, Party Political Broadcast

'Despite the efforts of decent Mr Dewar, the voters may yet conclude they are looking at the same old hacks in brand new suits.'

IAN BELL, *The Independent*
'At times like this you suddenly realise how dangerous the neglect of Scottish history in our schools and universities may turn out to be.'
MICHAEL FRY, *The Herald*
'...one of the things I hope will go is our chip on the shoulder about the English... The SNP has a

huge responsibility to articulate Scottish independence in a way that is pro-Scottish and not anti-English.'

ALEX SALMOND, *The Scotsman*

Scottish politics have never been more exciting. In *old Scotland new Scotland* Jeff Fallow takes us on a graphic voyage through Scotland's turbulent history, from earliest times through to the present day and beyond. This fast-track guide is the quick way to learn what your history teacher didn't tell you, essential reading for all who seek an understanding of Scotland and its history.

Eschewing the romanticisation of his country's past, Fallow offers a new perspective on an old nation. *'Too many people associate Scottish history with tartan trivia or outworn romantic myth. This book aims to blast that stubborn idea.'*

JEFF FALLOW

SOCIAL HISTORY

A Word for Scotland

Jack Campbell

with a foreword by Magnus Magnusson

ISBN 0 946487 48 0   PBK   £12.99

'A word for Scotland' was Lord Beaver-brook's hope when he founded the *Scottish Daily Express*. That word for Scotland quickly became, and was for many years, the national newspaper of Scotland.

The pages of *A Word For Scotland* exude warmth and a wry sense of humour. Jack Campbell takes us behind the scenes to meet the larger-than-life characters and ordinary people who made and recorded the stories. Here we hear the stories behind the stories that hit the headlines in this great yarn of journalism in action.

It would be true to say 'all life is here'. From the Cheapside Street fire of which cost the lives of 19 Glasgow firemen, to the theft of the Stone of Destiny, to the lurid exploits of serial killer Peter Manuel, to encounters with world boxing champions Benny Lynch and Cassius Clay - this book offers telling glimpses of the characters, events, joy and tragedy which make up Scotland's story in the 20th century.

'As a rookie reporter you were proud to work on it and proud to be part of it - it was fine newspaper right at the heartbeat of Scotland.'

RONALD NEIL, Chief Executive of BBC Production, and a reporter on the *Scottish Daily Express* (1963-68)

'This book is a fascinating reminder of Scottish journalism in its heyday. It will be read avidly by those journalists who take pride in their profession – and should be compulsory reading for those who don't.'

JACK WEBSTER, columnist on *The Herald* and *Scottish Daily Express* journalist (1960-80)

The Crofting Years

Francis Thompson

ISBN 0 946487 06 5   PBK   £6.95

Crofting is much more than a way of life. It is a storehouse of cultural, linguistic and moral values which holds together a scattered and struggling rural population. This book fills a blank in the written history of crofting over the last two centuries. Bloody conflicts and gunboat diplomacy, treachery, compassion, music and story: all figure in this mine of information on crofting in the Highlands and Islands of Scotland.

'I would recommend this book to all who are interested in the past, but even more so to those who are interested in the future survival of our way of life and culture'
STORNOWAY GAZETTE

'The book is a mine of information on many aspects of the past, among them the homes, the food, the music and the medicine of our crofting forebears.'
John M Macmillan, erstwhile CROFTERS COMMISSIONER FOR LEWIS AND HARRIS

Shale Voices

Alistair Findlay

foreword by Tam Dalyell MP

ISBN 0 946487 63 4   PBK   £10.99

ISBN 0 946487 78 2   HBK   £17.99

'He was at Addiewell oil works. Anyone goes in there is there for keeps.'

JOE, Electrician

'There's shale from here to Ayr, you see.'

DICK, a Drawer

'The way I describe it is, you're a coal miner and I'm a shale miner. You're a tramp and I'm a toff.'

HARRY, a Drawer

'There were sixteen or eighteen Simpsons... ...She was having one every dividend we would say.'
SISTERS, from Broxburn

Shale Voices offers a fascinating insight into shale mining, an industry that employed generations of Scots, had an impact on the social, political and cultural history of Scotland and gave birth to today's large oil companies. Author Alistair Findlay was born in the shale mining village of Winchburgh and is the fourth son of a shale miner, Bob Findlay, who became editor of the *West Lothian Courier*. *Shale Voices* combines oral history, local journalism and family history. The generations of communities involved in shale mining provide, in their own words, a unique documentation of the industry and its cultural and political impact.

Photographs, drawings, poetry and short stories make this a thought provoking and entertaining account. It is as much a joy to dip into and feast the eyes on as to read from cover to cover.

'Alistair Findlay has added a basic source material to

the study of Scottish history that is invaluable and will be of great benefit to future generations. Scotland owes him a debt of gratitude for undertaking this work.' TAM DALYELL MP

FOLKLORE

Scotland: Myth, Legend and Folklore

Stuart McHardy

ISBN: 0 946487 69 3 PBK 7.99

Who were the people who built the megaliths?

What great warriors sleep beneath the Hollow Hills?

Were the early Scottish saints just pagans in disguise?

Was King Arthur really Scottish?

When was Nessie first sighted?

This is a book about Scotland drawn from hundreds, if not thousands of years of story-telling. From the oral traditions of the Scots, Gaelic and Norse speakers of the past, it presents a new picture of who the Scottish are and where they come from. The stories that McHardy recounts may be hilarious, tragic, heroic, frightening or just plain bizzare, but they all provide an insight into a unique tradition of myth, legend and folklore that has marked both the language and landscape of Scotland.

The Supernatural Highlands

Francis Thompson

ISBN 0 946487 31 6 PBK £8.99

An authoritative exploration of the otherworld of the Highlander, happenings and beings hitherto thought to be outwith the ordinary forces of nature. A simple introduction to the way of life of rural Highland and Island communities, this new edition weaves a path through second sight, the evil eye, witchcraft, ghosts, fairies and other supernatural beings, offering new sight-lines on areas of belief once dismissed as folklore and superstition.

Tall Tales from an Island

Peter Macnab

ISBN 0 946487 07 3 PBK £8.99

Peter Macnab was born and reared on Mull. He heard many of these tales as a lad, and others he has listened to in later years.

There are humorous tales, grim tales, witty tales, tales of witchcraft, tales of love, tales of heroism, tales of treachery, historical tales and tales of yesteryear.

A popular lecturer, broadcaster and writer, Peter Macnab is the author of a number of books and articles about Mull, the island he knows so inti-

mately and loves so much. As he himself puts it in his introduction to this book 'I am of the unswerving opinion that nowhere else in the world will you find a better way of life, nor a finer people with whom to share it.'

'All islands, it seems, have a rich store of characters whose stories represent a kind of sub-culture without which island life would be that much poorer. Macnab has succeeded in giving the retelling of the stories a special Mull flavour, so much so that one can visualise the storytellers sitting on a bench outside the house with a few cronies, puffing on their pipes and listening with nodding approval.'

WEST HIGHLAND FREE PRESS

Tales from the North Coast

Alan Temperley

ISBN 0 946487 18 9 PBK £8.99

Seals and shipwrecks, witches and fairies, curses and clearances, fact and fantasy – the authentic tales in this collection come straight from the heart of a small Highland community. Children and adults alike respond to their timeless appeal. These *Tales of the North Coast* were collected in the early 1970s by Alan Temperley and young people at Farr Secondary School in Sutherland. All the stories were gathered from the area between the Kyle of Tongue and Strath Halladale, in scattered communities wonderfully rich in lore that had been passed on by word of mouth down the generations. This wide-ranging selection provides a satisying balance between intriguing tales of the supernatural and more everyday occurrences. The book also includes chilling eye-witness accounts of the notorious Strathnaver Clearances when tenants were given a few hours to pack up and get out of their homes, which were then burned to the ground.

Underlying the continuity through the generations, this new edition has a foreward by Jim Johnston, the head teacher at Farr, and includes the vigorous linocut images produced by the young people under the guidance of their art teacher, Elliot Rudie.

Since the original publication of this book, Alan Temperley has gone on to become a highly regarded writer for children.

'The general reader will find this book's spontaneity, its pictures by the children and its fun utterly charming.'
SCOTTISH REVIEW

'An admirable book which should serve as an encouragement to other districts to gather what remains of their heritage of folk-tales.'
SCOTTISH EDUCATION JOURNAL

Luath Storyteller: Highland Myths & Legends

George W. Macpherson

ISBN 1 84282 003 6 PBK £5.00

The mythical, the legendary, the true... This is the stuff of stories and storytellers, the stuff of an age-old tradition in almost every country in the world, and none more so than Scotland. Celtic heroes, Fairies, Druids, Selkies, Sea horses, Magicians, Giants, Viking invaders; all feature in this collection of traditional Scottish tales, the like of which

were told round camp fires centuries ago, and are still told today.

George W. Macpherson has dipped into his phenomenal repertoire of tales to compile this diverse collection of traditional stories, designed to be read aloud. Each has been passed from generation to generation, some are two and a half thousand years old.

From the Celtic legends of Cuchullin and Fionn to the mythical tales of seal-people and magicians these stories have a timeless quality. Often, strands of the stories will interweave and cross over, building a delicate tapestry of Scotland as a mystical, enchanted land. '*The result is vivid and impressive, conveying the tragic dignity of the ancient warrior, or the devoted love of the seal woman and her fisher mate. The personalities and circumstances of people long gone are brought fully to life by the power of the storyteller's words. The ancestors take form before us in the visual imagination.*' DR DONALD SMITH, THE SCOTTISH STORYTELLING CENTRE

FICTION

The Bannockburn Years
William Scott
ISBN 0 946487 34 0 PBK £7.95

The Great Melnikov
Hugh MacLachlan
ISBN 0 946487 42 1 PBK £7.95

The Strange Case of R L Stevenson
Richard Woodhead
ISBN 0 946487 86 3 HBK £16.99

But n Ben A Go Go
Matthew Fitt
ISBN 1 84282 014 1 PBK £6.99

CURRENT ISSUES

**Notes from the North
incorporating a Brief History of the Scots and the English**
Emma Wood
ISBN 0 946487 46 4 PBK £8.99

**Trident on Trial
the case for people's disarmament**
Angie Zelter
ISBN 1 84282 004 4 PBK £9.99

**Scotland - Land and Power
the agenda for land reform**
Andy Wightman
foreword by Lesley Riddoch
ISBN 0 946487 70 7 PBK £5.00

Broomie Law
Cinders McLeod
ISBN 0 946487 99 5 PBK £4.00

TRAVEL & LEISURE

Edinburgh and Leith Pub Guide
Stuart McHardy
ISBN 0 946487 80 4 PBK £4.95

Pilgrims in the Rough: St Andrews beyond the 19th Hole
Michael Tobert
ISBN 0 946487 74 X PBK £7.99

Let's Explore Edinburgh Old Town
Anne Bruce English
ISBN 0 946487 98 7 PBK £4.99

NATURAL SCOTLAND

Wild Scotland: The essential guide to finding the best of natural Scotland
James McCarthy
Photography by Laurie Campbell
ISBN 0 946487 37 5 PBK £8.99

**Scotland Land and People
An Inhabited Solitude**
James McCarthy
ISBN 0 946487 57 X PBK £7.99

The Highland Geology Trail
John L Roberts
ISBN 0 946487 36 7 PBK £4.99

Rum: Nature's Island
Magnus Magnusson
ISBN 0 946487 32 4 PBK £7.95

Red Sky at Night
John Barrington
ISBN 0 946487 60 X PBK £8.99

Listen to the Trees
Don MacCaskill
ISBN 0 946487 65 0 PBK £9.99

Wildlife: Otters – On the Swirl of the Tide
Bridget MacCaskill
ISBN 0 946487 67 7 PBK £9.99

Wildlife: Foxes – The Blood is Wild
Bridget MacCaskill
ISBN 0 946487 71 5 PBK £9.99

BIOGRAPHY

Tobermory Teuchter: A first-hand account of life on Mull in the early years of the 20th century
Peter Macnab
ISBN 0 946487 41 3 PBK £7.99

Bare Feet and Tackety Boots
Archie Cameron
ISBN 0 946487 17 0 PBK £7.95

The Last Lighthouse
Sharma Kraustopf
ISBN 0 946487 96 0 PBK £7.99

POETRY

Poems to be read aloud
Collected and with an introduction by Tom Atkinson
ISBN 0 946487 00 6 PBK £5.00

Scots Poems to be read aloud
Collected and with an introduction by Stuart McHardy
ISBN 0 946487 81 2 PBK £5.00

The Luath Burns Companion
John Cairney
ISBN 1 84282 000 1 PBK £10.00

Men & Beasts
Poems and Prose by Valerie Gillies
Photographs by Rebecca Marr
ISBN 0 946487 92 8 PBK £15.00

'Nothing but Heather!'
Gerry Cambridge
ISBN 0 946487 49 9 PBK £15.00

GENEALOGY

Scottish Roots: step-by-step guide for ancestor hunters
Alwyn James
ISBN 1 84282 007 9 PBK £9.99

Luath Press Limited

committed to publishing well written books worth reading

LUATH PRESS takes its name from Robert Burns, whose little collie Luath (*Gael.*, swift or nimble) tripped up Jean Armour at a wedding and gave him the chance to speak to the woman who was to be his wife and the abiding love of his life. Burns called one of *The Twa Dogs* Luath after Cuchullin's hunting dog in *Ossian's Fingal*. Luath Press was established in 1981 in the heart of Burns country, and is now based a few steps up the road from Burns' first lodgings on Edinburgh's Royal Mile.
Luath offers you distinctive writing with a hint of unexpected pleasures.

Most bookshops either carry our books in stock or can order them for you. To order direct from us, please send a £sterling cheque, postal order, international money order or your credit card details (number, address of cardholder and expiry date) to us at the address below. Please add post and packing as follows: UK – £1.00 per delivery address; overseas surface mail – £2.50 per delivery address; overseas airmail – £3.50 for the first book to each delivery address, plus £1.00 for each additional book by airmail to the same address. If your order is a gift, we will happily enclose your card or message at no extra charge.

Luath Press Limited
543/2 Castlehill
The Royal Mile
Edinburgh EH1 2ND
Scotland
Telephone: 0131 225 4326 (24 hours)
Fax: 0131 225 4324
email: gavin.macdougall@luath.co.uk
Website: www.luath.co.uk